THE Java™ Tutorial

Third Edition

A Short Course on the Basics

The Java™ Series

Lisa Friendly, Series Editor
Tim Lindholm, Technical Editor
Ken Arnold, Technical Editor of The Jini™ Technology Series
Jim Inscore, Technical Editor of The Java™ Series, Enterprise Edition

http://www.javaseries.com

ᵀᴴᴱ Java™ Tutorial
Third Edition

A Short Course on the Basics

Mary Campione
Kathy Walrath
Alison Huml

Handwritten annotation:
Q
pg 49
ps 53
70
73
79
106
110
122 – 123
143
✳ 206
↑ 321

ADDISON-WESLEY

Boston • San Francisco • New York • Toronto • Montreal
London • Munich • Paris • Madrid • Capetown
Sydney • Tokyo • Singapore • Mexico City

Library of Congress Cataloging-in-Publication Data

Campione, Mary.

    The Java tutorial : a short course on the basics / Mary Campione, Kathy Walrath, Alison Huml.

        p. cm. -- (The Java series)

    ISBN 0-201-70393-9 (alk. paper)

    1. Java (Computer program language) I. Walrath, Kathy. II. Huml, Alison. III. Title. IV. Series.

    QA76.73.J38 C365 2000

    005.13'3--dc21   00-038616

The publisher offers discounts on this book when ordered in quantity for special sales. For more information, please contact:

Pearson Education Corporate Sales Division
201 W. 103rd Street
Indianapolis, IN 46290
(800) 428-5331
corpsales@pearsoned.com

Visit us on the Web at www.awl.com/cseng/

Text printed on recycled and acid-free paper.

ISBN 0201703939

4 5 6 7 8 9 CRS 04 03 02 01

4th Printing   October 2001

Contents

Preface

SINCE the release of the original Java Development Kit in May of 1995, the engineering team at Sun Microsystems has been hard at work improving and enhancing the Java platform. We have been similarly laboring to update *The Java Tutorial* to reflect the work of the engineers.

This edition documents the APIs in the Java 2 Software Development Kit (SDK), v. 1.3. Because you might have to write or update code used with earlier releases of the Java platform, this book is also valid for versions 1.2 and 1.1.

Besides integrating v. 1.3 information into the text, we've added questions and exercises to help you practice what you learn. To help beginners avoid many common mistakes, an appendix is devoted to programming problems and their solutions. Convenient summaries at the end of each section are also new to this edition.

Like the first and second editions, this book is based on the online tutorial hosted at Sun Microsystems's Web site for the Java platform.

```
http://java.sun.com/docs/books/tutorial/index.html
```

Like the online version, this book reflects the latest advances in Java technology. Unlike the online version, this book solely focuses on the APIs needed by most beginning to intermediate programmers. Once you've mastered the material in this book, you can explore the rest of the Java platform on the Web site.

Our intent has always been to create a fun, easy-to-read, task-oriented programmer's guide with lots of practical examples to help people learn to program.

Who Should Read This Book?

The book is geared towards both novice and experienced programmers.

- *New programmers* can benefit most by reading the book from beginning to end, including the step by step instructions for compiling and running your first program in <u>Getting Started</u> (page 1).
- *Programmers experienced with procedural languages* such as C may wish start with the material on object-oriented concepts and features of the Java programming language.
- *Experienced object-oriented programmers* may want to jump feet first into more advanced trails, such as those on applets, essential classes, or user interfaces.

No matter what type of programmer you are, you can find a path through this book that fits your learning requirements.

How to Use This Book

This book is designed so that you can either read it straight through or skip around from topic to topic. Whenever a topic is discussed in another place, you'll see a link to that place in the tutorial. Links are underlined and are followed by page numbers, like this: <u>What Can Java Technology Do?</u> (page 5).

All the sample code used in this book is available online and on the accompanying CD. The CD icon in the margin indicates that the code is available. At the end of each chapter there is also a "Code Sample" section with a table that specifies the locations of the examples on the CD and online.

We're dedicated to keeping this book up-to-date with the most current information. To learn what's new since this book went to press, visit the following URL:

> `http://java.sun.com/docs/books/tutorial/books/3e/index.html`

Answers to Questions and Exercises

You can test your comprehension of each chapter by trying problems in the "Questions and Exercises" sections. The answers are all available online; here's a handy link to all the solution pages for this book:

> `http://java.sun.com/docs/books/tutorial/books/3e/toc.html`

Acknowledgments

Many Internet readers have helped us maintain and improve the quality of the tutorial by sending us email and cheerfully pointing out our numerous typos, broken links, and more importantly, areas of the tutorial that caused confusion or could benefit from rewriting.

Many members of the Java Software engineering and documentation team have given us counsel, answered our many questions, reviewed our material, and even made contributions to it. They also make Sun Microsystems a fun place to work. The list is long but we'd particularly like to note the contributions of Jennifer Ball, Brian Beck, Joshua Bloch, David Connelly, Chris Darke, Lisa Fenwick, Bill Foote, Carol Hayes, Herb Jellinek, Doug Kramer, Tim Lindholm, Marianne Mueller, Marla Parker, Mark Reinhold, John Rose, and Sharon Zakhour. We are also especially grateful for the talented writers at Sun who have contributed to the online tutorial as guest authors.

The Java programming language wouldn't exist without its creator, James Gosling. We'd like to thank James, not only for creating the language but also for staying involved as the Java platform develops.

Lisa Friendly, our manager and series editor, gave us the freedom and support necessary to do our work—and enjoy it.

Mike Hendrickson, our editorial advisor at Addison-Wesley, is always a calming influence and keeps us on schedule. Sarah Weaver was the superb and patient production manager on the book and Evelyn Pyle was our copy editor and grammar queen. The always cheerful and supportive Julie DiNicola and the whole team at Addison-Wesley have been a pleasure to work with.

Those who graciously helped with the first and second editions are thanked online at: http://java.sun.com/docs/books/tutorial/2e/book.html

Dedication

Mary: This book is dedicated to my husband, Richard Campione, for being my greatest friend. It's also dedicated to Sophia, a delightful child and a constant reminder of what's truly important.

Kathy: This book is dedicated to my husband, Nathan Walrath, and to our children, Laine and Cosmo. Nathan has done whatever it takes to help me get my work done, from distracting kids to dispensing advice and art criticism. Laine and Cosmo are not old enough to help but like their dad, they sure are fun.

Alison: This book is dedicated to everyone who put up with me during the book production. Highest honors go to my husband, Aron Hall, who helped to review chapters and lured me away from my computer for hikes in the mountains and down to Peet's Coffee and Tea.

Getting Started

THIS chapter gives a quick introduction to the Java™ technology. First, we explain what the Java platform is and what it can do. Next are step-by-step instructions on how to compile and run two simple programs on the Win32, the UNIX/Linux or the MacOS platforms.[1] After that, we take a look at the code for the two programs, so you can see how they work. The chapter ends with questions and exercises to test and expand your knowledge, followed by a table of download instructions for the code used in this chapter.

The software development kits (SDKs) that Sun Microsystems provides include a minimal set of tools to let you run and compile your programs. Serious developers are advised to use a professional Integrated Development Environment (IDE).[2] See Integrated Development Environments (page 540) for a list of IDEs.

---

[1] So, you're using a platform not listed here? Sun Microsystems maintains this list of third-party ports to other platforms: http://java.sun.com/cgi-bin/java-ports.cgi

[2] In fact, Java 2 SDK, Standard Edition v. 1.3, is available bundled with an IDE, the Forte™ for Java™, Community Edition. This version is included on this book's CD.

About the Java Technology

Talk about Java technology seems to be everywhere, but what exactly is it? The next two sections explain how it is both a programming language and a platform.

The Java Programming Language

The Java programming language is a high-level language that can be characterized by all the following buzzwords:[1]

- Simple
- Object oriented
- Distributed
- Interpreted

- Robust
- Secure
- Architecture neutral
- Portable

- High performance
- Multithreaded
- Dynamic

With most programming languages, you either compile or interpret a program so that you can run it on your computer. The Java programming language is unusual in that a program is both compiled and interpreted. With the compiler, first you translate a program into an inter-

---

[1] Each of these terms is explained in "The Java Language Environment," a white paper by James Gosling and Henry McGilton. You can find this white paper at http://java.sun.com/docs/white/langenv/index.html

mediate language called *Java bytecodes*—the platform-independent codes interpreted by the interpreter on the Java platform. The interpreter parses and runs each Java bytecode instruction on the computer. Compilation happens just once; interpretation occurs each time the program is executed. Figure 1 illustrates how this works.

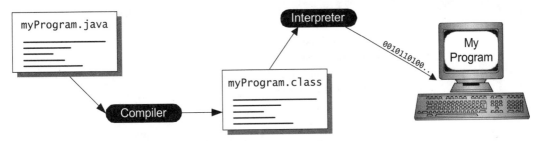

Figure 1   Programs written in the Java programming language are first compiled and then interpreted.

You can think of Java bytecodes as the machine code instructions for the *Java Virtual Machine* (Java VM). Every Java interpreter, whether it's a development tool or a Web browser that can run applets, is an implementation of the Java VM.

Java bytecodes help make "write once, run anywhere" possible. You can compile your program into bytecodes on any platform that has a Java compiler. The bytecodes can then be run on any implementation of the Java VM. That means that as long as a computer has a Java VM, the same program written in the Java programming language can run on Windows 2000, a Solaris workstation, or on an iMac, as shown in Figure 2.

The Java Platform

A *platform* is the hardware or software environment in which a program runs. We've already mentioned some of the most popular platforms, such as Windows 2000, Linux, Solaris, and MacOS. Most platforms can be described as a combination of the operating system and hardware. The Java platform differs from most other platforms in that it's a software-only platform that runs on top of other, hardware-based platforms.

The Java platform has two components:

- The *Java Virtual Machine* (Java VM)
- The *Java Application Programming Interface* (Java API)

You've already been introduced to the Java VM. It's the base for the Java platform and is ported onto various hardware-based platforms.

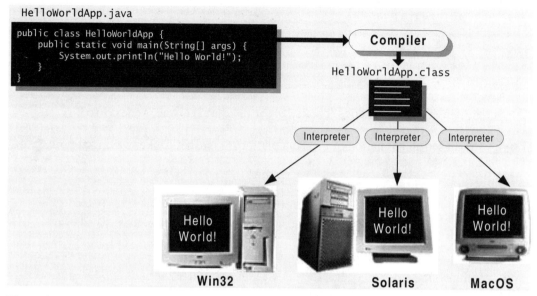

Figure 2   Programs can be written once and run on almost any platform.

The Java API is a large collection of ready-made software components that provide many useful capabilities, such as graphical user interface (GUI) widgets. The Java API is grouped into libraries of related classes and interfaces; these libraries are known as *packages*. The next section highlights what functionality some of the packages in the Java API provide.

Figure 3 depicts a program that's running on the Java platform. As the figure shows, the Java API and the virtual machine insulate the program from the hardware.

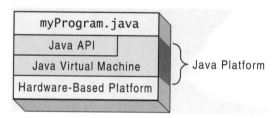

Figure 3   The Java API and the Java VM insulate a program from hardware dependencies.

Native code is code that, after you compile it, runs on a specific hardware platform. As a platform-independent environment, the Java platform can be a bit slower than native code. However, smart compilers, well-tuned interpreters, and just-in-time bytecode compilers can bring performance close to that of native code without threatening portability.

What Can Java Technology Do?

The most common types of programs written in the Java programming language are *applets* and *applications*. If you've surfed the Web, you're probably already familiar with applets. An applet is a program that adheres to certain conventions that allow it to run within a Java-enabled browser. To see a running applet, go to this page in the online version of this tutorial:

```
http://java.sun.com/docs/books/tutorial/getStarted/index.html
```

There you can see an animation of the Java platform's mascot, Duke, waving at you:

However, the Java programming language is not just for writing cute, entertaining applets for the Web. The general-purpose, high-level Java programming language is also a powerful software platform. Using the generous API, you can write many types of programs.

An application is a standalone program that runs directly on the Java platform. A special kind of application known as a *server* serves and supports clients on a network. Examples of servers are Web servers, mail servers, and print servers.

Another specialized program is a *servlet*. A servlet can almost be thought of as an applet that runs on the server side. Java servlets are a popular choice for building interactive Web applications, replacing the use of CGI scripts. Servlets are similar to applets in that they are run-time extensions of applications. Instead of working in browsers, though, servlets run within Java Web servers, configuring or tailoring the server.

How does the API support all these kinds of programs? It does so with packages of software components that provide a wide range of functionality. Every full implementation of the Java platform gives you the following features:

- **The essentials:** Objects, strings, threads, numbers, input and output, data structures, system properties, date and time, and so on.
- **Applets:** The set of conventions used by Java applets.
- **Networking:** URLs, TCP (Transmission Control Protocol), UDP (User Datagram Protocol) sockets, and IP (Internet Protocol) addresses.
- **Internationalization:** Help for writing programs that can be localized for users worldwide. Programs can automatically adapt to specific locales and be displayed in the appropriate language.

- **Security:** Both low level and high level, including electronic signatures, public and private key management, access control, and certificates.
- **Software components:** Known as JavaBeans™, can plug into existing component architectures.
- **Object serialization:** Allows lightweight persistence and communication via RMI (Remote Method Invocation).
- **Java Database Connectivity (JDBC™):** Provides uniform access to a wide range of relational databases.

The Java platform also has APIs for 2D and 3D graphics, accessibility, servers, collaboration, telephony, speech, animation, and more. Figure 4 depicts what is included in the Java 2 SDK.

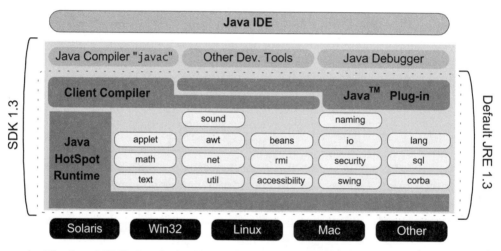

Figure 4   The Java 2 SDK, Standard Edition v. 1.3. The Java 2 Runtime Environment (JRE) consists of the Java VM, the Java platform core classes, and supporting files. The Java 2 SDK includes the JRE and development tools, such as compilers and debuggers.

This book covers the Java programming language and parts of the core API that beginning- to intermediate-level programmers will use most frequently. If you need additional information not found in this book, you can explore the other two books in *The Java Tutorial* series: *The JFC Swing Tutorial* and *The Java Tutorial Continued*. The contents of both books are included on the CD that accompanies this book and can be found in the online tutorial:

```
http://java.sun.com/docs/books/tutorial/index.html
```

How Will Java Technology Change My Life?

We can't promise you fame, fortune, or even a job if you learn the Java programming language. But it *is* likely to make your programs better, and it requires less effort than do other languages. We believe that the Java programming language will help you do the following:

- **Get started quickly:** Although the Java programming language is a powerful object-oriented language, it's easy to learn, especially for programmers already familiar with C or C++.

- **Write less code:** Comparisons of program metrics (class counts, method counts, and so on) suggest that a program written in the Java programming language can be four times smaller than the same program in C++.

- **Write better code:** The Java programming language encourages good coding practices, and its garbage collection helps you avoid memory leaks. Its object orientation, its JavaBeans component architecture, and its wide-ranging, extensible API let you reuse other people's code and introduce fewer bugs.

- **Develop programs more quickly:** Your development time may be twice as fast as writing the same program in C++. Why? You write fewer lines of code with the Java programming language, and it is a simpler programming language than C++.

- **Avoid platform dependencies with 100% Pure Java™:** You can keep your program portable by avoiding the use of libraries written in other languages. The 100% Pure Java™ Product Certification Program has a repository of historical process manuals, white papers, brochures, and similar materials online at: `http://java.sun.com/100percent/`

- **Write once, run anywhere:** Because 100% Pure Java programs are compiled into machine-independent bytecodes, they run consistently on any Java platform.

- **Distribute software more easily:** You can easily upgrade certain types of programs, such as applets, from a central server. Applets take advantage of the feature of allowing new classes to be loaded "on the fly," without recompiling the entire program.

Let's get started learning the Java programming language with a simple program, "Hello World." Depending on which platform you are using, you will want to read one of the next three sections: First Steps (Win32) (page 8) gives detailed instructions on compiling your first program on the Windows platform, First Steps (UNIX/Linux) (page 16) has instructions for the UNIX and Linux platforms, and First Steps (MacOS) (page 24) covers the MacOS platforms. Then don't miss the section A Closer Look at HelloWorld (page 32), which explains some basic features of the Java programming language as demonstrated in the `HelloWorld` program.

First Steps (Win32)

The following detailed instructions will help you write your first program. These instructions are for users on Win32 platforms, which include Windows 95/98 and Windows NT/2000. (UNIX and Linux instructions are on page 16. Users on MacOS platforms can find instructions on page 24.) We start with a checklist of what you need to write your first program. Next, we cover the steps to creating an application, steps to creating an applet, and explanations of error messages you may encounter.

A Checklist

To write your first program, you need

1. **The Java 2 SDK, Standard Edition:** The Java 2 SDK software is included on the CD that accompanies this book. You can download this platform to your PC or check `http://java.sun.com/products/` for the latest version.[1]
2. **A text editor:** In this example, we'll use NotePad, the simple editor included with the Windows platforms. To find NotePad, go to the `Start` menu and select `Programs` > `Accessories` > `NotePad`. You can easily adapt these instructions if you use a different text editor.

Note: You may want to consider using an IDE to help you write your programs. Java 2 SDK, Standard Edition v. 1.3, is available bundled with an IDE, the Forte™ for Java™, Community Edition. This version is included on this book's CD.

Creating Your First Application

Your first program, `HelloWorldApp`, will simply display the greeting "Hello World!" To create this program, you complete each of the following steps.

- **Create a source file.** A source file contains text, written in the Java programming language, that you and other programmers can understand. You can use any text editor to create and to edit source files.
- **Compile the source file into a bytecode file.** The compiler takes your source file and translates the text into instructions that the Java VM can understand. The compiler converts these instructions into a bytecode file.

---

[1] Before version 1.2, the software development kit (SDK) provided by Sun Microsystems was called the "JDK," or Java Development Kit.

- **Run the program contained in the bytecode file.** The Java interpreter installed on your computer implements the Java VM. This interpreter takes your bytecode file and carries out the instructions by translating them into instructions that your computer can understand.

Create a Source File

To create a source file, you have two options. You can save the file HelloWorldApp.java[1] on your computer and avoid a lot of typing. Then you can go straight to the second step of compiling the source file (page 10). Or, you can follow these longer instructions.

First, start NotePad. In a new document, type in the following code:

```
/**
 * The HelloWorldApp class implements an application that
 * displays "Hello World!" to the standard output.
 */
public class HelloWorldApp {
    public static void main(String[] args) {
        // Display "Hello World!"
        System.out.println("Hello World!");
    }
}
```

Be Careful When You Type: Type all code, commands, and file names exactly as shown. The compiler and interpreter are *case sensitive*, so you must capitalize consistently. In other words, HelloWorldApp is not equivalent to helloworldapp.

Second, save this code to a file. From the menu bar, select File > Save As. In the Save As dialog, do the following.

- Using the Save in drop-down menu, specify the folder (directory) where you'll save your file. In this example, the folder is java on the C drive.

- In the File name text box, type "HelloWorldApp.java", including the double quotation marks. The quotation marks force the file to be saved as a .java file rather than as a ".txt" text file.

- From the Save as type drop-down menu, choose Text Document.

---

[1] Throughout this book, we use the CD icon to indicate that the code (in this case, HelloWorldApp.java) is available on the CD and online. See Code Samples (page 43) for the file location on the CD and online.

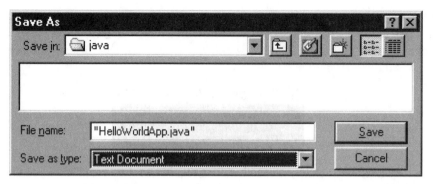

Figure 5   Saving the HelloWorldApp.java file with the correct .java extension.

When you're finished, the dialog box should look like Figure 5. Now click Save and exit NotePad.

Compile the Source File

From the Start menu, select the MS-DOS Prompt (Windows 95/98) or Command Prompt (Windows NT/2000) application. When the application launches, it should look like Figure 6.

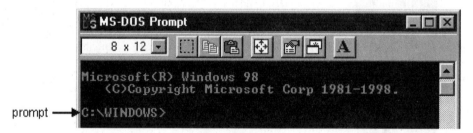

Figure 6   The prompt in the MS-DOS Prompt application.

The prompt shows your *current directory*. When you bring up the prompt for Windows 95/98, your current directory is usually WINDOWS on your C drive (as shown in Figure 6) or WINNT for Windows NT. To compile your source code file, change your current directory to the one in which your file is located. For example, if your source directory is java on the C drive, you would type the following command at the prompt and press Enter:

```
cd c:\java
```

Now the prompt should change to C:\java. To change to a directory on a different drive, you must type an extra command. As shown in Figure 7, to change to the java directory on the D drive, you must reenter the drive, d:.

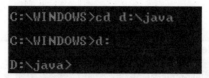

```
C:\WINDOWS>cd d:\java
C:\WINDOWS>d:
D:\java>
```

Figure 7   Changing to a directory on another drive requires an extra command—you must reenter the drive letter, followed by a colon.

In our example, the java directory is on the C drive. The dir command lists the files in your current directory. If your current directory is C:\java and you enter dir at the prompt, you should see your file (Figure 8).

Figure 8   HelloWorldApp.java listed in the current directory.

Now you can compile. At the prompt, type the following command and press Enter:

```
javac HelloWorldApp.java
```

If your prompt reappears without error messages, congratulations. You have successfully compiled your program. If you encounter errors, see <u>Error Explanations (Win32)</u> (page 14) to help you fix the problems.

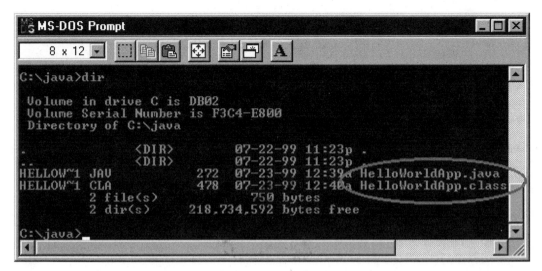

Figure 9   After you compile `HelloWorld.java`, the bytecode file, `HelloWorldApp.class`, is created in the same directory.

The compiler has generated a Java bytecode file, `HelloWorldApp.class`. At the prompt, type `dir` to see the new file that was generated (Figure 9). Now that you have a `.class` file, you can run your program.

Run the Program

In the same directory, enter the following command at the prompt:

```
java HelloWorldApp
```

Figure 10 shows what you should see.

Figure 10   When you run your `HelloWorldApp` program, you should see this result.

Creating Your First Applet

HelloWorldApp is an example of an *application*, a standalone program. Now you will create an *applet* called HelloWorld, which also displays the greeting "Hello World!" Unlike HelloWorldApp, however, the applet runs in a Java-enabled Web browser, such as the HotJava™ browser, Netscape Navigator, or Microsoft Internet Explorer.

To create this applet, you'll perform the basic steps as before: create a source file, compile the source file, and run the program. However, unlike for an application, you must also create an HTML file.

Create a Source File

You have two options to create a source file. You can save the files HelloWorld.java and Hello.html[1] on your computer and avoid a lot of typing. Then you can go straight to the second step of compiling the source file (page 14). Or, you can follow these instructions.

First, start NotePad. In a new document, type the following code:

```
import java.applet.Applet;
import java.awt.Graphics;

public class HelloWorld extends Applet {
    public void paint(Graphics g) {
        // Display "Hello world!"
        g.drawString("Hello world!", 50, 25);
    }
}
```

Save this code to a file called HelloWorld.java.

Second, you also need an HTML file to accompany your applet. Type the following code into a new NotePad document:

```
<HTML>
    <HEAD>
        <TITLE>A Simple Program</TITLE>
    </HEAD>
    <BODY>
        Here is the output of my program:
        <APPLET CODE="HelloWorld.class" WIDTH=150 HEIGHT=25>
        </APPLET>
    </BODY>
</HTML>
```

---

[1] HelloWorld.java and Hello.html are available on this book's CD and online. See Code Samples (page 43).

Save this code to a file called `Hello.html`.

Compile the Source File

 At the prompt, type the following command and press `Return`:

```
javac HelloWorld.java
```

The compiler should generate a Java bytecode file, `HelloWorld.class`.

Run the Program

Although you can use a Web browser to view your applets, you may find it easier to test your applets by using the simple `appletviewer` application that comes with the Java platform. To view the `HelloWorld` applet using `appletviewer`, enter at the prompt:

```
appletviewer Hello.html
```

Figure 11 shows what you should see.

Figure 11 The successful execution of the `HelloWorld` applet.

Congratulations! Your applet works. If you encounter errors, see <u>Common Problems and Their Solutions</u> (page 391) to help you fix the problems.

Error Explanations (Win32)

Here we list the most common errors users have when compiling and running their first application or applet using the Java 2 SDK or an earlier JDK. For more error explanations, consult the section <u>Common Problems and Their Solutions</u> (page 391).

Bad command or file name *(Windows 95/98)*

The name specified is not recognized as an internal or external command, operable program or batch file *(Windows NT/2000)*

If you receive this error, Windows cannot find the Java compiler, `javac`. Here's one way to tell Windows where to find `javac`. Suppose that you installed the Java 2 Software Development Kit in `C:\jdk1.3`. At the prompt, you would type the following command and press `Enter`:

```
C:\jdk1.3\bin javac HelloWorldApp.java
```

Note: If you choose this option, each time you compile or run a program, you must precede your `javac` and `java` commands with `c:\jdk1.3\bin` or the directory where you saved the Java 2 SDK, followed by `\bin`. The `bin` directory contains the compiler and interpreter. To avoid this extra typing, consult the section Update the PATH Variable (Win32) (page 541).

Exception in thread "main" java.lang.NoClassDefFoundError: HelloWorldApp

If you receive this error, the interpreter cannot find your bytecode file, `HelloWorldApp.class`.

One of the places `java` tries to find your bytecode file is your current directory. So, if your bytecode file is in C, you should change your current directory to that. To change your directory, type the following command at the prompt and press `Enter`:

```
cd c:
```

The prompt should change to `C:`. If you enter `dir` at the prompt, you should see your `.java` and `.class` files. Now enter `java HelloWorldApp` again.

If you still have problems, you might have to change your CLASSPATH variable. To see whether this is necessary, try clobbering the class path with the following command:

```
set CLASSPATH=
```

Now enter `java HelloWorldApp` again. If the program works now, you'll have to change your CLASSPATH variable. For more information, consult the section Path Help (page 540).

First Steps (UNIX/Linux)

These instructions tell you how to compile and run your first programs on UNIX and Linux platforms. (Win32 instructions are on page 8. Users on MacOS platforms can find instructions on page 24.) We start with a checklist of what you need to write your first program. Next, we cover the steps to creating an application, steps to creating an applet, and explanations of error messages you may encounter.

A Checklist

To write your first program, you will need

1. **The Java 2 SDK, Standard Edition:** The Java 2 SDK software is included on the CD that accompanies this book. You can download this SDK to your workstation or check `http://java.sun.com/products/` for the latest version.[1]

2. **A text editor:** In this example, we'll use Pico, an editor available on many UNIX-based platforms. You can easily adapt these instructions if you use a different text editor, such as vi or emacs.

These two items are all you need to write your first program.

Creating Your First Application

Your first program, `HelloWorldApp`, will simply display the greeting "Hello World!" To create this program, you will complete each of the following steps.

- **Create a source file.** A source file contains text, written in the Java programming language, that you and other programmers can understand. You can use any text editor to create and to edit source files.

- **Compile the source file into a bytecode file.** The compiler, `javac`, takes your source file and translates the text into instructions that the Java Virtual Machine can understand. The compiler converts these instructions into a bytecode file.

- **Run the program contained in the bytecode file.** The Java interpreter installed on your computer implements the Java VM. This interpreter takes your bytecode file and carries out the instructions by translating them into instructions that your computer can understand.

---

[1] The Linux platform was first supported in the Java 2 SDK, Standard Edition v. 1.3 release. Before version 1.2, the software development kit provided by Sun Microsystems was called the "JDK."

Create a Source File

You have two options. You can save the file `HelloWorldApp.java`[1] on your computer and avoid a lot of typing. Then you can go straight to the second step of compiling the file (page 18). Or, you can follow these (longer) instructions.

First, open a shell, or "terminal," window (Figure 12).

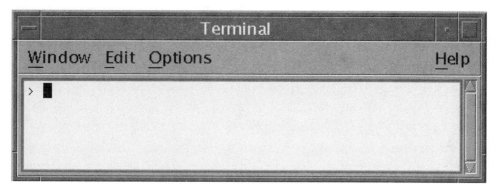

Figure 12 A UNIX terminal window.

When you first bring up the prompt, your current directory will usually be your home directory. You can change your current directory to your home directory at any time by typing `cd` at the prompt and then pressing `Return`.

We recommend that you keep the files you create in a separate directory. You can create a directory by using the command `mkdir`. For example, to create the directory `java` in your home directory, you would first change your current directory to your home directory by entering the following command:

    cd

Then you would enter the following command:

    mkdir java

To change your current directory to this new directory, you would then enter:

    cd java

Now you can start creating your source file. Start the Pico editor by typing `pico` at the prompt and pressing `Return`. If the system responds with the message **pico: command not**

---

[1] Throughout this book, we use the CD icon to indicate that the code (in this case, `HelloWorldApp.java`) is available on the CD and online. See <u>Code Samples</u> (page 43) for the file location on the CD and online.

found, Pico is probably unavailable. Consult your system administrator for more information, or use another editor.

When you start Pico, it will display a new, blank buffer. This is the area in which you will type your code.

Type the following code into the new buffer:

```
/**
 * The HelloWorldApp class implements an application that
 * displays "Hello World!" to the standard output.
 */
public class HelloWorldApp {
    public static void main(String[] args) {
        // Display "Hello World!"
        System.out.println("Hello World!");
    }
}
```

Be Careful When You Type: Type all code, commands, and file names exactly as shown. The compiler and interpreter are *case sensitive*, so you must capitalize consistently. In other words, HelloWorldApp is not equivalent to helloworldapp.

Save the code with the name HelloWorldApp.java by typing Ctrl-O in your Pico editor. On the bottom line of your editor, you will see the prompt File Name to write. Enter HelloWorldApp.java, preceded by the directory where you want to create the file. For example, if /home/myname/ is your home directory and you want to save HelloWorldApp.java in the directory /home/myname/java, you would type /home/myname/java/HelloWorldApp.java and press Return. Type Ctrl-X to exit Pico.

Compile the Source File

Bring up another shell window. To compile your source file, change your current directory to the one in which your file is located. For example, if your source directory is /home/myname/java, you would type the following command at the prompt and press Return:[1]

```
cd /home/myname/java
```

You can type pwd at the prompt to see your current directory. In this example, the current directory has been changed to /home/myname/java. If you enter ls at the prompt, you should see your file listed (Figure 13).

---

[1] You could also change to the source directory with two commands: Type cd, press Return, then type java and press Return. Typing cd alone changes you to your home directory (that is, to /home/myname).

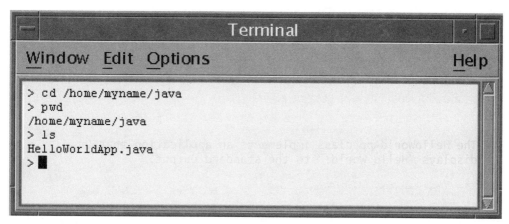

Figure 13 The `HelloWorldApp.java` file listed in the current directory.

Now you can compile. At the prompt, type the following command and press `Return`:

```
javac HelloWorldApp.java
```

If your prompt reappears without error messages, congratulations. You successfully compiled your program. If you encounter errors, see Common Problems and Their Solutions (page 391) to help you fix the problems.

The compiler has generated a bytecode file, `HelloWorldApp.class`. At the prompt, type `ls` to see the new file (Figure 14).

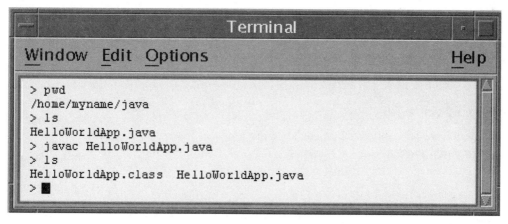

Figure 14 Compiling `HelloWorld.java` creates the bytecode file, `HelloWorldApp.class`, in the same directory.

Now that you have a `.class` file, you can run your program.

Run the Program

In the same directory, enter at the prompt: `java HelloWorldApp`. Figure 15 shows what you should see.

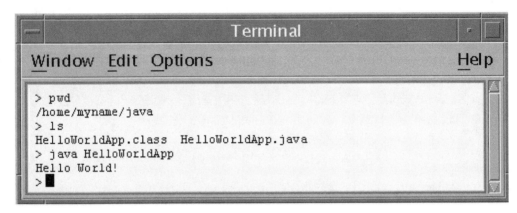

```
> pwd
/home/myname/java
> ls
HelloWorldApp.class   HelloWorldApp.java
> java HelloWorldApp
Hello World!
> █
```

Figure 15 Running the `HelloWorldApp` program.

Creating Your First Applet

`HelloWorldApp` is an example of an application, a standalone program. Now you will create an applet called `HelloWorld`, which also displays the greeting "Hello world!" Unlike `HelloWorldApp`, however, the applet runs in a Java-enabled Web browser, such as the HotJava browser, Netscape Navigator, or Microsoft Internet Explorer.

To create this applet, you'll perform the basic steps as before: create a source file, compile the source file, and run the program. However, unlike for an application, you must also create an HTML file.

Create a Source File

Again, you have two options. You can save the files `HelloWorld.java` and `Hello.html`[1] on your computer and avoid a lot of typing. Then you can go straight to Compile the Source File (page 21). Or, you can follow these instructions.

First, start Pico. Type the following code into a new buffer:

```
import java.applet.Applet;
```

---

[1] `HelloWorld.java` and `Hello.html` are available on this book's CD and online. See Code Samples (page 43).

```
import java.awt.Graphics;

public class HelloWorld extends Applet {
    public void paint(Graphics g) {
        // Display "Hello World!"
        g.drawString("Hello world!", 50, 25);
    }
}
```

Save this code to a file named `HelloWorld.java`. Type `Ctrl-X` to exit Pico.

Second, you also need an HTML file to accompany your applet. Restart Pico and type the following code into a new buffer:

```
<HTML>
    <HEAD>
        <TITLE>A Simple Program</TITLE>
    </HEAD>
    <BODY>
        Here is the output of my program:
        <APPLET CODE="HelloWorld.class" WIDTH=150 HEIGHT=25>
        </APPLET>
    </BODY>
</HTML>
```

Save this code to a file called `Hello.html` in the same directory as your `.java` file.

Compile the Source File

At the prompt, type the following command and press `Return`:

```
javac HelloWorld.java
```

The compiler should generate a Java bytecode file, `HelloWorld.class`.

Run the Program

Although you can use a Web browser to view your applets, you may find it easier to test your applets by using the simple `appletviewer` application that comes with the Java 2 SDK. To view the `HelloWorld` applet using `appletviewer`, enter at the prompt:

```
appletviewer Hello.html
```

Figure 16 The successful execution of the `HelloWorld` applet.

Figure 16 shows what you should see. Congratulations! Your applet works. If you encounter errors, see <u>Common Problems and Their Solutions</u> (page 391) to help you fix the problems.

Error Explanations (UNIX/Linux)

Here we list the most common errors users have when compiling and running their first application or applet. For more error explanations, consult the section <u>Common Problems and Their Solutions</u> (page 391).

`javac: Command not found`

   If you receive this error, the operating system cannot find the Java compiler, `javac`. Here's one way to tell it where to find `javac`. Suppose that you installed the Java 2 Software Development Kit in `/usr/local/jdk1.3`. At the prompt, you would type the following command and press `Return`:

```
/usr/local/jdk1.3/bin/javac HelloWorldApp.java
```

Note: If you choose this option, each time you compile or run a program, you must precede your `javac` and `java` commands with `/usr/local/jdk1.3/bin`. To avoid this extra typing, consult the section <u>Update the PATH Variable (UNIX)</u> (page 543) in the Appendix.

`Exception in thread "main" java.lang.NoClassDefFoundError: HelloWorldApp`

   If you receive this error, the interpreter cannot find your bytecode file, `HelloWorldApp.class`. One of the places the interpreter tries to find your bytecode file is your current directory. So, if your bytecode file is in `/home/myname/java/`, you should change your current directory to that directory. To change your directory, type the following command at the prompt and press `Return`:

```
cd /home/myname/java
```

Type pwd at the prompt; you should see /home/myname/java. If you type ls at the prompt, you should see your .java and .class files. Now enter java HelloWorldApp again.

If you still have problems, you might have to change your CLASSPATH variable. To see whether this is necessary, try clobbering the class path with the following command:

```
set CLASSPATH=
```

Now enter java HelloWorldApp again. If the program works now, you'll have to change your CLASSPATH variable. For more information, consult the section Path Help (page 540).

First Steps (MacOS)

The following detailed instructions will help you write your first program. These instructions are for users on MacOS platforms. (Users on Win32 platforms can find instructions on page 8. UNIX and Linux instructions are on page 16.) We start with a checklist of what you need to write your first program. Next, we cover the steps to creating an application and steps to creating an applet.

A Checklist

To write your first program, you need

1. **A development environment for the Java platform:** You can download the Macintosh Runtime Environment for Java Software Development Kit (MRJ SDK) from Apple's Web site at this address: `http://developer.apple.com/java/text/download.html`

2. **A runtime environment for the same version of the Java platform:** You can download the Macintosh Runtime Environment for Java (MRJ) from Apple's Web site: `http://developer.apple.com/java/text/download.html`

3. **Stuffit Expander 5.5 to open these files:** You can download this program from Aladdin Systems's Web site at this address: `http://www.aladdinsys.com/expander/expander_mac_login.html`

4. **A text editor:** In this example, we'll use SimpleText, the basic text editor included with the MacOS platforms. To find SimpleText, from the `File` menu, select `Find`, type `SimpleText`, and click the `Find` button. You can easily adapt these instructions if you use a different text editor.

Creating Your First Application

Your first program, `HelloWorldApp`, will simply display the greeting "Hello World!" To create this program, you complete each of the following steps.

- **Create a source file.** A source file contains text, written in the Java programming language, that you and other programmers can understand. You can use any text editor to create and to edit source files.

- **Compile the source file into a bytecode file.** The compiler takes your source file and translates the text into instructions that the Java Virtual Machine can understand. The compiler converts these instructions into a bytecode file.

- **Run the program contained in the bytecode file.** The Java interpreter installed on your computer implements the Java VM. This interpreter takes your bytecode file and carries out the instructions by translating them into instructions that your computer can understand.

Create a Source File

To create a source file, you have two options. You can save the file `HelloWorldApp.java`[1] on your computer and avoid a lot of typing. Then you can go straight to the second step of compiling the source file (page 26). Or, you can follow these longer instructions.

First, start SimpleText. In a new document, type in the following code:

```
/**
 * The HelloWorldApp class implements an application that
 * displays "Hello World!" to the standard output.
 */
public class HelloWorldApp {
    public static void main(String[] args) {
        // Display "Hello World!"
        System.out.println("Hello World!");
    }
}
```

Be Careful When You Type: Type all code, commands, and file names exactly as shown. The compiler and interpreter are *case sensitive*, so you must capitalize consistently. In other words, `HelloWorldApp` is not equivalent to `helloworldapp`.

Second, save this code to a file. From the menu bar, select `File` > `Save As`. In the `Save As` dialog, do the following.

- Specify the folder where you'll save your file. In this example, the folder is called `MRJ SDK 2.2.`
- In the `Save this document as:` text box, type `HelloWorldApp.java`.

---

[1] Throughout this book, we use the CD icon to indicate that the code (in this case, `HelloWorldApp.java`) is available on the CD and online. See <u>Code Samples</u> (page 43) for the file location on the CD and online.

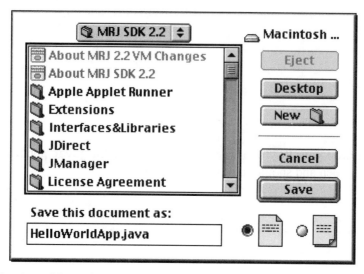

Figure 17 Saving the HelloWorldApp.java file.

When you're finished, the dialog box should look like Figure 17. Now click Save and exit
SimpleText.

Compile the Source File

Open the folder MRJ SDK 2.2 (or whatever you have named your folder); it should look
something like Figure 18.

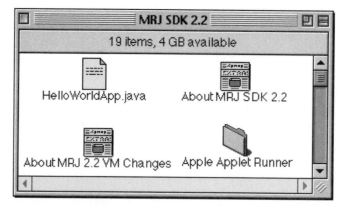

Figure 18 The contents of the MRJ SDK 2.2 folder.

From the MRJ SDK 2.2 folder, select Tools > JDK Tools. This last folder contains the program javac.

Figure 19 The javac icon.

Now drag and drop your HelloWorldApp.java file onto the javac application. The javac application will open and should look like Figure 20.

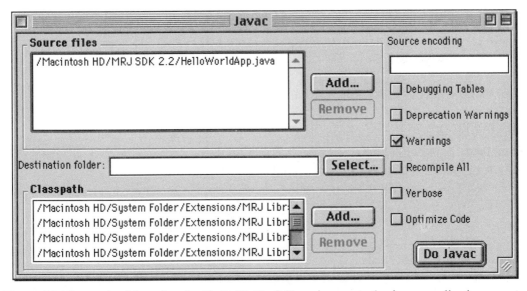

Figure 20 The result of dropping the file HelloWorldApp.java onto the javac application.

The Source Files text area shows the absolute path of the .java file we just created. Now there's nothing left to do except click the Do Javac button to compile your code. If a message like the one shown in Figure 21 appears without error messages, congratulations. You have successfully compiled your program.

Figure 21 The result of a successful compilation of HelloWorld.java.

The compiler has generated a Java bytecode file, `HelloWorldApp.class`. Look in the same folder where you saved the `.java` file to locate the `.class` file (Figure 22).

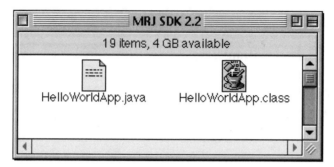

Figure 22 After you compile `HelloWorldApp.java`, the bytecode file, `HelloWorldApp.class`, is created in the same folder.

Now that you have a `.class` file, you can run your program.

Run the Program

From the MRJ SDK 2.2 folder, select the `Tools > Application Builders > JBindery`. The JBindery folder contains the JBindery application (Figure 23).

JBindery

Figure 23 The JBindery icon.

Drag and drop the `HelloWorldApp.class` file in the MRJ SDK 2.2 folder on top of the JBindery icon.

Note: A file called `HelloWorld.class` is included with the JBindery file. This file is not the one you created.

You should see the dialog shown in Figure 24.

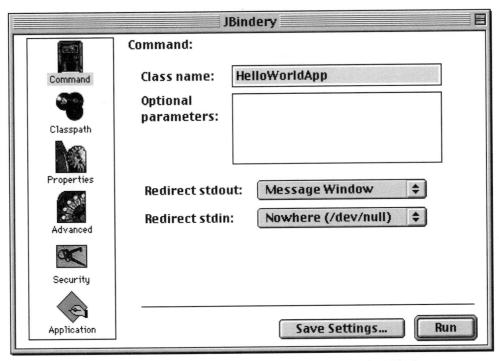

Figure 24 The result of dropping the HelloWorldApp.class file onto the JBindery program.

Click the Run button. Figure 25 shows what you should see.

Figure 25 The result of running the HelloWorldApp application.

Congratulations! You have just run your first program.

Creating Your First Applet

HelloWorldApp is an example of an *application*, a standalone program. Now you will create an *applet* called HelloWorld, which also displays the greeting "Hello world!" Unlike HelloWorldApp, however, the applet runs in a Java-enabled Web browser, such as the HotJava browser, Netscape Navigator, or Microsoft Internet Explorer.

To create this applet, you'll perform the basic steps as before: create a source file, compile the source file, and run the program. However, unlike for an application, you must also create an HTML file.

Create a Source File

You have two options to create a source file. You can save the files HelloWorld.java and Hello.html[1] on your computer and avoid a lot of typing. Then you can go straight to the second step of compiling the source file (page 31). Or, you can follow these instructions.

First, start SimpleText. In a new document, type the following code:

```
import java.applet.Applet;
import java.awt.Graphics;

public class HelloWorld extends Applet {
    public void paint(Graphics g) {
        // Display "Hello world!"
        g.drawString("Hello world!", 50, 25);
    }
}
```

Save this code to a file called HelloWorld.java.

Second, you also need an HTML file to accompany your applet. Type the following code into a new SimpleText document:

```
<HTML>
    <HEAD>
        <TITLE>A Simple Program</TITLE>
    </HEAD>
    <BODY>
        Here is the output of my program:
        <APPLET CODE="HelloWorld.class" WIDTH=150 HEIGHT=25>
        </APPLET>
    </BODY>
</HTML>
```

Save this code to a file called Hello.html. Make sure that your files HelloWorld.java and Hello.html are in the same folder.

---

[1] HelloWorld.java and Hello.html are available on this book's CD and online. See Code Samples (page 43).

Compile the Source File

Compile the HelloWorld.java source file using javac as before. The compiler should generate a bytecode file, HelloWorld.class.

Run the Program

Although you can use a Web browser to view your applets, you may find it easier to test your applets by using the simple Applet Runner application that comes with the Java platform. To view the HelloWorld applet using Applet Runner, select Apple Applet Runner in the MRJ SDK 2.2 folder (Figure 26).

Apple Applet Runner

Figure 26 The Apple Applet Runner icon.

Figure 27 shows what you should see.

Figure 27 The successful execution of the HelloWorld applet.

Congratulations! Your applet works. If you encounter errors, see Common Problems and Their Solutions (page 391) to help you fix the problems.

Error Explanation (MacOS)

If you drag and drop your .java file on top of the javac application and the file is only copied or moved on top of the javac application, you need to rebuild your desktop. To rebuild, you must restart you computer and press and hold the Apple and Alt keys until a confirmation dialog appears. Answer "yes" to the question asking whether you want to rebuild your desktop. When the rebuilding of your desktop is finished, you should be able to drag and drop the .java file onto javac to compile your program.

A Closer Look at HelloWorld

Now that you've compiled and run your first program, you may be wondering how it works
and how similar it is to other applications or applets. This section will first take a closer look
at the HelloWorldApp application and then the HelloWorld applet. Be aware that the following chapters, Object-Oriented Programming Concepts (page 45) and Language Basics (page
65), will go into much more detail than is presented in this section.

Explanation of an Application

Let's dissect the HelloWorldApp application. First, we will look at the comments in the code
before we touch on programming concepts, such as classes and methods.

```
/**
 * The HelloWorldApp class implements an application that
 * displays "Hello World!" to the standard output.
 */
public class HelloWorldApp {
    public static void main(String[] args) {
        System.out.println("Hello World!"); //Display the string.
    }
}
```

Comments

Comments make your code more readable; they help explain your code to others and serve
as reminder to yourself when you maintain your own code. The Java programming language
supports three kinds of comments:

/* *text* */
   The compiler ignores everything from the opening /* to the closing */.

/** *documentation* */
   This style indicates a documentation comment (*doc comment*, for short). As with the
   first kind of comment, the compiler ignores all the text within the comment. The SDK
   javadoc tool uses doc comments to automatically generate documentation. For more
   information on javadoc, see the tool documentation.[1]

// *text*
   The compiler ignores everything from the // to the end of the line.

---

[1] You can find the tool documentation online: http://java.sun.com/j2se/1.3/docs/tooldocs/tools.html

The boldface parts in the following code are comments:

```
/**
 * The HelloWorldApp class implements an application that
 * simply displays "Hello World!" to the standard output.
 */
class HelloWorldApp {
    public static void main(String[] args) {
        System.out.println("Hello World!"); //Display the string.
    }
}
```

Defining a Class

The first boldface line in this listing begins a *class definition block*:

```
/**
 * The HelloWorldApp class implements an application that
 * simply displays "Hello World!" to the standard output.
 */
class HelloWorldApp {
    public static void main(String[] args) {
        System.out.println("Hello World!"); //Display the string.
    }
}
```

A *class* is the basic building block of an object-oriented language, such as the Java programming language. A class is a blueprint that describes the state and the behavior associated with *instances* of that class. When you *instantiate* a class, you create an *object* that has the same states and behaviors as other instances of the same class. The state associated with a class or an object is stored in *member variables*. The behavior associated with a class or an object is implemented with *methods*, which are similar to the functions or procedures in procedural languages, such as C.

A recipe—say, Julia Child's recipe for ratatouille—is like a class. It's a blueprint for making a specific instance of the recipe. Her rendition of ratatouille is one instance of the recipe, and Mary Campione's is (quite) another.

A more traditional example from the world of programming is a class that represents a rectangle. The class defines variables for the origin, width, and height of the rectangle. The class might also define a method that calculates the area of the rectangle. An instance of the rectangle class, a rectangle object, contains the information for a specific rectangle, such as the dimensions of the floor of your office or the dimensions of this page.

This is simplest form of a class definition:

```
class Ratatouille {
    . . .                    //class definition block
}
```

The keyword `class` begins the class definition for a class named `Ratatouille`. The variables and the methods of the class are enclosed by the braces that begin and end the class definition block. The `HelloWorldApp` class has no variables and has a single method, named `main`.

The main Method

The entry point of every Java application is its `main` method. When you run an application with the Java interpreter, you specify the name of the class that you want to run. The interpreter invokes the `main` method defined in that class. The `main` method controls the flow of the program, allocates whatever resources are needed, and runs any other methods that provide the functionality for the application.

The boldface lines in the following listing begin and end the definition of the `main` method.

```
/**
 * The HelloWorldApp class implements an application that
 * simply displays "Hello World!" to the standard output.
 */
class HelloWorldApp {
    public static void main(String[] args) {
        System.out.println("Hello World!"); //Display the string.
    }
}
```

Every application must contain a `main` method declared like this:

```
public static void main(String[] args)
```

The `main` method declaration starts with three modifiers:

- `public`: Allows any class to call the `main` method
- `static`: Means that the `main` method is associated with the `HelloWorldApp` class as a whole instead of operating on an instance of the class
- `void`: Indicates that the `main` method does not return a value

When you invoke the interpreter, you give it the name of the class that you want to run. This class is the application's controlling class and must contain a `main` method. When invoked, the interpreter starts by calling the class's `main` method, which then calls all the other methods required to run the application. If you try to invoke the interpreter on a class that does not have a main method, the interpreter can't run your program. Instead, the interpreter displays an error message similar to this:

```
In class NoMain: void main(String argv[]) is not defined
```

As you can see from the declaration of the main method, it accepts a single argument: an array of elements of type String, like this:

```
public static void main(String[] args)
```

This array is the mechanism through which the Java Virtual Machine passes information to your application. Each String in the array is called a *command-line argument*. Command-line arguments let users affect the operation of the application without recompiling it. The HelloWorldApp application ignores its command-line arguments, so there isn't much more to discuss here.

Using Classes and Objects

The HelloWorldApp application is about the simplest program you can write that actually does something. Because it is such a simple program, it doesn't need to define any classes except HelloWorldApp.

However, the application does *use* another class, System, that is part of the Java API. The System class provides system-independent access to system-dependent functionality. One feature provided by the System class is the *standard output stream*—a place to send text that usually refers to the terminal window in which you invoked the Java interpreter.

Impurity Alert! Using the standard output stream isn't recommended in 100% Pure Java programs. However, it's fine to use during the development cycle. We use it in many of our example programs because otherwise, our code would be longer and more difficult to read.

The following boldface line shows HelloWorldApp's use of the standard output stream to display the string Hello World:

```
/**
 * The HelloWorldApp class implements an application that
 * simply displays "Hello World!" to the standard output.
 */
```

```
class HelloWorldApp {
    public static void main(String[] args) {
        System.out.println("Hello World!"); //Display the string.
    }
}
```

This one line of code uses both a *class variable* and an *instance method.*

Let's take a look at the first segment of the statement:

```
System.out.println("Hello World!");
```

The construct `System.out` is the full name of the `out` variable in the `System` class. The application never instantiates the `System` class but instead refers to `out` directly through the class. The reason is that `out` is a *class variable*—a variable associated with a class rather than with an object. The Java Virtual Machine allocates a class variable once per class, no matter how many instances of that class exist. The Java programming language also has the notion of *class methods* used to implement class-specific behaviors.

Although `System`'s `out` variable *is* a class variable, it *refers* to an instance of the `Print-Stream` class (another Java API-provided class that implements an easy-to-use output stream). When it is loaded into the application, the `System` class instantiates `PrintStream` and assigns the new `PrintStream` object to the `out` class variable. Now that you have an instance of a class, you can call one of its *instance methods*:

```
System.out.println("Hello World!");
```

An instance method implements behavior specific to a particular object—an instance of a class.

The Java programming language also has *instance variables*. An instance variable is a member variable associated with an object rather than with a class. Each time you instantiate a class, the new object gets its own copy of all the instance variables defined in its class.

If this discussion of member variables, methods, instances, and classes has left you with nothing but questions, the chapters Object-Oriented Programming Concepts (page 45) and Language Basics (page 65) can help.

The Anatomy of an Applet

By following the steps outlined in Creating Your First Applet (page 13 for Win32 and page 20 for UNIX/Linux), you created an applet—a program to be included in HTML pages and executed in Java-enabled browsers. Remember that an applet is a program that adheres to some conventions that allow it to run within a Java-enabled browser.

Here again is the code for the HelloWorld applet:

```
import java.applet.Applet;
import java.awt.Graphics;

public class HelloWorld extends Applet {
    public void paint(Graphics g) {
        g.drawString("Hello world!", 50, 25);
    }
}
```

Importing Classes and Packages

HelloWorld.java begins with two import statements that import the Applet and Graphics classes:

```
import java.applet.Applet;
import java.awt.Graphics;

public class HelloWorld extends Applet {
    public void paint(Graphics g) {
        g.drawString("Hello world!", 50, 25);
    }
}
```

By importing classes or packages, a class can easily refer to classes in other packages. In the Java programming language, packages are used to group classes, similar to the way libraries group C functions. If you removed the first two lines, you could still compile and run the program, but you could do so only if you changed the rest of the code like this (as shown in boldface):

```
public class HelloWorld extends java.applet.Applet {
    public void paint(java.awt.Graphics g) {
        g.drawString("Hello world!", 50, 25);
    }
}
```

As you can see, importing the Applet and Graphics classes lets the program refer to them later without any prefixes. The java.applet. and java.awt. prefixes tell the compiler which packages it should search for the Applet and Graphics classes. The java.applet package contains classes that are essential to applets. The java.awt package contains classes used by all programs with a GUI.

You might have noticed that the HelloWorldApp application uses the System class without any prefix, yet it does not import the System class. The reason is that the System class is part of the java.lang package, and everything in the java.lang package is automatically imported into every program written in the Java programming language.

You can import not only individual classes but also entire packages. Here's an example:

```
import java.applet.*;
import java.awt.*;

public class HelloWorld extends Applet {
    public void paint(Graphics g) {
        g.drawString("Hello world!", 50, 25);
    }
}
```

Every class is in a package. If the source code for a class doesn't have a package statement at the top declaring in which package the class is, the class is in the *default package*. Almost all the example classes in this tutorial are in the default package, java.lang.

Within a package, all classes can refer to one another without prefixes. For example, the java.awt package's Component class refers to the same package's Graphics class without any prefixes and without importing the Graphics class.

Defining an Applet Subclass

The first boldface line of the following listing begins a block that defines the HelloWorld class:

```
import java.applet.Applet;
import java.awt.Graphics;

public class HelloWorld extends Applet {
    public void paint(Graphics g) {
        g.drawString("Hello world!", 50, 25);
    }
}
```

The extends keyword indicates that HelloWorld is a subclass of the Applet class. In fact, every applet must define a subclass of the Applet class. Applets inherit a great deal of functionality from the Applet class, ranging from the ability to communicate with the browser to the ability to present a graphical user interface (GUI). You will learn more about subclasses in the chapter Object-Oriented Programming Concepts (page 45).

Implementing Applet Methods

The boldface lines of the following listing implement the paint method:

```
import java.applet.Applet;
import java.awt.Graphics;

public class HelloWorld extends Applet {
    public void paint(Graphics g) {
        g.drawString("Hello world!", 50, 25);
    }
}
```

The HelloWorld applet implements just one method: paint. Every applet should implement at least one of the following methods: init, start, or paint. Unlike applications, applets do *not* need to implement a main method.

Applets are designed to be included in HTML pages. Using the <APPLET> HTML tag, you specify (at a minimum) the location of the Applet subclass and the dimensions of the applet's on-screen display area. The applet's coordinate system starts at (0, 0), which is at the upper-left corner of the applet's display area. In the previous code snippet, the string Hello world! is drawn starting at location (50, 25), which is at the bottom of the applet's display area.

Running an Applet

When it encounters an <APPLET> tag, a Java-enabled browser reserves on-screen space for the applet, loads the Applet subclass onto the computer on which it is executing, and creates an instance of the Applet subclass.[1]

The boldface lines of the following listing comprise the <APPLET> tag that includes the Hello-World applet in an HTML page:

```
<HTML>
    <HEAD>
        <TITLE> A Simple Program </TITLE>
    </HEAD>
    <BODY>
        Here is the output of my program:
        <APPLET CODE="HelloWorld.class" WIDTH=150 HEIGHT=25>
        </APPLET>
    </BODY>
</HTML>
```

---

[1] You might use other tags to include applets, such as <OBJECT> or <EMBED>, but we show the <APPLET> tag for simplicity.

The <APPLET> tag specifies that the browser should load the class whose compiled code (bytecodes) is in the file named HelloWorld.class. The browser looks for this file in the same directory as the HTML document that contains the tag.

When it finds the class file, the browser loads it over the network, if necessary, onto the computer on which the browser is running. The browser then creates an instance of the class. If you include an applet twice in one HTML page, the browser loads the class file once and creates two instances of the class.

The WIDTH and HEIGHT attributes are like the attributes of the same name in an <IMG> tag: They specify the size in pixels of the applet's display area. Most browsers do not let the applet resize itself to be larger or smaller than this display area. For example, all the drawing that the HelloWorld applet does in its paint method occurs within the 150 x 25 pixel display area reserved by the <APPLET> tag.

Questions and Exercises

Questions

1. When you compile a program written in the Java language, the compiler converts the human-readable source file into platform-independent code that a Java Virtual Machine can understand. What is this platform-independent code called?

2. Which of the following is *not* a valid comment:

   a. `/** comment */`

   b. `/* comment */`

   c. `/* comment`

   d. `// comment`

3. In *The Java Tutorial*, what is the URL of the page that describes Khwarazm? (*Hint:* You can find the answer by going to `http://java.sun.com/docs/books/tutorial/` and clicking on the link to the Search page where you can perform a search.)

4. a. What is the highest version number of the Java 2 SDK, Standard Edition, that is available for download (early-access releases included)? (*Hint:* You can find the answer at `http://java.sun.com/j2se/`)

   b. What is the highest version number for an SDK that you can download and use in shipping products (that is, not an early-access release)?

   c. What is the lowest version number for an SDK that you can download? (Note that "SDK" used to be called "JDK.")

5. a. Which bug has the highest number of votes at the Java Developer Connection? Give the bug number, description, and number of votes. (*Hint:* Look for the answer at `http://developer.java.sun.com/developer/bugParade/`)

   b. Does the bug report give a workaround? If so, what is it?

6. What is the first thing you should check if the interpreter returns the error:
   ```
   Exception in thread "main" java.lang.NoClassDefFoundError:
   HelloWorldApp.java.
   ```

Exercises

1. Change the `HelloWorldApp.java` program so that it displays `Hola Mundo!` instead of `Hello World!`

2. Get the following file from the online Tutorial:

    `http://java.sun.com/docs/books/tutorial/getStarted/QandE/Useless.java`

    Compile and run this program. What is the output?

3. You can find a slightly modified version of `HelloWorldApp` here:

    `http://java.sun.com/docs/books/tutorial/getStarted/QandE/HelloWorldApp2.java`

    The program has an error. Fix the error so that the program successfully compiles and runs. What was the error?

4. Change the height of the `HelloWorld` applet from 25 to 50. Describe what the modified applet looks like.

5. Download the following two source files:

    `http://java.sun.com/docs/books/tutorial/getStarted/QandE/FirstClass.java`

    `http://java.sun.com/docs/books/tutorial/getStarted/QandE/SecondClass.java`

    Compile the files, and then run the resulting program. What is the output? If you have trouble compiling the files but have successfully compiled before, try unsetting the `CLASSPATH` environment variable as described in Path Help (page 540), and then compile again.

Answers

You can find answers to these Questions and Exercises online:

`http://java.sun.com/docs/books/tutorial/getStarted/QandE/answers.html`

Code Samples

Table 1 lists the code samples used in this chapter and where you can find the code online and on the CD that accompanies this book.

Table 1 Code Samples in Getting Started

Code Sample (where discussed)	CD Location	Online Location
HelloWorldApp.java (page 9, page 18, and page 25)	JavaTutorial/getStarted/ application/example/ HelloWorldApp.java	http://java.sun.com/docs/ books/tutorial/getStarted/ application/example/ HelloWorldApp.java
HelloWorld.java (page 13, page 20, and page 30)	JavaTutorial/getStarted/ applet/example/HelloWorld.java	http://java.sun.com/docs/ books/tutorial/getStarted/ applet/example/HelloWorld.java
HelloWorld.html (page 13, page 21, and page 30)	JavaTutorial/getStarted/ applet/example/Hello.html	http://java.sun.com/docs/ books/tutorial/getStarted/ applet/example/Hello.html

Note: The section Common Problems and Their Solutions (page 391) contains solutions to common problems that Tutorial readers have encountered.

Object-Oriented
Programming Concepts

IF you've never used an object-oriented language before, you need to understand the underlying concepts before you begin writing code. You need to understand what an object is, what a class is, how objects and classes are related, and how objects communicate by using messages. The first few sections of this chapter describe the concepts behind object-oriented programming. The last section shows how these concepts translate into code.

What Is an Object?

Objects are key to understanding object-oriented technology. You can look around you now and see many examples of real-world objects: your dog, your desk, your television set, your bicycle.

These real-world objects share two characteristics: They all have *state* and *behavior*. For example, dogs have state (name, color, breed, hungry) and behavior (barking, fetching, and wagging tail). Bicycles have state (current gear, current pedal cadence, two wheels, number of gears) and behavior (braking, accelerating, slowing down, changing gears).

Software objects are modeled after real-world objects in that they too have state and behavior. A software object maintains its state in one or more *variables*. A variable is an item of data named by an identifier. A software object implements its behavior with *methods*. A method is a function (subroutine) associated with an object.

Definition: An object is a software bundle of variables and related methods.

You can represent real-world objects by using software objects. You might want to represent real-world dogs as software objects in an animation program or a real-world bicycle as a software object in the program that controls an electronic exercise bike. You can also use software objects to model abstract concepts. For example, an *event* is a common object used in Graphical User Interface (GUI) window systems to represent the action of a user pressing a mouse button or a key on the keyboard. Figure 28 is a common visual representation of a software object.

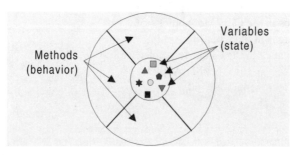

Figure 28   A software object.

Everything that the software object knows (state) and can do (behavior) is expressed by the variables and the methods within that object. A software object that modeled your real-world bicycle would have variables that indicated the bicycle's current state: Its speed is 10 mph, its pedal cadence is 90 rpm, and its current gear is the 5th gear. These variables are formally known as *instance variables* because they contain the state for a particular bicycle object, and in object-oriented terminology, a particular object is called an *instance*. Figure 29 illustrates a bicycle modeled as a software object.

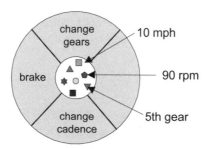

Figure 29 A bicycle modeled as a software object.

In addition to its variables, the software bicycle would also have methods to brake, change the pedal cadence, and change gears. (The bike would not have a method for changing the speed of the bicycle, as the bike's speed is just a side effect of what gear it's in, how fast the rider is pedaling, whether the brakes are on, and how steep the hill is.) These methods are formally known as *instance methods* because they inspect or change the state of a particular bicycle instance.[1]

The object diagrams show that the object's variables make up the center, or nucleus, of the object. Methods surround and hide the object's nucleus from other objects in the program. Packaging an object's variables within the protective custody of its methods is called *encapsulation*. This conceptual picture of an object—a nucleus of variables packaged within a protective membrane of methods—is an ideal representation of an object and is the ideal that designers of object-oriented systems strive for. However, it's not the whole story. Often, for practical reasons, an object may wish to expose some of its variables or to hide some of its methods. In the Java™ programming language, an object can specify one of four access levels for each of its variables and methods. The access level determines which other objects and classes can access that variable or method. Refer to the section <u>Controlling Access to Members of a Class</u> (page 193) for details.

Encapsulating related variables and methods into a neat software bundle is a simple yet powerful idea that provides two primary benefits to software developers.

---

[1] Only the state and the behavior related to the object are included in the object. For example, your bicycle (probably) doesn't have a name, and it can't run, bark, or fetch. Thus, there are no variables or methods for those states and behaviors in the bicycle class.

- **Modularity:** The source code for an object can be written and maintained independently of the source code for other objects. Also, an object can be easily passed around in the system. You can give your bicycle to someone else, and it will still work.
- **Information hiding:** An object has a public interface that other objects can use to communicate with it. The object can maintain private information and methods that can be changed at any time without affecting the other objects that depend on it. You don't need to understand the gear mechanism on your bike to use it.

What Is a Message?

A single object alone is generally not very useful. Instead, an object usually appears as a component of a larger program or application that contains many other objects. Through the interaction of these objects, programmers achieve higher-order functionality and more complex behavior. Your bicycle hanging from a hook in the garage is just a bunch of titanium alloy and rubber; by itself, the bicycle is incapable of any activity. The bicycle is useful only when another object (you) interacts with it (pedal).

Software objects interact and communicate with each other by sending *messages* to each other. When object A wants object B to perform one of B's methods, object A sends a message to object B (Figure 30).

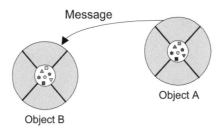

Figure 30 Objects interact by sending each other messages.

Sometimes, the receiving object needs more information so that it knows exactly what to do; for example, when you want to change gears on your bicycle, you have to indicate which gear you want. This information is passed along with the message as *parameters*.

Figure 31 shows the three components that comprise a message:

- The object to which the message is addressed (`YourBicycle`)
- The name of the method to perform (`changeGears`)
- Any parameters needed by the method (`lowerGear`)

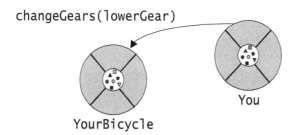

Figure 31 Messages use parameters to pass along extra information that the object needs—in this case, which gear the bicycle should be in.

These three components are enough information for the receiving object to perform the desired method. No other information or context is required.

Messages provide two important benefits.

- An object's behavior is expressed through its methods, so (aside from direct variable access) message passing supports all possible interactions between objects.
- Objects don't need to be in the same process or even on the same machine to send and receive messages back and forth to each other.

What Is a Class?

In the real world, you often have many objects of the same kind. For example, your bicycle is just one of many bicycles in the world. Using object-oriented terminology, we say that your bicycle object is an instance of the class of objects known as bicycles. Bicycles have some state (current gear, current cadence, two wheels) and behavior (change gears, brake) in common. However, each bicycle's state is independent of and can be different from that of other bicycles.

When building bicycles, manufacturers take advantage of the fact that bicycles share characteristics, building many bicycles from the same blueprint. It would be very inefficient to produce a new blueprint for every individual bicycle manufactured.

In object-oriented software, it's also possible to have many objects of the same kind that share characteristics: rectangles, employee records, video clips, and so on. Like the bicycle manufacturers, you can take advantage of the fact that objects of the same kind are similar and you can create a blueprint for those objects. A software blueprint for objects is called a *class* (Figure 32).

can an object be restricted from using a method within its class?

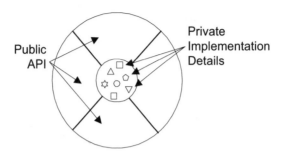

Figure 32 A visual representation of a class.

Definition: A class is a blueprint, or prototype, that defines the variables and the methods common to all objects of a certain kind.

The class for our bicycle example would declare the instance variables necessary to contain the current gear, the current cadence, and so on, for each bicycle object. The class would also declare and provide implementations for the instance methods that allow the rider to change gears, brake, and change the pedaling cadence, as shown in Figure 33.

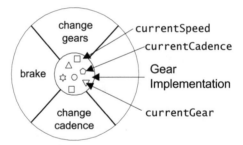

Figure 33 The bicycle class.

After you've created the bicycle class, you can create any number of bicycle objects from the class. When you create an instance of a class, the system allocates enough memory for the object and all its instance variables. Each instance gets its own copy of all the instance variables defined in the class (Figure 34).

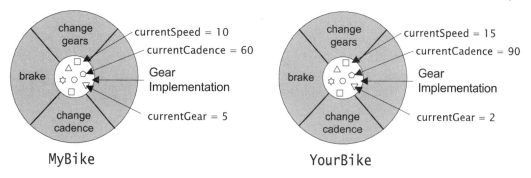

Figure 34 MyBike and YourBike are two different instances of the Bike class. Each instance has its own copy of the instance variables defined in the Bike class but has different values for these variables.

In addition to instance variables, classes can define *class variables*. A class variable contains information that is shared by all instances of the class. For example, suppose that all bicycles had the same number of gears. In this case, defining an instance variable to hold the number of gears is inefficient; each instance would have its own copy of the variable, but the value would be the same for every instance. In such situations, you can define a class variable that contains the number of gears. All instances share this variable. If one object changes the variable, it changes for all other objects of that type. A class can also declare *class methods*. You can invoke a class method directly from the class, whereas you must invoke instance methods on a particular instance. *method acts on all objects w/in class?*

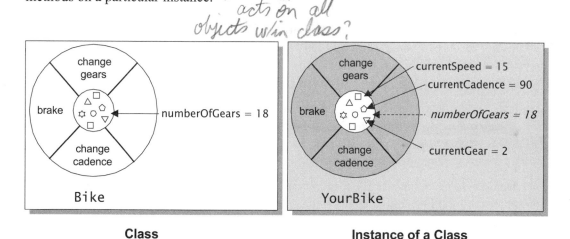

Class **Instance of a Class**

Figure 35 YourBike, an instance of Bike, has access to the numberOfGears variable in the Bike class; however, the YourBike instance does not have a copy of this class variable.

The section <u>Understanding Instance and Class Members</u> (page 198) discusses instance variables and methods and class variables and methods in detail.

Objects provide the benefit of modularity and information hiding. Classes provide the benefit of reusability. Bicycle manufacturers reuse the same blueprint over and over again to build lots of bicycles. Software programmers use the same class, and thus the same code, over and over again to create many objects.

Objects versus Classes

You probably noticed that the illustrations of objects and classes look very similar. And indeed, the difference between classes and objects is often the source of some confusion. In the real world, it's obvious that classes are not themselves the objects they describe: A blueprint of a bicycle is not a bicycle. However, it's a little more difficult to differentiate classes and objects in software. This is partially because software objects are merely electronic models of real-world objects or abstract concepts in the first place. But it's also because the term "object" is sometimes used to refer to both classes and instances.

In the figures, the class is not shaded, because it represents a blueprint of an object rather than an object itself. In comparison, an object is shaded, indicating that the object exists and that you can use it.

What Is Inheritance?

Generally speaking, objects are defined in terms of classes. You know a lot about an object by knowing its class. Even if you don't know what a penny-farthing is, if I told you it was a bicycle, you would know that it had two wheels, handle bars, and pedals.

Object-oriented systems take this a step further and allow classes to be defined in terms of other classes. For example, mountain bikes, racing bikes, and tandems are all kinds of bicycles. In object-oriented terminology, mountain bikes, racing bikes, and tandems are all *subclasses* of the bicycle class. Similarly, the bicycle class is the *superclass* of mountain bikes, racing bikes, and tandems. This relationship is shown in Figure 36.

Each subclass *inherits* state (in the form of variable declarations) from the superclass. Mountain bikes, racing bikes, and tandems share some states: cadence, speed, and the like. Also, each subclass inherits methods from the superclass. Mountain bikes, racing bikes, and tandems share some behaviors: braking and changing pedaling speed, for example.

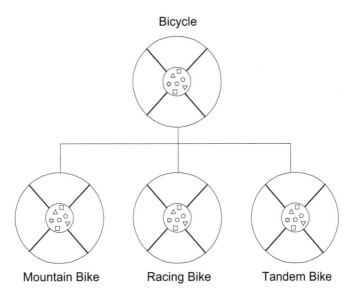

Figure 36 The hierarchy of bicycle classes.

However, subclasses are not limited to the state and behaviors provided to them by their superclass. Subclasses can add variables and methods to the ones they inherit from the superclass. Tandem bicycles have two seats and two sets of handle bars; some mountain bikes have an extra set of gears with a lower gear ratio.

Subclasses can also *override* inherited methods and provide specialized implementations for those methods. For example, if you had a mountain bike with an extra set of gears, you would override the "change gears" method so that the rider could use those new gears.

You are not limited to just one layer of inheritance. The inheritance tree, or class *hierarchy*, can be as deep as needed. Methods and variables are inherited down through the levels. In general, the farther down in the hierarchy a class appears, the more specialized its behavior.

The Object class is at the top of class hierarchy, and each class is its descendant (directly or indirectly). A variable of type Object can hold a reference to any object, such as an instance of a class or an array. Object provides behaviors that are required of all objects running in the Java Virtual Machine. For example, all classes inherit Object's toString method, which returns a string representation of the object. The section <u>Managing Inheritance</u> (page 204) covers the Object class in detail.

Inheritance offers the following benefits:

- Subclasses provide specialized behaviors from the basis of common elements provided by the superclass. Through the use of inheritance, programmers can reuse the code in the superclass many times.

- Programmers can implement superclasses called *abstract classes* that define "generic" behaviors. The abstract superclass defines and may partially implement the behavior, but much of the class is undefined and unimplemented. Other programmers fill in the details with specialized subclasses.

What Is an Interface?

In English, an interface is a device or a system that unrelated entities use to interact. According to this definition, a remote control is an interface between you and a television set, the English language is an interface between two people, and the protocol of behavior enforced in the military is the interface between people of different ranks. Within the Java programming language, an *interface* is a device that unrelated objects use to interact with each other.[1] An interface is probably most analogous to a protocol (an agreed on behavior). In fact, other object-oriented languages have the functionality of interfaces, but they call their interfaces protocols.

Definition: An interface is a device that unrelated objects use to interact with each other. An object can implement multiple interfaces.

The bicycle class and its class hierarchy define what a bicycle can and cannot do in terms of its "bicycleness." But bicycles interact with the world on other terms. For example, a bicycle in a store could be managed by an inventory program. An inventory program doesn't care what class of items it manages, as long as each item provides certain information, such as price and tracking number. Instead of forcing class relationships on otherwise unrelated items, the inventory program sets up a protocol of communication. This protocol comes in the form of a set of constant and method definitions contained within an interface. The inventory interface would define, but not implement, methods that set and get the retail price, assign a tracking number, and so on.

To work in the inventory program, the bicycle class must agree to this protocol by implementing the interface. When a class implements an interface, the class agrees to implement all the methods defined in the interface. Thus, the bicycle class would provide the implementations for the methods that set and get retail price, assign a tracking number, and so on.

You use an interface to define a protocol of behavior that can be implemented by any class anywhere in the class hierarchy. Interfaces are useful for the following:

---

[1]   Unrelated objects are not related by class hierarchy.

- Capturing similarities among unrelated classes without artificially forcing a class relationship
- Declaring methods that one or more classes are expected to implement
- Revealing an object's programming interface without revealing its class

How Do These Concepts Translate into Code?

Now that you have a conceptual understanding of object-oriented programming, let's look at how these concepts get translated into code. Figure 37 is a snapshot of an applet named ClickMe. A spot appears when you click the mouse within the applet's bounds.

Figure 37 The ClickMe applet.

The ClickMe applet is a relatively simple program and the code for it is short. However, if you don't have much experience with programming, you might find the code daunting. We don't expect you to understand everything in this program right away, and this section won't explain every detail. The intent is to expose you to some source code and to associate it with the concepts and terminology you just learned. You will learn the details in later chapters.

The Source Code and the Applet Tag for ClickMe

To compile this applet, you need two source files: ClickMe.java[1] and Spot.java.[2] These source files contain the code for two classes. In addition to these two classes, the applet uses some classes provided by the Java platform. You can compile the ClickMe.java and Spot.java files by invoking the compiler on ClickMe.java. See Common Problems and Their Solutions (page 391) if you have any trouble compiling.

To run the applet, you first need to create an HTML file with the following applet tag in it.

---

[1] ClickMe.java is included on the CD and is available online. See Code Samples (page 63).

[2] Spot.java is included on the CD and is available online. See Code Samples (page 63).

```
<applet code="ClickMe.class"
        width="300" height="150">
</applet>
```

Then load the page into your browser or the appletviewer tool. Figure 38 shows where to put the files for the ClickMe applet.

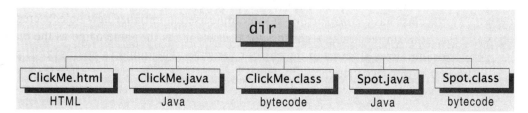

Figure 38 A sample directory structure showing where files for the ClickMe applet are stored.

Objects in the ClickMe Applet

Many objects play a part in this applet. The two most obvious ones are the ones you can see: the applet itself and the spot, which is red on-screen.

The browser creates the applet object when it encounters the applet tag in the HTML code containing the applet. The applet tag provides the name of the class from which to create the applet object. In this case, the class name is ClickMe.

The ClickMe applet in turn creates an object to represent the spot on the screen. Every time you click the mouse in the applet, the applet moves the spot by changing the object's *x* and *y* location and repainting itself. The spot does not draw itself; the applet draws the spot, based on information contained within the spot object.

Besides these two obvious objects, other, nonvisible objects play a part in this applet. Three objects represent the three colors used in the applet (black, white, and red); an event object represents the user action of clicking the mouse, and so on.

Classes in the ClickMe Applet

Because the object that represents the spot on the screen is very simple, let's look at its class, named Spot. It declares three instance variables: size contains the spot's radius, x contains the spot's current horizontal location, and y contains the spot's current vertical location:

```
public class Spot {
    //instance variables
    public int size;
    public int x, y;
```

```
    //constructor
    public Spot(int intSize) {
        size = intSize;
        x = -1;
        y = -1;
    }
}
```

Additionally, the class has a *constructor*—a subroutine used to initialize new objects created from the class. You can recognize a constructor because it has the same name as the class. The constructor initializes all three of the object's variables. The initial value of size is provided as an argument to the constructor by the caller (intSize). The x and y variables are set to -1, indicating that the spot is not on-screen when the applet starts up.

The applet creates a new spot object when the applet is initialized. Here's the relevant code from the applet class:

```
private Spot spot = null;
private static final int RADIUS = 7;
...
spot = new Spot(RADIUS);
```

The first line shown declares a variable named spot whose data type is Spot, the class from which the object is created, and initializes the variable to null.[1] The second line declares an integer variable named RADIUS whose value is 7. Finally, the last line shown creates the object; new allocates memory space for the object. Spot(RADIUS) calls the constructor you saw previously and passes in the value of RADIUS. Thus, the spot object's size is set to 7, as shown in Figure 39.

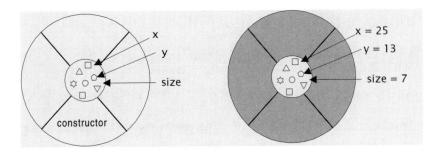

Figure 39 The figure on the left is a representation of the Spot class. The figure on the right is a spot object.

---

[1] The keyword null is used to specify an undefined value for variables that refer to objects.

Messages in the ClickMe Applet

As you know, object A can use a message to request that object B do something, and a message has three components:

- The object to which the message is addressed
- The name of the method to perform
- Any parameters the method needs

Here are two lines of code from the `ClickMe` applet:

```
g.setColor(Color.white);
g.fillRect(0, 0, getSize().width - 1, getSize().height - 1);
```

Both are messages from the applet to an object named g—a `Graphics` object that knows how to draw simple on-screen shapes and text. This object is provided to the applet when the browser instructs the applet to draw itself. The first line sets the color to white; the second fills a rectangle the size of the applet, thus painting the extent of the applet's area white.

Figure 40 highlights each message component in the first message.

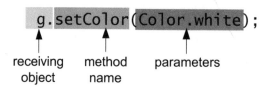

Figure 40 The message components of a message in the `ClickMe` applet.

Inheritance in the ClickMe Applet

To run in a browser, an object must be an applet. This means that the object must be an instance of a class that derives from the `Applet` class provided by the Java platform.

The `ClickMe` applet object is an instance of the `ClickMe` class, which is declared like this:

```
public class ClickMe extends Applet implements MouseListener {
    ...
}
```

The `extends Applet` clause makes `ClickMe` a subclass of `Applet`. `ClickMe` inherits a lot of capability from its superclass, including the ability to be initialized, started, and stopped by the browser; to draw within an area on a browser page; and to register to receive mouse events. Along with these benefits, the ClickMe class has certain obligations: Its painting code must be in a method called paint, its initialization code must be in a method called init, and so on:

```
public void init() {
    ... // ClickMe's initialization code here
}

public void paint(Graphics g) {
    ... // ClickMe's painting code here
}
```

Interfaces in the ClickMe Applet

The ClickMe applet responds to mouse clicks by displaying a red spot at the click location. If an object wants to be notified of mouse clicks, the event system requires that the object implement the MouseListener interface. The object must also register as a mouse listener.

The MouseListener interface declares five methods, each of which is called for a different kind of mouse event: when the mouse is clicked, when the mouse moves outside of the applet, and so on. Even though the applet is interested only in mouse clicks, it must implement all five methods. The methods for the events that the applet isn't interested in are empty.

The complete code for the ClickMe applet follows. The code that participates in mouse event handling is in boldface:

```
import java.applet.Applet;
import java.awt.*;
import java.awt.event.*;

public class ClickMe extends Applet implements MouseListener {
    private Spot spot = null;
    private static final int RADIUS = 7;

    public void init() {
        addMouseListener(this);
    }

    public void paint(Graphics g) {
        // draw a black border and a white background
        g.setColor(Color.white);
        g.fillRect(0, 0, getSize().width - 1, getSize().height - 1);
        g.setColor(Color.black);
        g.drawRect(0, 0, getSize().width - 1, getSize().height - 1);
```

```
        // draw the spot
        g.setColor(Color.red);
        if (spot != null) {
            g.fillOval(spot.x - RADIUS, spot.y - RADIUS,
                    RADIUS * 2, RADIUS * 2);
        }
    }

    public void mousePressed(MouseEvent event) {
        if (spot == null) {
            spot = new Spot(RADIUS);
        }
        spot.x = event.getX();
        spot.y = event.getY();
        repaint();
    }

    public void mouseClicked(MouseEvent event) {}
    public void mouseReleased(MouseEvent event) {}
    public void mouseEntered(MouseEvent event) {}
    public void mouseExited(MouseEvent event) {}
}
```

API Documentation

The ClickMe applet inherits a lot of capability from its superclass. To learn more about how ClickMe works, you need to learn about its superclass, Applet. How do you find that information? You can find detailed descriptions of every class in the API documentation, which constitutes the specification for the classes that make up the Java platform.

The API documentation for the Java 2 Platform is online at java.sun.com. The documentation is also included on the CD that accompanies this book. When appropriate, this book has footnotes providing the URLs to the API documents for particular classes. It's helpful to have the API documentation for all releases you use bookmarked in your browser.

- API documents for Java 2 Platform, Standard Edition, v. 1.3[1]
- API documents for Java 2 Platform, Standard Edition, v. 1.2[2]
- API documents for JDK 1.1[3]
- API documents for JDK 1.0.2[4]

---

[1]   http://java.sun.com/j2se/1.3/docs/api/index.html
[2]   http://java.sun.com/products/jdk/1.2/docs/api/index.html
[3]   http://java.sun.com/products/jdk/1.1/docs/api/packages.html
[4]   http://java.sun.com/products/jdk/1.0.2/api/index.html

To learn more about all the classes and interfaces from the Java platform used by the `ClickMe` applet, you can look at the API documentation for these classes:

- `java.applet.Applet`[1]
- `java.awt.Graphics`[2]
- `java.awt.Color`[3]
- `java.awt.event.MouseListener`[4]
- `java.awt.event.MouseEvent`[5]

Summary

This discussion glossed over many details and left some things unexplained, but you should have some understanding now of what object-oriented concepts look like in code. You should now have a general understanding of the following:

- That a class is a prototype for objects
- That objects are created from classes
- That an object's class is its type
- How to create an object from a class
- What constructors are
- How to initialize objects
- What the code for a class looks like
- What class variables and methods are
- What instance variables and methods are
- How to find out what a class's superclass is
- That an interface is a protocol of behavior
- What it means to implement an interface

[1]   http://java.sun.com/j2se/1.3/docs/api/java/applet/Applet.html
[2]   http://java.sun.com/j2se/1.3/docs/api/java/awt/Graphics.html
[3]   http://java.sun.com/j2se/1.3/docs/api/java/awt/Color.html
[4]   http://java.sun.com/j2se/1.3/docs/api/java/awt/event/MouseListener.html
[5]   http://java.sun.com/j2se/1.3/docs/api/java/awt/event/MouseEvent.html

Questions and Exercises

Questions

Use the API documentation to answer these questions.

1. The applet uses `Color.red` to set the drawing color to red. What other colors can you get by name like this?

2. How would you specify other colors, such as purple? (*Hint:* Purple is made up of equal parts red and blue.)

3. What `Graphics` method would you use to draw a filled square?

4. What `Graphics` method would you call to draw text?

Exercises

Note: The point of these exercises is to encourage you to read code and to use the API documentation. We haven't yet given you any detailed information about how to write code, but you might be surprised at how much you can do.

Use what you learned from the preceding questions to make the following modifications to the `ClickMe` applet.

1. Modify the applet to draw a green square instead of a red spot.

2. Modify the applet to display your name in purple instead of a red spot.

Remember that to compile this program, you need two source files: `ClickMe.java`[1] and `Spot.java`.[2] To run the program, you need to supply `appletviewer` with an HTML file, such as `ClickMe.html`,[3] that has the appropriate applet tag.

Answers

You can find answers to these Questions and Exercises online:

```
http://java.sun.com/docs/books/tutorial/java/concepts/QandE/
answers.html
```

---
[1] `ClickMe.java` is included on the CD and is available online. See <u>Code Samples</u> (page 63).
[2] `Spot.java` is included on the CD and is available online. See <u>Code Samples</u> (page 63).
[3] `ClickMe.html` is included on the CD and is available online. See <u>Code Samples</u> (page 63).

Code Samples

Table 2 lists the code samples used in this chapter and where you can find the code online and on the CD that accompanies this book.

Table 2   Code Samples in Object-Oriented Programming Concepts

Code Sample (where discussed)	CD Location	Online Location
Spot.java (page 56)	JavaTutorial/java/concepts/example-1dot1/Spot.java	http://java.sun.com/docs/books/tutorial/java/concepts/example-1dot1/Spot.java
ClickMe.java (page 58)	JavaTutorial/java/concepts/example-1dot1/ClickMe.java	http://java.sun.com/docs/books/tutorial/java/concepts/example-1dot1/ClickMe.java
ClickMe.html (page 58)	JavaTutorial/java/concepts/example-1dot1/ClickMe.html	http://java.sun.com/docs/books/tutorial/java/concepts/example-1dot1/ClickMe.html

Note: The section <u>Common Problems and Their Solutions</u> (page 391) contains solutions to common problems Tutorial readers have encountered.

Language Basics

T HE BasicsDemo program[1] that follows adds the numbers from 1 to 10 and displays the result:

```java
public class BasicsDemo {
    public static void main(String[] args) {
        int sum = 0;
        for (int i = 1; i <= 10; i++) {
            sum += i;
        }
        System.out.println("Sum = " + sum);
    }
}
```

The output from this program is:

```
Sum = 55
```

Even a small program such as this uses many of the traditional features of the Java™ programming language, including variables, operators, and control flow statements. The code might look a little mysterious now. But this chapter teaches what you need to know about the nuts and bolts of the Java programming language to understand this program.

This chapter has four sections. The first section, Variables (page 67), discusses data types, how to initialize variables, and how to refer to variables within blocks of code.

---

[1] BasicsDemo.java is included on the CD and is available online. See Code Samples (page 117).

The Operators (page 76) section details how you perform various operations, such as arithmetic and assignment operations. Expressions, Statements, and Blocks (page 94) covers the building blocks of your code. And finally, the last section, Control Flow Statements (page 99), shows you how to control the flow of your program with such statements as `if-else` and `while`.

Variables

An object stores its state in variables.

Definition: A *variable* is an item of data named by an identifier.

You must explicitly provide a name and a type for each variable you want to use in your program. The variable's name must be a legal *identifier*—an unlimited series of Unicode[1] characters that begins with a letter. You use the variable name to refer to the data that the variable contains. The variable's type determines what values it can hold and what operations can be performed on it. To give a variable a type and a name, you write a variable *declaration*, which generally looks like this:

```
type name
```

In addition to the name and the type that you explicitly give a variable, a variable has *scope*. The section of code where the variable's simple name can be used is the variable's scope. The variable's scope is determined implicitly by the location of the variable declaration, that is, where the declaration appears in relation to other code elements. You'll learn more about scope in the section Scope (page 72).

The boldface type in the following program, called MaxVariablesDemo,[2] highlights all the variable declarations in the program:

```java
public class MaxVariablesDemo {
    public static void main(String args[]) {

        // integers
        byte largestByte = Byte.MAX_VALUE;
        short largestShort = Short.MAX_VALUE;
        int largestInteger = Integer.MAX_VALUE;
        long largestLong = Long.MAX_VALUE;

        // real numbers
        float largestFloat = Float.MAX_VALUE;
        double largestDouble = Double.MAX_VALUE;

        // other primitive types
```

---

[1] Unicode is a 16-bit character set defined by ISO 10646.
[2] MaxVariablesDemo.java is included on the CD and is available online. See Code Samples (page 117).

```
char aChar = 'S';
boolean aBoolean = true;

// display them all
System.out.println("The largest byte value is "
                    + largestByte);
System.out.println("The largest short value is "
                    + largestShort);
System.out.println("The largest integer value is "
                    + largestInteger);
System.out.println("The largest long value is "
                    + largestLong);

System.out.println("The largest float value is "
                    + largestFloat);
System.out.println("The largest double value is "
                    + largestDouble);

if (Character.isUpperCase(aChar)) {
    System.out.println("The character " + aChar
                        + " is upper case.");
} else {
    System.out.println("The character " + aChar
                        + " is lower case.");
}
System.out.println("The value of aBoolean is " + aBoolean);
        }
    }
```

The output from this program is:

```
The largest byte value is 127
The largest short value is 32767
The largest integer value is 2147483647
The largest long value is 9223372036854775807
The largest float value is 3.40282e+38
The largest double value is 1.79769e+308
The character S is upper case.
The value of aBoolean is true
```

The following sections further explore the various aspects of variables, including data types, names, scope, initialization, and final variables. The MaxVariablesDemo program uses two items with which you might not yet be familiar and are not covered in this section: several constants named MAX_VALUE and an if-else statement. Each MAX_VALUE constant is defined in one of the number classes provided by the Java platform and is the largest value that can be assigned to a variable of that numeric type. These classes are covered in the section The

Number Classes (page 150). The `if-else` statement is covered later in this chapter in the section The if-else Statements (page 102).

Data Types

Every variable must have a data type. A variable's data type determines the values that the variable can contain and the operations that can be performed on it. For example, in the Max-VariablesDemo program, the declaration `int largestInteger` declares that `largest-Integer` has an integer data type (`int`). Integers can contain only integral values (both positive and negative). You can perform arithmetic operations, such as addition, on integer variables.

The Java programming language has two categories of data types: *primitive* and *reference*. A variable of primitive type contains a single value of the appropriate size and format for its type: a number, a character, or a boolean value. For example, an integer value is 32 bits of data in a format known as two's complement, the value of a char is 16 bits of data formatted as a Unicode character, and so on.

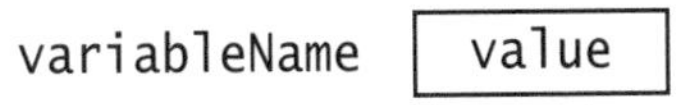

variableName | value |

Figure 41 A variable of primitive type contains a value of a particular size and format.

Table 3 lists, by keyword, all the primitive data types supported by the Java platform, their sizes and formats, and a brief description of each. The MaxVariablesDemo program declares one variable of each primitive type.

Table 3 Primitive Data Types[a]

	Keyword	**Description**	**Size/Format**
Integers	`byte`	Byte-length integer	8-bit signed two's-complement integers
	`short`	Short integer	16-bit signed two's-complement integers
	`int`	Integer	32-bit signed two's-complement integers
	`long`	Long integer	64-bit signed two's-complement integers
Real Numbers	`float`	Single-precision floating point	32-bit IEEE 754 floating-point numbers
	`double`	Double-precision floating point	64-bit IEEE 754 floating-point numbers
Other Types	`char`	A single Unicode character	16-bit Unicode character
	`boolean`	A boolean value (`true` or `false`)	8-bit/1-bit (8 bits of space, 1 bit of data)

a. The size and format information is provided for experienced programmers who like details of this sort. If you don't know what two's complement or IEEE 754 is, don't worry about it. You don't need to.

Purity Tip: In other programming languages, the format and the size of primitive data types can depend on the system on which the program is running. In contrast, the Java programming language specifies the size and the format of its primitive data types. Hence, you don't have to worry about system dependencies.

You can put a literal primitive value directly in your code. For example, if you need to assign the value 4 to an integer variable, you can write this:

```
int anInt = 4;
```

The digit 4 is a literal integer value. Table 4 gives some examples of literal values of various primitive types.

Table 4   Examples of Literal Values and Their Data Types

Literal	Data Type
178	int
8864L	long
37.266	double
37.266D	double
87.363F	float
26.77e3	double
'c'	char
true	boolean
false	boolean

Generally speaking, a series of digits with no decimal point is typed as an integer. You can specify a long integer by putting an 'L' or 'l' after the number. 'L' is preferred, as it cannot be confused with the digit '1'. A series of digits with a decimal point is of type double. You can specify a float by putting an 'f' or 'F' after the number. A literal character value is any single Unicode character between single quote marks. The two boolean literals are simply true and false.

Arrays, classes, and interfaces are *reference* types. The value of a reference type variable, in contrast to that of a primitive type, is a reference to (an address of) the value or set of values represented by the variable (Figure 42). A reference is called a pointer, or a memory address in other languages. The Java programming language does not support the explicit use of addresses like other languages do. You use the variable's name instead.

reference variables

Figure 42 A variable of reference type contains a reference to (an address of) an object or an array.

Variable Names

A program refers to a variable's value by the variable's name. For example, when it displays the value of the `largestByte` variable, the `MaxVariablesDemo` program uses the name `largestByte`. A name, such as `largestByte`, that's composed of a single identifier, is called a *simple name*. Simple names are in contrast to *qualified* names, which a class uses to refer to a member variable that's in another object or class. This topic is covered further in the section Using Objects (page 126).

In the Java programming language, the following must hold true for a simple name.

- It must be a legal identifier. Recall from page 67 that an identifier is an unlimited series of Unicode characters that begins with a letter.
- It must not be a keyword,[1] a boolean literal (`true` or `false`), or the reserved word `null`.
- It must be unique within its scope. A variable may have the same name as a variable whose declaration appears in a different scope. In some situations, a variable may share names with another variable, which is declared in a nested scope. Scope is covered in the next section.

By Convention: Variable names begin with a lowercase letter, and class names begin with an uppercase letter. If a variable name consists of more than one word, the words are joined together, and each word after the first begins with an uppercase letter, like this: `isVisible`. The underscore character (`_`) is acceptable anywhere in a name, but by convention is used only to separate words in constants (because constants are all caps by convention and thus cannot be case-delimited).

---

[1] All the keywords in the Java programming language are listed in the section Java Programming Language Keywords (page 535).

Scope

A variable's scope is the region of a program within which the variable can be referred to by its simple name. Secondarily, scope also determines when the system creates and destroys memory for the variable. Scope is distinct from visibility, which applies only to member variables and determines whether the variable can be used from outside of the class within which it is declared. Visibility is set with an access modifier. See the section Controlling Access to Members of a Class (page 193) for more information.

The location of the variable declaration within your program establishes its scope. There are four categories of scope, as shown in Figure 43.

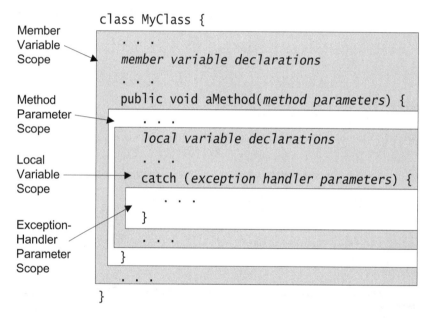

Figure 43 The four categories of scope: member variable, method parameter, local variable, and exception-handler parameter.

A member variable is a member of a class or an object. It is declared within a class but outside of any method or constructor. A member variable's scope is the entire declaration of the class. However, the declaration of a member needs to appear before it is used when the use is in a member initialization expression. For information about declaring member variables, refer to the section Declaring Member Variables (page 181).

You declare local variables within a block of code. In general, the scope of a local variable extends from its declaration to the end of the code block in which it was declared. In Max-VariablesDemo, all the variables declared within the main method are local variables. The scope of each variable in that program extends from the declaration of the variable to the end of the main method—indicated by the second to last right brace (}) in the program code.

Parameters are formal arguments to methods or constructors and are used to pass values into methods and constructors. The scope of a parameter is the entire method or constructor for which it is a parameter. The chapter <u>Classes and Inheritance</u> (page 177) discusses writing methods in the section <u>Defining Methods</u> (page 182), which talks about passing values into methods through parameters.

Exception-handler parameters are similar to parameters but are arguments to an exception handler rather than to a method or a constructor. The scope of an exception-handler parameter is the code block between { and } that follow a catch statement. The chapter <u>Handling Errors Using Exceptions</u> (page 243) talks about using exceptions to handle errors and shows you how to write an exception handler that has a parameter.

Consider the following code sample:

```
if (...) {
    int i = 17;
    ...
}
System.out.println("The value of i = " + i);    // error
```

The final line won't compile, because the local variable i is out of scope. The scope of i is the block of code between the { and }. The i variable does not exist anymore after the closing }. Either the variable declaration needs to be moved outside of the if statement block, or the println method call needs to be moved into the if statement block.

Variable Initialization

Local variables and member variables can be initialized with an assignment statement when they're declared. The data type of the variable must match the data type of the value assigned to it. The MaxVariablesDemo program provides initial values for all its local variables when they are declared. The local variable declarations from that program follow, with the initialization code set in boldface:

```
// integers
byte largestByte = Byte.MAX_VALUE;
short largestShort = Short.MAX_VALUE;
int largestInteger = Integer.MAX_VALUE;
long largestLong = Long.MAX_VALUE;

// real numbers
float largestFloat = Float.MAX_VALUE;
double largestDouble = Double.MAX_VALUE;
```

```
// other primitive types
char aChar = 'S';
boolean aBoolean = true;
```

Parameters and exception-handler parameters cannot be initialized in this way. The value for a parameter is set by the caller.

Final Variables

You can declare a variable in any scope to be `final`. The value of a final variable cannot change after it has been initialized. Such variables are similar to constants in other programming languages.

To declare a final variable, use the `final` keyword in the variable declaration before the type:

```
final int aFinalVar = 0;
```

The previous statement declares a final variable and initializes it, all at once. Subsequent attempts to assign a value to `aFinalVar` result in a compiler error. You may defer initialization of a final *local* variable. Simply declare the local variable and initialize it later, like this:

```
final int blankfinal;
   . . .
blankfinal = 0;
```

A final local variable that has been declared but not yet initialized is called a *blank final*. Again, once a final local variable has been initialized, it cannot be set, and any later attempts to assign a value to `blankfinal` result in a compile-time error.

By Convention: Names of constant values are spelled in all capital letters. For example:
```
final double AVOGADRO = 6.023e23;
```

Summary of Variables

When you declare a variable, you explicitly set the variable's name and data type. The Java programming language has two categories of data types: primitive and reference. A variable of primitive type contains a value. Table 3 (page 69) shows all the primitive data types along with their sizes and formats. A variable of reference type contains a reference to a value. Arrays, classes, and interfaces are reference types.

The location of a variable declaration implicitly sets the variable's scope, which determines what section of code may refer to the variable by its simple name. There are four categories of scope: member variable scope, local variable scope, parameter scope, and exception-handler parameter scope.

You can provide an initial value for a variable within its declaration by using the assignment operator (=). You can declare a variable as final. The value of a final variable cannot change after it's been initialized.

Questions and Exercises: Variables

Questions

1. Which of the following are valid variable names?

```
int
anInt
i
i1
1
thing1
1thing
ONE-HUNDRED
ONE_HUNDRED
something2do
```

2. Answer the following questions about the `BasicsDemo` program shown on page 65.

   a. What is the name of each variable declared in the program? Remember that method parameters are also variables.

   b. What is the data type of each variable?

   c. What is the scope of each variable?

Exercises

1. Modify the `MaxVariablesDemo` program shown on page 67 so that `aBoolean` has a different value.

2. Rewrite the `MaxVariablesDemo` program to display the minimum value of each integer data type. You can guess what the names of these variables are, or you can look them up in the API documentation.

3. Can you guess the name of a method in the `Character` class that you can use instead of `isUpperCase` to determine the capitalization of a character? Modify the `MaxVariablesDemo` program to use that method instead of `isUpperCase`.

Answers

You can find answers to these Questions and Exercises online:

```
http://java.sun.com/docs/books/tutorial/java/nutsandbolts/QandE/
answers_variables.html
```

Operators

An operator performs a function on one, two, or three operands. An operator that requires one operand is called a *unary operator*. For example, ++ is a unary operator that increments the value of its operand by 1. An operator that requires two operands is a *binary operator*. For example, = is a binary operator that assigns the value from its right-hand operand to its left-hand operand. And finally, a *ternary operator* is one that requires three operands. The Java programming language has one ternary operator, ?:, which is a short-hand if-else statement.

The unary operators support either prefix or postfix notation. *Prefix notation* means that the operator appears *before* its operand:

```
operator op          //prefix notation
```

Postfix notation means that the operator appears *after* its operand:

```
op operator          //postfix notation
```

All the binary operators use *infix notation*, which means that the operator appears *between* its operands:

```
op1 operator op2     //infix notation
```

The ternary operator is also infix; each component of the operator appears between operands:

```
op1 ? op2 : op3      //infix notation
```

In addition to performing the operation, an operator returns a value. The return value and its type depend on the operator and the type of its operands. For example, the arithmetic operators, which perform such basic arithmetic operations as addition and subtraction, return numbers—the result of the arithmetic operation. The data type returned by an arithmetic operator depends on the type of its operands: If you add two integers, you get an integer back. An operation is said to *evaluate to* its result.

We divide the operators into these categories:

- Arithmetic operators
- Relational and conditional operators
- Shift and bitwise operators
- Assignment operators
- Other operators

Arithmetic Operators

The Java programming language supports various arithmetic operators for all floating-point and integer numbers. These operators are + (addition), - (subtraction), * (multiplication), / (division), and % (modulo). Table 5 summarizes the binary arithmetic operations in the Java programming language.

Table 5   Binary Arithmetic Operators

Operator	Use	Description
+	op1 + op2	Adds op1 and op2; also used to concatenate strings
-	op1 - op2	Subtracts op2 from op1
*	op1 * op2	Multiplies op1 by op2
/	op1 / op2	Divides op1 by op2
%	op1 % op2	Computes the remainder of dividing op1 by op2

Here's an example program, ArithmeticDemo,[1] that defines two integers and two double-precision floating-point numbers and uses the five arithmetic operators to perform different arithmetic operations. This program also uses + to concatenate strings. The arithmetic operations are shown in boldface:

```
public class ArithmeticDemo {
    public static void main(String[] args) {

        //a few numbers
        int i = 37;
        int j = 42;
        double x = 27.475;
        double y = 7.22;
        System.out.println("Variable values...");
        System.out.println("    i = " + i);
        System.out.println("    j = " + j);
        System.out.println("    x = " + x);
        System.out.println("    y = " + y);

        //adding numbers
        System.out.println("Adding...");
```

---

[1] ArithmeticDemo.java is included on the CD and is available online. See <u>Code Samples</u> (page 117).

```
        System.out.println("    i + j = " + (i + j));
        System.out.println("    x + y = " + (x + y));

        //subtracting numbers
        System.out.println("Subtracting...");
        System.out.println("    i - j = " + (i - j));
        System.out.println("    x - y = " + (x - y));

        //multiplying numbers
        System.out.println("Multiplying...");
        System.out.println("    i * j = " + (i * j));
        System.out.println("    x * y = " + (x * y));

        //dividing numbers
        System.out.println("Dividing...");
        System.out.println("    i / j = " + (i / j));
        System.out.println("    x / y = " + (x / y));

        //computing the remainder resulting from dividing numbers
        System.out.println("Computing the remainder...");
        System.out.println("    i % j = " + (i % j));
        System.out.println("    x % y = " + (x % y));

        //mixing types
        System.out.println("Mixing types...");
        System.out.println("    j + y = " + (j + y));
        System.out.println("    i * x = " + (i * x));
    }
}
```

The output from this program is:

```
Variable values...
    i = 37
    j = 42
    x = 27.475
    y = 7.22
Adding...
    i + j = 79
    x + y = 34.695
Subtracting...
    i - j = -5
    x - y = 20.255
Multiplying...
    i * j = 1554
    x * y = 198.37
Dividing...
    i / j = 0
```

```
    x / y = 3.8054
Computing the remainder...
    i % j = 37
    x % y = 5.815
Mixing types...
    j + y = 49.22
    i * x = 1016.58
```

Note that when an integer and a floating-point number are used as operands to a single arithmetic operation, the result is floating point. The integer is implicitly converted to a floating-point number before the operation takes place. Table 6 summarizes the data type returned by the arithmetic operators, based on the data type of the operands. The necessary conversions take place before the operation is performed.

Table 6   Data Types Returned by Arithmetic Operators

Data Type of Result	Data Type of Operands
long	Neither operand is a `float` or a `double` (integer arithmetic); at least one operand is a `long`.
int	Neither operand is a `float` or a `double` (integer arithmetic); neither operand is a `long`.
double	At least one operand is a `double`.
float	At least one operand is a `float`; neither operand is a `double`.

In addition to the binary forms of + and -, each of these operators has unary versions that perform the following operations, as shown in Table 7.

Table 7   Unary Arithmetic Operators

Operator	Use	Description
+	+op	Promotes op to `int` if it's a `byte`, `short`, or `char`
-	-op	Arithmetically negates op

Two shortcut arithmetic operators are ++, which increments its operand by 1, and --, which decrements its operand by 1. Either ++ or -- can appear before *(prefix)* or after *(postfix)* its operand. The prefix version, ++op/--op, evaluates to the value of the operand *after* the increment/decrement operation. The postfix version, op++/op--, evaluates to the value of the operand *before* the increment/decrement operation.

The following program, called SortDemo,[1] uses ++ twice and -- once.

```java
public class SortDemo {
    public static void main(String[] args) {
        int[] arrayOfInts = { 32, 87, 3, 589, 12, 1076,
                              2000, 8, 622, 127 };

        for (int i = arrayOfInts.length; --i >= 0; ) {
            for (int j = 0; j < i; j++) {
                if (arrayOfInts[j] > arrayOfInts[j+1]) {
                    int temp = arrayOfInts[j];
                    arrayOfInts[j] = arrayOfInts[j+1];
                    arrayOfInts[j+1] = temp;
                }
            }
        }

        for (int i = 0; i < arrayOfInts.length; i++) {
            System.out.print(arrayOfInts[i] + " ");
        }
        System.out.println();
    }
}
```

This program puts ten integer values into an array—a fixed-length structure that can hold multiple values of the same type—then sorts them. The boldface line of code declares an array referred to by arrayOfInts, creates the array, and puts ten integer values into it. The program uses arrayOfInts.length to get the number of elements in the array. Individual elements are accessed with this notation: arrayOfInts[*index*], where *index* is an integer indicating the position of the element within the array. Note that indices begin at 0. You'll get more details and examples for arrays in the section <u>Arrays</u> (page 165).

The output from this program is a list of numbers sorted from lowest to highest:

```
3 8 12 32 87 127 589 622 1076 2000
```

Let's look at how the SortDemo program uses -- to help control the outer of its two nested sorting loops. Here's the statement that controls the outer loop:

```java
for (int i = arrayOfInts.length; --i >= 0; ) {
    ...
}
```

---

[1] SortDemo.java is included on the CD and is available online. See <u>Code Samples</u> (page 117).

The for statement is a looping construct, which you'll meet later in this chapter. What's important here is the code set in boldface, which continues the for loop as long as the value returned by --i is greater than or equal to 0. Using the prefix version of -- means that the last iteration of this loop occurs when i is equal to 0. If we change the code to use the postfix version of --, the last iteration of this loop occurs when i is equal to -1, which is incorrect for this program because i is used as an array index and -1 is not a valid array index.

The other two loops in the program use the postfix version of ++. In both cases, the version used doesn't really matter, because the value returned by the operator isn't used for anything. When the return value of one of these shortcut operations isn't used for anything, convention prefers the postfix version.

The shortcut increment/decrement operators are summarized in Table 8.

Table 8   Shortcut Increment and Decrement Operators

Operator	Use	Description
++	op++	Increments op by 1; evaluates to the value of op before it was incremented
++	++op	Increments op by 1; evaluates to the value of op after it was incremented
--	op--	Decrements op by 1; evaluates to the value of op before it was decremented
--	--op	Decrements op by 1; evaluates to the value of op after it was decremented

Relational and Conditional Operators

A relational operator compares two values and determines the relationship between them. For example, != returns true if its two operands are unequal. Table 9 summarizes the relational operators.

Table 9   Relational Operators

Operator	Use	Description
>	op1 > op2	Returns true if op1 is greater than op2
>=	op1 >= op2	Returns true if op1 is greater than or equal to op2
<	op1 < op2	Returns true if op1 is less than op2
<=	op1 <= op2	Returns true if op1 is less than or equal to op2
==	op1 == op2	Returns true if op1 and op2 are equal
!=	op1 != op2	Returns true if op1 and op2 are not equal

Following is an example, `RelationalDemo`,[1] that defines three integer numbers and uses the relational operators to compare them:

```java
public class RelationalDemo {
    public static void main(String[] args) {

        //a few numbers
        int i = 37;
        int j = 42;
        int k = 42;
        System.out.println("Variable values...");
        System.out.println("    i = " + i);
        System.out.println("    j = " + j);
        System.out.println("    k = " + k);

        //greater than
        System.out.println("Greater than...");
        System.out.println("    i > j is " + (i > j));      //false
        System.out.println("    j > i is " + (j > i));      //true
        System.out.println("    k > j is " + (k > j));      //false

        //greater than or equal to
        System.out.println("Greater than or equal to...");
        System.out.println("    i >= j is " + (i >= j));    //false
        System.out.println("    j >= i is " + (j >= i));    //true
        System.out.println("    k >= j is " + (k >= j));    //true

        //less than
        System.out.println("Less than...");
        System.out.println("    i < j is " + (i < j));      //true
        System.out.println("    j < i is " + (j < i));      //false
        System.out.println("    k < j is " + (k < j));      //false

        //less than or equal to
        System.out.println("Less than or equal to...");
        System.out.println("    i <= j is " + (i <= j));    //true
        System.out.println("    j <= i is " + (j <= i));    //false
        System.out.println("    k <= j is " + (k <= j));    //true

        //equal to
        System.out.println("Equal to...");
        System.out.println("    i == j is " + (i == j));    //false
        System.out.println("    k == j is " + (k == j));    //true
```

---

[1] `RelationalDemo.java` is included on the CD and is available online. See Code Samples (page 117).

```
              //not equal to
              System.out.println("Not equal to...");
              System.out.println("    i != j is " + (i != j));   //true
              System.out.println("    k != j is " + (k != j));   //false

       }
   }
```

Here's the output from this program:

```
       Variable values...
           i = 37
           j = 42
           k = 42
       Greater than...
           i > j is false
           j > i is true
           k > j is false
       Greater than or equal to...
           i >= j is false
           j >= i is true
           k >= j is true
       Less than...
           i < j is true
           j < i is false
           k < j is false
       Less than or equal to...
           i <= j is true
           j <= i is false
           k <= j is true
       Equal to...
           i == j is false
           k == j is true
       Not equal to...
           i != j is true
           k != j is false
```

Relational operators often are used with conditional operators to construct more complex decision-making expressions. The Java programming language supports six conditional operators—five binary and one unary—shown in Table 10 (page 84).

One such operator is &&, which performs the *conditional* AND operation. You can use two different relational operators along with && to determine whether both relationships are true. The following line of code uses this technique to determine whether an array index is

Table 10   Conditional Operators

Operator	Use	Description
&&	op1 && op2	Returns `true` if op1 and op2 are both `true`; conditionally evaluates op2
||	op1 || op2	Returns `true` if either op1 or op2 is `true`; conditionally evaluates op2
!	!op	Returns `true` if op is `false`
&	op1 & op2	Returns `true` if op1 and op2 are both boolean and both `true`; always evaluates op1 and op2 If both operands are numbers, performs bitwise AND operation
|	op1 | op2	Returns `true` if both op1 and op2 are boolean, and either op1 or op2 is `true`; always evaluates op1 and op2 If both operands are numbers, performs bitwise inclusive OR operation
^	op1 ^ op2	Returns true if op1 and op2 are different, that is, if one or the other of the operands, but not both, is true

between two boundaries. It determines whether the index is both greater than or equal to 0 and less than `NUM_ENTRIES`, which is a previously defined constant value.

```
0 <= index && index < NUM_ENTRIES
```

Note that in some instances, the second operand to a conditional operator may not be evaluated. Consider this code segment:

```
(numChars < LIMIT) && (...)
```

The **&&** operator will return `true` only if *both* operands are `true`. So, if numChars is greater than or equal to `LIMIT`, the left-hand operand for **&&** is `false`, and the return value of **&&** can be determined without evaluating the right-hand operand. In such a case, the interpreter will not evaluate the right-hand operand. This has important implications if the right-hand operand has side effects, such as reading from a stream, updating a value, or making a calculation.

When both operands are boolean, the operator & performs the same operation as &&. However, & always evaluates both of its operands and returns `true` if both are `true`. Likewise, when the operands are boolean, | performs the same operation as is similar to ||. The | operator always evaluates both of its operands and returns `true` if at least one of its operands is `true`. When their operands are numbers, & and | perform bitwise manipulations. The next section, <u>Shift and Bitwise Operators</u> (page 85), has more information.

Shift and Bitwise Operators

A shift operator performs bit manipulation on data by shifting the bits of its first operand right or left. Table 11 summarizes the shift operators available in the Java programming language.

Table 11   Shift Operators

Operator	Use	Description
<<	op1 << op2	Shift bits of op1 left by distance op2; fills with zero bits on the right-hand side
>>	op1 >> op2	Shift bits of op1 right by distance op2; fills with highest (sign) bit on the left-hand side
>>>	op1 >>> op2	Shift bits of op1 right by distance op2; fills with zero bits on the left-hand side

Each operator shifts the bits of the left-hand operand over by the number of positions indicated by the right-hand operand. The shift occurs in the direction indicated by the operator itself. For example, the following statement shifts the bits of the integer 13 to the right by one position:

```
13 >> 1;
```

The binary representation of the number 13 is 1101. The result of the shift operation is 1101 shifted to the right by one position—110, or 6 in decimal. The right-hand bits are filled with 0s as needed.

Table 12 shows the four operators the Java programming language provides to perform bitwise functions on their operands.

Table 12   Bitwise Operators

Operator	Use	Description
&	op1 & op2	Bitwise AND, if both operands are numbers Conditional AND, if both operands are boolean
|	op1 | op2	Bitwise inclusive OR, if both operands are numbers Conditional OR, if both operands are boolean
^	op1 ^ op2	Bitwise exclusive OR (XOR)
~	~op2	Bitwise complement

When its operands are numbers, the & operation performs the bitwise AND function on each parallel pair of bits in each operand. The AND function sets the resulting bit to 1 if the corresponding bit in both operands is 1, as shown in Table 13.

Table 13   Bitwise AND (op1 & op2)

Bit in op1	Corresponding Bit in op2	Result
0	0	0
0	1	0
1	0	0
1	1	1

Suppose that you were to AND the values 13 and 12, like this: 13 & 12. The result of this operation is 12 because the binary representation of 12 is 1100, and the binary representation of 13 is 1101.

```
  1101     // 13
& 1100     // 12
_____

  1100     // 12
```

If both operand bits are 1, the AND function sets the resulting bit to 1; otherwise, the resulting bit is 0. So, when you line up the two operands and perform the AND function, you can see that the two high-order bits (the two bits farthest to the left of each number) of each operand are 1. Thus, the resulting bit in the result is also 1. The low-order bits evaluate to 0 because either one or both bits in the operands are 0.

When both of its operands are numbers, the | operator performs the *inclusive or* operation, and ^ performs the *exclusive or* (XOR) operation. *Inclusive or* means that if either of the two bits is 1, the result is 1. Table 14 shows the results of an *inclusive or* operation.

Table 14   Bitwise Inclusive Or (op1 | op2)

Bit in op1	Corresponding Bit in op2	Result
0	0	0
0	1	1
1	0	1
1	1	1

Table 15   Bitwise Exclusive Or (op1 ∧ op2)

Bit in op1	Corresponding Bit in op2	Result
0	0	0
0	1	1
1	0	1
1	1	0

Exclusive or means that if the two operand bits are different, the result is 1; otherwise, the result is 0. Table 15 shows the results of an *exclusive or* operation.

And finally, the complement operator (~) inverts the value of each bit of the operand: If the operand bit is 1, the result is 0; if the operand bit is 0, the result is 1. For example, ~1011 (11) is 0100 (4)

Among other things, bitwise manipulations are useful for managing sets of boolean flags. Suppose, for example, that your program had several boolean flags that indicated the state of various components in your program: is it visible, is it draggable, and so on. Rather than define a separate boolean variable to hold each flag, you could define a single variable, flags, for all of them. Each bit within flags would represent the current state of one of the flags. You would then use bit manipulations to set and to get each flag.

First, set up constants that indicate the various flags for your program. These flags should each be a different power of 2 to ensure that each bit is used by only one flag. Define a variable, flags, whose bits would be set according to the current state of each flag. The following code sample initializes flags to 0, which means that all flags are false (none of the bits are set):

```
static final int VISIBLE = 1;
static final int DRAGGABLE = 2;
static final int SELECTABLE = 4;
static final int EDITABLE = 8;

int flags = 0;
```

To set the visible flag when something became visible, you would use this statement:

```
flags = flags | VISIBLE;
```

To test for visibility, you could then write:

```
if ((flags & VISIBLE) == VISIBLE) {
    ...
}
```

Here's the complete program, BitwiseDemo,[1] that includes this code:

```
public class BitwiseDemo {

    static final int VISIBLE = 1;
    static final int DRAGGABLE = 2;
    static final int SELECTABLE = 4;
    static final int EDITABLE = 8;

    public static void main(String[] args) {
        int flags = 0;

        flags = flags | VISIBLE;
        flags = flags | DRAGGABLE;
        if ((flags & VISIBLE) == VISIBLE) {
            if ((flags & DRAGGABLE) == DRAGGABLE) {
                System.out.println("Flags are Visible and Draggable.");
            }
        }

        flags = flags | EDITABLE;
        if ((flags & EDITABLE) == EDITABLE) {
            System.out.println("Flags are now also Editable.");
        }
    }
}
```

Here's the output from this program:

```
Flags are Visible and Draggable.
Flags are now also Editable.
```

Assignment Operators

You use the basic assignment operator, =, to assign one value to another. The MaxVariablesDemo program uses = to initialize all its local variables:

---

[1] BitwiseDemo.java is included on the CD and is available online. See Code Samples (page 117). BitwiseDemo is based on a program sent to us by reader Ric Stattin.

```
// integers
byte largestByte = Byte.MAX_VALUE;
short largestShort = Short.MAX_VALUE;
int largestInteger = Integer.MAX_VALUE;
long largestLong = Long.MAX_VALUE;

// real numbers
float largestFloat = Float.MAX_VALUE;
double largestDouble = Double.MAX_VALUE;

// other primitive types
char aChar = 'S';
boolean aBoolean = true;
```

The Java programming language also provides several shortcut assignment operators that allow you to perform an arithmetic, shift, or bitwise operation and an assignment operation all with one operator. Suppose that you wanted to add a number to a variable and assign the result back into the variable, like this:

```
i = i + 2;
```

You can shorten this statement by using the shortcut operator +=, like this:

```
i += 2;
```

The two previous lines of code are equivalent. Table 16 lists the shortcut assignment operators and their lengthy equivalents.

Table 16   Shortcut Assignment Operators

	Operator	**Use**	**Equivalent to**
Arithmetic Shortcuts	+=	op1 += op2	op1 = op1 + op2
	-=	op1 -= op2	op1 = op1 - op2
	*=	op1 *= op2	op1 = op1 * op2
	/=	op1 /= op2	op1 = op1 / op2
	%=	op1 %= op2	op1 = op1 % op2
Bitwise Shortcuts	&=	op1 &= op2	op1 = op1 & op2
	|=	op1 |= op2	op1 = op1 | op2
	^=	op1 ^= op2	op1 = op1 ^ op2
Shift Shortcuts	<<=	op1 <<= op2	op1 = op1 << op2
	>>=	op1 >>= op2	op1 = op1 >> op2
	>>>=	op1 >>>= op2	op1 = op1 >>> op2

Other Operators

The Java programming language also supports the operators in Table 17. These operators are covered in other parts of this book.

Table 17   Other Operators

Operator	Description
?:	Shortcut if-else statement The if-else Statements (page 102)
[]	Used to declare arrays, to create arrays, and to access array elements Creating and Using Arrays (page 165)
.	Used to form qualified names Using Objects (page 126)
(*params*)	Delimits a comma-separated list of parameters Defining Methods (page 182)
(*type*)	Casts (converts) a value to the specified type
new	Creates a new object or array Creating Objects (page 122) and Creating and Using Arrays (page 165)
instanceof	Determines whether its first operand is an instance of its second operand

Summary of Operators

Table 18 lists all the operators supported by the Java programming language.

Table 18   All the Operators

Operator	Use	Description
+	op1 + op2	Adds op1 and op2; also used to concatenate strings
+	+op	Promotes op to int if it's a byte, short, or char
-	op1 - op2	Subtracts op2 from op1
-	-op	Arithmetically negates op
*	op1 * op2	Multiplies op1 by op2
/	op1 / op2	Divides op1 by op2
%	op1 % op2	Computes the remainder of dividing op1 by op2
++	op++	Increments op by 1; evaluates to the value of op before it was incremented

Table 18   All the Operators

++	++op	Increments op by 1; evaluates to the value of op after it was incremented
--	op--	Decrements op by 1; evaluates to the value of op before it was decremented
--	--op	Decrements op by 1; evaluates to the value of op after it was decremented
>	op1 > op2	Returns true if op1 is greater than op2
>=	op1 >= op2	Returns true if op1 is greater than or equal to op2
<	op1 < op2	Returns true if op1 is less than op2
<=	op1 <= op2	Returns true if op1 is less than or equal to op2
==	op1 == op2	Returns true if op1 and op2 are equal
!=	op1 != op2	Returns true if op1 and op2 are not equal
&&	op1 && op2	Returns true if op1 and op2 are both true; conditionally evaluates op2
||	op1 || op2	Returns true if either op1 or op2 is true; conditionally evaluates op2
!	!op	Returns true if op is false
&	op1 & op2	Returns true if op1 and op2 are both boolean and both true; always evaluates op1 and op2
|	op1 | op2	Returns true if both op1 and op2 are boolean, and either op1 or op2 is true; always evaluates op1 and op2
^	op1 ^ op2	Returns true if op1 and op2 are different, that is, if one, but not both, of the operands is true
>>	op1 >> op2	Shift bits of op1 right by distance op2; fills with zero bits on the right-hand side
<<	op1	Shift bits of op1 left by distance op2; fills with the highest (sign) bit on the left-hand side
>>>	op1 >>> op2	Shift bits of op1 right by distance op2; fills with zero bits on the left-hand side
&	op1 & op2	Bitwise AND, if both operands are numbers Logical AND, if both operands are boolean
|	op1 | op2	Bitwise OR, if both operands are numbers Logical OR, if both operands are boolean
^	op1 ^ op2	Bitwise XOR
~	~op2	Bitwise complement
=	op1 = op2	Assigns the value of op2 to op1

Table 18   All the Operators

+=	op1 += op2	Equivalent to op1 = op1 + op2
-=	op1 -= op2	Equivalent to op1 = op1 - op2
*=	op1 *= op2	Equivalent to op1 = op1 * op2
/=	op1 /= op2	Equivalent to op1 = op1 / op2
%=	op1 %= op2	Equivalent to op1 = op1 % op2
&=	op1 &= op2	Equivalent to op1 = op1 & op2
|=	op1 |= op2	Equivalent to op1 = op1 | op2
^=	op1 ^= op2	Equivalent to op1 = op1 ^ op2
<<=	op1 <<= op2	Equivalent to op1 = op1 << op2
>>=	op1 >>= op2	Equivalent to op1 = op1 >> op2
>>>=	op1 >>>= op2	Equivalent to op1 = op1 >>> op2
?:	op1 ? op2 : op3	If op1 is true, returns op2; otherwise, returns op3
[]		Used to declare arrays, to create arrays, and to access array elements. Creating and Using Arrays (page 165)
.		Used to form long names. Using Objects (page 126)
(params)		Delimits a comma-separated list of parameters. Defining Methods (page 182)
(type)		Casts (converts) a value to the specified type.
new		Creates a new object or array. Creating Objects (page 122) and Creating and Using Arrays (page 165)
instanceof	op1 instanceof op2	Returns true if op1 is an instance of op2

Questions and Exercises: Operators

Questions

1. Consider the following code snippet:

   ```
   arrayOfInts[j] > arrayOfInts[j+1]
   ```

   What operators does the code contain?

2. Consider the following code snippet:

   ```
   int i = 10;
   int n = i++%5;
   ```

a. What are the values of i and n after the code is executed? *n=10 N=0*

b. What are the final values of i and n if instead of using the postfix increment operator (i++), you use the prefix version (++i)? *i=11 , N = 11/5 = 2.2 = ,2 =0*

3. a. What is the value of i after the following code snippet executes? *declaring Int*

```
int i = 8;
i >>=2;
```
0010 = 2

b. What is the value of i after the following code snippet executes?

```
int i = 17;
i >>=1;
```
10001 *i =0 1000 = 8*

Exercises

1. Write a program that tests whether a floating-point number is zero. (*Hint:* You shouldn't generally use the equality operator == with floating-point numbers, as floating-point numbers by nature are difficult to match exactly. Instead, test whether the number is close to zero.) *US = 6.85062 * #Francs*

2. Write a program that calculates the number of U.S. dollars equivalent to a given number of French francs. Assume an exchange rate of 6.85062 francs per dollar. If you want to control the format of the numbers your program displays, you can use the DecimalFormat class, which is discussed in the section <u>Formatting Numbers with Custom Formats</u> (page 156). *1 dollar = 10 francs*

3. Write a program that uses the bits in a single integer to represent the true/false data shown in Figure 44. *dollar = # francs/6.85062*

20 francs / 10 = 2

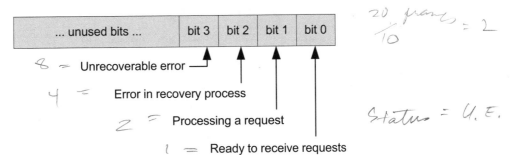

8 =   4 =   2 =   1 =

Status = U.E.

Figure 44   Bits in a single integer represent the true and false data.

Include in the program a variable named status, and have the program print the meaning of status. For example, if status is 1 (only bit 0 is set), the program should print something like this:

```
Ready to receive requests
```

a. Show your code.

b. What is the output when status is 8?   *U, E* (handwritten)

c. What is the output when status is 7?   *E, R, I, P, P, R, R, R.* (handwritten)

Answers

You can find answers to these Questions and Exercises online:

```
http://java.sun.com/docs/books/tutorial/java/nutsandbolts/QandE/
answers_operators.html
```

Expressions, Statements, and Blocks

Variables and operators, which you met in the previous two sections, are basic building blocks of programs. You combine literals, variables, and operators to form expressions—segments of code that perform computations and return values. Certain expressions can be made into statements—complete units of execution. By grouping statements together with braces—{ and }—you create blocks of code.

This section covers expressions, statements, and blocks. The next section discusses a kind of statement, called a control flow statement, that affects the flow of your program.

Expressions

Expressions perform the work of a program. Among other things, expressions are used to compute and to assign values to variables and to help control the execution flow of a program. The job of an expression is twofold: to perform the computation indicated by the elements of the expression and to return a value that is the result of the computation.

Definition: An *expression* is a series of variables, operators, and method calls (constructed according to the syntax of the language) that evaluates to a single value.

As discussed in the previous section, operators return a value, so the use of an operator is an expression. This partial listing of the MaxVariablesDemo program shows some of the program's expressions in boldface:

```
// other primitive types
char aChar = 'S';
boolean aBoolean = true;

// display them all
System.out.println("The largest byte value is " + largestByte);
...
```

```
if (Character.isUpperCase(aChar)) {
    ...
}
```

Each expression performs an operation and returns a value, as shown in Table 19.

Table 19   Expressions in the MaxVariablesDemo Program

Expression	Action	Value Returned
aChar = 'S'	Assign the character 'S' to the character variable aChar	The value of aChar after the assignment ('S')
"The largest byte value is " + largestByte	Concatenate the string "The largest byte value is " and the value of largestByte converted to a string	The resulting string: The largest byte value is 127
Character.isUpperCase(aChar)	Call the method isUpperCase	The return value of the method: true

The data type of the value returned by an expression depends on the elements used in the expression. The expression aChar = 'S' returns a character because the assignment operator returns a value of the same data type as its operands, and aChar and 'S' are characters. As you see from the other expressions, an expression can return a boolean value, a string, and so on.

The Java programming language allows you to construct compound expressions from various smaller expressions as long as the data type required by one part of the expression matches the data type of the other. Here's an example of a compound expression:

```
x * y * z
```

In this particular example, the order in which the expression is evaluated is unimportant because the results of multiplication are independent of order; the outcome is always the same, no matter what order you apply the multiplications. However, this is not true of all expressions. For example, the following expression gives different results, depending on whether you perform the addition or the division operation first:

```
x + y / 100        //ambiguous
```

You can specify exactly how you want an expression to be evaluated, using balanced parentheses—(and). For example, to make the previous expression unambiguous, you could write:

```
(x + y) / 100        //unambiguous, recommended
```

If you don't explicitly indicate the order in which you want the operations in a compound expression to be performed, the order is determined by the *precedence* assigned to the operators in use within the expression. Operators with a higher precedence get evaluated first. For example, the division operator has a higher precedence than does the addition operator. Thus, the two following statements are equivalent:

```
x + y / 100
x + (y / 100)          //unambigous, recommended
```

When writing compound expressions, you should be explicit and indicate with parentheses which operators should be evaluated first. This will make your code easier to read and to maintain.

Table 20 shows the precedence assigned to the operators in the Java platform. The operators in this table are listed in precedence order: The higher in the table an operator appears, the higher its precedence. Operators with higher precedence are evaluated before operators with a relatively lower precedence. Operators on the same line have equal precedence.

Table 20   Operator Precedence

Highest Precedence	Postfix operators	`[] . (params) expr++ expr--`
	Unary operators	`++expr --expr +expr -expr ~ !`
	Creation or cast	`new (type)expr`
	Multiplicative	`* / %`
	Additive	`+ -`
	Shift	`> >>>`
	Relational	`< > <= >= instanceof`
	Equality	`== !=`
	Bitwise AND	`&`
	Bitwise exclusive OR	`^`
	Bitwise inclusive OR	`|`
	Conditional AND	`&&`
	Conditional OR	`||`
	Shortcut if-else	`?:`
Lowest Precedence	Assignment	`= += -= *= /= %= &= ^= |= <<= >>= >>>=`

When operators of equal precedence appear in the same expression, a rule must govern which is evaluated first. All binary operators except for the assignment operators are evaluated from left to right. Assignment operators are evaluated right to left.

Statements

Statements are roughly equivalent to sentences in natural languages. A *statement* forms a complete unit of execution. The following types of expressions can be made into a statement by terminating the expression with a semicolon (;):

- Assignment expressions
- Any use of ++ or --
- Method calls
- Object creation expressions

These kinds of statements are called *expression statements*. Here are some examples of expression statements:

```
aValue = 8933.234;                        //assignment statement
aValue++;                                 //increment statement
System.out.println(aValue);               //method call statement
Integer integerObject = new Integer(4);   //object creation statement
```

In addition to these kinds of expression statements, there are two other kinds of statements. A *declaration statement* declares a variable. You've seen many examples of declaration statements.

```
double aValue = 8933.234;              // declaration statement
```

A *control flow statement* regulates the order in which statements get executed. The for loop and the if statement are both examples of control flow statements. You'll learn about control flow statements in the section <u>Control Flow Statements</u> (page 99).

Blocks

A *block* is a group of zero or more statements between balanced braces and can be used anywhere a single statement is allowed. The following listing shows two blocks from the MaxVariablesDemo program, each containing a single statement:

```
if (Character.isUpperCase(aChar)) {
    System.out.println("The character " + aChar + " is upper case.");
```

```
} else {
    System.out.println("The character " + aChar + " is lower case.");
}
```

Summary of Expressions, Statements, and Blocks

An expression is a series of variables, operators, and method calls (constructed according to the syntax of the language) that evaluates to a single value. You can write compound expressions by combining expressions as long as the types required by all the operators involved in the compound expression are correct. When writing compound expressions, you should be explicit and indicate with parentheses which operators should be evaluated first.

If you choose not to use parentheses in a compound expression, the Java platform evaluates it in the order dictated by operator precedence. Table 20 (page 96) shows the relative precedence assigned to the operators in the Java platform.

A statement forms a complete unit of execution and is terminated with a semicolon (;). There are three kinds of statements: expression statements, declaration statements, and control flow statements.

You can group zero or more statements together into a block with braces: { and }. Even though not required, we recommend using blocks with control flow statements even if only one statement is in the block.

Questions and Exercises: Expressions, Statements, and Blocks

Questions

1. What are the data types of the following expressions, assuming that i's type is int?

```
i > 0
i = 0
i++
(float)i
i == 0
"aString" + i
```

2. Consider the following expression:

```
i--%5>0
```

a. What is the result of the expression, assuming that the value of i is initially 10?

b. Modify the expression so that it has the same result but is easier for programmers to read.

Exercises

1. Write a program to confirm your answers to questions 2a and 2b.

Answers

You can find answers to these Questions and Exercises online:

```
http://java.sun.com/docs/books/tutorial/java/nutsandbolts/QandE/
answers_expressions.html
```

Control Flow Statements

When you write a program, you type statements into a file. Without control flow statements, the interpreter executes these statements in the order they appear in the file from left to right, top to bottom. You can use *control flow statements* in your programs to conditionally execute statements, to repeatedly execute a block of statements, and to otherwise change the normal, sequential flow of control. For example, in the following code snippet, the `if` statement conditionally executes the `System.out.println` statement within the braces, based on the return value of `Character.isUpperCase(aChar)`:

```
char c;
...
if (Character.isUpperCase(aChar)) {
    System.out.println("The character " + aChar + " is upper case.");
}
```

How many levels are required to implement a method?

The Java programming language provides several control flow statements, which are listed in Table 21.

Table 21   Control Flow Statements

Statement Type	Keywords
Looping	`while, do-while, for`
Decision making	`if-else, switch-case`
Exception handling	`try-catch-finally, throw`
Branching	`break, continue, label:, return`

In the sections that follow, you will see the following notation to describe the general form of a control flow statement.

```
control flow statement details {
    statement(s)
}
```

Technically, the braces, { and }, are not required if the block contains only one statement. However, we recommend that you always use { and }, because the code is easier to read and it helps to prevent errors when modifying code.

The while and do-while Statements

You use a *while* statement to continually execute a block while a condition remains true. The general syntax of the while statement is:

```
while (expression) {
    statement(s)
}
```

First, the while statement evaluates *expression*, which must return a boolean value. If the expression returns true, the while statement executes the statement(s) in the while block. The while statement continues testing the expression and executing its block until the expression returns false.

The following example program, called WhileDemo,[1] uses a while statement (shown in boldface) to step through the characters of a string, appending each character from the string to the end of a string buffer until it encounters the letter g. You will learn more about the String and StringBuffer classes in the next chapter, Object Basics and Simple Data Objects (page 119).

```
public class WhileDemo {
    public static void main(String[] args) {
        String copyFromMe = "Copy this string until you " +
                            "encounter the letter 'g'.";
        StringBuffer copyToMe = new StringBuffer();

        int i = 0;
        char c = copyFromMe.charAt(i);

        while (c != 'g') {
            copyToMe.append(c);
            c = copyFromMe.charAt(++i);
        }
        System.out.println(copyToMe);
    }
}
```

---

[1] WhileDemo.java is included on the CD and is available online. See Code Samples (page 117).

The value printed by the last line is: Copy this strin.

The Java programming language provides another statement that is similar to the while statement—the do-while statement. The general syntax of do-while is:

```
do {
    statement(s)
} while (expression);
```

Statements within the block associated with a do-while are executed at least once. Instead of evaluating the expression at the top of the loop, do-while evaluates the expression at the bottom.

Here's the previous program rewritten to use do-while (shown in boldface) and renamed to DoWhileDemo:[1]

```
public class DoWhileDemo {
    public static void main(String[] args) {
        String copyFromMe = "Copy this string until you " +
                            "encounter the letter 'g'.";
        StringBuffer copyToMe = new StringBuffer();

        int i = 0;
        char c = copyFromMe.charAt(i);

        do {
            copyToMe.append(c);
            c = copyFromMe.charAt(++i);
        } while (c != 'g');
        System.out.println(copyToMe);
    }
}
```

The value printed by the last line is: Copy this strin.

The for Statement

The *for* statement provides a compact way to iterate over a range of values. The general form of the for statement can be expressed like this:

```
for (initialization; termination; increment) {
    statement(s)
}
```

---

[1] DoWhileDemo.java is included on the CD and is available online. See Code Samples (page 117).

The *initialization* is an expression that initializes the loop—it's executed once at the beginning of the loop. The *termination* expression determines when to terminate the loop. This expression is evaluated at the top of each iteration of the loop. When the expression evaluates to false, the loop terminates. Finally, *increment* is an expression that gets invoked after each iteration through the loop. All these components are optional. In fact, to write an infinite loop, you omit all three expressions:

```
for ( ; ; ) {    // infinite loop
    ...
}
```

Often, for loops are used to iterate over the elements in an array or the characters in a string. The following sample, ForDemo,[1] uses a for statement (shown in boldface) to iterate over the elements of an array and to print them:

```
public class ForDemo {
    public static void main(String[] args) {
        int[] arrayOfInts = { 32, 87, 3, 589, 12,
                             1076, 2000, 8, 622, 127 };

        for (int i = 0; i < arrayOfInts.length; i++) {
            System.out.print(arrayOfInts[i] + " ");
        }
        System.out.println();
    }
}
```

The output of the program is: 32 87 3 589 12 1076 2000 8 622 127.

Notice that you can declare a local variable within the initialization expression of a for loop. The scope of this variable extends from its declaration to the end of the block governed by the for statement so it can be used in the termination and increment expressions as well. If the variable that controls a for loop is not needed outside of the loop, it's best to declare the variable in the initialization expression. The names i, j, and k are often used to control for loops; declaring them within the for loop initialization expression limits their life span and reduces errors.

The if-else Statements

The if statement enables your program to selectively execute other statements, based on some criteria. For example, suppose that your program prints debugging information, based on the value of a boolean variable named DEBUG. If DEBUG is true, your program prints

---

[1] ForDemo.java is included on the CD and is available online. See Code Samples (page 117).

debugging information, such as the value of a variable, such as x. Otherwise, your program proceeds normally. A segment of code to implement this might look like this:

```
if (DEBUG) {
    System.out.println("DEBUG: x = " + x);
}
```

This is the simplest version of the if statement: The block governed by the if is executed if a condition is true. Generally, the simple form of if can be written like this:

```
if (expression) {
    statement(s)
}
```

What if you want to perform a different set of statements if the expression is false? You use the else statement for that. Consider another example. Suppose that your program needs to perform different actions, depending on whether the user clicks the OK button or another button in an alert window. Your program could do this by using an if statement along with an else statement:

```
    . . .
    // response is either OK or CANCEL depending
    // on the button that the user pressed
    . . .
if (response == OK) {
    // code to perform OK action
} else {
    // code to perform Cancel action
}
```

The else block is executed if the if part is false. Another form of the else statement, else if, executes a statement based on another expression. An if statement can have any number of companion else if statements but only one else. Following is a program, IfElseDemo,[1] that assigns a grade based on the value of a test score: an A for a score of 90% or above, a B for a score of 80% or above, and so on:

```
public class IfElseDemo {
    public static void main(String[] args) {

        int testscore = 76;
        char grade;

        if (testscore >= 90) {
            grade = 'A';
```

---

[1] IfElseDemo.java is included on the CD and is available online. See Code Samples (page 117).

```
        } else if (testscore >= 80) {
            grade = 'B';
        } else if (testscore >= 70) {
            grade = 'C';
        } else if (testscore >= 60) {
            grade = 'D';
        } else {
            grade = 'F';
        }
        System.out.println("Grade = " + grade);
    }
}
```

The output from this program is:

```
Grade = C
```

You may have noticed that the value of testscore can satisfy more than one of the expressions in the compound if statement: 76 >= 70 and 76 >= 60. However, as the runtime system processes a compound if statement such as this one, once a condition is satisfied, the appropriate statements are executed (grade = 'C';), and control passes out of the if statement without evaluating the remaining conditions.

The Java programming language supports an operator, ?:, that is a compact version of an if statement. Recall this statement from the MaxVariablesDemo program:

```
if (Character.isUpperCase(aChar)) {
    System.out.println("The character " + aChar + " is upper case.");
} else {
    System.out.println("The character " + aChar + " is lower case.");
}
```

Here's how you could rewrite that statement, using the ?: operator (shown in boldface):

```
System.out.println("The character " + aChar + " is " +
                   (Character.isUpperCase(aChar) ? "upper" : "lower") +
                   "case.");
```

The ?: operator returns the string "upper" if the isUpperCase method returns true. Otherwise, it returns the string "lower". The result is concatenated with other parts of a message to be displayed. Using ?: makes sense here because the if statement is secondary to the call to the println method. Once you get used to this construct, it also makes the code easier to read.

The switch Statement

Use the switch statement to conditionally perform statements based on an integer expression. Following is a sample program, SwitchDemo,[1] that declares an integer named month whose value supposedly represents the month in a date. The program displays the name of the month, based on the value of month, using the switch statement:

```java
public class SwitchDemo {
    public static void main(String[] args) {

        int month = 8;
        switch (month) {
            case 1:  System.out.println("January"); break;
            case 2:  System.out.println("February"); break;
            case 3:  System.out.println("March"); break;
            case 4:  System.out.println("April"); break;
            case 5:  System.out.println("May"); break;
            case 6:  System.out.println("June"); break;
            case 7:  System.out.println("July"); break;
            case 8:  System.out.println("August"); break;
            case 9:  System.out.println("September"); break;
            case 10: System.out.println("October"); break;
            case 11: System.out.println("November"); break;
            case 12: System.out.println("December"); break;
        }
    }
}
```

The switch statement evaluates its expression, in this case the value of month, and executes the appropriate case statement. Thus, the output of the program is August. Of course, you could implement this by using an if statement:

```java
int month = 8;
if (month == 1) {
    System.out.println("January");
} else if (month == 2) {
    System.out.println("February");
}
. . . // and so on
```

Deciding whether to use an if statement or a switch statement is a judgment call. You can decide which to use, based on readability and other factors. An if statement can be used to make decisions based on ranges of values or conditions, whereas a switch statement can

---

[1] SwitchDemo.java is included on the CD and is available online. See Code Samples (page 117).

make decisions based only on a single integer value. Also, the value provided to each `case` statement must be unique.

Another point of interest in the `switch` statement is the break statement after each `case`. Each `break` statement terminates the enclosing `switch` statement, and the flow of control continues with the first statement following the `switch` block. The `break` statements are necessary because without them, the case statements fall through. That is, without an explicit `break`, control will flow sequentially through subsequent `case` statements. Following is an example, `SwitchDemo2`,[1] that illustrates why it might be useful to have `case` statements fall through:

```java
public class SwitchDemo2 {
    public static void main(String[] args) {

        int month = 2;
        int year = 2000;
        int numDays = 0;

        switch (month) {
        case 1:
        case 3:
        case 5:
        case 7:
        case 8:
        case 10:
        case 12:
            numDays = 31;
            break;
        case 4:
        case 6:
        case 9:
        case 11:
            numDays = 30;
            break;
        case 2:
            if ( ((year % 4 == 0) && !(year % 100 == 0))
                  || (year % 400 == 0) )
                numDays = 29;
            else
                numDays = 28;
            break;
        }
        System.out.println("Number of Days = " + numDays);
    }
}
```

why should case 2 be tested here 1st? (handwritten annotation)

---

[1] `SwitchDemo2.java` is included on the CD and is available online. See Code Samples (page 117).

The output from this program is:

```
Number of Days = 29
```

Technically, the final break is not required, because flow would fall out of the switch statement anyway. However, we recommend using a break for the last case statement just in case you need to add more case statements later. This makes modifying the code easier and less error prone. You will see break used to terminate loops in the section <u>Branching Statements</u> (page 108).

Finally, you can use the default statement at the end of the switch to handle all values that aren't explicitly handled by one of the case statements:

```
int month = 8;
. . .
switch (month) {
    case 1:  System.out.println("January"); break;
    case 2:  System.out.println("February"); break;
    case 3:  System.out.println("March"); break;
    case 4:  System.out.println("April"); break;
    case 5:  System.out.println("May"); break;
    case 6:  System.out.println("June"); break;
    case 7:  System.out.println("July"); break;
    case 8:  System.out.println("August"); break;
    case 9:  System.out.println("September"); break;
    case 10: System.out.println("October"); break;
    case 11: System.out.println("November"); break;
    case 12: System.out.println("December"); break;
    default: System.out.println("Hey, that's not a valid month!"); break;
}
```

Exception-Handling Statements

The Java programming language provides a mechanism known as *exceptions* to help programs report and handle errors. When an error occurs, the program throws an exception. What does this mean? It means that the normal flow of the program is interrupted and that the runtime environment attempts to find an *exception handler*—a block of code that can handle a particular type of error. The exception handler can attempt to recover from the error or, if it determines that the error is unrecoverable, provide a gentle exit from the program.

Three statements play a part in handling exceptions.

- The try statement identifies a block of statements within which an exception might be thrown.

- The `catch` statement must be associated with a `try` statement and identifies a block of statements that can handle a particular type of exception. The statements are executed if an exception of a particular type occurs within the `try` block.
- The `finally` statement must be associated with a `try` statement and identifies a block of statements that are executed regardless of whether an error occurs within the `try` block.

Here's the general form of these statements:

```
try {
    statement(s)
} catch (exceptiontype name) {
    statement(s)
} finally {
    statement(s)
}
```

This has been a brief overview of the statements provided by the Java programming language used in reporting and handling errors. However, other factors and considerations, such as the difference between runtime and checked exceptions and the hierarchy of exceptions classes, which represent various types of exceptions, play a role in using the exception mechanism. The chapter <u>Handling Errors Using Exceptions</u> (page 243) provides a complete discussion on this subject.

Branching Statements

The Java programming language supports three branching statements:

- The `break` statement
- The `continue` statement
- The `return` statement

The `break` statement and the `continue` statement, which are covered next, can be used with or without a label. A *label* is an identifier placed before a statement. The label is followed by a colon (`:`):

```
statementName: someJavaStatement ;
```

You'll see an example of a label within the context of a program in the next section.

The break Statement

The `break` statements has two forms: unlabeled and labeled. You saw the unlabeled form of the `break` statement used with `switch` earlier. As noted there, an unlabeled `break` terminates the enclosing `switch` statement, and flow of control transfers to the statement immediately following the `switch`. You can also use the unlabeled form of the `break` statement to terminate a `for`, `while`, or `do-while` loop. The following sample program, `BreakDemo`,[1] contains a `for` loop that searches for a particular value within an array:

```
public class BreakDemo {
    public static void main(String[] args) {

        int[] arrayOfInts = { 32, 87, 3, 589, 12, 1076,
                              2000, 8, 622, 127 };
        int searchfor = 12;

        int i = 0;
        boolean foundIt = false;

        for ( ; i < arrayOfInts.length; i++) {
            if (arrayOfInts[i] == searchfor) {
                foundIt = true;
                break;
            }
        }

        if (foundIt) {
            System.out.println("Found " + searchfor + " at index " + i);
        } else {
            System.out.println(searchfor + "not in the array");
        }
    }
}
```

The `break` statement, shown in boldface, terminates the `for` loop when the value is found. The flow of control transfers to the statement following the enclosing `for`, which is the `print` statement at the end of the program.

The output of this program is:

```
Found 12 at index 4
```

The unlabeled form of the break statement, `break`, is used to terminate the innermost `switch`, `for`, `while`, or `do-while`; the labeled form terminates an outer statement, which is identified by the label specified in the `break` statement. The following program, `BreakWith-LabelDemo`,[2] is similar to the previous one, but it searches for a value in a two-dimensional

---

[1] `BreakDemo.java` is included on the CD and is available online. See Code Samples (page 117).

[2] `BreakWithLabelDemo.java` is included on the CD and is available online. See Code Samples (page 117).

array. Two nested for loops traverse the array. When the value is found, a labeled break terminates the statement labeled search, which is the outer for loop:

```java
public class BreakWithLabelDemo {
    public static void main(String[] args) {

        int[][] arrayOfInts = { { 32, 87, 3, 589 },
                                { 12, 1076, 2000, 8 },
                                { 622, 127, 77, 955 }
                              };
        int searchfor = 12;

        int i = 0;
        int j = 0;
        boolean foundIt = false;

    search:
        for ( ; i < arrayOfInts.length; i++) {
            for (j = 0; j < arrayOfInts[i].length; j++) {
                if (arrayOfInts[i][j] == searchfor) {
                    foundIt = true;
                    break search;
                }
            }
        }

        if (foundIt) {
          System.out.println("Found " + searchfor + " at " + i + ", " + j);
        } else {
            System.out.println(searchfor + "not in the array");
        }

    }
}
```

The output of this program is:

```
Found 12 at 1, 0
```

This syntax can be a little confusing. The break statement terminates the labeled statement; it does not transfer the flow of control to the label. The flow of control transfers to the statement immediately following the labeled (terminated) statement.

The continue Statement

You use the continue statement to skip the current iteration of a for, while, or do-while loop. The unlabeled form skips to the end of the innermost loop's body and evaluates the boolean expression that controls the loop, basically skipping the remainder of this iteration of the loop. The following program, ContinueDemo,[1] steps through a string buffer, checking each letter. If the current character is not a p, the continue statement skips the rest of the loop and proceeds to the next character. If it is a p, the program increments a counter and converts the p to an uppercase letter:

```java
public class ContinueDemo {
    public static void main(String[] args) {

        StringBuffer searchMe = new StringBuffer(
                "peter piper picked a peck of pickled peppers");
        int max = searchMe.length();
        int numPs = 0;

        for (int i = 0; i < max; i++) {
            //interested only in p's
            if (searchMe.charAt(i) != 'p')
                continue;

            //process p's
            numPs++;
            searchMe.setCharAt(i, 'P');
        }
        System.out.println("Found " + numPs + " p's in the string.");
        System.out.println(searchMe);
    }
}
```

Here is the output of this program:

```
Found 9 p's in the string.
Peter PiPer Picked a Peck of Pickled PePPers
```

The labeled form of the continue statement skips the current iteration of an outer loop marked with the given label. The following example program, ContinueWithLabelDemo,[2] uses nested loops to search for a substring within another string. Two nested loops are required: one to iterate over the substring and one to iterate over the string being searched. This program uses the labeled form of continue to skip an iteration in the outer loop:

```java
public class ContinueWithLabelDemo {
    public static void main(String[] args) {
```

---

[1] ContinueDemo.java is included on the CD and is available online. See Code Samples (page 117).
[2] ContinueWithLabelDemo.java is included on the CD and is available online. See Code Samples (page 117).

```
        String searchMe = "Look for a substring in me";
        String substring = "sub";
        boolean foundIt = false;

        int max = searchMe.length() - substring.length();

    test:
        for (int i = 0; i <= max; i++) {
            int n = substring.length();
            int j = i;
            int k = 0;
            while (n-- != 0) {
                if (searchMe.charAt(j++) != substring.charAt(k++)) {
                    continue test;
                }
            }
            foundIt = true;
            break test;
        }
        System.out.println(foundIt ? "Found it" : "Didn't find it");
    }
}
```

Here is the output from this program:

```
Found it
```

The return Statement

The last of the branching statements is the `return` statement. You use `return` to exit from the current method. The flow of control returns to the statement that follows the original method call. The `return` statement has two forms: one that returns a value and one that doesn't. To return a value, simply put the value (or an expression that calculates the value) after the `return` keyword:

```
return ++count;
```

The data type of the value returned by `return` must match the type of the method's declared return value. When a method is declared `void`, use the form of `return` that doesn't return a value:

```
return;
```

For information about writing methods for your classes, refer to the section <u>Defining Methods</u> (page 182).

Summary of Control Flow Statements

For controlling the flow of a program, the Java programming language has three loop constructs, a flexible if-else statement, a switch statement, exception-handling statements, and branching statements.

Loops

Use the while statement to loop over a block of statements while a boolean expression remains true. The expression is evaluated at the top of the loop:

```
while (boolean expression) {
    statement(s)
}
```

Use the do-while statement to loop over a block of statements while a boolean expression remains true. The expression is evaluated at the bottom of the loop, so the statements within the do-while block execute at least once:

```
do {
    statement(s)
} while (expression);
```

The for statement loops over a block of statements and includes an initialization expression, a termination condition expression, and an increment expression:

```
for (initialization ; termination ; increment) {
    statements
}
```

Decision-Making Statements

The Java programming language has two decision-making statements: if-else and switch. The more general-purpose statement is if; use switch to make multiple-choice decisions based on a single integer value.

The following is the most basic if statement whose single statement block is executed if the boolean expression is true:

```
if (boolean expression) {
    statement(s)
}
```

Here's an if statement with a companion else statement. The if statement executes the first block if the boolean expression is true; otherwise, it executes the second block:

```
if (boolean expression) {
    statement(s)
} else {
    statement(s)
}
```

You can use `else if` to construct compound `if` statements:

```
if (boolean expression) {
    statement(s)
} else if (boolean expression) {
    statement(s)
} else if (boolean expression) {
    statement(s)
} else {
    statement(s)
}
```

The `switch` statement evaluates an integer expression and executes the appropriate `case` statement:

```
switch (integer expression) {
    case integer expression:
        statement(s)
        break;
    ...
    default:
        statement(s)
        break;
}
```

Exception-Handling Statements

Use the `try`, `catch`, and `finally` statements to handle exceptions. Exception handling is covered in detail in the chapter <u>Handling Errors Using Exceptions</u> (page 243).

```
try {
    statement(s)
} catch (exceptiontype name) {
    statement(s)
} finally {
    statement(s)
}
```

Branching Statements

Some branching statements change the flow of control in a program to a labeled statement. You label a statement by placing a legal identifier (the label) followed by a colon (:) before the statement:

```
statementName: someJavaStatement
```

Use the unlabeled form of the `break` statement to terminate the innermost `switch`, `for`, `while`, or do-`while` statement:

```
break;
```

Use the labeled form of the `break` statement to terminate an outer `switch`, `for`, `while`, or do-`while` statement with the given label:

```
break label;
```

A `continue` statement terminates the current iteration of the innermost loop and evaluates the boolean expression that controls the loop:

```
continue;
```

The labeled form of the `continue` statement skips the current iteration of the loop with the given label:

```
continue label;
```

Use `return` to terminate the current method:

```
return;
```

You can return a value to the method's caller by using the form of `return` that takes a value:

```
return value;
```

Questions and Exercises: Control Flow

Questions

1. Look at the `SortDemo` program on page 80. What control flow statements does it contain?

2. What's wrong with the following code snippet:

```java
if (i = 1) {
    /* do something */
}
```

3. Look at the WhileDemo program on page 100 and the DoWhileDemo program on page 101. What would the output be from each program if you changed the value of each program's copyFromMe string to "golly gee. this is fun."? Explain why you think each program will have the predicted output.

Exercises

1. Consider the following code snippet.

```java
if (aNumber >= 0)
    if (aNumber == 0) System.out.println("first string");
else System.out.println("second string");
System.out.println("third string");
```

   a. What output do you think the code will produce if aNumber is 3?

   b. Write a test program containing the code snippet; make aNumber 3. What is the output of the program? Is it what you predicted? Explain why the output is what it is. In other words, what is the control flow for the code snippet?

   c. Using only spaces and line breaks, reformat the code snippet to make the control flow easier to understand.

   d. Use braces—{ and }—to further clarify the code. The use of braces also reduces the possibility of errors by future maintainers of the code.

Answers

You can find answers to these Questions and Exercises online:

```
http://java.sun.com/docs/books/tutorial/java/nutsandbolts/QandE/
answers_flow.html
```

Code Samples

Table 22 lists the code samples used in this chapter and where you can find the code online and on the CD that accompanies this book.

Table 22   Code Samples in Language Basics

Code Sample (where discussed)	CD Location	Online Location
`BasicsDemo.java` (page 65)	`JavaTutorial/java/ nutsandbolts/example/ BasicsDemo.java`	`http://java.sun.com/docs/ books/tutorial/java/ nutsandbolts/example/ BasicsDemo.java`
`MaxVariablesDemo.java` (page 67)	`JavaTutorial/java/ nutsandbolts/ example-1dot1/ MaxVariablesDemo.java`	`http://java.sun.com/docs/ books/tutorial/java/ nutsandbolts/ example-1dot1/ MaxVariablesDemo.java`
`ArithmeticDemo.java` (page 77)	`JavaTutorial/java/ nutsandbolts/example/ ArithmeticDemo.java`	`http://java.sun.com/docs/ books/tutorial/java/ nutsandbolts/example/ ArithmeticDemo.java`
`SortDemo.java` (page 80)	`JavaTutorial/java/ nutsandbolts/example/ SortDemo.java`	`http://java.sun.com/docs/ books/tutorial/java/ nutsandbolts/example/ SortDemo.java`
`RelationalDemo.java` (page 82)	`JavaTutorial/java/ nutsandbolts/example/ RelationalDemo.java`	`http://java.sun.com/docs/ books/tutorial/java/ nutsandbolts/example/ RelationalDemo.java`
`BitwiseDemo.java` (page 88)	`JavaTutorial/java/ nutsandbolts/example/ BitwiseDemo.java`	`http://java.sun.com/docs/ books/tutorial/java/ nutsandbolts/example/ BitwiseDemo.java`
`WhileDemo.java` (page 100)	`JavaTutorial/java/ nutsandbolts/example/ WhileDemo.java`	`http://java.sun.com/docs/ books/tutorial/java/ nutsandbolts/example/ WhileDemo.java`
`DoWhileDemo.java` (page 101)	`JavaTutorial/java/ nutsandbolts/example/ DoWhileDemo.java`	`http://java.sun.com/docs/ books/tutorial/java/ nutsandbolts/example/ DoWhileDemo.java`

Table 22   Code Samples in Language Basics

ForDemo.java (page 102)	JavaTutorial/java/ nutsandbolts/example/ ForDemo.java	http://java.sun.com/docs/ books/tutorial/java/ nutsandbolts/example/ ForDemo.java
IfElseDemo.java (page 103)	JavaTutorial/java/ nutsandbolts/example/ IfElseDemo.java	http://java.sun.com/docs/ books/tutorial/java/ nutsandbolts/example/ IfElseDemo.java
SwitchDemo.java (page 105)	JavaTutorial/java/ nutsandbolts/example/ SwitchDemo.java	http://java.sun.com/docs/ books/tutorial/java/ nutsandbolts/example/ SwitchDemo.java
SwitchDemo2.java (page 106)	JavaTutorial/java/ nutsandbolts/example/ SwitchDemo2.java	http://java.sun.com/docs/ books/tutorial/java/ nutsandbolts/example/ SwitchDemo2.java
BreakDemo.java (page 109)	JavaTutorial/java/ nutsandbolts/example/ BreakDemo.java	http://java.sun.com/docs/ books/tutorial/java/ nutsandbolts/example/ BreakDemo.java
BreakWithLabelDemo.java (page 110)	JavaTutorial/java/ nutsandbolts/example/ BreakWithLabelDemo.java	http://java.sun.com/docs/ books/tutorial/java/ nutsandbolts/example/ BreakWithLabelDemo.java
ContinueDemo.java (page 111)	JavaTutorial/java/ nutsandbolts/example/ ContinueDemo.java	http://java.sun.com/docs/ books/tutorial/java/ nutsandbolts/example/ ContinueDemo.java
ContinueWithLabelDemo.java (page 111)	JavaTutorial/java/ nutsandbolts/example/ ContinueWithLabelDemo.java	http://java.sun.com/docs/ books/tutorial/java/ nutsandbolts/example/ ContinueWithLabelDemo.java

Note: The section <u>Common Problems and Their Solutions</u> (page 391) contains solutions to common problems Tutorial readers have encountered.

4

Object Basics and Simple Data Objects

THIS chapter begins with a general discussion about the life cycle of objects. The information presented applies to objects of all types and includes how to create an object, how to use it, and, finally, how the system cleans up the object when it's no longer being used.

Next, this chapter shows you how to use objects of the following types. Classes for these objects are provided by the Java™ platform.

- Character data—either a single character or a series of characters—can be stored and manipulated by one of three classes in java.lang: Character, String, and StringBuffer.
- To work with numeric data, you use the number classes. The Number class is the superclass for all number classes in the Java platform. Its subclasses include Float, Integer, and so on.
- You can group values of the same type within arrays. Arrays are supported directly by the Java programming language; there is no array class. Arrays are implicit extensions of the Object class, so you can assign an array to a variable whose type is declared as Object.

The Java platform groups its classes into functional packages. Instead of writing your own classes, you can use one provided by the platform. Most of the classes discussed in this chapter are members of the java.lang package.[1] All the classes in the java.lang package are available to your programs automatically.

---

[1] http://java.sun.com/j2se/1.3/docs/api/java/lang/package-summary.html

The Life Cycle of an Object

A typical program creates many objects, which interact by sending messages. Through these object interactions, a program can implement a GUI, run an animation, or send and receive information over a network. Once an object has completed the work for which it was created, its resources are recycled for use by other objects.

Here's a small program, called CreateObjectDemo,[1] that creates three objects: one Point object and two Rectangle objects.[2]

```java
public class CreateObjectDemo {

    public static void main(String[] args) {
        // declare and create a point object and two rectangle objects
        Point origin_one = new Point(23, 94);
        Rectangle rect_one = new Rectangle(origin_one, 100, 200);
        Rectangle rect_two = new Rectangle(50, 100);

        // display rect_one's width, height, and area
        System.out.println("Width of rect_one: " + rect_one.width);
        System.out.println("Height of rect_one: " + rect_one.height);
        System.out.println("Area of rect_one: " + rect_one.area());

        // set rect_two's position
        rect_two.origin = origin_one;

        // display rect_two's position
        System.out.println("X Position of rect_two: "
                            + rect_two.origin.x);
        System.out.println("Y Position of rect_two: "
                            + rect_two.origin.y);

        // move rect_two and display its new position
        rect_two.move(40, 72);
        System.out.println("X Position of rect_two: "
                            + rect_two.origin.x);
        System.out.println("Y Position of rect_two: "
                            + rect_two.origin.y);
    }
}
```

After creating the objects, this program manipulates the objects and displays some information about them. Here's the output from the program:

```
Width of rect_one: 100
Height of rect_one: 200
Area of rect_one: 20000
X Position of rect_two: 23
```

---

[1] CreateObjectDemo.java, Rectangle.java, and Point.java are included on the CD and are available online. See Code Samples (page 174).

[2] This example contains code for the Point and Rectangle classes so that you can see code for simple classes. However, instead of our Point and Rectangle classes, you should use the ones provided by the Java platform in the java.awt package.

```
Y Position of rect_two: 94
X Position of rect_two: 40
Y Position of rect_two: 72
```

This section uses this example to describe the life cycle of an object within a program. From this, you can learn how to write code that creates and uses an object and how the system cleans it up.

Creating Objects

As you know, a class provides the blueprint for objects; you create an object from a class. Each of the following statements taken from the CreateObjectDemo program creates an object;

[handwritten: →Point   = new Point (23,94); ? where's the object?]

```
Point origin_one = new Point(23, 94);
Rectangle rect_one = new Rectangle(origin_one, 100, 200);
Rectangle rect_two = new Rectangle(50, 100);
```

The first line creates an object from the Point class. The second and third lines each create an object from the Rectangle class.

Each statement has the following three parts:

1. **Declaration:** The code set in boldface in the previous listing are all variable declarations that associate a name with a type. When you create an object, you do not have to declare a variable to refer to it. However, a variable declaration often appears on the same line as the code to create an object.

2. **Instantiation:** The new keyword is an operator that creates the new object (allocates space for it).

3. **Initialization:** The new operator is followed by a call to a constructor. For example, Point(23, 94) is a call to Point's only constructor. The constructor initializes the new object.

Declaring a Variable to Refer to an Object

From the section <u>Variables</u> (page 67) in Chapter 3, you learned that to declare a variable, you write:

```
type name
```

This notifies the Java platform that you will use *name* to refer to a particular item of data whose type is *type*.

In addition to the primitive types, such as `int` and `boolean`, provided directly by the Java programming language, classes and interfaces are also types. To declare a variable to refer to an object, you use the name of a class or an interface as the variable's type. The sample program uses both the `Point` and the `Rectangle` class names as types to declare variables:

```
Point origin_one = new Point(23, 94);
Rectangle rect_one = new Rectangle(origin_one, 100, 200);
Rectangle rect_two = new Rectangle(50, 100);
```

Declarations do not create new objects. The code `Point origin_one` does not create a new `Point` object; it just declares a variable, named `origin_one`, that will be used to refer to a `Point` object. The reference is empty until assigned, as illustrated in Figure 45. An empty reference is known as a *null reference*.

Figure 45 A reference variable, such as `origin_one`, contains a null reference until a value is assigned to it.

To create an object, you instantiate a class with the new operator.

Instantiating an Object

The new operator instantiates a class by allocating memory for a new object. The new operator requires a single, postfix argument: a call to a constructor. The name of the constructor provides the name of the class to instantiate. The constructor initializes the new object.

The new operator returns a reference to the object it created. Often, this reference is assigned to a variable of the appropriate type. If the reference is not assigned to a variable, the object is unreachable after the statement in which the new operator appears finishes executing.

→ why would you need an object you can't reach?

Initializing an Object

Here's the code for the `Point`[1] class:

```
public class Point {
    public int x = 0;
    public int y = 0;
    //A constructor!
    public Point(int x, int y) {
        this.x = x;
        this.y = y;
    }
}
```

---

[1] `Point.java` is included on the CD and is available online. See <u>Code Samples</u> (page 174).

This class contains a single constructor. You can recognize a constructor because it has the same name as the class and has no return type. The constructor in the `Point` class takes two integer arguments, as declared by the code (`int x`, `int y`). The following statement provides 23 and 94 as values for those arguments:

```
Point origin_one = new Point(23, 94);
```

The effect of the previous line of code can be illustrated in Figure 46:

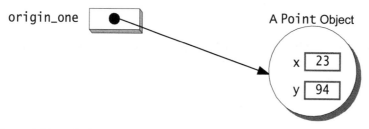

Figure 46 The variable `origin_one` contains a reference to the `Point` object.

Here's the code for the `Rectangle`[1] class, which contains four constructors:

```
public class Rectangle {
    public int width = 0;
    public int height = 0;
    public Point origin;

    //Four constructors
    public Rectangle() {
        origin = new Point(0, 0);
    }

    public Rectangle(Point p) {
        origin = p;
    }

    public Rectangle(int w, int h) {
        this(new Point(0, 0), w, h);
    }

    public Rectangle(Point p, int w, int h) {
        origin = p;
        width = w;
        height = h;
    }
```

[1] `Rectangle.java` is included on the CD and is available online. See Code Samples (page 174).

```
//A method for moving the rectangle
public void move(int x, int y) {
    origin.x = x;
    origin.y = y;
}

//A method for computing the area of the rectangle
public int area() {
    return width * height;
}
}
```

How do I know if this is class object or method [handwritten annotation]

Each constructor lets you provide initial values for different aspects of the rectangle: the origin, width, and height. You can set the values for all three or none. If a class has multiple constructors, they all have the same name but a different number of arguments or different typed arguments. The Java platform differentiates the constructors, based on the number and the type of the arguments. When the Java platform encounters the following code, it knows to call the constructor in the Rectangle class that requires a Point argument followed by two integer arguments:

```
Rectangle rect_one = new Rectangle(origin_one, 100, 200);
```

This call initializes the rectangle's origin variable to the Point object referred to by origin_one. The code also sets width to 100 and height to 200. Now there are two references to the same Point object; an object can have multiple references to it, as shown in Figure 47:

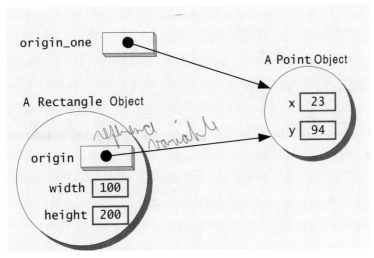

Figure 47 Multiple references can refer to the same object.

The following line of code calls the constructor that requires two integer arguments, which provide the initial values for width and height. If you inspect the code within the constructor, you will see that it creates a new Point object whose x and y values are initialized to 0:

```
Rectangle rect_two = new Rectangle(50, 100);
```

The Rectangle constructor used in the following statement doesn't take any arguments, so it's called a *no-argument constructor*:

```
Rectangle rect = new Rectangle();
```

If a class does not explicitly declare any constructors, the Java platform automatically provides a no-argument constructor, called the *default constructor*, that does nothing. Thus, all classes have at least one constructor.

This section talked about how to use a constructor. The section <u>Providing Constructors for Your Classes</u> (page 186) explains how to write constructors for your classes.

Using Objects

Once you've created an object, you probably want to use it for something. You may need information from it, want to change its state, or have it perform some action. You can use an object in one of two ways:

- Manipulate or inspect its variables
- Call its methods

Referencing an Object's Variables

The following is the general form of a *qualified name*, which is also known as a long name:

```
objectReference.variableName
```

You may use a simple name for an instance variable when the instance variable is in scope—that is, within code for the object's class. Code that is outside the object's class must use a qualified name. For example, the code in the CreateObjectDemo class is outside the code for the Rectangle class. So to refer to the origin, width, and height variables within the Rectangle object named rect_one, the CreateObjectDemo class must use the names rect_one.origin, rect_one.width, and rect_one.height, respectively. The program uses two of these names to display the width and the height of rect_one:

```
System.out.println("Width of rect_one: " + rect_one.width);
System.out.println("Height of rect_one: " + rect_one.height);
```

Attempting to use the simple names `width` and `height` from the code in the `CreateObject-Demo` class doesn't make sense—those variables exist only within an object—and results in a compiler error.

Later, the program uses similar code to display information about `rect_two`. Objects of the same type have their own copy of the same instance variables. Thus, each `Rectangle` object has variables named `origin`, `width`, and `height`. When you access an instance variable through an object reference, you reference that particular object's variable. The two objects `rect_one` and `rect_two` in the `CreateObjectDemo` program have different `origin`, `width`, and `height` variables.

The first part of the variable's qualified name, *objectReference*, must be a reference to an object. You can use the name of a reference variable here, as in the previous examples, or you can use any expression that returns an object reference. Recall that the new operator returns a reference to an object. So you could use the value returned from new to access a new object's variables:

```java
int height = new Rectangle().height;
```

This statement creates a new `Rectangle` object and immediately gets its height. In essence, the statement calculates the default height of a `Rectangle`. Note that after this statement has been executed, the program no longer has a reference to the created `Rectangle`, because the program never stored the reference in a variable. The object is unreferenced, and its resources can be recycled by the Java platform.

A Word about Variable Access

The direct manipulation of an object's variables by other objects and classes is discouraged because it's possible to set the variables to values that don't make sense. For example, consider the `Rectangle` class from the previous section. Using that class, you can create a rectangle whose width and height are negative, which, for some applications, doesn't make sense.

Ideally, instead of allowing direct manipulation of variables, a class would provide methods through which other objects can inspect or change variables. These methods ensure that the values of the variables make sense for objects of that type. Thus, the `Rectangle` class would provide methods called `setWidth`, `setHeight`, `getWidth`, and `getHeight` for setting and getting the width and the height. The methods for setting the variables would report an error if the caller tried to set the width or the height to a negative number. The other advantage of using methods instead of direct variable access is that the class can change the type and the names of the variables it uses for storing the width and the height without affecting its clients.

However, in practical situations, it sometimes makes sense to allow direct access to an object's variables. For example, both the `Point` class and the `Rectangle` class allow free access to their member variables by declaring them `public`. This keeps these classes small and simple. Also, it keeps them generally useful. Some applications might allow rectangles with negative widths and heights.

The Java programming language provides an access control mechanism whereby classes can determine what other classes can have direct access to its variables. A class should protect variables against direct manipulation by other objects if those manipulations could result in values that don't make sense for objects of that type. Changes to these variables should be controlled by method calls. If a class grants access to its variables, you can assume that you can inspect and change those variables without adverse effects. To learn more about the access control mechanism, refer to the section Controlling Access to Members of a Class (page 193) in Chapter 5. Also, by making the variables accessible, they become part of the class's API, which means that the writer of the class should not change their names or their types.

Calling an Object's Methods

You also use qualified names to call an object's method. To form the qualified name of a method, you append the method name to an object reference, with an intervening period (.). Also, you provide, within enclosing parentheses, any arguments to the method. If the method does not require any arguments, use empty parentheses.

```
objectReference.methodName(argumentList);
```

or

```
objectReference.methodName();
```

The `Rectangle` class has two methods: `area` to compute the rectangle's area and `move` to change the origin. Here's the `CreateObjectDemo` code that calls these two methods:

```
System.out.println("Area of rect_one: " + rect_one.area());
...
rect_two.move(40, 72);
```

The first statement calls `rect_one`'s `area` method and displays the results. The second line moves `rect_two` because the `move` method assigns new values to the object's `origin.x` and `origin.y`.

As with instance variables, *objectReference* must be a reference to an object. You can use a variable name, but you also can use any expression that returns an object reference. The `new` operator returns an object reference, so you can use the value returned from `new` to call a new object's methods:

```
new Rectangle(100, 50).area()
```

The expression new Rectangle(100, 50) returns an object reference that refers to a Rectangle object. As shown, you can use the dot notation to call the new Rectangle's area method to compute the area of the new rectangle.

Some methods, such as area, return a value. For methods that return a value, you can use the method call in expressions. You can assign the return value to a variable, use it to make decisions, or control a loop. This code assigns the value returned by area to a variable:

```
int areaOfRectangle = new Rectangle(100, 50).area();
```

Remember, invoking a method on a particular object is the same as sending a message to that object. In this case, the object that area is invoked on is the rectangle returned by the constructor.

A Word about Method Access

The methods in our Point and Rectangle classes are all declared public, so they are accessible to any other class. Sometimes, a class needs to restrict access to its methods. For example, a class might have a method that only subclasses are allowed to call. A class can use the same mechanism to control access to its methods as it uses to control access to its variables. To learn more about the access control mechanism, refer to the section Controlling Access to Members of a Class (page 193).

Cleaning Up Unused Objects

Some object-oriented languages require that you keep track of all the objects you create and that you explicitly destroy them when they are no longer needed. Managing memory explicitly is tedious and error prone. The Java platform allows you to create as many objects as you want (limited, of course, by what your system can handle), and you don't have to worry about destroying them. The Java runtime environment deletes objects when it determines that they are no longer being used. This process is called *garbage collection*.

An object is eligible for garbage collection when there are no more references to that object. References that are held in a variable are usually dropped when the variable goes out of scope. Or, you can explicitly drop an object reference by setting the variable to the special value null. Remember that a program can have multiple references to the same object; all references to an object must be dropped before the object is eligible for garbage collection.

The Garbage Collector

The Java runtime environment has a garbage collector that periodically frees the memory used by objects that are no longer referenced. The garbage collector does its job automatically, although, in some situations, you may want to run the garbage collection explicitly by calling the gc method in the System class. For instance, you might want to run the garbage collector after a section of code that creates a large amount of garbage or before a section of code that needs a lot of memory.

Finalization

Before an object gets garbage-collected, the garbage collector gives the object an opportunity to clean up after itself through a call to the object's `finalize` method. This process is known as *finalization*.

Most programmers don't have to worry about implementing the `finalize` method. In rare cases, however, a programmer might have to implement a `finalize` method to release resources, such as native peers, that aren't under the control of the garbage collector.

The `finalize` method is a member of the Object class, which is the top of the Java platform's class hierarchy and a superclass of all classes. A class can override the `finalize` method to perform any finalization necessary for objects of that type. If you override `final-ize`, your implementation of the method should call `super.finalize` as the last thing it does. The section Overriding and Hiding Methods (page 204) talks more about how to override methods.

Summary of Objects

You create an object from a class by using the new operator and a constructor. The new operator returns a reference to the object that was created. You can assign the reference to a variable or use it directly.

A class controls access to its instance variables and methods by using the Java platform's access mechanism. Instance variables and methods that are accessible to code outside of the class that they are declared in can be referred to by using a qualified name. The qualified name of an instance variable looks like this:

```
objectReference.variableName
```

The qualified name of a method looks like this:

```
objectReference.methodName(argumentList)
    or
objectReference.methodName()
```

The garbage collector automatically cleans up unused objects. An object is unused if the program holds no more references to it. You can explicitly drop a reference by setting the variable holding the reference to `null`.

Questions and Exercises: Objects

Some of the following questions and exercises refer to the `Point` and `Rectangle` classes. Use the classes shown on page 123 and page 124, respectively.

Questions

1. What's wrong with the following program?

```
public class SomethingIsWrong {
    public static void main(String[] args) {
        Rectangle myRect;
        myRect.width = 40;
        myRect.height = 50;
        System.out.println("myRect's area is " + myRect.area());
    }
}
```

→ no constructor ; no = new Rectangle (40,50)

2. The following code creates one `Point` object and one `Rectangle` object. How many references to those objects exist after the code executes? Is either object eligible for garbage collection?

```
...
Point point = new Point(2,4);
Rectangle rectangle = new Rectangle(point, 20, 20);
point = null;
...
```

point   0
rectangle   1

3. How does a program destroy an object that it creates? *Through GC*

Exercises

1. Fix the program called `SomethingIsWrong` shown in question 1.

2. Given the following class, write some code that creates an instance of the class, initializes its two member variables, and then displays the value of each member variable.

```
public class NumberHolder {
    public int anInt;
    public float aFloat;
}
```

Answers

You can find answers to these Questions and Exercises online:

```
http://java.sun.com/docs/books/tutorial/java/data/QandE/
objects-answers.html
```

Characters and Strings

The Java platform contains three classes that you can use when working with character data:

- Character[1]—A class whose instances can hold a single character value. This class also defines handy methods that can manipulate or inspect single-character data.
- String[2]—A class for working with immutable (unchanging) data composed of multiple characters.
- StringBuffer[3]—A class for storing and manipulating mutable data composed of multiple characters.

Characters

An object of Character type contains a single character value. You use a Character object instead of a primitive char variable when an object is required—for example, when passing a character value into a method that changes the value or when placing a character value into a data structure, such as a vector, that requires objects.

The following sample program, CharacterDemo,[4] creates a few character objects and displays some information about them. The code that is related to the Character class is shown in boldface:

```
public class CharacterDemo {
    public static void main(String args[]) {
        Character a = new Character('a');
        Character a2 = new Character('a');
        Character b = new Character('b');

        int difference = a.compareTo(b);

        if (difference == 0) {
            System.out.println("a is equal to b.");
        } else if (difference < 0) {
            System.out.println("a is less than b.");
        } else if (difference > 0) {
            System.out.println("a is greater than b.");
        }
```

---

[1] http://java.sun.com/j2se/1.3/docs/api/java/lang/Character.html
[2] http://java.sun.com/j2se/1.3/docs/api/java/lang/String.html
[3] http://java.sun.com/j2se/1.3/docs/api/java/lang/StringBuffer.html
[4] CharacterDemo.java is included on the CD and is available online. See Code Samples (page 174). This program requires Java 2 SDK 1.2 to run because it uses the compareTo method, which was added to the Character class for that release.

```
System.out.println("a is "
                + ((a.equals(a2)) ? "equal" : "not equal")
                + " to a2.");
        System.out.println("The character " + a.toString() + " is "
            + (Character.isUpperCase(a.charValue()) ? "upper" : "lower")
            + "case.");
    }
}
```

The following is the output from this program:

```
a is less than b.
a is equal to a2.
The character a is lowercase.
```

The CharacterDemo program calls the following constructors and methods provided by the Character class:

- Character(char)—The Character class's only constructor, which creates a Character object containing the value provided by the argument. Once a Character object has been created, the value it contains cannot be changed.

- compareTo(Character)[1]—An instance method that compares the values held by two character objects: the object on which the method is called (a in the example) and the argument to the method (b in the example). This method returns an integer indicating whether the value in the current object is greater than, equal to, or less than the value held by the argument. A letter is greater than another letter if its numeric value is greater.

- equals(Object)—An instance method that compares the value held by the current object with the value held by another. This method returns true if the values held by both objects are equal.

- toString()—An instance method that converts the object to a string. The resulting string is one character in length and contains the value held by the character object.

- charValue()—An instance method that returns the value held by the character object as a primitive char value.

- isUpperCase(char)—A class method that determines whether a primitive char value is uppercase. This is one of many Character class methods that inspect or manipulate character data. Table 23 lists several other useful class methods the Character class provides.

---

[1] The compareTo method was added to the Character class for Java 2 SDK v. 1.2.

Table 23 Useful Class Methods in the `Character` Class

Method	Description
`boolean isUpperCase(char)` `boolean isLowerCase(char)`	Determines whether the specified primitive `char` value is upper- or lowercase, respectively.
`char toUpperCase(char)` `char toLowerCase(char)`	Returns the upper- or lowercase form of the specified primitive `char` value.

`boolean isLetter(char)`
`boolean isDigit(char)`
`boolean isLetterOrDigit(char)`
	Determines whether the specified primitive `char` value is a letter, a digit, or a letter or a digit, respectively.

`boolean isWhitespace(char)`[a]	Determines whether the specified primitive `char` value is white space according to the Java platform.
`boolean isSpaceChar(char)`[b]	Determines whether the specified primitive `char` value is a white-space character according to the Unicode specification.
`boolean isJavaIdentifierStart(char)`[c] `boolean isJavaIdentifierPart(char)`[d]	Determines whether the specified primitive `char` value can be the first character in a legal identifier or be a part of a legal identifier, respectively.

a. Added to the Java platform for the 1.1 release. Replaces `isSpace(char)`, which is deprecated.

b. Added to the Java platform for the 1.1 release.

c. Added to the Java platform for the 1.1 release. Replaces `isJavaLetter(char)`, which is deprecated.

d. Added to the Java platform for the 1.1 release. Replaces `isJavaLetterOrDigit(char)`, which is deprecated.

Strings and String Buffers

The Java platform provides two classes, `String` and `StringBuffer`, that store and manipulate strings—character data consisting of more than one character. The `String` class provides for strings whose value will not change. For example, if you write a method that requires string data and the method is not going to modify the string in any way, pass a `String` object into the method. The `StringBuffer` class provides for strings that will be modified; you use string buffers when you know that the value of the character data will change. You typically use string buffers for constructing character data dynamically: for example, when reading text data from a file. Because strings are constants, they are more efficient to use than are string buffers and can be shared. So it's important to use strings when you can.

Following is a sample program called `StringsDemo`,[1] which reverses the characters of a string. This program uses both a string and a string buffer.

---

[1] `StringsDemo.java` is included on the CD and is available online. See Code Samples (page 174). Note that instead of explicitly writing code to reverse the characters of a string, you should use the `reverse` method in the `StringBuffer` class.

```
public class StringsDemo {
    public static void main(String[] args) {
        String palindrome = "Dot saw I was Tod";
        int len = palindrome.length();
        StringBuffer dest = new StringBuffer(len);

        for (int i = (len - 1); i >= 0; i--) {
            dest.append(palindrome.charAt(i));
        }
        System.out.println(dest.toString());
    }
}
```

The output from this program is:

```
doT saw I was toD
```

In addition to highlighting the differences between strings and string buffers, this section discusses several features of the String and StringBuffer classes: creating strings and string buffers, using accessor methods to get information about a string or string buffer, and modifying a string buffer.

Creating Strings and String Buffers

A string is often created from a *string literal*—a series of characters enclosed in double quotes. For example, when it encounters the following string literal, the Java platform creates a String object whose value is Gobbledygook.

```
"Gobbledygook"
```

The StringsDemo program uses this technique to create the string referred to by the palindrome variable:

```
String palindrome = "Dot saw I was Tod";
```

You can also create String objects as you would any other Java object: using the new keyword and a constructor. The String class provides several constructors that allow you to provide the initial value of the string, using different sources, such as an array of characters, an array of bytes, or a string buffer. Table 24 shows the constructors provided by the String class.

Table 24   Constructors in the `String` Class[a]

Constructor	Description
`String()`	Creates an empty string.

`String(byte[])`
`String(byte[], int, int)`
`String(byte[], int, int, String)`
`String(byte[], String)`
	Creates a string whose value is set from the contents of an array of bytes. The two integer arguments, when present, set the offset and the length, respectively, of the subarray from which to take the initial values. The `String` argument, when present, specifies the character encoding to use to convert bytes to characters.

`String(char[])` `String(char[], int, int)`	Creates a string whose value is set from the contents of an array of characters. The two integer arguments, when present, set the offset and the length, respectively, of the subarray from which to take the initial values.
`String(String)`	Creates a string whose value is set from another string. Using this constructor with a literal string argument is not recommended, because it creates two identical strings.
`String(StringBuffer)`	Creates a string whose value is set from a string buffer.

a. The `String` class defines other constructors not listed in this table. Those constructors have been deprecated, and their use is not recommended.

Here's an example of creating a string from a character array:

```
char[] helloArray = { 'h', 'e', 'l', 'l', 'o' };
helloString = new String(helloArray);
System.out.println(helloString);
```

The last line of this code snippet displays: `hello`.

You must always use `new` to create a string buffer. The `StringBuffer` class has three constructors, as described in Table 25.

Table 25   Constructors in the `StringBuffer` Class

Constructor	Description
`StringBuffer()`	Creates an empty string buffer whose initial capacity is 16 characters.
`StringBuffer(int)`	Creates an empty string buffer with the specified initial capacity.
`StringBuffer(String)`	Creates a string buffer whose value is initialized by the specified `String`. The capacity of the string buffer is the length of the original string plus 16.

The `StringsDemo` program creates the string buffer referred to by `dest`, using the constructor that sets the buffer's capacity:

```
String palindrome = "Dot saw I was Tod";
int len = palindrome.length();
StringBuffer dest = new StringBuffer(len);
```

This code creates the string buffer with an initial capacity equal to the length of the string referred to by the name `palindrome`. This ensures only one memory allocation for `dest` because it's just big enough to contain the characters that will be copied to it. By initializing the string buffer's capacity to a reasonable first guess, you minimize the number of times memory must be allocated for it. This makes your code more efficient because memory allocation is a relatively expensive operation.

Getting the Length of a String or a String Buffer

Methods used to obtain information about an object are known as *accessor methods*. One accessor method that you can use with both strings and string buffers is the `length` method, which returns the number of characters contained in the string or the string buffer. After the following two lines of code have been executed, `len` equals 17:

```
String palindrome = "Dot saw I was Tod";
int len = palindrome.length();
```

In addition to `length`, the `StringBuffer` class has a method called `capacity`, which returns the amount of space allocated for the string buffer rather than the amount of space used. For example, the capacity of the string buffer referred to by `dest in the StringsDemo program never changes, although its length increases by 1` for each iteration of the loop. Figure 48 shows the capacity and the length of `dest` after nine characters have been appended to it.

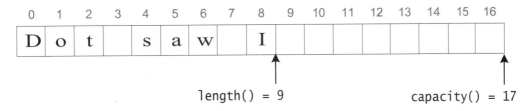

Figure 48 A string buffer's length is the number of characters it contains; a string buffer's capacity is the number of character spaces that have been allocated.

The `String` class doesn't have a `capacity` method, because a string cannot change.

Getting Characters by Index from a String or a String Buffer

You can get the character at a particular index within a string or a string buffer by using the charAt accessor. The index of the first character is 0; the index of the last is length()-1. For example, the following code gets the character at index 9 in a string:

```
String anotherPalindrome = "Niagara. O roar again!";
char aChar = anotherPalindrome.charAt(9);
```

Indices begin at 0, so the character at index 9 is '0', as illustrated in Figure 49:

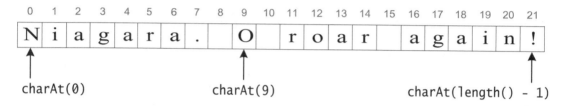

Figure 49 Use the charAt method to get a character at a particular index.

The figure also shows that to compute the index of the last character of a string, you have to subtract 1 from the value returned by the length method.

If you want to get more than one character from a string or a string buffer, you can use the substring method. The substring method has two versions, as shown in Table 26.

Table 26   The substring Methods in the String and StringBuffer Classes[a]

Method	Description
String substring(int) String substring(int, int)	Returns a new string that is a substring of this string or string buffer. The first integer argument specifies the index of the first character. The second integer argument is the index of the last character -1. The length of the substring is therefore the first int minus the second int. If the second integer is not present, the substring extends to the end of the original string.

a. The substring methods were added to the StringBuffer class for Java 2 SDK 1.2.

The following code gets from the Niagara palindrome the substring that extends from index 11 to index 15, which is the word "roar":

```
String anotherPalindrome = "Niagara. O roar again!";
String roar = anotherPalindrome.substring(11, 15);
```

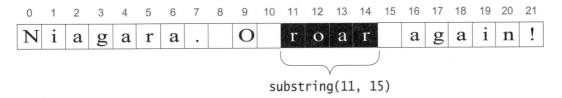

Figure 50 Use the `substring` method to get part of a string or string buffer.

Remember that indices begin at 0 (Figure 50).

Searching for a Character or a Substring within a String

The `String` class provides two accessor methods that return the position within the string of a specific character or substring: `indexOf` and `lastIndexOf`. The `indexOf` method searches forward from the beginning of the string, and `lastIndexOf` searches backward from the end of the string. Table 27 describes the various forms of the `indexOf` and the `lastIndexOf` methods.

Table 27 The `indexOf` and `lastIndexOf` Methods in the `String` Class

Method	Description
`int indexOf(int)` `int lastIndexOf(int)`	Returns the index of the first (last) occurrence of the specified character.
`int indexOf(int, int)` `int lastIndexOf(int, int)`	Returns the index of the first (last) occurrence of the specified character, searching forward (backward) from the specified index.
`int indexOf(String)` `int lastIndexOf(String)`	Returns the index of the first (last) occurrence of the specified string.
`int indexOf(String, int)` `int lastIndexOf(String, int)`	Returns the index of the first (last) occurrence of the specified string, searching forward (backward) from the specified index.

The `StringBuffer` class does not support the `indexOf` or the `lastIndexOf` methods. If you need to use these methods on a string buffer, first convert the string buffer to a string by using the `toString` method.

The following class, `Filename`,[1] illustrates the use of `lastIndexOf` and `substring` to isolate different parts of a file name.

---

[1] `Filename.java` is included on the CD and is available online. See <u>Code Samples</u> (page 174).

Note: The methods in the following class don't do any error checking and assume that their argument contains a full directory path and a file name with an extension. If these methods were production code, they would verify that their arguments were properly constructed.

```java
// This class assumes that the string used to initialize
// fullPath has a directory path, filename, and extension.
// The methods won't work if it doesn't.
public class Filename {
    private String fullPath;
    private char pathSeparator, extensionSeparator;

    public Filename(String str, char sep, char ext) {
        fullPath = str;
        pathSeparator = sep;
        extensionSeparator = ext;
    }

    public String extension() {
        int dot = fullPath.lastIndexOf(extensionSeparator);
        return fullPath.substring(dot + 1);
    }

    public String filename() {
        int dot = fullPath.lastIndexOf(extensionSeparator);
        int sep = fullPath.lastIndexOf(pathSeparator);
        return fullPath.substring(sep + 1, dot);
    }

    public String path() {
        int sep = fullPath.lastIndexOf(pathSeparator);
        return fullPath.substring(0, sep);
    }
}
```

Here's a small program, named `FilenameDemo`,[1] that constructs a `Filename` object and calls all its methods:

```java
public class FilenameDemo {
    public static void main(String[] args) {
        Filename myHomePage = new Filename("/home/mem/index.html",
                                           '/', '.');
        System.out.println("Extension = " + myHomePage.extension());
```

---

[1] `FilenameDemo.java` is included on the CD and is available online. See Code Samples (page 174).

```
        System.out.println("Filename = " + myHomePage.filename());
        System.out.println("Path = " + myHomePage.path());
    }
}
```

And here's the output from `FilenameDemo`:

```
Extension = html
Filename = index
Path = /home/mem
```

As shown in Figure 51, our `extension` method uses `lastIndexOf` to locate the last occurrence of the period (.) in the file name. Then `substring` uses the return value of `lastIndexOf` to extract the file name extension—that is, the substring from the period to the end of the string. This code assumes that the file name has a period in it; if the file name does not have a period, `lastIndexOf` returns -1, and the `substring` method throws a `StringIndexOutOfBoundsException`.

Figure 51 The use of `lastIndexOf` and `substring` in the `extension` method in the `Filename` class.

Also, notice that the `extension` method uses `dot + 1` as the argument to `substring`. If the period character (.) is the last character of the string, `dot + 1` is equal to the length of the string, which is 1 larger than the largest index into the string (because indices start at 0). This is a legal argument to `substring` because that method accepts an index equal to but not greater than the length of the string and interprets it to mean "the end of the string."

Comparing Strings and Portions of Strings

The `String` class has several methods for comparing strings and portions of strings. Table 28 lists and describes these methods.

Table 28 Methods in the String Class for Comparing Strings[a]

Method	Description
boolean endsWith(String) boolean startsWith(String) boolean startsWith(String, int)	Returns true if this string ends with or begins with the substring specified as an argument to the method. The integer argument, when present, indicates the offset within the original string at which to begin looking.
int compareTo(String) int compareTo(Object)* int compareToIgnoreCase(String)*	Compares two strings lexicographically and returns an integer indicating whether this string is greater than (result is > 0), equal to (result is = 0), or less than (result is < 0) the argument. The Object argument is converted to a string before the comparison takes place. The compareToIgnoreCase method ignores case; thus, "a" and "A" are considered equal.
boolean equals(Object) boolean equalsIgnore- Case(String)	Returns true if this string contains the same sequence of characters as the argument. The Object argument is converted to a string before the comparison takes place. The equalsIgnoreCase method ignores case; thus, "a" and "A" are considered equal.
boolean regionMatches(int, String, int, int) boolean regionMatches(boolean, int, String, int, int)	Tests whether the specified region of this string matches the specified region of the String argument. The boolean argument indicates whether case should be ignored; if true, the case is ignored when comparing characters.

a. Methods marked with * were added to the String class for Java 2 SDK 1.2.

The following program, RegionMatchesDemo,[1] uses the regionMatches method to search for a string within another string:

```
public class RegionMatchesDemo {
    public static void main(String[] args) {

        String searchMe = "Green Eggs and Ham";
        String findMe = "Eggs";
        int len = findMe.length();
        boolean foundIt = false;

        int i = 0;
        while (!searchMe.regionMatches(i, findMe, 0, len)) {
            i++;
            foundIt = true;
        }
```

---

[1] RegionMatchesDemo.java is included on the CD and is available online. See Code Samples (page 174).

```
            if (foundIt) {
                System.out.println(searchMe.substring(i, i+len));
            }
        }
    }
}
```

The output from this program is Eggs.

The program steps through the string referred to by searchMe one character at a time. For each character, the program calls the regionMatches method to determine whether the substring beginning with the current character matches the string for which the program is looking.

Manipulating Strings

The String class has several methods that appear to modify a string. Of course, strings can't be modified, so what these methods really do is create and return a second string that contains the result, as indicated in Table 29.

Table 29   Methods in the String Class for Manipulating Strings

Method	Description
String concat(String)	Concatenates the String argument to the end of this string. If the length of the argument is 0, the original string object is returned.
String replace(char, char)	Replaces all occurrences of the character specified as the first argument with the character specified as the second argument. If no replacements are necessary, the original string object is returned.
String trim()	Removes white space from both ends of this string.
String toLowerCase() String toUpperCase()	Converts this string to lower- or uppercase. If no conversions are necessary, these methods return the original string.

Here's a small program, BostonAccentDemo,[1] that uses the replace method to translate a string into the Bostonian dialect:

```
    public class BostonAccentDemo {
        private static void bostonAccent(String sentence) {
            char r = 'r';
            char h = 'h';
            String translatedSentence = sentence.replace(r, h);
            System.out.println(translatedSentence);
        }
```

---

[1]   BostonAccentDemo.java is included on the CD and is available online. See Code Samples (page 174).

```
public static void main(String[] args) {
    String translateThis = "Park the car in Harvard yard.";
    bostonAccent(translateThis);
    }
}
```

→ method for use by all members of Boston Accent Demo?

The `replace` method switches all the r's to h's in the `sentence` string so that the output of this program is:

```
Pahk the cah in Hahvahd yahd.
```

Modifying String Buffers

As you know, string buffers can change. The `StringBuffer` class provides various methods for modifying the data within a string buffer. Table 30 summarizes the methods used to modify a string buffer.

Table 30   Methods for Modifying a String Buffer[a]

Method	Description

`StringBuffer append(boolean)`
`StringBuffer append(char)`
`StringBuffer append(char[])`
`StringBuffer append(char[], int, int)`
`StringBuffer append(double)`
`StringBuffer append(float)`
`StringBuffer append(int)`
`StringBuffer append(long)`
`StringBuffer append(Object)`
`StringBuffer append(String)`
	Appends the argument to this string buffer. The data is converted to a string before the append operation takes place.

`StringBuffer delete(int, int)` * `StringBuffer deleteCharAt(int)` *	Deletes the specified character(s) in this string buffer.

`StringBuffer insert(int, boolean)`
`StringBuffer insert(int, char)`
`StringBuffer insert(int, char[])`
`StringBuffer insert(int, char[], int, int)` *
`StringBuffer insert(int, double)`
`StringBuffer insert(int, float)`
`StringBuffer insert(int, int)`
`StringBuffer insert(int, long)`
`StringBuffer insert(int, Object)`
`StringBuffer insert(int, String)`
	Inserts the second argument into the string buffer. The first integer argument indicates the index before which the data is to be inserted. The data is converted to a string before the insert operation takes place.

`StringBuffer replace(int, int, String)` * `void setCharAt(int, char)`	Replaces the specified character(s) in this string buffer.
`StringBuffer reverse()`	Reverses the sequence of characters in this string buffer.

a. Methods marked with * were added to the `StringBuffer` class for Java 2 SDK 1.2.

You saw the append method in action in the StringsDemo program at the beginning of this section. Here's a program, InsertDemo,[1] that uses the insert method to insert a string into a string buffer:

```
public class InsertDemo {
    public static void main(String[] args) {
        StringBuffer palindrome = new StringBuffer(
                        "A man, a plan, a canal; Panama.");
        palindrome.insert(15, "a cat, ");
        System.out.println(palindrome);
    }
}
```

The output from this program is still a palindrome:

```
A man, a plan, a cat, a canal; Panama.[2]
```

With insert, you specify the index *before* which you want the data inserted. In the example, 15 specifies that "a cat, " is to be inserted before the first a in a canal. To insert data at the beginning of a string buffer, use an index of 0. To add data at the end of a string buffer, use an index equal to the current length of the string buffer or use append.

If the operation that modifies a string buffer causes the size of the string buffer to grow beyond its current capacity, the string buffer allocates more memory. As mentioned previously, memory allocation is a relatively expensive operation, and you can make your code more efficient by initializing a string buffer's capacity to a reasonable first guess.

Strings and the Compiler

The compiler uses the String and the StringBuffer classes behind the scenes to handle literal strings and concatenation. As you know, you specify literal strings between double quotes:

```
"Hello World!"
```

You can use literal strings anywhere you would use a String object. For example, System.out.println accepts a string argument, so you could use a literal string there:

```
System.out.println("Might I add that you look lovely today.");
```

---

[1] InsertDemo.java is included on the CD and is available online. See <u>Code Samples</u> (page 174).
[2] Palindrome by Jim Saxe.

You can also use `String` methods directly from a literal string:

```
int len = "Goodbye Cruel World".length();
```

 Because the compiler automatically creates a new string object for every literal string it encounters, you can use a literal string to initialize a string:

```
String s = "Hola Mundo";
```

The preceding construct is equivalent to, but more efficient than, this one, which ends up creating two identical strings:

```
String s = new String("Hola Mundo");    //don't do this
```

You can use + to concatenate strings:

```
String cat = "cat";
System.out.println("con" + cat + "enation");
```

Behind the scenes, the compiler uses string buffers to implement concatenation. The preceding example compiles to:

```
String cat = "cat";
System.out.println(new StringBuffer().append("con").
                        append(cat).append("enation").toString());
```

You can also use the + operator to append to a string values that are not themselves strings:

```
System.out.println("You're number " + 1);
```

The compiler implicitly converts the nonstring value (the integer 1 in the example) to a string object before performing the concatenation operation.

Summary of Characters and Strings

Use a `Character` object to contain a single character value, use a `String` object to contain a sequence of characters that won't change, and use a `StringBuffer` object to construct or to modify a sequence of characters dynamically. Refer to the tables listed in Table 31 for details about constructors and methods in these classes.

Table 31 Useful Tables for `String` and `StringBuffer`

Number	Table Title	Page
Table 23	Useful Class Methods in the `Character` Class	(page 134)
Table 24	Constructors in the `String` Class	(page 136)
Table 25	Constructors in the `StringBuffer` Class	(page 136)
Table 26	The `substring` Methods in the `String` and `StringBuffer` Classes	(page 138)
Table 27	The `indexOf` and `lastIndexOf` Methods in the `String` Class	(page 139)
Table 28	Methods in the `String` Class for Comparing Strings	(page 142)
Table 29	Methods in the `String` Class for Manipulating Strings	(page 143)
Table 30	Methods for Modifying a String Buffer	(page 144)

Here's a fun program, `Palindrome`,[1] that determines whether a string is a palindrome. This program uses many methods from the `String` and the `StringBuffer` classes:

```
public class Palindrome {
    public static boolean isPalindrome(String stringToTest) {
        String workingCopy = removeJunk(stringToTest);
        String reversedCopy = reverse(workingCopy);

        return reversedCopy.equalsIgnoreCase(workingCopy);
    }

    protected static String removeJunk(String string) {
        int i, len = string.length();
        StringBuffer dest = new StringBuffer(len);
        char c;

        for (i = (len - 1); i >= 0; i--) {
            c = string.charAt(i);
            if (Character.isLetterOrDigit(c)) {
                dest.append(c);
            }
        }
```

---

[1] `Palindrome.java` is included on the CD and is available online. See <u>Code Samples</u> (page 174). To save space, we've removed the comments from the code. The online version is well commented.

```
        return dest.toString();
    }

    protected static String reverse(String string) {
        StringBuffer sb = new StringBuffer(string);

        return sb.reverse().toString();
    }

    public static void main(String[] args) {
        String string = "Madam, I'm Adam.";

        System.out.println();
        System.out.println("Testing whether the following "
                            + "string is a palindrome:");
        System.out.println("     " + string);
        System.out.println();

        if (isPalindrome(string)) {
            System.out.println("It IS a palindrome!");
        } else {
            System.out.println("It is NOT a palindrome!");
        }
        System.out.println();
    }
}
```

The output from this program is:

```
Testing whether the following string is a palindrome:
    Madam, I'm Adam.

It IS a palindrome!
```

Questions and Exercises: Characters and Strings

Questions

1. What is the initial capacity of the following string buffer?
   ```
   StringBuffer sb = new StringBuffer("Able was I ere I saw Elba.");
   ```

2. Consider the following line of code:
   ```
   String hannah = "Did Hannah see bees? Hannah did.";
   ```

   a. What is the value displayed by the expression hannah.length()?

   b. What is the value returned by the method call hannah.charAt(12)?

   c. Write an expression that refers to the letter b in the string referred to by hannah.

d. How long is the string returned by the following expression? What is the string?

```
"Was it a car or a cat I saw?".substring(9, 12)
```

3. In the following program, what is the value of `result` after each numbered line executes?

```java
public class ComputeResult {
    public static void main(String[] args) {
        String original = "software";
        StringBuffer result = new StringBuffer("hi");
        int index = original.indexOf('a');
/*1*/   result.setCharAt(0, original.charAt(0));
/*2*/   result.setCharAt(1, original.charAt(original.length()-1));
/*3*/   result.insert(1, original.charAt(4));
/*4*/   result.append(original.substring(1,4));
/*5*/   result.insert(3, (original.substring(index, index+2) + " "));

        System.out.println(result);
    }
}
```

Exercises

1. Show two ways to concatenate the following two strings together to get `"Hi, mom."`:

   ```java
   String hi = "Hi, ";
   String mom = "mom.";
   ```

2. Write a program that computes your initials from your full name and displays them.

3. An anagram is a word or a phrase made by transposing the letters of another word or phrase; for example, "parliament" is an anagram of "partial men," and "software" is an anagram of "swear oft." Write a program that figures out whether one string is an anagram of another string. The program should ignore white space and punctuation.

Answers

You can find answers to these Questions and Exercises online:

```
http://java.sun.com/docs/books/tutorial/java/data/QandE/
characters-answers.html
```

Numbers

This section begins with a discussion of the `Number` class in `java.lang` and its subclasses. In particular, this section talks about why you might need these classes, points out the common methods and class variables they have in common, and shows you how to convert instances to strings.

Additionally, this section talks about other classes you might need to work with numbers. For instance, if you need to display a number in a particular format, you can use the `Number-Format` and `DecimalFormat` classes in `java.text` to format them. Also, the `Math` class in `java.lang` contains class methods that perform mathematical functions beyond those provided by the language. This class has methods for the trigonometric functions, exponential functions, and so on.

The Number Classes

Figure 52 shows the class hierarchy for the number classes the Java platform provides.

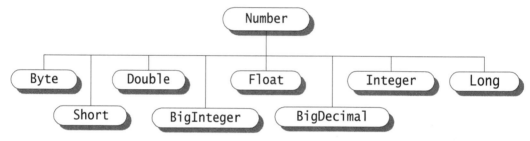

Figure 52 The class hierarchy of `Number`.

In addition to the number classes, the Java platform includes the `Boolean`,[1] `Character`,[2] and `Void`[3] classes, which together with the number classes are known as the *type-wrapper classes*.

You might wonder why the type-wrapper classes are necessary, as they seem to duplicate the primitive data types. The type-wrapper classes have several uses.

- You can store a value of primitive type in a type-wrapper object whenever an object is required. For example, the `Vector` class can hold only objects, so if you want to put numbers in a vector, you wrap each value in a type-wrapper object and provide that object to the vector.

- The classes define useful variables, such as `MIN_VALUE` and `MAX_VALUE`, that provide general information about the data type. The classes also define useful methods for converting values to other types, for converting to strings, and so on.

- The classes are used in reflection, part of the Java platform that allows programs to gather information about any object or class in the Java VM.

---

[1] http://java.sun.com/j2se/1.3/docs/api/java/lang/Boolean.html
[2] http://java.sun.com/j2se/1.3/docs/api/java/lang/Character.html
[3] http://java.sun.com/j2se/1.3/docs/api/java/lang/Void.html

Furthermore, `BigInteger` and `BigDecimal` extend the primitive data types in that they allow for arbitrary-precision numbers (numbers that might not fit into any of the primitive data types). Note that whereas the other classes are in the `java.lang` package, `BigDecimal` and `BigInteger` are in `java.math`.

Here's an example, called `NumberDemo`,[1] that creates two `Float` objects and one `Double` object and then uses `compareTo` and `equals` to compare them:

```
public class NumberDemo {
    public static void main(String args[]) {
        Float floatOne = new Float(14.78f - 13.78f);
        Float oneAgain = new Float(1.0);
        Double doubleOne = new Double(1.0);

        int difference = floatOne.compareTo(oneAgain);

        if (difference == 0) {
            System.out.println("floatOne is equal to oneAgain.");
        } else if (difference < 0) {
            System.out.println("floatOne is less than oneAgain.");
        } else if (difference > 0) {
            System.out.println("floatOne is greater than oneAgain.");
        }

        System.out.println("floatOne is "
                        + ((floatOne.equals(doubleOne))
                            ? "equal" : "not equal")
                        + " to doubleOne.");


    }
}
```

The output from this program might surprise you a little:

```
floatOne is equal to oneAgain.
floatOne is not equal to doubleOne.
```

Even though the values contained in `floatOne` and `doubleOne` are both numerically equal to 1, they are considered unequal because the objects are of different types.

Table 32 lists the instance methods that all the subclasses of the `Number` class contain, including the `compareTo` and `equals` methods used in the preceding example.

---

[1] `NumberDemo.java` is included on the CD and is available online. See <u>Code Samples</u> (page 174). This program requires SDK1.2 to run because it uses the `compareTo` method, which was added in that release.

Table 32   Instance Methods Common to the Number Classes

Method	Description
byte byteValue()[a] short shortValue()[b] int intValue() long longValue() float floatValue() double doubleValue()	Convert the value of this number object to the primitive data types of byte, short, int, long, float, and double.
int compareTo(Integer)[c] int compareTo(Object)[d]	Compare this number object to the argument. This method returns a number less than, equal to, or greater than 0, indicating that this number object is, respectively, less than, equal to, or greater than the argument.
boolean equals(Object)	Determine whether this number object is equal to the argument.

a. Added to the Number class and its subclasses for JDK 1.1.
b. Added to the Number class and its subclasses for JDK 1.1.
c. Added to the Number subclasses for Java 2 SDK 1.2.
d. Added to the Number subclasses for Java 2 SDK 1.2.

As a group, the Number subclasses also contain some useful constants. Recall the MaxVariablesDemo program shown on page 67 in the chapter <u>Language Basics</u> (page 65). That program displays the value of the MAX_VALUE constant for each of the following classes: Byte, Short, Integer, Long, Float, and Double. Each of these classes defines this constant, which contains the largest value that can be held by an instance of that class. Each of these classes also defines a constant named MIN_VALUE, which contains the smallest value that can be held by an instance of that class. To refer to one of these constants, you concatenate the class name, with a dot (.), with the constant name, like this: Integer.MIN_VALUE.

Table 33 lists other useful constants in the Float and Double classes:

Table 33   Other Useful Constants in the Float and Double Classes

Constant	Description
Float.NaN Double.NaN	Not a Number. Returned by certain methods in the java.lang.Math class when the result is undefined for the arguments passed to the method.
Float.NEGATIVE_INFINITY Double.NEGATIVE_INFINITY	The negative infinity value for a float or a double.
Float.POSITIVE_INFINITY Double.POSITIVE_INFINITY	The positive infinity value for a float or a double.

Converting Strings to Numbers

Sometimes, a program ends up with numeric data in a string object—a value entered by the user, for example. The numeric type-wrapper classes (Byte, Integer, Double, Float, Long, and Short) each provide a class method named valueOf that converts a string to an object of that type. Here's a small example, ValueOfDemo,[1] that gets two strings from the command line, converts them to numbers, and performs arithmetic operations on the values:

```java
public class ValueOfDemo {
    public static void main(String[] args) {

        //this program requires two arguments on the command line
        if (args.length == 2) {

            //convert strings to numbers
            float a = Float.valueOf(args[0]).floatValue();
            float b = Float.valueOf(args[1]).floatValue();

            //do some arithmetic
            System.out.println("a + b = " + (a + b) );
            System.out.println("a - b = " + (a - b) );
            System.out.println("a * b = " + (a * b) );
            System.out.println("a / b = " + (a / b) );
            System.out.println("a % b = " + (a % b) );
        } else {
            System.out.println("This program requires two "
                                + "command-line arguments.");
        }
    }
}
```

The following is the output from the program when you use 4.5 and 87.2 for the command line arguments:

```
a + b = 91.7
a - b = -82.7
a * b = 392.4
a / b = 0.0516055
a % b = 4.5
```

---

[1] ValueOfDemo.java is included on the CD and is available online. See <u>Code Samples</u> (page 174).

Converting Numbers to Strings

Sometimes, you need to convert a number to a string because you need to operate on the value in its string form. All classes inherit a method called `toString` from the `Object` class. The type-wrapper classes override this method to provide a reasonable string representation of the value held by the number object. The following program, `ToStringDemo`,[1] uses the `toString` method to convert a number to a string. Next, the program uses some string methods to compute the number of digits before and after the decimal point:

```
public class ToStringDemo {
    public static void main(String[] args) {
        String s = Double.toString(858.48);
        int dot = s.indexOf('.');

        System.out.println(s.substring(0, dot).length()
                            + " digits before decimal point.");
        System.out.println(s.substring(dot+1).length()
                            + " digits after decimal point.");
    }
}
```

The output from this program is:

```
3 digits before decimal point.
2 digits after decimal point.
```

The `toString` method called by this program is the class method. Each of the number classes has an instance method called `toString`, which you call on an instance of that type.

You don't have to explicitly call the `toString` method to display numbers with the `System.out.println` method or when concatenating numeric values to a string. The Java platform handles the conversion by calling `toString` implicitly.

Formatting Numbers

The `toString` method is handy for simple conversions, but you might not like the format of its output. For instance, a floating-point number that represents a monetary value in your program should perhaps be formatted with only two decimal points. To get more control over the format of the output of your program, you can use the `NumberFormat`[2] class and its subclass, `DecimalFormat`,[3] to format primitive-type numbers, such as `double`, and their cor-

---

[1] `ToStringDemo.java` is included on the CD and is available online. See Code Samples (page 174).
[2] http://java.sun.com/j2se/1.3/docs/api/java/text/NumberFormat.html
[3] http://java.sun.com/j2se/1.3/docs/api/java/text/DecimalFormat.html

responding wrapper objects, such as `Double`. The `NumberFormat` and `DecimalFormat` classes are in the `java.text` package.

The following code example formats a `Double`. The `getNumberInstance` method is a factory method that returns an instance of `NumberFormat`. The `format` method accepts the `Double` as an argument and returns the formatted number in a string:

```
Double amount = new Double(345987.246);
NumberFormat numberFormatter;
String amountOut;

numberFormatter = NumberFormat.getNumberInstance();
amountOut = numberFormatter.format(amount);
System.out.println(amountOut);
```

The last line of code prints 345,987.246.

Note: The output you see when you run the previous code snippet might be different from that shown because the `NumberFormat` and the `DecimalFormat` classes are *locale-sensitive*—they tailor their output according to locale. A locale is an object that identifies a specific geographical, political, or cultural region. The locale is not explicitly set in the previous code snippet; thus, the number format object uses the default locale for the current invocation of the Java VM. The output shown here is the output you get when the default locale specifies the United States. You can use the `Locale.getDefault` method to figure out what the current default locale is, and you can use `Locale.setDefault` to change it.

An alternative to changing the default locale for the current invocation of the Java VM is to specify the locale when you create a number format object. Instead of using the default locale, the number format object uses the one specified when it was created. Here's how you would create a number format object that tailors its output for France:

```
NumberFormat numberFormatter =
              NumberFormat.getNumberInstance(Locale.FRANCE);
```

This note applies to all the format examples, including those that use the `DecimalFormat` class, in the rest of this section. For more information, refer to "Internationalization" in *The Java Tutorial Continued* book, which is also available online and on this book's CD.

Formatting Currencies

If you're writing business applications, you'll probably need to format and to display currencies. You format currencies in the same manner as numbers, except that you call `getCurrencyInstance` to create a formatter. When you invoke the `format` method, it returns a string that includes the formatted number and the appropriate currency sign.

This code example shows how to format currency:

```
Double currency = new Double(9876543.21);
NumberFormat currencyFormatter;
String currencyOut;

currencyFormatter = NumberFormat.getCurrencyInstance();
currencyOut = currencyFormatter.format(currency);
System.out.println(currencyOut);
```

The last line of code prints: $9,876,543.21.

Formatting Percentages

You can also use the methods of the NumberFormat class to format percentages. To get the formatter, invoke the getPercentInstance method. With this formatter, a decimal fraction, such as 0.75, is displayed as 75%.

The following code sample shows how to format a percentage:

```
Double percent = new Double(0.75);
NumberFormat percentFormatter;
String percentOut;

percentFormatter = NumberFormat.getPercentInstance();
percentOut = percentFormatter.format(percent);
System.out.println(percentOut);
```

The last line of code prints 75%.

Formatting Numbers with Custom Formats

You can use the DecimalFormat class to format decimal numbers into strings. This class allows you to control the display of leading and trailing zeros, prefixes and suffixes, grouping (thousands) separators, and the decimal separator. If you want to change formatting symbols, such as the decimal separator, you can use the DecimalFormatSymbols[1] class, also in the java.text package, in conjunction with DecimalFormat. These classes offer a great deal of flexibility in the formatting of numbers, but they can make your code more complex.

The text that follows uses examples that demonstrate the DecimalFormat and the Decimal-FormatSymbols classes. The code examples in this material are from a sample program called DecimalFormatDemo.[2]

---

[1] http://java.sun.com/j2se/1.3/docs/api/java/text/DecimalFormatSymbols.html
[2] DecimalFormatDemo.java is included on the CD and is available online. See <u>Code Samples</u> (page 174).

Constructing Patterns

You specify the formatting properties of DecimalFormat with a string pattern. The pattern determines what the formatted number looks like. The example that follows creates a formatter by passing a pattern string to the DecimalFormat constructor. The format method accepts a double value as an argument and returns the formatted number in a string:

```
DecimalFormat myFormatter = new DecimalFormat(pattern);
String output = myFormatter.format(value);
System.out.println(value + " " + pattern + " " + output);
```

The output for the preceding lines of code is described in Table 34. The value is the number, a double, that is to be formatted. The pattern is the String that specifies the formatting properties. The output, which is a string, represents the formatted number.

Table 34   Output from DecimalFormatDemo Program

Value	Pattern	Output	Explanation
123456.789	###,###.###	123,456.789	The pound sign (#) denotes a digit, the comma is a placeholder for the grouping separator, and the period is a placeholder for the decimal separator.
123456.789	###.##	123456.79	The value has three digits to the right of the decimal point, but the pattern has only two. The format method handles this by rounding up.
123.78	000000.000	000123.780	The pattern specifies leading and trailing zeros, because the 0 character is used instead of the pound sign (#).
12345.67	$###,###.###	$12,345.67	The first character in the pattern is the dollar sign ($). Note that it immediately precedes the leftmost digit in the formatted output.
12345.67	\u00A5###,###.###	¥12,345.67	The pattern specifies the currency sign for Japanese yen (¥) with the Unicode value 00A5.

Altering the Formatting Symbols

You can use the DecimalFormatSymbols class to change the symbols that appear in the formatted numbers produced by the format method. These symbols include the decimal separator, the grouping separator, the minus sign, and the percent sign, among others.

The next example demonstrates the DecimalFormatSymbols class by applying a strange format to a number. The unusual format is the result of the calls to the setDecimalSeparator, setGroupingSeparator, and setGroupingSize methods.

```
DecimalFormatSymbols unusualSymbols =
                    new DecimalFormatSymbols(currentLocale);
unusualSymbols.setDecimalSeparator('|');
unusualSymbols.setGroupingSeparator('^');

String strange = "#,##0.###";
DecimalFormat weirdFormatter =
                new DecimalFormat(strange, unusualSymbols);
weirdFormatter.setGroupingSize(4);

String bizarre = weirdFormatter.format(12345.678);
System.out.println(bizarre);
```

When run, this example prints the number in a bizarre format:

```
1^2345|678
```

Beyond Basic Arithmetic

The Java programming language supports basic arithmetic computation with its arithmetic operators: +, -, *, /, and %. In the `java.lang` package, the Java platform provides a class called `Math`[1] that provides methods and variables for doing more advanced mathematical computation, such as computing the sine of an angle, or raising a number to a certain power.

The methods in the `Math` class are class methods, so you call them directly from the class, like this:

```
Math.round(34.87);
```

The first set of methods in the `Math` class that we are going to look at perform various basic mathematical functions, such as computing a number's absolute value and rounding numbers. Table 35 lists and describes these methods.

Table 35 Basic Mathematical Functions Implemented by Methods in the `Math` Class

Method	Description

`double abs(double)`
` float abs(float)`
`   int abs(int)`
`  long abs(long)`
	Returns the absolute value of the argument.

`double ceil(double)`	Returns the smallest `double` value that is greater than or equal to the argument and is equal to a mathematical integer.

---

[1] http://java.sun.com/j2se/1.3/docs/api/java/lang/Math.html

Table 35 Basic Mathematical Functions Implemented by Methods in the Math Class

`double floor(double)`	Returns the largest `double` value that is less than or equal to the argument and is equal to a mathematical integer.
`double rint(double)`	Returns the `double` value that is closest in value to the argument and is equal to a mathematical integer.
`long round(double)` `int round(float)`	Returns the closest `long` or `int`, as indicated by the method's return value, to the argument.

The following program, `BasicMathDemo`,[1] illustrates how to use some of these methods:

```java
public class BasicMathDemo {
    public static void main(String[] args) {
        double aNumber = -191.635;

        System.out.println("The absolute value of " + aNumber + " is "
                           + Math.abs(aNumber));
        System.out.println("The ceiling of " + aNumber + " is "
                           + Math.ceil(aNumber));
        System.out.println("The floor of " + aNumber + " is "
                           + Math.floor(aNumber));
        System.out.println("The rint of " + aNumber + " is "
                           + Math.rint(aNumber));
    }
}
```

Here's the output from this program:

```
The absolute value of -191.635 is 191.635
The ceiling of -191.635 is -191
The floor of -191.635 is -192
The rint of -191.635 is -192
```

Two other basic methods in the Math class are `min` and `max`. Table 36 shows the different forms of the `min` and `max` methods, which compare two numbers and return the smaller or larger, respectively, of the two.

---

[1] `BasicMathDemo.java` is included on the CD and is available online. See <u>Code Samples</u> (page 174).

Table 36 Comparative Functions Implemented by Methods in the Math Class

Method	Description

`double min(double, double)`
`  float min(float, float)`
`    int min(int, int)`
`   long min(long, long)`
	Returns the smaller of the two arguments.

`double max(double, double)`
`  float max(float, float)`
`    int max(int, int)`
`   long max(long, long)`
	Returns the larger of the two arguments.

MinDemo,[1] shown following, uses `min` to figure out the smaller of two values:

```
public class MinDemo {
    public static void main(String[] args) {
        double enrollmentPrice = 45.875;
        double closingPrice = 54.375;
        System.out.println("Your purchase price is: $"
                        + Math.min(enrollmentPrice, closingPrice));
    }
}
```

The program correctly prints the smaller price:

```
Your purchase price is: $45.875
```

The next set of methods provided by the Math class are exponential functions. In addition to these functions, you can get the value of *e*, the base of the natural logarithms, by using Math.E.

Table 37 Exponential Functions Implemented by Methods in the Math Class

Method	Description
`double exp(double)`	Returns the base of the natural logarithms, *e*, to the power of the argument.
`double log(double)`	Returns the natural logarithm of the argument.
`double pow(double, double)`	Returns of value of the first argument raised to the power of the second argument.
`double sqrt(double)`	Returns the square root of the argument.

---

[1] MinDemo.java is included on the CD and is available online. See <u>Code Samples</u> (page 174).

The following program, ExponentialDemo,[1] displays the value of *e*, then calls each of the methods listed in the previous table on arbitrarily chosen numbers:

```
public class ExponentialDemo {
    public static void main(String[] args) {
        double x = 11.635;
        double y = 2.76;

        System.out.println("The value of e is " + Math.E);
        System.out.println("exp(" + x + ") is " + Math.exp(x));
        System.out.println("log(" + x + ") is " + Math.log(x));

        System.out.println("pow(" + x + ", " + y + ") is "
                    + Math.pow(x, y));
        System.out.println("sqrt(" + x + ") is " + Math.sqrt(x));
    }
}
```

Here's the output you'll see when you run ExponentialDemo:

```
The value of e is 2.71828
exp(11.635) is 112984
log(11.635) is 2.45402
pow(11.635, 2.76) is 874.008
sqrt(11.635) is 3.41101
```

The Math class provides a collection of trigonometric functions, which are summarized in Table 38. The value passed into each of these methods is an angle expressed in radians. You can use the toDegrees and toRadians methods[2] to convert from degrees to radians and back. Also, you can use Math.PI to get the value of π.

Table 38 Trigonometric Functions Implemented by Methods in the Math Class

Method	Description
double sin(double)	Returns the sine of the specified double value.
double cos(double)	Returns the cosine of the specified double value.
double tan(double)	Returns the tangent of the specified double value.
double asin(double)	Returns the arc sine of the specified double value.
double acos(double)	Returns the arc cosine of the specified double value.
double atan(double)	Returns the arc tangent of the specified double value.

[1] ExponentialDemo.java is included on the CD and is available online. See Code Samples (page 174).
[2] The toDegrees and toRadians methods were added to the Math class for Java 2 SDK 1.2.

Table 38   Trigonometric Functions Implemented by Methods in the `Math` Class

`double atan2(double)`	Converts rectangular coordinates (b, a) to polar (r, theta).
`double toDegrees(double)`[a] `double toRadians(double)`[a]	Converts the argument to degrees or radians as indicated by the method name.

a. Added to the `Math` class for Java 2 SDK 1.2.

Here's a program, `TrigonometricDemo`,[1] that uses each of these methods to compute various trigonometric values for a 45-degree angle:

```java
public class TrigonometricDemo {
    public static void main(String[] args) {
        double degrees = 45.0;
        double radians = Math.toDegrees(degrees);

        System.out.println("The value of pi is " + Math.PI);
        System.out.println("The sine of " + degrees + " is "
                            + Math.sin(radians));
        System.out.println("The cosine of " + degrees + " is "
                            + Math.cos(radians));
        System.out.println("The tangent of " + degrees + " is "
                            + Math.tan(radians));
        System.out.println("The arc sine of " + degrees + " is "
                            + Math.asin(radians));
        System.out.println("The arc cosine of " + degrees + " is "
                            + Math.acos(radians));
        System.out.println("The arc tangent of " + degrees + " is "
                            + Math.atan(radians));
    }
}
```

The output of this program is as follows:

```
The value of pi is 3.141592653589793
The sine of 45.0 is 0.8060754911159176
The cosine of 45.0 is -0.5918127259718502
The tangent of 45.0 is -1.3620448762608377
The arc sine of 45.0 is NaN
The arc cosine of 45.0 is NaN
The arc tangent of 45.0 is 1.570408475869457
```

Notice that `NaN` is displayed when the result is undefined for the argument passed into the method. `NaN` is the acronym for Not a Number. Various methods in the `Math` class return this value when the result of a particular function is undefined for the argument passed into the

---

[1]   `TrigonometricDemo.java` is included on the CD and is available online. See Code Samples (page 174).
    This program requires Java 2 SDK 1.2 because it uses the `toDegrees` method.

method. Both the `Double` and `Float` classes contain constants called `NaN`. By comparing the return value of a method to one of these constants, your program can determine whether the `NaN` value is returned from a method. Thus, your program can do something reasonable when the mathematical result of a method call is undefined.

The last `Math` method that we'll cover is `random`. The `random` method returns a pseudo-randomly selected number between 0.0 and 1.0. The range includes 0.0 but not 1.0. In other words: `0.0 <= Math.random() < 1.0`. To get a number in a different range, you can perform arithmetic on the value returned by the `random` method. For example, to generate an integer between 1 and 10, you would write:

```
int number = (int)(Math.random() * 10 + 1);
```

By multiplying the value by 10, the range of possible values becomes `0.0 <= number < 10.0`. By then adding 1, the range of possible values becomes `1.0 <= number < 11.0`. Finally, by converting the number to an integer with an explicit cast (`int`), the value is as desired: an integer value between 1 and 10.

Using `Math.random` is fine if you need to generate a single number. If you need to generate a series of random numbers, you should create an instance of `java.util.Random` and call methods on that object to generate numbers. The `RandomBag` class[1] in the online Bingo example uses this technique to generate a random series of bingo balls. The `Math.random` method uses an instance of `java.util.Random` to generate its numbers.

Summary of Numbers

You use an instance of one of the `Number` classes—`Byte`, `Double`, `Float`, `Integer`, `Long`, and `Short`—to contain a number of primitive type. You can also use `BigInteger` and `BigDecimal` for arbitrary-precision numbers.

The `Number` classes include class methods and constants, which are useful in a variety of ways. The `MIN_VALUE` and `MAX_VALUE` constants contain the smallest and largest values that can be contained by an object of that type. The `byteValue`, `shortValue`, and similar methods convert one numeric type to another. The `valueOf` method converts a string to a number, and the `toString` method converts a number to a string.

To format a number to display to an end user, you use the `NumberFormat` class in the `java.text` package. When using `NumberFormat`, you can get a default format for decimal numbers, percentages, or currency. Or, you can design a custom format using patterns.

The `Math` class contains a variety of class methods for performing mathematical functions. This class includes the trigonometric functions, such as computing sine, cosine, and so on.

---

[1] `RandomBag.java` is included on the CD and is available online. See <u>Code Samples</u> (page 174).

Math also includes functions for logarithm calculations, as well as basic arithmetic functions, such as rounding. Finally, Math contains a method, random, for generating random numbers.

Questions and Exercises: Numbers

Questions

1. Use the API documentation to find the answers to the following questions:

   a. What Integer method can you use to convert an int into a string that expresses the number in hexadecimal? For example, what method converts the integer 65 into the string "41"?

   b. What two Integer methods would you use to convert a string expressed in base 5 into the equivalent int? For example, how would you convert the string "230" into the integer value 65? Show the code you would use to accomplish this task.

   c. What Double method can you use to detect whether a floating-point number has the special value Not a Number (NaN)?

2. What is the value of the following expression, and why?

   ```
   new Integer(1).equals(new Long(1))
   ```

Exercises

1. Change MaxVariablesDemo (java/nutsandbolts/variables.html) to show minimum values instead of maximum values. You can delete all code related to the variables aChar and aBoolean. What is the output?

2. Create a program that reads an unspecified number of integer arguments from the command line and adds them together. For example, suppose that you enter the following:

   ```
   java Adder 1 3 2 10
   ```

   The program should display 16 and then exit. The program should display an error message if the user enters only one argument. You can base your program on ValueOf-Demo.java.

3. Create a program that is similar to the previous one but has the following differences:

   * Instead of reading integer arguments, it reads floating-point arguments.

   * It displays the sum of the arguments, using exactly two digits to the right of the decimal point.

   For example, suppose that you enter the following:

   ```
   java FPAdder 1 1e2 3.0 4.754
   ```

   The program would display 108.75. Depending on your locale, the decimal point might be a comma (,) instead of a period (.).

Answers

You can find answers to these Questions and Exercises online:

```
http://java.sun.com/docs/books/tutorial/java/data/QandE/
numbers-answers.html
```

Arrays

An array is a structure that holds multiple values of the same type. The length of an array is established when the array is created (at runtime). After creation, an array is a fixed-length structure (Figure 53).

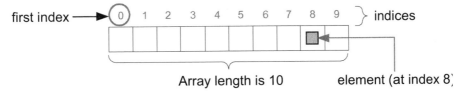

Figure 53 An array with ten elements. Indices begin at 0 and end at the array length minus 1.

An *array element* is one of the values within an array and is accessed by its position within the array. Array indices begin at 0 and end at the array length minus 1.

If you want to store data of different types in a single structure or if you need a structure whose size can change dynamically, use a `Collection` implementation, such as `Vector`, instead of an array. Refer to the section <u>Collections</u> in Appendix B (page 467) for more on the subject.

Creating and Using Arrays

Here is a simple program, called `ArrayDemo`,[1] that creates the array, puts some values in it, and displays the values:

```
public class ArrayDemo {
    public static void main(String[] args) {
        // declare an array of integers
        int[] anArray;

        // create an array of integers
```

---

[1] `ArrayDemo.java` is included on the CD and is available online. See <u>Code Samples</u> (page 174).

```
        anArray = new int[10];

        // assign a value to each array element and print
        for (int i = 0; i < anArray.length; i++) {
            anArray[i] = i;
            System.out.print(anArray[i] + " ");
        }
        System.out.println();
    }
}
```

The output from this program is:

```
0 1 2 3 4 5 6 7 8 9
```

Declaring a Variable to Refer to an Array

The following line of code from the sample program declares an array variable:

```
int[] anArray;          // declares an array of integers
```

Like declarations for variables of other types, an array declaration has two components: the array's type and the array's name. An array's type is written *type*[], where *type* is the data type of the elements contained within the array, and [] indicates that this is an array. Remember that all the elements within an array are of the same type. The sample program uses int[], so the array called anArray will be used to hold integer data. Here are declarations for arrays that hold other types of data:

```
float[] anArrayOfFloats;
boolean[] anArrayOfBooleans;
Object[] anArrayOfObjects;
String[] anArrayOfStrings;
```

You can write an array declaration like this:

```
float anArrayOfFloats[];     //this form is discouraged
```

However, convention discourages this form because the brackets identify the array type, and so they should appear with the type designation, not with the array name.

As with declarations for variables of other types, the declaration for an array variable does not create an array and does not allocate any memory to contain array elements. The code must create the array explicitly and assign it to anArray.

Creating an Array

You create an array explicitly by using the new operator. The next statement in the sample program allocates an array with enough memory for ten integer elements and assigns the array to the variable anArray declared earlier:

```
anArray = new int[10];   // creates an array of integers
```

In general, when creating an array, you use the new operator, plus the data type of the array elements, plus the number of elements desired enclosed within brackets—[and]:

```
new elementType[arraySize]
```

If the new statement were omitted from the sample program, the compiler would print an error like the following one, and compilation would fail:

```
ArrayDemo.java:4: Variable anArray may not have been initialized.
```

Array Initializers

You can use a shortcut syntax for creating and initializing an array. Here's an example:

```
boolean[] answers = { true, false, true, true, false };
```

The length of the array is determined by the number of values provided between { and }.

Accessing an Array Element

Now that some memory has been allocated for the array, the program assigns values to the array elements:

```
for (int i = 0; i < anArray.length; i++) {
    anArray[i] = i;
    System.out.print(anArray[i] + " ");
}
```

This part of the code shows that to refer to an array element, either to assign a value to it or to get its value, you append brackets to the array name. The value between the brackets indicates (with a variable or other expression) the index of the element to access.

Getting the Size of an Array

To get the size of an array, you write:

```
arrayreference.length
```

Be Careful: Programmers new to the Java programming language are tempted to follow `length` with an empty set of parentheses. This doesn't work, because `length` is not a method, as with the `String` class, but rather a property provided by the Java platform for all arrays.

The `for` loop in our sample program iterates over each element of `anArray`, assigning values to its elements. The `for` loop uses `anArray.length` to determine when to terminate the loop.

Arrays of Objects

Arrays can hold reference types and primitive types. You create an array with reference types in much the same way you create an array with primitive types. Here's a small program, `ArrayOfStringsDemo`,[1] that creates an array containing three string objects. It then prints the strings in all lowercase letters:

```java
public class ArrayOfStringsDemo {
    public static void main(String[] args) {
        String[] anArray = { "String One",
                             "String Two",
                             "String Three" };

        for (int i = 0; i < anArray.length; i++) {
            System.out.println(anArray[i].toLowerCase());
        }
    }
}
```

The output from this program is:

```
string one
string two
string three
```

This program creates and populates the array in a single statement by using an array initializer. The next program, `ArrayOfIntegersDemo`,[2] populates the array with `Integer` objects. Notice that the program creates one `Integer` object and places it in the array during each iteration of the `for` loop:

---

[1] `ArrayOfStringsDemo.java` is included on the CD and is available online. See <u>Code Samples</u> (page 174).

[2] `ArrayOfIntegersDemo.java` is included on the CD and is available online. See <u>Code Samples</u> (page 174).

```
public class ArrayOfIntegersDemo {
    public static void main(String[] args) {
        Integer[] anArray = new Integer[5];

        for (int i = 0; i < anArray.length; i++) {
            anArray[i] = new Integer(i);
            System.out.println(anArray[i]);
        }
    }
}
```

The output from this program is:

```
0
1
2
3
4
```

The following line of code taken from the `ArrayOfIntegersDemo` program creates an array without putting any elements in it:

```
Integer[] anArray = new Integer[5];
```

This brings us to a potential stumbling block, often encountered by new programmers, when using arrays that contain objects. After the previous line of code is executed, the array called anArray exists and has enough room to hold five integer objects. However, the array doesn't contain any objects yet. It is empty. The program must explicitly create objects and put them in the array. This might seem obvious; however, many beginners assume that the previous line of code creates the array and creates five empty objects in it. Thus, they end up writing code like the following, which generates a `NullPointerException`:

```
Integer[] anArray = new Integer[5];

for (int i = 0; i < anArray.length; i++) {
    //ERROR: the following line gives a runtime error
    System.out.println(anArray[i]);
}
```

This problem is most likely to occur when the array is created in a constructor or other initializer and then used somewhere else in the program.

Arrays of Arrays

Arrays can contain arrays. ArrayOfArraysDemo[1] creates an array and uses an initializer to populate it with four subarrays:

```java
public class ArrayOfArraysDemo {
    public static void main(String[] args) {
        String[][] cartoons =
        {
            { "Flintstones", "Fred", "Wilma", "Pebbles", "Dino" },
            { "Rubbles", "Barney", "Betty", "Bam Bam" },
            { "Jetsons", "George", "Jane", "Elroy", "Judy",
              "Rosie", "Astro" },
            { "Scooby Doo Gang", "Scooby Doo", "Shaggy", "Velma",
              "Fred", "Daphne" }
        };

        for (int i = 0; i < cartoons.length; i++) {
            System.out.print(cartoons[i][0] + ": ");
            for (int j = 1; j < cartoons[i].length; j++) {
                System.out.print(cartoons[i][j] + " ");
            }
            System.out.println();
        }
    }
}
```

The output from this program is:

```
Flintstones: Fred Wilma Pebbles Dino
Rubbles: Barney Betty Bam Bam
Jetsons: George Jane Elroy Judy Rosie Astro
Scooby Doo Gang: Scooby Doo Shaggy Velma Fred Daphne
```

Notice that the subarrays are all of different lengths. The subarrays can be referred to with cartoons[0], cartoons[1], and so on.

As with arrays of objects, you must explicitly create the subarrays within an array. So if you don't use an initializer, you need to write code as in the following program, called ArrayOfArraysDemo2.[2]

```java
public class ArrayOfArraysDemo2 {
    public static void main(String[] args) {
```

---

[1] ArrayOfArraysDemo.java is included on the CD and is available online. See Code Samples (page 174).

[2] ArrayOfArraysDemo2.java is included on the CD and is available online. See Code Samples (page 174).

```
    //length of subarrays unspecified
    int[][] aMatrix = new int[4][];

     //populate matrix
    for (int i = 0; i < aMatrix.length; i++) {
        //create subarray
        aMatrix[i] = new int[5];
        for (int j = 0; j < aMatrix[i].length; j++) {
            aMatrix[i][j] = i + j;
        }
    }

    //print matrix
    for (int i = 0; i < aMatrix.length; i++) {
        for (int j = 0; j < aMatrix[i].length; j++) {
            System.out.print(aMatrix[i][j] + " ");
        }
        System.out.println();
    }
}
}
```

The output from this program is:

```
0 1 2 3 4
1 2 3 4 5
2 3 4 5 6
3 4 5 6 7
```

You must specify the length of an array when you create it. For an array that contains subarrays, you specify the length of the primary array when you create it but don't have to specify the length of any of the subarrays until you create them.

Copying Arrays

Use System's arraycopy method to efficiently copy data from one array into another. The arraycopy method requires five arguments:

```
public static void arraycopy(Object source, int srcIndex, Object dest,
                             int destIndex, int length)
```

The two Object arguments indicate the array to copy from and the array to copy to. The three integer arguments indicate the starting location in the source and destination arrays and the number of elements to copy. Figure 54 illustrates how the copy takes place.

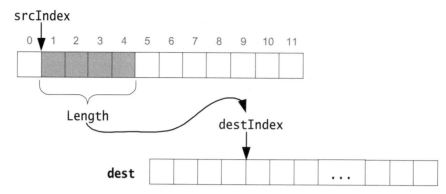

Figure 54   Copying the contents of one array to another.

The following program, ArrayCopyDemo,[1] uses arraycopy to copy some elements from the
copyFrom array to the copyTo array:

```
public class ArrayCopyDemo {
    public static void main(String[] args) {
        char[] copyFrom = { 'd', 'e', 'c', 'a', 'f', 'f', 'e',
                            'i', 'n', 'a', 't', 'e', 'd' };
        char[] copyTo = new char[7];

        System.arraycopy(copyFrom, 2, copyTo, 0, 7);
        System.out.println(new String(copyTo));
    }
}
```

The output from this program is:

```
caffein
```

The arraycopy method call in this example program begins the copy at element number 2 in the source array. Recall that array indices start at 0, so that the copy begins at the array element 'c'. The arraycopy method call puts the copied elements into the destination array (copyTo) beginning at the first element (element 0). The arraycopy method copies seven elements: c, a, f, f, e, i, and n. In essence, it takes the caffein out of decaffeinated (Figure 55).

---

[1] ArrayCopyDemo.java is included on the CD and is available online. See <u>Code Samples</u> (page 174).

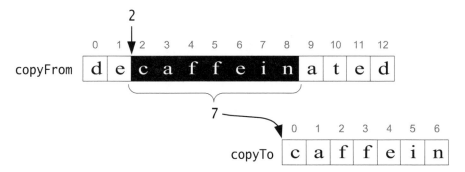

Figure 55 Copying `caffein` from `decaffeinated` into another array.

Note that the destination array must be allocated before you call `arraycopy` and must be large enough to contain the data being copied.

Summary of Arrays

An array is a fixed-length data structure that can contain multiple objects of the same type. An array can contain any type of object, including arrays. To declare an array, you use the type of object that the array can contain and brackets.

The length of the array must be specified when it is created. You can use the `new` operator to create an array, or you can use an array initializer. Once created, the size of the array cannot change. To get the length of the array, you use the `length` attribute.

An element within an array can be accessed by its index. Indices begin at 0 and end at the length of the array minus 1.

To copy an array, use the `arraycopy` method in the `System` class.

Questions and Exercises: Arrays

Questions

1. What is the index of `Brighton` in the following array?

```
String[] skiResorts = {
    "Whistler Blackcomb", "Squaw Valley", "Brighton",
    "Snowmass", "Sun Valley",  "Taos"
};
```

2. Write an expression that refers to the string `Brighton` within the array.

String [ ] P

ski resorts =

System, out, printLn (ski.resorts [2])';

2

String[]

3. What is the value of the expression `skiResorts.length`? *6*

4. What is the index of the last item in the array? *5*

5. What is the value of the expression `skiResorts[4]`? *Sun Valley*

Exercises

1. The following program contains a bug. Find it and fix it.

```java
public class WhatHappens {
    public static void main(String[] args) {
        StringBuffer[] stringBuffers = new StringBuffer[10];

        for (int i = 0; i < stringBuffers.length; i++) {
            stringBuffers[i].append("String Buffer at index" + i);
        }
    }
}
```

length - Null because no obj put in array

Answers

You can find answers to these Questions and Exercises online:

```
http://java.sun.com/docs/books/tutorial/java/data/QandE/
arrays-answers.html
```

Code Samples

Table 39 lists the code samples used in this chapter and where you can find the code online and on the CD that accompanies this book.

Table 39   Code Samples in Object Basics and Simple Data Objects

Code Sample	CD Location	Online Location
CreateObjectDemo.java (page 121)	JavaTutorial/java/data/ example/CreateObject- Demo.java	http://java.sun.com/docs/ books/tutorial/java/ data/example/ CreatObjectDemo.java
Point.java (page 123)	JavaTutorial/java/data/ example/Point.java	http://java.sun.com/docs/ books/tutorial/java/ data/example/Point.java
Rectangle.java (page 124)	JavaTutorial/java/data /example/Rectangle.java	http://java.sun.com/docs/ books/tutorial/java/data/ example/Rectangle.java

Table 39   Code Samples in Object Basics and Simple Data Objects

`CharacterDemo.java`
(page 132)
	`JavaTutorial/java/data/`
	`example/CharacterDemo.java`
		`http://java.sun.com/docs/`
		`books/tutorial/java/data/`
		`example/CharacterDemo.java`

`StringsDemo.java`
(page 134)
	`JavaTutorial/java/data/`
	`example/StringsDemo.java`
		`http://java.sun.com/docs/`
		`books/tutorial/java/data/`
		`example/StringsDemo.java`

`Filename.java`
(page 139)
	`JavaTutorial/java/data/`
	`example/Filename.java`
		`http://java.sun.com/docs/`
		`books/tutorial/java/data/`
		`example/Filename.java`

`FilenameDemo.java`
(page 140)
	`JavaTutorial/java/data/`
	`example/FilenameDemo.java`
		`http://java.sun.com/docs/`
		`books/tutorial/java/data/`
		`example/FilenameDemo.java`

`RegionMatchesDemo.java`
(page 142)
	`JavaTutorial/java/`
	`data/example/`
	`RegionMatchesDemo.java`
		`http://java.sun.com/docs/`
		`books/tutorial/java/`
		`data/example/`
		`RegionMatchesDemo.java`

`BostonAccentDemo.java`
(page 143)
	`JavaTutorial/java/`
	`data/example/`
	`BostonAccentDemo.java`
		`http://java.sun.com/docs/`
		`books/tutorial/java/`
		`data/example/`
		`BostonAccentDemo.java`

`InsertDemo.java`
(page 145)
	`JavaTutorial/java/data/`
	`example/InsertDemo.java`
		`http://java.sun.com/docs/`
		`books/tutorial/java/data/`
		`example/InsertDemo.java`

`Palindrome.java`
(page 147)
	`JavaTutorial/java/data/`
	`example/Palindrome.java`
		`http://java.sun.com/docs/`
		`books/tutorial/java/data/`
		`example/Palindrome.java`

`NumberDemo.java`
(page 151)
	`JavaTutorial/java/data/`
	`example/NumberDemo.java`
		`http://java.sun.com/docs/`
		`books/tutorial/java/data/`
		`example/NumberDemo.java`

`ValueOfDemo.java`
(page 153)
	`JavaTutorial/java/data/`
	`example/ValueOfDemo.java`
		`http://java.sun.com/docs/`
		`books/tutorial/java/data/`
		`example/ValueOfDemo.java`

`ToStringDemo.java`
(page 154)
	`JavaTutorial/java/data/`
	`example/ToStringDemo.java`
		`http://java.sun.com/docs/`
		`books/tutorial/java/data/`
		`example/ToStringDemo.java`

`DecimalFormatDemo.java`
(page 156)
	`JavaTutorial/java/`
	`data/example/`
	`DecimalFormatDemo.java`
		`http://java.sun.com/docs/`
		`books/tutorial/java/`
		`data/example/`
		`DecimalFormatDemo.java`

`BasicMathDemo.java`
(page 159)
	`JavaTutorial/java/data/`
	`example/BasicMathDemo.java`
		`http://java.sun.com/docs/`
		`books/tutorial/java/data/`
		`example/BasicMathDemo.java`

Table 39   Code Samples in Object Basics and Simple Data Objects

`MinDemo.java`
(page 160)
	`JavaTutorial/java/data/`
	`example/MinDemo.java`
		`http://java.sun.com/docs/`
		`books/tutorial/java/data/`
		`example/MinDemo.java`

`ExponentialDemo.java`
(page 161)
	`JavaTutorial/java/`
	`data/example/`
	`ExponentialDemo.java`
		`http://java.sun.com/docs/`
		`books/tutorial/java/`
		`data/example/Exponential-`
		`Demo.java`

`TrigonometricDemo.java`
(page 162)
	`JavaTutorial/java/`
	`data/example/`
	`TrigonometricDemo.java`
		`http://java.sun.com/docs/`
		`books/tutorial/java/`
		`data/example/Trigonomet-`
		`ricDemo.java`

`RandomBagDemo.java`
(page 163)
	`JavaTutorial/java/data/`
	`example/RandomBagDemo.java`
		`http://java.sun.com/docs/`
		`books/tutorial/java/data/`
		`example/RandomBagDemo.java`

`ArrayDemo.java`
(page 165)
	`JavaTutorial/java/data/`
	`example/ArrayDemo.java`
		`http://java.sun.com/docs/`
		`books/tutorial/java/data/`
		`example/ArrayDemo.java`

`ArrayOfStringsDemo.java`
(page 168)
	`JavaTutorial/java/`
	`data/example/`
	`ArrayOfStringsDemo.java`
		`http://java.sun.com/docs/`
		`books/tutorial/java/`
		`data/example/`
		`ArrayOfStringsDemo.java`

`ArrayOfIntegersDemo.java`
(page 168)
	`JavaTutorial/java/`
	`data/example/`
	`ArrayOfIntegersDemo.java`
		`http://java.sun.com/docs/`
		`books/tutorial/java/`
		`data/example/`
		`ArrayOfIntegersDemo.java`

`ArrayOfArraysDemo.java`
(page 170)
	`JavaTutorial/java/`
	`data/example/`
	`ArrayOfArraysDemo.java`
		`http://java.sun.com/docs/`
		`books/tutorial/java/`
		`data/example/`
		`ArrayOfArraysDemo.java`

`ArrayOfArraysDemo2.java`
(page 170)
	`JavaTutorial/java/`
	`data/example/`
	`ArrayOfArraysDemo2.java`
		`http://java.sun.com/docs/`
		`books/tutorial/java/`
		`data/example/`
		`ArrayOfArraysDemo2.java`

`ArrayCopyDemo.java`
(page 172)
	`JavaTutorial/java/`
	`data/example/`
	`ArrayCopyDemo.java`
		`http://java.sun.com/docs/`
		`books/tutorial/java/data/`
		`example/ArrayCopyDemo.java`

The section <u>Common Problems and Their Solutions</u> (page 391) contains solutions to common problems.

5

Classes and Inheritance

WITH the knowledge you now have of the basics of the Java programming language and creating and using objects, you can learn to write your own classes. In this chapter, you will find information about defining your own classes, including declaring member variables, writing methods, inheriting variables and methods from superclasses, nesting classes within other classes, and so on.

Creating Classes

This section shows you the main components of a class by using a small example that implements a stack—a data structure whose items are added and removed in a last-in-first-out (LIFO) fashion. Figure 56 lists the <u>Stack</u>[1] <u>class</u> and identifies the structure of the code.

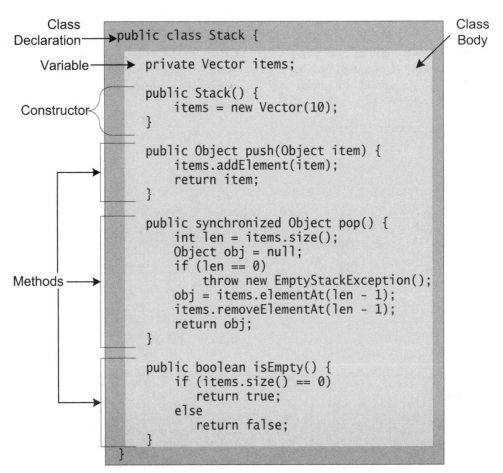

Figure 56   The Stack class and the structure of a class definition.

---

[1]   Stack.java is included on the CD and is available online. See <u>Code Samples</u> (page 224).

A class definition has two main components: the *class declaration* and the *class body*. The class declaration is the first line of code in a class. At a minimum, the class declaration declares the name of the class.

The class body follows the class declaration and appears between braces—{ and }. The class body contains all the code that provides for the life cycle of the objects created from the class: constructors for initializing new objects, declarations for the variables that provide the state of the class and its objects, and methods to implement the behavior of the class and its objects. The Stack class defines one member variable within the class body—the items vector. The Stack class also defines one constructor—a no-argument constructor—and three methods: push, pop, and isEmpty.

Declaring a Class

You've seen many class definitions of the following form:

```
class MyClass {
    //member variable and method declarations
}
```

The first line of code is called the class declaration. The preceding class declaration is a minimal class declaration; it contains only those components of a class declaration that are required. Certain aspects of this class, though unspecified, are assumed. The most important is that the direct superclass of MyClass is the Object class. You can provide more information about the class, such as the name of its superclass, whether it implements any interfaces, whether it can be subclassed, and so on, within the class declaration.

Figure 57 shows all the possible components of a class declaration in the order they should or must appear. The right-hand side describes the purpose of each component. The required

public	Class is publicly accessible.
abstract	Class cannot be instantiated.
final	Class cannot be subclassed.
class *NameOfClass*	Name of the Class.
extends *Super*	Superclass of the class.
implements *Interfaces*	Interfaces implemented by the class.

{
    ClassBody
}	

Figure 57 The components of a class declaration and their purposes.

components are shown in boldface. All the other components are optional, and each appears on a line by itself within the diagram (thus, extends *Super* is a single component), but you don't have to write your code that way. Italic indicates an identifier, such as the name of a class or an interface. If you do not explicitly declare the optional items, the Java™ platform assumes certain defaults: a nonpublic, nonabstract, nonfinal subclass of Object that implements no interfaces.

The following list provides a few more details about each class declaration component. The list also provides references to this chapter's sections that talk about what each component means, how to use each, and how it affects your class, other classes, and your program.

public
> The public modifier declares that the class can be used by any other class. Without the public modifier, your class can be used only by classes in the same package. Look in the section <u>Creating and Using Packages</u> (page 234) for information.

abstract
> The abstract modifier declares that the class cannot be instantiated. For a discussion about when abstract classes are appropriate and how to write them, see the section <u>Writing Abstract Classes and Methods</u> (page 214).

final
> The final modifier declares that the class cannot be subclassed. The section <u>Writing Final Classes and Methods</u> (page 213) discusses the reasons for writing final classes.

class *NameOfClass*
> The class keyword indicates to the compiler that this is a class declaration. The name of the class—*NameOfClass*—follows the class keyword.

extends *Super*
> The extends clause identifies *Super* as the superclass of the class, thereby inserting the class within the class hierarchy. The section <u>Managing Inheritance</u> (page 204) discusses the responsibilities and benefits of subclasses.

implements *Interfaces*
> To declare that your class implements one or more interfaces, use the keyword implements followed by a comma-separated list of the names of the interfaces implemented by the class. Details about writing your own interfaces and how to use them can be found in the section <u>Creating and Using Interfaces</u> (page 228).

Declaring Member Variables

Stack uses the following line of code to define its single member variable:

```
private Vector items;
```

This code declares a member variable and not another type of variable, such as a local variable, because the declaration appears within the class body but outside any methods or constructors. The member variable declared is named `items` and its data type is `Vector`, which is a class provided by the Java platform. Also, the `private` keyword identifies `items` as a private member. This means that only the `Stack` class has access to it.

The declaration of the `items` vector is a simple member variable declaration, but declarations can be more complex. You can specify not only type, name, and access level but also other attributes, including whether the variable is a class variable and whether it's a constant. Figure 58 shows all the possible components of a member variable declaration.

accessLevel	Indicates the access level for this member.
`static`	Declares a class member.
`final`	Indicates that it is constant.
`transient`	This variable is transient.
`volatile`	This variable is volatile.
type name	The type and the name of the variable.

Figure 58 The possible components of a member variable declaration and their purposes. Only the type and the name are required. The rest are optional.

Each component of a member variable declaration is further defined and discussed in later sections of this chapter, as follows:

accessLevel
Lets you control what other classes have access to a member variable by specifying one of four access levels: public, protected, package, and private. You control access to methods in the same way. Controlling Access to Members of a Class (page 193) covers access levels in detail.

static
Declares that this is a class variable rather than an instance variable. You also use `static` to declare class methods. Understanding Instance and Class Members (page 198) talks about instance and class variables.

final

Indicates that the value of this member cannot change. The following variable declaration defines a constant named AVOGADRO, whose value is Avogadro's number (6.023×10^{23}) and cannot be changed:

```
final double AVOGADRO = 6.023e23;
```

It's a compile-time error if your program ever tries to change a final variable. By convention, the names of constant values are spelled in uppercase letters.

transient

Marks member variables that should not be serialized. This component is used in object serialization, which is covered in the chapter I/O: Reading and Writing (page 313).

volatile

Prevents the compiler from performing certain optimizations on a member. This advanced feature, used by few programmers, is outside the scope of this book.

type

Like other variables, a member variable must have a type. You can use primitive type names, such as int, float, or boolean. Or, you can use reference types, such as array, object, or interface names.

name

A member variable's name can be any legal identifier and, by convention, begins with a lowercase letter. A member variable cannot have the same name as any other member variable in the same class.

Defining Methods

Figure 59 shows the code for Stack's push method. This method puts the object argument onto the top of the stack and returns the object.

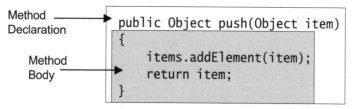

Figure 59   The push method and the structure of a method definition.

Like a class, a method definition has two major parts: the *method declaration* and the *method body*. The method declaration defines all the method's attributes, such as access

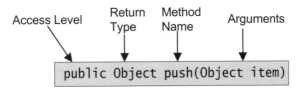

Figure 60   The components of the method declaration for the push method.

level, return type, name, and arguments, as shown in Figure 60. The method body is where all the action takes place. It contains the instructions that implement the method.

The only required elements of a method declaration are the method's name, return type, and a pair of parentheses: (and). A method declaration can provide more information about the method, including the return type of the method, the number and type of the arguments required by the method, and which other classes and objects can call the method. Figure 61 shows all possible elements of a method declaration.

accessLevel	Access level for this method.
static	This is a class method.
abstract	This method is not implemented.
final	Method cannot be overwritten.
native	Method implemented in another language.
synchronized	Method requires a monitor to run.
returnType methodName	The return type and method name.
(*paramlist*)	The list of arguments.
throws exceptions	The exceptions thrown by this method.

Figure 61   The possible components of a method declaration and their purposes.

Each element of a method declaration can be further defined and is discussed as indicated in the following list:

accessLevel
> As with member variables, you control what other classes have access to a method by using one of four access levels: public, protected, package, and private. The section Controlling Access to Members of a Class (page 193) covers access levels in detail.

static
> As with member variables, static declares this method as a class method rather than as an instance method. The section Understanding Instance and Class Members (page 198) talks about declaring instance and class methods.

abstract

An abstract method has no implementation and must be a member of an abstract class. Refer to the section <u>Writing Abstract Classes and Methods</u> (page 214) for information about why you might want to write an abstract method and how such methods affect subclasses.

final

A final method cannot be overridden by subclasses. The section <u>Writing Final Classes and Methods</u> (page 213) discusses why you might want to write final methods, how they affect subclasses, and whether you might want to write a final class instead.

native

If you have a significant library of functions written in another language, such as C, you may wish to preserve that investment and to use those functions from a program written in the Java programming language. Methods implemented in another language are called native methods and are declared as such, using the `native` keyword. Learn about writing native methods with the Java Native Interface.[1]

synchronized

Concurrently running threads often invoke methods that operate on the same data. Mark these methods with the `synchronized` keyword to ensure that the threads access information in a thread-safe manner. Synchronizing method calls is covered in the chapter <u>Threads: Doing Two or More Tasks at Once</u> (page 269). Take particular note of the section <u>Synchronizing Threads</u> (page 291).

returnType

A method must declare the data type of the value that it returns. If your method does not return a value, use the keyword `void` for the return type. The section <u>Returning a Value from a Method</u> (page 190) talks about the issues related to returning values from a method.

methodName

A method name can be any legal identifier. You need to consider code conventions, name overloading, and method overriding when naming a method. These topics are covered next.

(*parameterList*)

You pass information into a method through its arguments. See the section <u>Passing Information into a Method or a Constructor</u> (page 187).

throws *exceptionList*

If your method throws any checked exceptions, your method declaration must indicate the type of those exceptions. See the chapter <u>Handling Errors Using Exceptions</u> (page 243) for information. In particular, refer to the section <u>Specifying the Exceptions Thrown by a Method</u> (page 255).

---

[1] You can learn more about the Java Native Interface in the book *The Java Tutorial Continued* and online at http://java.sun.com/docs/books/tutorial/jni/index.html

Two of these components comprise the *method signature*: the method's name and the parameter list.

Naming a Method

Although a method name can be any legal identifier, code conventions[1] restrict method names. In general, method names should be verbs and should be in mixed case, with the first letter in lowercase and the first letter of each internal word in uppercase. Here are some examples:

```
toString
compareTo
isDefined
setX
getX
```

A method name should not be the same as the class name, because constructors are named for the class. The JavaBeans™ naming conventions[2] further describe how to name methods for setting and getting properties.

Typically, a method has a unique name within its class. However, three situations might cause a method to have the same name as other methods in the class or in a superclass: overriding methods, hiding methods, and name overloading.

A method with the same signature and return type as a method in a superclass *overrides* or *hides* the superclass method. The section Overriding and Hiding Methods (page 204) describes what each means, shows you how to override and to hide methods, and discusses related issues.

The Java programming language supports *name overloading* for methods, which means that multiple methods in the same class can share the same name if they have different parameter lists. Suppose that you have a class that can draw various types of data (strings, integers, and so on) and that contains a method for drawing each data type. In other languages, you have to think of a new name for each method, for example, drawString, drawInteger, drawFloat, and so on. In the Java programming language, you can use the same name for all the drawing methods but pass a different type of argument to each method. Thus, the data drawing class might declare three methods named draw, each of which takes a different type of argument.

---

[1]   Sun Microsystems' code conventions for the Java programming language are available online at http://java.sun.com/docs/codeconv/

[2]   The JavaBeans naming conventions are outlined in the JavaBeans specification, available online at http://java.sun.com/beans/spec.html

```
public class DataArtist {
    ...
    public void draw(String s) {
        ...
    }
    public void draw(int i) {
        ...
    }
    public void draw(float f) {
        ...
    }
}
```

Overloaded methods are differentiated by the number and the type of the arguments passed into the method. In the code sample, draw(String s) and draw(int i) are distinct and unique methods because they require different argument types. You cannot declare more than one method with the same name and the same number and type of arguments, because the compiler cannot tell them apart. The compiler does not consider return type when differentiating methods, so you cannot declare two methods with the same signature even if they have a different return type.

Providing Constructors for Your Classes

All classes have at least one constructor. A constructor is used to initialize a new object of that type and has the same name as the class. For example, the name of the Stack class's single constructor is Stack:

```
public Stack() {
    items = new Vector(10);
}
```

A constructor is not a method, so it has no return type. A constructor is called by the new operator, which automatically returns the newly created object. You cannot use the return statement in a constructor.

Following is another constructor that could be defined by the Stack class. This particular constructor sets the initial size of the stack according to its integer argument:

```
public Stack(int initialSize) {
    items = new Vector(initialSize);
}
```

Both constructors share the same name, Stack, but they have different argument lists. As with methods, the Java platform differentiates constructors on the basis of the number of arguments in the list and their types. You cannot write two constructors that have the same number and type of arguments for the same class, because the platform would not be able to tell them apart. Doing so causes a compile-time error.

When writing a class, you should provide it with whatever constructors make sense for that class. Recall the `Rectangle` class on page 124. That class contains four constructors that allow the user to initialize a new rectangle object in a variety of ways. You don't have to provide any constructors for your class if that's what makes sense. The runtime system automatically provides a no-argument, default constructor for any class that contains no constructors. The default provided by the runtime system doesn't do anything.

You can use one of the following access specifiers in a constructor's declaration to control what other classes can call the constructor:

private
> Only this class can use this constructor. If all constructors within a class are private, the class might contain public class methods (called *factory methods*) that create and initialize an instance of this class. Other classes can use the factory methods to create an instance of this class.

protected
> Subclasses of this class and classes in the same package can use this constructor.

public
> Any class can use this constructor.

no specifier
> Gives package access. Only classes within the same package as this class can use this constructor.

Constructors provide a way to initialize a new object. The section Initializing Instance and Class Members (page 201) describes other ways you can provide for the initialization of your class and a new object created from the class. That section also discusses when and why you would use each technique.

Passing Information into a Method or a Constructor

The declaration for a method or a constructor declares the number and the type of the arguments for that method or constructor. For example, the following is a method that computes the monthly payments for a home loan, based on the amount of the loan, the interest rate, the length of the loan (the number of periods), and the future value of the loan:

```
public double computePayment(double loanAmt, double rate,
                             double futureValue, int numPeriods) {
    double I, partial1, denominator, answer;
    I = rate / 100.0;
```

```
        partial1 = Math.pow((1 + I), (0.0 - numPeriods));
        denominator = (1 - partial1) / I;
        answer = ((-1 * loanAmt) / denominator)
                    - ((futureValue * partial1) / denominator);
        return answer;
    }
```

This method takes four arguments: the loan amount, the interest rate, the future value, and the number of periods. The first three are double-precision floating-point numbers, and the fourth is an integer.

As with this method, the set of arguments to any method or constructor is a comma-separated list of variable declarations, where each variable declaration is a type/name pair. As you can see from the body of the computePayment method, you simply use the argument name to refer to the argument's value.

Argument Types

You can pass an argument of any data type into a method or a constructor. This includes primitive data types, such as doubles, floats, and integers, as you saw in the computePayment method, and reference data types, such as classes and arrays. Here's an example of a factory method that accepts an array as an argument. In this example, the method creates a new Polygon object and initializes it from a list of Points (assume that Point is a class that represents an *x, y* coordinate):

```
    public static Polygon polygonFrom(Point[] listOfPoints) {
        ...
    }
```

The Java programming language doesn't let you pass methods into methods. But you can pass an object into a method and then invoke the object's methods.

Argument Names

When you declare an argument to a method or a constructor, you provide a name for that argument. This name is used within the method body to refer to the data.

The name of an argument must be unique in its scope. It cannot be the same as the name of another argument for the same method or constructor, the name of a local variable within the method or constructor, or the name of any parameter to a catch clause within the same method or constructor.

An argument can have the same name as one of the class's member variables. If this is the case, the argument is said to *hide* the member variable. Hiding member variables can make your code difficult to read and is conventionally used only within constructors and methods that set a particular member variable. For example, consider the following Circle class and its setOrigin method:

```
public class Circle {
    private int x, y, radius;
    public void setOrigin(int x, int y) {
        ...
    }
}
```

The Circle class has three member variables: x, y, and radius. The setOrigin method accepts two arguments, each of which has the same name as one of the member variables. Each method argument hides the member variable that shares its name. So using the simple names x or y within the body of the method refers to the argument, *not* to the member variable. To access the member variable, you must use a qualified name. See the section Using the this Keyword (page 192) for details.

Pass by Value

Arguments are *passed by value*. When invoked, a method or a constructor receives the value of the variable passed in. When the argument is of primitive type, "pass by value" means that the method cannot change its value. When the argument is of reference type, "pass by value" means that the method cannot change the object reference but can invoke the object's methods and modify the accessible variables within the object.

To get a better idea of what this means, let's look at a method called getRGBColor within a class called Pen. This method is attempting to return three values by setting the values of its arguments:

```
public class Pen {
    private int redValue, greenValue, blueValue;
    ...
    //This method does not work as intended.
    public void getRGBColor(int red, int green, int blue) {
        red = redValue;
        green = greenValue;
        blue = blueValue;
    }
}
```

This simply does not work. The red, green, and blue variables exist only within the scope of the getRGBColor method. When that method returns, those variables are gone and any changes to them lost.

Let's rewrite the `getRGBColor` method so that it does what was intended. First, we need a new type of object, `RGBColor`, that can hold the red, green, and blue values of a color in RGB space:

```
public class RGBColor {
    public int red, green, blue;
}
```

Now we can rewrite `getRGBColor` so that it accepts an `RGBColor` object as an argument. The `getRGBColor` method returns the current color of the pen by setting the `red`, `green`, and `blue` member variables of its `RGBColor` argument:

```
public class Pen {
    private int redValue, greenValue, blueValue;
    ...
    public void getRGBColor(RGBColor aColor) {
        aColor.red = redValue;
        aColor.green = greenValue;
        aColor.blue = blueValue;
    }
}
```

The changes made to the `RGBColor` object within the `getRGBColor` method persist after the method returns, because `aColor` is a reference to an object that exists outside the scope of the method.

Returning a Value from a Method

You declare a method's return type in its method declaration. Within the body of the method, you use the `return` statement to return the value. Any method declared `void` doesn't return a value and cannot contain a `return` statement. Any method that is not declared `void` must contain a `return` statement. Let's look at the `isEmpty` method in the `Stack` class:

```
public boolean isEmpty() {
    if (items.size() == 0) {
        return true;
    } else {
        return false;
    }
}
```

The data type of the return value must match the method's declared return type; you can't return an integer value from a method declared to return a boolean. The declared return type for the isEmpty method is boolean, and the implementation of the method returns the boolean value true or false, depending on the outcome of a test.

The isEmpty method returns a primitive type. A method can return a reference type. For example, Stack declares the pop method that returns the Object reference type:

```
public synchronized Object pop() {
    int len = items.size();
    Object obj = null;
    if (len == 0) {
        throw new EmptyStackException();
    }
    obj = items.elementAt(len - 1);
    items.removeElementAt(len - 1);
    return obj;
}
```

[handwritten annotations: "Variable?", "// ck if anything too pop", "is obj an object?", "Obj refers to 4th item or is it 4th object", "return ref to item 4"]

When a method uses a class name as its return type, such as pop does, the class of the type of the returned object must be either a subclass of or the exact class of the return type. Suppose that you have a class hierarchy in which ImaginaryNumber is a subclass of java.lang.Number, which is in turn a subclass of Object, as illustrated in Figure 62.

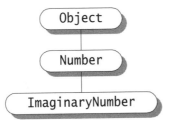

Figure 62 ImaginaryNumber is a subclass of java.lang.Number, which is a subclass of Object.

Now suppose that you have a method declared to return a Number:

```
public Number returnANumber() {
    ...
}
```

The returnANumber method can return an ImaginaryNumber but not an Object. ImaginaryNumber is a Number because it's a subclass of Number. However, an Object is not necessarily a Number—it could be a String or another type.

You also can use interface names as return types. In this case, the object returned must implement the specified interface.

Using the this Keyword

Within an instance method or a constructor, this is a reference to the *current object*—the object whose method or constructor is being called. You can refer to any member of the current object from within an instance method or a constructor by using this. The most common reason for doing so is that a member variable is hidden by an argument to the method or the constructor.

For example, the following constructor for the HSBColor class initializes the object's member variables according to the arguments passed into the constructor. Each argument to the constructor hides one of the object's member variables, so this constructor must refer to the object's member variables through this:

```java
public class HSBColor {
    private int hue, saturation, brightness;
    public HSBColor (int hue, int saturation, int brightness) {
        this.hue = hue;
        this.saturation = saturation;
        this.brightness = brightness;
    }
}
```

From within a constructor, you can also use the this keyword to call another constructor in the same class. Doing so is called an *explicit constructor invocation*. Here's another Rectangle class, with a different implementation from the one shown on page 124:

```java
public class Rectangle {
    private int x, y;
    private int width, height;
    public Rectangle() {
        this(0, 0, 0, 0);
    }
    public Rectangle(int width, int height) {
        this(0, 0, width, height);
    }
    public Rectangle(int x, int y, int width, int height) {
        this.x = x;
        this.y = y;
        this.width = width;
        this.height = height;
    }
    ...
}
```

This class contains a set of constructors. Each constructor initializes some or all of the rectangle's member variables. The constructors provide a default value for any member variable whose initial value is not provided by an argument. For example, the no-argument constructor calls the four-argument constructor, using 0s as default values. As before, the compiler determines which constructor to call, based on the number and the type of arguments.

If present, an explicit constructor invocation must be the first line in the constructor.

Controlling Access to Members of a Class

An access specifier determines whether other classes can use a particular member variable or call a particular method. The Java programming language supports four distinct access levels for member variables and methods: private, protected, public, and, if left unspecified, package.[1] Table 40 shows the access permitted by each level.

Table 40   Access Levels

Specifier	Class	Package	Subclass	World
private	✔	–	–	–
no specifier	✔	✔	–	–
protected	✔	✔	✔[a]	–
public	✔	✔	✔	✔

a. The protected/subclass case has an interesting twist discussed in detail on page 197.

The first column indicates whether the class itself has access to the member defined by the access specifier. As you can see, a class always has access to its own members. The second column indicates whether classes in the same package as the class (regardless of their parentage) have access to the member. A package groups related classes and interfaces and provides access protection and namespace management. You'll learn more about packages in the section Creating and Using Packages (page 234). The third column indicates whether subclasses of the class—regardless of which package they are in—have access to the member. The fourth column indicates whether all classes have access to the member.

Access levels affect you in two ways. First, when you use classes that come from another source, such as the classes in the Java platform, access levels determine which members of those classes your classes can use. Second, when you write a class, you need to decide what access level every member variable and every method in your class should have. One way of

---

[1] The 1.0 release of the Java programming language supported five access levels: the four listed plus private protected. The private protected access level is not supported in versions of the JDK higher than 1.0; you should not use it.

thinking about access levels is in terms of the API: Access levels directly affect the public API of a class and determine which members of the class can be used by other classes. You need to put as much effort into deciding the access level for a member as you put into making other decisions about your class's API, such as naming methods.

Let's look at a collection of classes and see access levels in action. Figure 63 shows the four classes that comprise this example and how they are related.

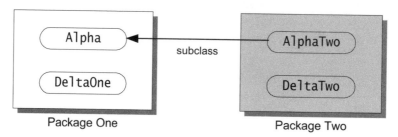

Figure 63 The classes and packages that comprise the example used to illustrate access levels.

Here's a listing of a class, Alpha,[1] whose members other classes will be trying to access. Alpha contains one member variable and one method per access level. Alpha is in a package called One:

```
package One;

public class Alpha {

    //member variables
    private    int iamprivate = 1;
               int iampackage = 2;        //package access
    protected int iamprotected = 3;
    public     int iampublic = 4;

    //methods
    private    void privateMethod() {
        System.out.println("iamprivate Method");
    }

    /*       */void packageMethod() {    //package access
        System.out.println("iampackage Method");
    }
    protected  void protectedMethod() {
        System.out.println("iamprotected Method");
    }
```

---

[1] Alpha.java is included on the CD and is available online. See <u>Code Samples</u> (page 224).

```
public     void publicMethod() {
    System.out.println("iampublic Method");
}

public static void main(String[] args) {
    Alpha a = new Alpha();
    a.privateMethod();     //legal
    a.packageMethod();     //legal
    a.protectedMethod();   //legal
    a.publicMethod();      //legal

    System.out.println("iamprivate: " + a.iamprivate);     //legal
    System.out.println("iampackage: " + a.iampackage);     //legal
    System.out.println("iamprotected: " + a.iamprotected); //legal
    System.out.println("iampublic: " + a.iampublic);       //legal

}
}
```

As you can see, Alpha can refer to all its member variables and all its methods, as shown by the Class column in Table 40. The output from this program is:

```
iamprivate Method
iampackage Method
iamprotected Method
iampublic Method
iamprivate: 1
iampackage: 2
iamprotected: 3
iampublic: 4
```

A member's access level determines which *classes* have access to that member, not which *instances* have access. So, for example, instances of the same class have access to one another's private members. Thus, we can add to the Alpha class an instance method that compares the current Alpha object (this) to another object, based on their iamprivate variables:

```
package One;
public class Alpha {
    ...
    public boolean isEqualTo(Alpha anotherAlpha) {

        if (this.iamprivate == anotherAlpha.iamprivate) {     //legal
            return true;
        } else {
            return false;
        }
    }
}
```

Now consider the following class, DeltaOne,[1] which is in the same package as Alpha. The methods and the variables this class can use are predicted by the Package column in Table 40:

```java
package One;
public class DeltaOne {
    public static void main(String[] args) {
        Alpha a = new Alpha();
      //a.privateMethod();       //illegal
        a.packageMethod();       //legal
        a.protectedMethod();     //legal
        a.publicMethod();        //legal


      //System.out.println("iamprivate: " + a.iamprivate);      //illegal
        System.out.println("iampackage: " + a.iampackage);       //legal
        System.out.println("iamprotected: " + a.iamprotected);   //legal
        System.out.println("iampublic: " + a.iampublic);         //legal
    }
}
```

DeltaOne cannot refer to the `iamprivate` variable or invoke `privateMethod` but can access the other members of Alpha. If you remove the comment from the lines of code that are commented out and try to compile the class, the compiler will generate errors. Here's the output from the program when you run it as shown:

```
iampackage Method
iamprotected Method
iampublic Method
iampackage: 2
iamprotected: 3
iampublic: 4
```

is this possible

The next class, AlphaTwo,[2] is a subclass of Alpha but is in a different package. You can predict what member variables and methods it can use by looking at the Subclass column in Table 40:

```java
package Two;
import One.*;

public class AlphaTwo extends Alpha {
    public static void main(String[] args) {
        Alpha a = new Alpha();
```

---

[1] `DeltaOne.java` is included on the CD and is available online. See <u>Code Samples</u> (page 224).
[2] `AlphaTwo.java` is included on the CD and is available online. See <u>Code Samples</u> (page 224).

```
    //a.privateMethod();        //illegal
    //a.packageMethod();        //illegal
    //a.protectedMethod();      //illegal
      a.publicMethod();         //legal

    //System.out.println("iamprivate: " + a.iamprivate);     //illegal
    //System.out.println("iampackage: " + a.iampackage);     //illegal
    //System.out.println("iamprotected: " + a.iamprotected); //illegal
      System.out.println("iampublic: " + a.iampublic);       //legal

      AlphaTwo a2 = new AlphaTwo();
      a2.protectedMethod();                                  //legal
      System.out.println("iamprotected: " + a2.iamprotected);//legal
    }
}
```

This particular case has an interesting twist. Note that AlphaTwo cannot call protected-Method or access iamprotected on the Alpha instance but can call protectedMethod and access iamprotected on an instance of AlphaTwo. The protected access level allows a subclass to refer to a protected member only through an object reference that is the same type as the class or one of its subclasses. If AlphaTwo had subclasses, it could call protectedMethod through a reference to an instance of any of its subclasses. The output displayed when running AlphaTwo is:

```
iampublic Method
iampublic: 4
iamprotected Method
iamprotected: 3
```

Finally, DeltaTwo[1] is not related through the class hierarchy to Alpha and is in a different package than Alpha. As the World column in Table 40 shows, DeltaTwo can access only the public members of Alpha:

```
package Two;
import One.*;

public class DeltaTwo {

    public static void main(String[] args) {
        Alpha alpha = new Alpha();
    //alpha.privateMethod();      //illegal
    //alpha.packageMethod();      //illegal
    //alpha.protectedMethod();    //illegal
      alpha.publicMethod();       //legal
```

---

[1] DeltaTwo.java is included on the CD and is available online. See Code Samples (page 224).

```
//System.out.println("iamprivate: " + a.iamprivate);    //illegal
//System.out.println("iampackage: " + a.iampackage);    //illegal
//System.out.println("iamprotected: " + a.iamprotected); //illegal
  System.out.println("iampublic: " + a.iampublic);      //legal
    }
}
```

Here's the output from DeltaTwo:

```
iampublic Method
iampublic: 4
```

Tips on Choosing an Access Level: If other programmers use your class, you want to ensure that errors from misuse cannot happen. Access levels can help you do this. The following tips can help you decide what access level is appropriate for a particular member.

- Use the most restrictive access level that makes sense for a particular member. Use private unless you have a good reason not to.
- Avoid public member variables except for constants.[1] Public member variables tend to link you to a particular implementation and can lead to bugs and misuse. Furthermore, if a member variable can be changed only by calling a method, you can notify other classes or objects of the change. Notification is impossible if you allow public access to a member variable. You might decide to grant public access if doing so gives you significant performance gains.
- Limit the number of protected and package member variables.
- If a member variable is a JavaBeans property, it must be private.

Understanding Instance and Class Members

You learned briefly about instance and class members in Chapter 2, Object-Oriented Programming Concepts (page 45). This section shows you how to declare and to use class and instance members. The following class, AClass,[2] declares an instance member variable, an instance method, a class variable, a class method, and main, which is a class method:

```
public class AClass {

    public int instanceInteger = 0;
    public int instanceMethod() {
        return instanceInteger;
    }
```

---

[1] Many of the examples in the tutorial use public member variables. Examples and nonproduction code don't have to live up to the rigid design standards that an API does.

[2] AClass.java is included on the CD and is available online. See Code Samples (page 224).

```
public static int classInteger = 0;
public static int classMethod() {
    return classInteger;
}

public static void main(String[] args) {
    AClass anInstance = new AClass();
    AClass anotherInstance = new AClass();

    //Refer to instance members through an instance.
    anInstance.instanceInteger = 1;
    anotherInstance.instanceInteger = 2;
    System.out.println(anInstance.instanceMethod());
    System.out.println(anotherInstance.instanceMethod());

    //Illegal to refer directly to instance members
    //from a class method
    //System.out.println(instanceMethod());     //illegal
    //System.out.println(instanceInteger);      //illegal

    //Refer to class members through the class...
    AClass.classInteger = 7;
    System.out.println(classMethod());

    //...or through an instance.
    System.out.println(anInstance.classMethod());

    //Instances share class variables
    anInstance.classInteger = 9;
    System.out.println(anInstance.classMethod());
    System.out.println(anotherInstance.classMethod());
}
}
```

Here's the output from the program:

```
1
2
7
7
9
9
```

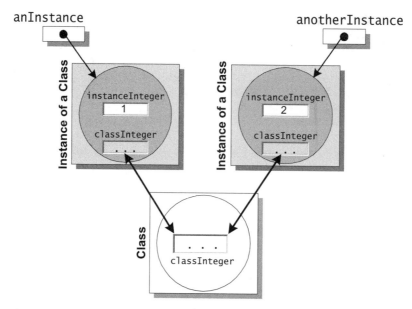

Figure 64 The objects in the `AClass` example and their instance and class member variables.

Figure 64 shows the objects and member variables in the program and how they are related.

Unless otherwise specified, a member declared within a class is an instance member. So `instanceInteger` and `instanceMethod` are both instance members. The runtime system creates one copy of each instance variable for each instance of a class created by a program. Thus, the objects referred to by `anInstance` and `anotherInstance` each have their own copy of `instanceInteger`. You can access an instance member and call an instance method only through a reference to an instance. If you remove the two slashes from the beginning of the lines marked `illegal` and try to compile the program, the compiler will display an error message.

An instance variable is in contrast to a *class variable*, which is declared by using the `static` modifier. Besides the `main` method, `AClass` declares one class variable and one class method, called `classInteger` and `classMethod`, respectively. The runtime system allocates a class variable once per class, regardless of the number of instances created of that class. The system allocates memory for a class variable the first time it encounters the class. All instances of that class share the same copy of the class's class variables. You can access class variables either through an instance or through the class itself. Similarly, class methods can be invoked on the class or through an instance reference. Note that when the program changes the value of `classVariable`, its value changes for all instances.

Initializing Instance and Class Members

You can provide an initial value for a class or an instance member variable in its declaration:

```
public class BedAndBreakfast {
    public static final int MAX_CAPACITY = 10; //initialize to 10
    private boolean full = false;               //initialize to false
}
```

This works well for member variables of primitive data types. Sometimes, it even works when creating arrays and objects. But this form of initialization has limitations.

- The initialization must be expressed in an assignment statement. For example, you can't use an if-else statement.
- The initialization expression cannot call any method that is declared to throw a non-runtime (checked) exception.
- If the initialization expression calls a method that throws a runtime exception, such as NullPointerException, it cannot do error recovery.

If these limitations prevent you from initializing a member variable in its declaration, you have to put the initialization code elsewhere. To initialize a class member variable, put the initialization code in a static initialization block, as the following section shows. To initialize an instance member variable, put the initialization code in a constructor.

Using Static Initialization Blocks

Figure 65 shows an example of a static initialization block.

```
import java.util.ResourceBundle;
class Errors {
    static ResourceBundle errorStrings;
    static {
        try {
            errorStrings = ResourceBundle.getBundle("ErrorStrings");
        } catch (java.util.MissingResourceException e) {
            // error recovery code here
        }
    }
}
```

Figure 65   A static initialization block can be used to initialize class member variables.

The `errorStrings` resource bundle must be initialized in a static initialization block because the `getBundle` method can throw an exception if the bundle cannot be found. The code should perform error recovery. Also, `errorStrings` is a class member, so it should not be initialized in a constructor. A *static initialization block* begins with the `static` keyword and is a normal block of code enclosed in braces: { and }.

A class can have any number of static initialization blocks that appear anywhere in the class body. The runtime system guarantees that static initialization blocks and static initializers are called in the order (left to right, top to bottom) that they appear in the source code.

Initializing Instance Members

If you want to initialize an instance variable and cannot do it in the variable declaration for the reasons cited previously, put the initialization in the constructor(s) for the class. If the `errorStrings` bundle in the previous example were an instance variable rather than a class variable, you'd move the code that initializes `errorStrings` to a constructor for the class, as follows:

```
import java.util.ResourceBundle;
class Errors {
    ResourceBundle errorStrings;
    Errors() {
        try {
            errorStrings = ResourceBundle.getBundle("ErrorStrings");
        } catch (java.util.MissingResourceException e) {
            // error recovery code here
        }
    }
}
```

Summary of Creating Classes

A class definition has two parts: a class declaration and a class body. For details about the components of a class declaration, refer to Figure 57. The class body contains member variables, methods, and constructors for the class. A class uses member variables to contain state and uses methods to implement behavior. Figure 58 shows all the possible components of a member variable declaration and Figure 61 shows all possible components of a method declaration. Constructors initialize a new instance of a class and have the same name as the class.

You control access to member variables and methods in the same way: by using an access specifier, such as `private` or `public`, in the member's declaration. Table 40 (page 193) shows the access specifiers and the effect of each.

You specify a class member variable or a class method by using the `static` keyword in the member's declaration. A member that is not declared as `static` is implicitly an instance member. Class variables are shared by all instance of a class and can be accessed through the class name. Instances of a class get their own copy of each instance variable, which must be accessed through an instance reference.

Questions and Exercises: Creating Classes

Questions

1. Consider the following class:

```java
public class IdentifyMyParts {
    public static int x = 7;
    public int y = 3;
}
```

a. How many class variables does the `IdentifyMyParts` class contain? What are their names? *1, x*

b. How many instance variables does the `IdentifyMyParts` class contain? What are their names? *1, y*

c. What is the output from the following code:

```java
IdentifyMyParts a = new IdentifyMyParts();
IdentifyMyParts b = new IdentifyMyParts();
a.y = 5;
b.y = 6;
a.x = 1;
b.x = 2;
System.out.println("a.y = " + a.y);
System.out.println("b.y = " + b.y);
System.out.println("a.x = " + a.x);
System.out.println("b.x = " + b.x);
```

Exercises

1. Write a class whose instances represent a playing card from a deck of cards.

2. Write a class whose instances represents a deck of cards.

3. Write a small program to test your deck and card classes. The program can be as simple as creating a deck of cards and displaying its cards.

Answers

You can find answers to these Questions and Exercises online:

```
http://java.sun.com/docs/books/tutorial/java/javaOO/QandE/
creating-answers.html
```

Managing Inheritance

The `Object` class, defined in the `java.lang` package, defines and implements behavior that every class needs. As depicted in Figure 66, many classes derive from `Object`, many classes derive from those classes, and so on, forming a hierarchy of classes.

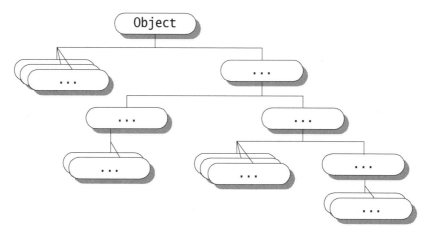

Figure 66   All classes are descendants of the `Object` class.

At the top of the hierarchy, `Object` is the most general of all classes. Classes near the bottom of the hierarchy provide for more specialized behavior. A *subclass* derives from another class. The term *superclass* refers to a class's direct ancestor or to any of its ascendant classes. Every class has one and only one immediate superclass.

A subclass inherits all the member variables and methods from its superclass. However, the subclass might not have access to an inherited member variable or method. For example, a subclass cannot access a private member inherited from its superclass. One might say, then, that the item was not inherited at all. But the item *is* inherited. This becomes important when using an inner class, which does have access to its enclosing class's private members. Note that constructors are not members and so are not inherited by subclasses.

Overriding and Hiding Methods

An instance method in a subclass with the same signature and return type as an instance method in the superclass *overrides* the superclass's method. (Remember that a method's signature is its name and the number and the type of its arguments.) The ability of a subclass to override a method allows a class to inherit from a superclass whose behavior is "close enough" and then to modify behavior as needed. For example, the `Object` class contains an instance method called `toString` that returns a string representation of an instance of that type. Every class inherits this method. The implementation in `Object` is not very useful for subclasses; thus, we recommend overriding this method to provide better information for your classes. It's particularly useful for debugging. Here's an example of overriding toString:

```
public class MyClass {
    private int anInt = 4;
    //Overrides toString in Object class.
    public String toString() {
        return "Instance of MyClass. anInt = " + anInt;
    }
}
```

The overriding method has the same name, number and type of arguments, and return value as the method it overrides. The overriding method can have a different throws clause as long as it doesn't specify any types not specified by the throws clause in the overridden method. Also, the access specifier for the overriding method can allow more but not less access than the overridden method. For example, a protected method in the superclass can be made public but not private.

A subclass cannot override methods that are declared final in the superclass (by definition, final methods cannot be overridden). If you attempt to override a final method, the compiler displays an error message. The section Writing Final Classes and Methods (page 213) discusses final methods in detail.

A subclass must override methods that are declared abstract in the superclass, or the subclass itself must be abstract. The section Writing Abstract Classes and Methods (page 214) discusses abstract classes and methods in detail.

Recall from page 185 that the Java programming language allows you to overload methods by changing the number or the type of arguments to the method. You can also overload methods in a superclass. Here's an example of overloading the toString method:

```
public class MyClass {
    private int anInt = 4;
    //Overrides toString in Object class.
    public String toString() {
        return "Instance of MyClass. anInt = " + anInt;
    }
    //Overloads toString method name to provide additional functionality.
    public String toString(String prefix) {
        return prefix + ": " + toString();
    }
}
```

As illustrated by the preceding example, you might overload a superclass method to provide additional functionality. When writing a method that has the same name as a method in a superclass, double check the return values and the argument lists to make sure that you are overloading or overriding as you intended.

If a subclass defines a class method with the same signature as a class method in the superclass, the method in the subclass *hides* the one in the superclass. The distinction between hiding and overriding has important implications. Let's look at an example to see why. This example contains two classes. The first is Planet,[1] which contains one instance method and one class method:

```java
public class Planet {
    public static void hide() {
        System.out.println("The hide method in Planet.");
    }
    public void override() {
        System.out.println("The override method in Planet.");
    }
}
```

The second class, a subclass of Planet, is called Earth:[2]

```java
public class Earth extends Planet {
    public static void hide() {
        System.out.println("The hide method in Earth.");
    }
    public void override() {
        System.out.println("The override method in Earth.");
    }

    public static void main(String[] args) {
        Earth myEarth = new Earth();
        Planet myPlanet = (Planet)myEarth;
        myPlanet.hide();
        myPlanet.override();
    }
}
```

The Earth class overrides the instance method in Planet called override and hides the class method in Planet called hide. The main method in this class creates an instance of Earth, casts it to a Planet reference, and then calls both the hide and the override methods on the instance. The output from this program is as follows:

---

[1] Planet.java is included on the CD and is available online. See Code Samples (page 224).
[2] Earth.java is included on the CD and is available online. See Code Samples (page 224).

```
The hide method in Planet.
The override method in Earth.
```

The version of the hidden method that gets invoked is the one in the superclass, and the version of the overridden method that gets invoked is the one in the subclass. For class methods, the runtime system invokes the method defined in the compile-time type of the reference on which the method is called. In the example, the compile-time type of myPlanet is Planet. Thus, the runtime system invokes the hide method defined in Planet. For instance methods, the runtime system invokes the method defined in the runtime type of the reference on which the method is called. In the example, the runtime type of myPlanet is Earth. Thus, the runtime system invokes the override method defined in Earth.

An instance method cannot override a static method, and a static method cannot hide an instance method. Table 41 summarizes what happens when you define a method with the same signature as a method in a superclass.

Table 41   The effect of defining a method with the same signature as the superclass's method.

	Superclass Instance Method	**Superclass Static Method**
Instance Method	Overrides (must also have the same return type)	Generates a compile-time error
Static Method	Generates a compile-time error	Hides

Hiding Member Variables

Within a class, a member variable that has the same name as a member variable in the superclass *hides* the superclass's member variable, even if their types are different. Within the subclass, the member variable in the superclass cannot be referenced by its simple name. Instead, the member variable must be accessed through super, which is covered in the next section. Generally speaking, we don't recommend hiding member variables.

Using super

If your method overrides one of its superclass's methods, you can invoke the overridden method through the use of super. You can also use super to refer to a hidden member variable. Consider this class, Superclass:[1]

```
public class Superclass {
    public boolean aVariable;
```

---

[1] Superclass.java is included on the CD and is available online. See <u>Code Samples</u> (page 224).

```
        public void aMethod() {
            aVariable = true;
        }
    }
```

Now, here's a subclass, called `Subclass`,[1] that overrides `aMethod` and hides `aVariable`:

```
    public class Subclass extends Superclass {
        public boolean aVariable;        //hides aVariable in Superclass
        public void aMethod() {          //overrides aMethod in Superclass
            aVariable = false;
            super.aMethod();
            System.out.println(aVariable);
            System.out.println(super.aVariable);
        }
    }
```

Within `Subclass`, the simple name `aVariable` refers to the one declared in `SubClass`, which hides the one declared in `Superclass`. Similarly, the simple name `aMethod` refers to the one declared in `Subclass`, which overrides the one in `Superclass`. So to refer to `aVariable` and `aMethod` inherited from `Superclass`, `Subclass` must use a qualified name, using `super` as shown. Thus, the print statements in `Subclass`'s `aMethod` displays the following:

```
    false
    true
```

You can also use `super` within a constructor to invoke a superclass's constructor. The following code sample is a partial listing of a subclass of `Thread`—a core class used to implement multitasking behavior—which performs an animation. The constructor for `AnimationThread` sets up some default values, such as the frame speed and the number of images, and then loads the images:

```
    class AnimationThread extends Thread {
        int framesPerSecond;
        int numImages;
        Image[] images;

        AnimationThread(int fps, int num) {
            super("AnimationThread");
            this.framesPerSecond = fps;
            this.numImages = num;
            this.images = new Image[numImages];
```

---

[1] `Subclass.java` is included on the CD and is available online. See Code Samples (page 224).

```
        for (int i = 0; i <= numImages; i++) {
            ...
            // Load all the images.
            ...
        }
    }
    ...
}
```

The line set in boldface is an explicit superclass constructor invocation that calls a constructor provided by the superclass of `AnimationThread`, namely, `Thread`. This particular `Thread` constructor takes a `String` that sets the name of `Thread`. If present, an explicit superclass constructor invocation must be the first statement in the subclass constructor: An object should perform the higher-level initialization first. If a constructor does not explicitly invoke a superclass constructor, the Java runtime system automatically invokes the no-argument constructor of the superclass before any statements within the constructor are executed.

Being a Descendant of Object

The Object[1] class sits at the top of the class hierarchy tree. Every class is a descendant, direct or indirect, of the `Object` class. This class defines the basic state and behavior that all objects must have, such as the ability to compare oneself to another object, to convert to a string, to wait on a condition variable, to notify other objects that a condition variable has changed, and to return the class of the object.

The following is a list of handy methods that the `Object` class provides:

- `clone`
- `equals` and `hashCode`
- `finalize`
- `toString`
- `getClass`
- `notify`, `notifyAll`, and `wait`

With the exception of `notify`, `notifyAll`, and `wait`, these methods are covered in the sections that follow. The `notify`, `notifyAll`, and `wait` methods all play a part in synchronizing the activities of independently running threads in a program. Refer to the chapter Threads: Doing Two or More Tasks at Once (page 269).

---

[1] http://java.sun.com/j2se/1.3/docs/api/java/lang/Object.html

The clone Method

You use the `clone` method to create an object from an existing object. To create a clone, you write:

```
aCloneableObject.clone();
```

`Object`'s implementation of this method checks to see whether the object on which `clone` was invoked implements the `Cloneable` interface. If the object does not, the method throws a `CloneNotSupportedException`. Even though `Object` implements the `clone` method, the `Object` class is not declared to implement the `Cloneable` interface, so classes that don't explicitly implement the interface are not cloneable. If the object on which `clone` was invoked does implement the `Cloneable` interface, `Object`'s implementation of the `clone` method creates an object of the same type as the original object and initializes the new object's member variables to have the same values as the original object's corresponding member variables.

The simplest way to make your class cloneable, then, is to add `implements Cloneable` to your class's declaration. For some classes, the default behavior of `Object`'s `clone` method works just fine. Other classes need to override `clone` to get correct behavior.

Consider a `Stack` class that contains a member variable referring to a `Vector`. If `Stack` relies on `Object`'s implementation of `clone`, the original stack and its clone refer to the same vector. Changing one stack changes the other, which is undesirable behavior.

Here is an appropriate implementation of `clone` for our `Stack` class, which clones the vector to ensure that the original stack and its clone do not refer to the same vector:

```
public class Stack implements Cloneable {
    private Vector items;
    ...
    // code for Stack's methods and constructor not shown
    protected Object clone() {
        try {
            Stack s = (Stack)super.clone(); // clone the stack
            s.items = (Vector)items.clone();// clone the vector
            return s;      // return the clone
        } catch (CloneNotSupportedException e) {
            //This shouldn't happen because
            //Stack and Vector are Cloneable.
            throw new InternalError();
        }
    }
}
```

The implementation for `Stack`'s `clone` method is relatively simple. First, it calls `Object`'s implementation of the `clone` method by calling `super.clone`, which creates and initializes a `Stack` object. At this point, the original stack and its clone refer to the same vector. Next, the method clones the vector.

Be Careful: The `clone` method should never use `new` to create the clone and should not call constructors. Instead, the method should call `super.clone`, which creates an object of the correct type and allows the hierarchy of superclasses to perform the copying necessary to get a proper clone.

The equals and hashCode Methods

The `equals` method compares two objects for equality and returns `true` if they are equal. The `equals` method provided in the `Object` class uses the identity operator (`==`) to determine whether two objects are equal. If the objects compared are the exact same object, the method returns `true`.

However, for some classes, two distinct objects of that type might be considered equal if they contain the same information. Consider this code that tests two `Integers`, `one` and `anotherOne`, for equality:

```
Integer one = new Integer(1), anotherOne = new Integer(1);
if (one.equals(anotherOne)) {
    System.out.println("objects are equal");
}
```

This program displays `objects are equal` even though `one` and `anotherOne` reference two distinct objects. They are considered equal because the objects compared contain the same integer value.

You should override the `equals` method only if the identity operator is not appropriate for your class. If you override `equals`, override `hashCode` as well.

The value returned by `hashCode` is an `int` that maps an object into a bucket in a hash table. An object must always produce the same hash code. However, objects can share hash codes (they aren't necessarily unique). Writing a "correct" hashing function is easy—always return the same hash code for the same object. Writing an "efficient" hashing function—one that provides a sufficient distribution of objects over the buckets—is difficult and is outside the scope of this book.

Even so, the hashing function for some classes is relatively obvious. For example, an obvious hash code for an `Integer` object is its integer value. For an example of a class that overrides the `equals` and `hashCode` methods, see the `BingoBall` class in <u>BINGO!</u>[1]

---

[1] http://java.sun.com/docs/books/tutorial/together/index.html

The finalize Method

The Object class provides a method, finalize, that cleans up an object before it is garbage collected. This method's role during garbage collection was discussed previously, in the section Cleaning Up Unused Objects (page 129). The finalize method is called automatically by the system, and most classes do not need to override it. Thus, you can generally ignore this method.

The toString Method

The Object's toString method returns a String representation of the object. You can use toString along with System.out.println to display a text representation of an object, such as an instance of Double:

```
System.out.println(new Double(Math.PI).toString());
```

The String representation for an object depends entirely on the object. The String representation of a Double object is the double value displayed as text. Thus, the previous line of code displays 3.14159.

The toString method is very useful for debugging. You should override this method in all your classes.

The getClass Method

The getClass method returns a runtime representation of the class of an object. This method returns a Class object, which you can query for information about the class, such as its name, its superclass, and the names of the interfaces it implements. You cannot override getClass. The following method gets and displays the class name of an object:

```
void PrintClassName(Object obj) {
    System.out.println("The Object's class is "
                        + obj.getClass().getName());
}
```

One handy use of a Class object is to create a new instance of a class without knowing what the class is at compile time. The following sample method creates a new instance of the same class as obj, which can be any class that inherits from Object:

```
Object createNewInstanceOf(Object obj) {
    return obj.getClass().newInstance();
}
```

If you already know the name of the class, you can also get a Class object from a class name. The following two lines are equivalent ways to get a Class object for the String class:

```
String.class¹
Class.forName("String")
```

The first is more efficient than the second.

Writing Final Classes and Methods

Final Classes

You can declare that your class is final, that is, that your class cannot be subclassed. You might want to do this for two reasons: (1) to increase system security by preventing system subversion, and (2) for reasons of good object-oriented design.

1. *Security:* One mechanism that hackers use to subvert systems is to create a subclass of a class and to then substitute the subclass for the original. The subclass looks and feels like the original class but does vastly different things, possibly causing damage or getting into private information. To prevent this kind of subversion, you can declare your class to be final and thereby prevent any subclasses from being created. The String class is a final class for just this reason. This class is so vital to the operation of the Java platform that it must guarantee that whenever a method or an object uses a String, it gets exactly a java.lang.String and not another kind of string. This ensures that all strings have no strange, inconsistent, undesirable, or unpredictable properties.

   If you try to compile a subclass of a final class, the compiler prints an error message and refuses to compile your program. In addition, the Java runtime system ensures that the subversion is not taking place at the bytecode level. It does this by checking to make sure that a class is not a subclass of a final class.

2. *Design:* You may also wish to declare a class as final for object-oriented design reasons. You may think that your class is "perfect" or that, conceptually, your class should have no subclasses.

To specify that your class is final, use the keyword final before the class keyword in your class declaration. For example, if you wanted to declare your (perfect) ChessAlgorithm class as final, its declaration should look like this:

```
final class ChessAlgorithm {
    ...
}
```

Any subsequent attempts to subclass ChessAlgorithm will result in a compiler error.

---

¹　The *type*.class construct was added to the Java platform for the 1.1 release.

Final Methods

If declaring an entire class final is too heavy-handed for your needs, you can declare some or all of the class's methods final instead. Use the final keyword in a method declaration to indicate that the method cannot be overridden by subclasses. The Object class does this; some of its methods are final, and some are not.

You might wish to make a method final if it has an implementation that should not be changed and it is critical to the consistent state of the object. For example, instead of making your ChessAlgorithm class final, you might want the nextMove method to be final instead:

```
class ChessAlgorithm {
    ...
    final void nextMove(ChessPiece pieceMoved,
                        BoardLocation newLocation) {
        ...
    }
    ...
}
```

Writing Abstract Classes and Methods

Abstract Classes

Sometimes, a class that you define represents an abstract concept and, as such, should not be instantiated. Take, for example, food in the real world. Have you ever seen an instance of food? No. What you see instead are instances of carrot, apple, and chocolate chip cookies. Food represents the abstract concept of what we can eat. It doesn't make sense for an instance of food to exist.

Similarly, in object-oriented programming, you may want to model an abstract concept without being able to create an instance of it. For example, the Number class represents the abstract concept of numbers. It makes sense to model numbers in a program, but it doesn't make sense to create a generic number object. Instead, the Number class makes sense only as a superclass to such classes as Integer and Float, both of which implement specific kinds of numbers. A class such as Number, which represents an abstract concept and should not be instantiated, is called an *abstract class*. An abstract class can only be subclassed; it cannot be instantiated.

To declare that your class is an abstract class, use the keyword abstract before the class keyword in your class declaration:

```
abstract class Number {
    ...
}
```

If you attempt to instantiate an abstract class, the compiler displays an error message.

Abstract Methods

An abstract class can contain *abstract methods*—methods with no implementation. In this way, an abstract class can define a complete programming interface for its subclasses but allows its subclasses to fill in the implementation details of those methods. In practice, abstract classes provide a complete or partial implementation of at least one method. If an abstract class contains only abstract method declarations, it should be implemented as an interface instead. Interfaces are covered in the section <u>Creating and Using Interfaces</u> (page 228).

Let's look at an example of when you might want to create an abstract class with an abstract method in it. In an object-oriented drawing application, you can draw circles, rectangles, lines, Bézier curves, and so on. These graphic objects all have certain states (position, bounding box) and behaviors (move, resize, draw) in common. You can take advantage of these similarities and declare them all to inherit from the same parent object—for example, GraphicObject, as shown in Figure 67.

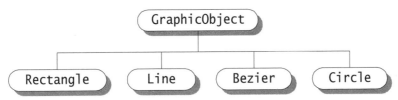

Figure 67 Classes Rectangle, Line, Bezier, and Circle inherit certain states and behavior from their common parent, GraphicObject.

Graphic objects are substantially different in many ways: drawing a circle is quite different from drawing a rectangle. The graphic objects cannot share these types of states or behavior. On the other hand, all GraphicObjects must know how to draw themselves; they just differ in how they are drawn. This is a perfect situation for an abstract superclass.

First, you would declare an abstract class, GraphicObject, to provide member variables and methods that were wholly shared by all subclasses, such as the current position and the moveTo method. GraphicObject also declares abstract methods for methods, such as draw, that need to be implemented by all subclasses but that are implemented in entirely different ways (no default implementation in the superclass makes sense). The GraphicObject class would look something like this:

```
abstract class GraphicObject {
    int x, y;
    ...
```

```
            void moveTo(int newX, int newY) {
                ...
            }
            abstract void draw();
        }
```

Each nonabstract subclass of `GraphicObject`, such as `Circle` and `Rectangle`, must provide an implementation for the draw method:

```
        class Circle extends GraphicObject {
            void draw() {
                ...
            }
        }
        class Rectangle extends GraphicObject {
            void draw() {
                ...
            }
        }
```

[handwritten margin note: why not just create a class called GraphicObj w/ method draw & override?]

An abstract class is not required to have an abstract method in it. But any class that has an abstract method in it or that does not provide an implementation for any abstract methods declared in its superclasses or implemented interfaces *must* be declared as an abstract class.

Summary of Managing Inheritance

Except for the `Object` class, a class has exactly one direct superclass. A class inherits member variables and methods from all its superclasses, whether direct or indirect. A subclass can override methods that it inherits, or it can hide variables or methods that it inherits. Table 41 on page 207 shows the effect of declaring a method with the same signature as a method in the superclass.

The `Object` class is the top of the class hierarchy. All classes are descendants from this class and inherit methods from it. Useful methods inherited from `Object` include `toString`, `equals`, `clone`, `getClass`, `wait`, `notify`, and `notifyAll`.

You can prevent a class from being subclassed by using the `final` keyword in the class's declaration. Similarly, you can prevent a method from being overridden by subclasses by declaring it as a final method.

An abstract class can only be subclassed; it cannot be instantiated. An abstract class can contain abstract methods—methods that are declared but not implemented. Subclasses provide the implementations for abstract methods.

Questions and Exercises: Managing Inheritance

Questions

1. Consider the following two classes:

```
public class ClassA {
    public void methodOne(int i) {
    }
    public void methodTwo(int i) {
    }
    public static void methodThree(int i) {
    }
    public static void methodFour(int i) {
    }
}

public class ClassB extends ClassA {
    public static void methodOne(int i) {
    }
    public void methodTwo(int i) {
    }
    public void methodThree(int i) {
    }
    public static void methodFour(int i) {
    }
}
```

a. Which method overrides a method in the superclass? *method Two*

b. Which method hides a method in the superclass? *method four*

c. What do the other methods do? *1, 3 are invalid*

2. Consider the `Card`, `Deck`, and `DisplayDeck` classes you wrote for exercise 1 on page 203. What `Object` methods should each of these classes override?

Exercises

1. Write the implementations for the methods that you answered in question 2.

2. Write an abstract class. Write at least two of its nonabstract subclasses.

Answers

You can find answers to these Questions and Exercises online:

```
http://java.sun.com/docs/books/tutorial/java/javaOO/QandE/
inherit-answers.html
```

Implementing Nested Classes

You can define a class as a member of another class. Such a class is called a *nested class* and is illustrated here:

```
class EnclosingClass {
    ...
    class ANestedClass {
        ...
    }
}
```

Definition: A nested class is a member of another class.

You use nested classes to reflect and to enforce the relationship between two classes. You should define a class within another class when the nested class makes sense only in the context of its enclosing class or when it relies on the enclosing class for its function. For example, a text cursor might make sense only in the context of a text component.

As a member of its enclosing class, a nested class has a special privilege: It has unlimited access to its enclosing class's members, even if they are declared private.[1] However, this special privilege isn't really special at all. It is fully consistent with the meaning of private and the other access specifiers. The access specifiers restrict access to members for classes *outside* the enclosing class. The nested class is *inside* its enclosing class so that it has access to its enclosing class's members.

Like other members, a nested class can be declared static (or not). A static nested class is called just that: a *static nested class*. A nonstatic nested class is called an *inner class*.

```
class EnclosingClass {
    ...
    static class StaticNestedClass {
        ...
    }
    class InnerClass {
        ...
    }
}
```

---

[1] Owing to a bug in the JDK 1.1 compiler, an inner class cannot call a private method in its enclosing class in that release. The workaround is to use package access instead of private. This bug has been fixed.

As with static methods and variables, which we call class methods and variables, a static nested class is associated with its enclosing class. And like class methods, a static nested class cannot refer directly to instance variables or methods defined in its enclosing class—it can use them only through an object reference.

As with instance methods and variables, an inner class is associated with an instance of its enclosing class and has direct access to that object's instance variables and methods. Also, because an inner class is associated with an instance, it cannot define any static members itself.

To help further differentiate the terms nested class and inner class, it's useful to think about them in the following way. The term nested class reflects the *syntactic relationship between two classes*; that is, syntactically, the code for one class appears within the code of another. In contrast, the term inner class reflects the *relationship between objects that are instances of the two classes*. Consider the following classes:

```
class EnclosingClass {
    ...
    class InnerClass {
        ...
    }
}
```

The interesting feature about the relationship between these two classes is not that `Inner-Class` is syntactically defined within `EnclosingClass`. Rather, it's that an instance of `InnerClass` can exist only within an instance of `EnclosingClass` and that it has direct access to the instance variables and methods of its enclosing instance. Figure 68 illustrates this idea.

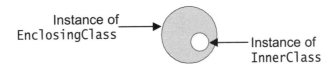

Figure 68   An instance of `InnerClass` can exist only within an instance of `EnclosingClass`.

You may encounter nested classes of both kinds in the Java platform API and be required to use them. However, most nested classes that you write will probably be inner classes.

Definition: An *inner class* is a nested class whose instance exists within an instance of its enclosing class. An inner class has direct access to the instance members of its enclosing instance.

Inner Classes

To help you get a handle on inner classes and what they are good for, let's revisit the `Stack` class. Suppose that you want to add to this class a feature that lets another class enumerate the elements in the stack, using the `java.util.Iterator`[1] interface. This interface contains three method declarations:

```
public boolean hasNext();
public Object next();
public void remove();
```

`Iterator` defines the interface for stepping once through the elements within an ordered set in order. You use it like this:

```
while (hasNext()) {
    next()
}
```

The `Stack` class itself should not implement the `Iterator` interface, because of certain limitations imposed by the API of the `Iterator` interface: Two separate objects could not enumerate the items in the `Stack` concurrently, because there's no way of knowing who's calling the `next` method; the enumeration could not be restarted, because the `Iterator` interface doesn't have methods to support that; and the enumeration could be invoked only once, because the `Iterator` interface doesn't have methods for going back to the beginning. Instead, a helper class should do the work for `Stack`.

The helper class must have access to the `Stack`'s elements and also must be able to access them directly because the `Stack`'s public interface supports only LIFO access. This is where inner classes come in.

Here's a `Stack` implementation that defines a helper class, called `StackIterator`, for enumerating the stack's elements:

```
public class Stack {
    private Vector items;

    ...//code for Stack's methods and constructors not shown...

    public Iterator iterator() {
        return new StackIterator();
    }
```

---

[1] http://java.sun.com/j2se/1.3/docs/api/java/util/Iterator.html
The `Iterator` interface was added to the Java 2 SDK 1.2 release. If you are using a JDK release, use the `java.util.Enumeration` interface instead.

```
class StackIterator implements Iterator {
    int currentItem = items.size() - 1;

    public boolean hasNext() {
        ...
    }
    public Object next() {
        ...
    }
    public void remove() {
        ...
    }
}
}
```

Note that the StackIterator class refers directly to Stack's items instance variable.

Inner classes are used primarily to implement helper classes like the one shown in this example. If you plan on handling user-interface events, you'll need to know about using inner classes because the event-handling mechanism makes extensive use of them.

You can declare an inner class without naming it. Here's yet another version of the Stack class, in this case using an *anonymous* class for its iterator:

```
public class Stack {
    private Vector items;

    ...//code for Stack's methods and constructors not shown...

    public Iterator iterator() {
        return new Iterator() {
            int currentItem = items.size() - 1;
            public boolean hasNext() {
                ...
            }
            public Object next() {
                ...
            }
            public void remove() {
                ...
            }
        }
    }
}
```

Anonymous classes can make code difficult to read. You should limit their use to those classes that are very small (no more than a method or two) and whose use is well understood, such as event-handling classes.

Other Facts about Nested Classes

Like other classes, nested classes can be declared abstract or final. The meaning of these two modifiers for nested classes is the same as for other classes. Also, you may use the access specifiers—private, public, and protected—to restrict access to nested classes, just as you do to other class members.

Any nested class, not just anonymous ones, can be declared in any block of code. A nested class declared within a method or other smaller block of code has access to any final, local variables in scope.

Summary of Nested Classes

A class defined within another class is called a nested class. Like other members of a class, a nested class can be declared static or not. A nonstatic nested class is called an inner class. An instance of an inner class can exist only within an instance of its enclosing class and has access to its enclosing class's members even if they are declared private.

Questions and Exercises: Nested Classes

Questions

1. Match each situation in the first column with the most appropriate type of nested class in the second column.

a. The only users of this nested class will be instances of the enclosing class or instances of the enclosing class's subclasses.	1. anonymous inner class
b. Anyone can use this nested class.	2. protected inner class
c. Only instances of the declaring class need to use this nested class, and a particular instance might use it several times.	3. public static nested class
d. This tiny nested class is used just once, to create an object that implements an interface.	4. protected static nested class
e. This nested class has information about its enclosing class (not about instances of the enclosing class) and is used only by its enclosing class and perhaps their subclasses.	5. private static nested class
f. Similar situation as the preceding (choice e), but not intended to be used by subclasses.	6. private inner class

2. The program `Problem.java`[1] doesn't compile. What do you need to do to make it compile? Why?

3. Use the 1.3 API documentation for the `Box` class (in the `javax.swing` package) to help you answer the following questions.

   a. What static nested class does `Box` define?

   b. What inner class does `Box` define?

   c. What is the superclass of `Box`'s inner class?

   d. Which of `Box`'s nested classes can you use from any class?

   e. How do you create an instance of `Box`'s `Filler` class?

Exercises

1. First, get the source file `InnerClassDemo.java`[2]

   a. Compile and run `InnerClassDemo.java`.[3]

   b. Make a copy of `InnerClassDemo`. Add to it an inner class named `MyActionListener` that implements the `ActionListener` interface.[4] The `ActionListener` interface defines a single method. Put the following code into your implementation of the method: `quit();`

   Delete the double forward slashes (`//`) in front of the following line of code:

   ```
   //button.addActionListener(new MyActionListener());
   ```

   Now compile and run the program. What is the difference in behavior between this version and the previous version of `InnerClassDemo`?

   c. Make a copy of the program you created in exercise 1b. Change your `ActionListener` implementation to be an anonymous inner class. (*Hint:* The program has another anonymous inner class, a `WindowAdapter`, which you can refer to for syntax help.)

2. Get the file `Class1.java`.[5]

   a. Compile and run `Class1`. What is the output?

---

[1] You can find `Problem.java` on the CD and online at: http://java.sun.com/docs/books/tutorial/java/javaOO/QandE/Problem.java

[2] You can find `InnerClassDemo.java` on the CD and online at: http://java.sun.com/docs/books/tutorial/java/javaOO/QandE/Problem.java

[3] If you have problems, see Compiling and Running Swing Programs (page 353).

[4] http://java.sun.com/products/jdk/1.3/docs/api/java/awt/event/ActionListener.html

[5] http://java.sun.com/docs/books/tutorial/java/javaOO/QandE/Class1.java

b. Create a file called Class2.java that defines subclasses of both Class1 and its inner class, InnerClass1. (Call the subclasses Class2 and InnerClass2, respectively.) InnerClass2 should override the getAnotherString method to return "InnerClass2 version of getAnotherString invoked". Class2 should define one constructor and one method:

- A no-argument constructor that initializes the inherited ic instance variable to be an instance of InnerClass2

- A main method that creates an instance of Class2 and invokes displayStrings on that instance

What is the output when you run Class2?

Answers

You can find answers to these Questions and Exercises online:

```
http://java.sun.com/docs/books/tutorial/java/javaOO/QandE/
nested-answers.html
```

Code Samples

Table 42 lists the code samples used in this chapter and where you can find the code online and on the CD that accompanies this book.

Table 42   Code Samples in Classes and Inheritance

Code Sample	CD Location	Online Location
Stack.java (page 178)	JavaTutorial/java/classes/ example/Stack.java	http://java.sun.com/docs/books/ tutorial/java/classes/example/ Stack.java
Alpha.java (page 194)	JavaTutorial/java/classes/ example/One/Alpha.java	http://java.sun.com/docs/books/ tutorial/java/classes/example/ One/Alpha.java
DeltaOne.java (page 196)	JavaTutorial/java/classes/ example/One/DeltaOne.java	http://java.sun.com/docs/books/ tutorial/java/classes/example/ One/DeltaOne.java
AlphaTwo.java (page 196)	JavaTutorial/java/classes/ example/Two/AlphaTwo.java	http://java.sun.com/docs/books/ tutorial/java/classes/example/ Two/AlphaTwo.java

Table 42   Code Samples in Classes and Inheritance

DeltaTwo.java (page 197)	JavaTutorial/java/classes/ example/Two/DeltaTwo.java	http://java.sun.com/docs/books/ tutorial/java/classes/example/ Two/DeltaTwo.java
AClass.java (page 198)	JavaTutorial/java/classes/ example/AClass.java	http://java.sun.com/docs/books/ tutorial/java/classes/example/ AClass.java
Planet.java (page 206)	JavaTutorial/java/classes/ example/Planet.java	http://java.sun.com/docs/books/ tutorial/java/classes/example/ Planet.java
Earth.java (page 206)	JavaTutorial/java/classes/ example/Earth.java	http://java.sun.com/docs/books/ tutorial/java/classes/example/ Earth.java
Superclass.java (page 207)	JavaTutorial/java/classes/ example/Superclass.java	http://java.sun.com/docs/books/ tutorial/java/classes/example/ Superclass.java
Subclass.java (page 208)	JavaTutorial/java/classes/ example/Subclass.java	http://java.sun.com/docs/books/ tutorial/java/classes /example/ Subclass.java

The section Common Problems and Their Solutions (page 391) contains solutions to common problems *Tutorial* readers have encountered.

6

Interfaces and Packages

THIS chapter talks about two more Java™ programming language features that help you to manage relationships between classes that might not otherwise be related by the class hierarchy. First, you learn how to write and use an interface—a protocol of communication between objects. Second, you will learn how to bundle classes and interfaces into packages.

Creating and Using Interfaces

The section <u>What Is an Interface?</u> (page 54) provided an introduction to interfaces. This section goes further, showing you how to create and to use interfaces and talking about why you would use an interface instead of a class.

An *interface* defines a protocol of behavior that can be implemented by any class anywhere in the class hierarchy. An interface defines a set of methods but does not implement them. A class that implements the interface agrees to implement all the methods defined in the interface, thereby agreeing to certain behavior.

Definition: An *interface* is a named collection of method definitions (without implementations). An interface can also declare constants.

Because an interface is simply a list of unimplemented, and therefore abstract, methods, you might wonder how an interface differs from an abstract class. The differences are significant.

- An interface cannot implement any methods, whereas an abstract class can.
- A class can implement many interfaces but can have only one superclass.
- An interface is not part of the class hierarchy. Unrelated classes can implement the same interface.

Let's set up the example we'll be using in this section. Suppose that you have written a class that can watch stock prices coming over a data feed. This class allows other classes to register to be notified when the value of a particular stock changes. First, your class, which we'll call StockMonitor, would implement a method that lets other objects register for notification:

```
public class StockMonitor {
    public void watchStock(StockWatcher watcher,
                        String tickerSymbol, double delta) {
        ...
    }
}
```

The first argument to this method is a StockWatcher object. StockWatcher is the name of an interface whose code you will see in the next section. That interface declares one method: valueChanged. An object that wants to be notified of stock changes must be an instance of a class that implements this interface and thus implements the valueChanged method. The other two arguments provide the symbol of the stock to watch and the amount of change that the watcher considers interesting enough to be notified of. When the StockMonitor class detects an interesting change, it calls the valueChanged method of the watcher.

The watchStock method ensures, through the data type of its first argument, that all registered objects implement the valueChanged method. It makes sense to use an interface data type here because it matters only that registrants implement a particular method. If Stock-Monitor had used a class name as the data type, that would artificially force a class relationship on its users. Because a class can have only one superclass, it would also limit what type of objects can use this service. By using an interface, the registered object's class could be anything—Applet or Thread, for instance—thus allowing any class anywhere in the class hierarchy to use this service.

Defining an Interface

Figure 69 shows that an interface definition has two components: the interface declaration and the interface body. The interface declaration declares various attributes about the interface, such as its name and whether it extends other interfaces. The interface body contains the constant and the method declarations for that interface.

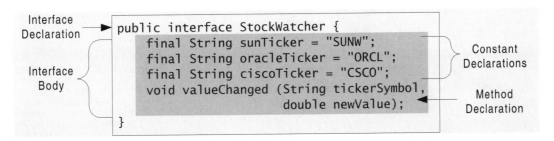

Figure 69 The StockWatcher interface and the structure of an interface definition.

```
public interface StockWatcher {
    final String sunTicker = "SUNW";
    final String oracleTicker = "ORCL";
    final String ciscoTicker = "CSCO";
    void valueChanged(String tickerSymbol, double newValue);
}
```

The interface shown in Figure 69 is the StockWatcher interface mentioned previously. This interface defines three constants, which are the ticker symbols of watchable stocks. This interface also declares, but does not implement, the valueChanged method. Classes that implement this interface provide the implementation for that method.

The Interface Declaration

Figure 70 shows all possible components of an interface declaration.

`public`	Makes this interface public.
`interface InterfaceName`	Class cannot be instantiated.
`Extends SuperInterfaces`	This interface's superinterfaces.
`{`	
`InterfaceBody`	
`}`	

Figure 70 The possible components of an interface declaration and their purposes.

Two elements are required in an interface declaration—the `interface` keyword and the name of the interface. The `public` access specifier indicates that the interface can be used by any class in any package. If you do not specify that your interface is public, your interface will be accessible only to classes that are defined in the same package as the interface.

An interface declaration can have one other component: a list of superinterfaces. An interface can extend other interfaces, just as a class can extend or subclass another class. However, whereas a class can extend only one other class, an interface can extend any number of interfaces. The list of superinterfaces is a comma-separated list of all the interfaces extended by the new interface.

The Interface Body

The interface body contains method declarations for all the methods included in the interface. A method declaration within an interface is followed by a semicolon (;) because an interface does not provide implementations for the methods declared within it. All methods declared in an interface are implicitly `public` and `abstract`.

An interface can contain constant declarations in addition to method declarations. All constant values defined in an interface are implicitly `public`, `static`, and `final`.

Member declarations in an interface disallow the use of some declaration modifiers; you cannot use `transient`, `volatile`, or `synchronized` in a member declaration in an interface. Also, you may not use the `private` and `protected` specifiers when declaring members of an interface.

Note: Previous releases of the Java platform allowed you to use the `abstract` modifier on interface declarations and on method declarations within interfaces. However, this is unnecessary, because interfaces and their methods are implicitly abstract. You should not use `abstract` in your interface declarations or in your method declarations within interfaces.

Implementing an Interface

An interface defines a protocol of behavior. A class that implements an interface adheres to the protocol defined by that interface. To declare a class that implements an interface, include an `implements` clause in the class declaration. Your class can implement more than one interface (the Java platform supports multiple inheritance for interfaces), so the `implements` keyword is followed by a comma-separated list of the interfaces implemented by the class.

By Convention: The `implements` clause follows the `extends` clause, if it exists.

Here's a partial example of an applet that implements the `StockWatcher` interface:

```
public class StockApplet extends Applet implements StockWatcher {
    ...
    public void valueChanged(String tickerSymbol, double newValue) {
        if (tickerSymbol.equals(sunTicker)) {
            ...
        } else if (tickerSymbol.equals(oracleTicker)) {
            ...
        } else if (tickerSymbol.equals(ciscoTicker)) {
            ...
        }
    }
}
```

Note that this class refers to each constant defined in `StockWatcher`, `sunTicker`, `oracle-Ticker`, and `ciscoTicker`, by its simple name. Classes that implement an interface inherit the constants defined within that interface. So those classes can use simple names to refer to the constants. Any other class can use an interface's constants with a qualified name, like this:

```
StockWatcher.sunTicker
```

When a class implements an interface, it is essentially signing a contract. Either the class must implement all the methods declared in the interface and its superinterfaces, or the class must be declared `abstract`. The method signature—the name and the number and type of arguments—in the class must match the method signature as it appears in the interface. The `StockApplet` implements the `StockWatcher` interface, so the applet provides an implementation for the `valueChanged` method. The method ostensibly updates the applet's display or otherwise uses this information.

Using an Interface as a Type

When you define a new interface, you are defining a new reference data type. You can use interface names anywhere you can use any other data type name. Recall that the data type for the first argument to the watchStock method in the StockMonitor class is StockWatcher:

```
public class StockMonitor {
    public void watchStock(StockWatcher watcher,
                           String tickerSymbol, double delta) {
        ...
    }
}
```

Only an instance of a class that implements the interface can be assigned to a reference variable whose type is an interface name. So only instances of a class that implements the StockWatcher interface can register to be notified of stock value changes. StockWatcher objects are guaranteed to have a valueChanged method.

Interfaces Cannot Grow

Suppose that you want to add some functionality to StockWatcher. For instance, suppose that you want to add a method that reports the current stock price, regardless of whether the value changed:

```
public interface StockWatcher {
    final String sunTicker = "SUNW";
    final String oracleTicker = "ORCL";
    final String ciscoTicker = "CSCO";
    void valueChanged(String tickerSymbol, double newValue);
    void currentValue(String tickerSymbol, double newValue);
}
```

However, if you make this change, all classes that implement the old StockWatcher interface will break because they don't implement the interface anymore! Programmers relying on this interface will protest loudly.

Try to anticipate all uses for your interface up front and specify it completely from the beginning. Given that this is often impossible, you may need either to create more interfaces later or to break your customer's code. For example, you could create a StockWatcher subinterface called StockTracker that declared the new method:

```
public interface StockTracker extends StockWatcher {
    void currentValue(String tickerSymbol, double newValue);
}
```

Now users of your code can choose to upgrade to the new interface or to stick with the old interface.

Summary of Interfaces

An interface defines a protocol of communication between two objects. An interface definition is comprised of a declaration and a body. The section The Interface Declaration (page 230) shows all possible components of an interface declaration. The interface body contains declarations, but no implementations, for a set of methods. An interface might also contain constant definitions. A class that implements an interface must implement all the methods declared in the interface. An interface name can be used anywhere a type can be used.

Questions and Exercises: Interfaces

Questions

1. What methods would a class that implements the `java.util.Iterator` interface[1] have to implement?

2. What is wrong with the following interface?

```
public interface SomethingIsWrong {
    public void aMethod(int aValue) {
        System.out.println("Hi Mom");
    }
}
```

3. Fix the interface in question 2.

4. Is the following interface valid?

```
public interface Marker {
}
```

Exercises

1. Write a class that implements the `Iterator` interface found in the `java.util` package. The ordered data for this exercise is the 13 cards in a suit from a deck of cards. The first call to `next` returns 2, the subsequent call returns the next highest card, 3, and so on, up to `Ace`. Write a small `main` method to test your class.

2. Suppose that you have written a time server, which periodically notifies its clients of the current date and time. Write an interface that the server could use to enforce a particular protocol on its clients.

---

[1] `Iterator` was introduced to the Java platform in the 1.2 release. If you are using a prior release, answer this question with regard to the `Enumerator` interface instead.

Answers

You can find answers to these Questions and Exercises online:

```
http://java.sun.com/docs/books/tutorial/java/interpack/QandE/
interfaces-answers.html
```

Creating and Using Packages

To make classes easier to find and to use, to avoid naming conflicts, and to control access, programmers bundle groups of related classes and interfaces into packages.

Definition: A *package* is a collection of related classes and interfaces providing access protection and namespace management.

The classes and interfaces that are part of the Java platform are members of various packages that bundle classes by function: fundamental classes are in java.lang, classes for reading and writing (input and output) are in java.io, and so on. You can put your classes and interfaces in packages, too.

Let's look at a set of classes and examine why you might want to put them in a package. Suppose that you write a group of classes that represent a collection of graphic objects, such as circles, rectangles, lines, and points. You also write an interface, Draggable, that classes implement if they can be dragged with the mouse by the user:

```
//in the Graphic.java file
public abstract class Graphic {
    ...
}

//in the Circle.java file
public class Circle extends Graphic implements Draggable {
    ...
}

//in the Rectangle.java file
public class Rectangle extends Graphic implements Draggable {
    ...
}

//in the Draggable.java file
public interface Draggable {
    ...
}
```

You should bundle these classes and the interface in a package for several reasons:

- You and other programmers can easily determine that these classes and interfaces are related.
- You and other programmers know where to find classes and interfaces that provide graphics-related functions.
- The names of your classes won't conflict with class names in other packages, because the package creates a new namespace.
- You can allow classes within the package to have unrestricted access to one another yet still restrict access for classes outside the package.

Creating a Package

To create a package, you put a class or an interface in it. To do this, you put a `package` statement at the top of the source file in which the class or the interface is defined. For example, the following code appears in the source file `Circle.java` and puts the `Circle` class in the `graphics` package:

```
package graphics;

public class Circle extends Graphic implements Draggable {
    . . .
}
```

The `Circle` class is a public member of the `graphics` package.

You must include a `package` statement at the top of every source file that defines a class or an interface that is to be a member of the `graphics` package. So you would also include the statement in `Rectangle.java` and so on:

```
package graphics;

public class Rectangle extends Graphic implements Draggable {
    . . .
}
```

The scope of the `package` statement is the entire source file, so all classes and interfaces defined in `Circle.java` and `Rectangle.java` are also members of the `graphics` package. If you put multiple classes in a single source file, only one may be public, and it must share the name of the source file's base name.[1] Only public package members are accessible from outside the package.

---

[1] Some compilers might allow more than one public file per `.java` file. However, we recommend that you use the convention one public class per file, because it makes public classes easier to find and works for all compilers.

If you do not use a `package` statement, your class or interface ends up in the *default package*, which is a package that has no name. Generally speaking, the default package is only for small or temporary applications or when you are just beginning development. Otherwise, classes and interfaces belong in named packages.

Naming a Package

With programmers all over the world writing classes and interfaces using the Java programming language, it is likely that two programmers will use the same name for two different classes. In fact, the previous example does just that: It defines a `Rectangle` class when there is already a `Rectangle` class in the `java.awt` package. Yet the compiler allows both classes to have the same name. Why? Because they are in different packages, and the fully qualified name of each class includes the package name. That is, the fully qualified name of the `Rectangle` class in the `graphics` package is `graphics.Rectangle`, and the fully qualified name of the `Rectangle` class in the `java.awt` package is `java.awt.Rectangle`.

This generally works just fine unless two independent programmers use the same name for their packages. What prevents this? Convention.

By Convention: Companies use their reversed Internet domain name in their package names, like this: `com.company.package`. Some companies now choose to drop the first element—`com.` in this example—from their package names. Name collisions that occur within a single company need to be handled by convention within that company, perhaps by including the region or the project name after the company name, for example, `com.company.region.package`.

Using Package Members

Only public package members are accessible outside the package in which they are defined. To use a public package member from outside its package, you must do one or more of the following:

- Refer to the member by its long (qualified) name
- Import the package member
- Import the member's entire package

Each is appropriate for different situations, as explained in the following sections.

Referring to a Package Member by Name

So far, the examples in this book have referred to classes and interfaces by their simple names, such as `Rectangle` and `StockWatcher`. You can use a package member's simple name if the code you are writing is in the same package as that member or if the member's package has been imported.

However, if you are trying to use a member from a different package and that package has not been imported, you must use the member's qualified name, which includes the package name. This is the qualified name for the `Rectangle` class declared in the `graphics` package in the previous example:

```
graphics.Rectangle
```

You could use this long name to create an instance of `graphics.Rectangle`:

```
graphics.Rectangle myRect = new graphics.Rectangle();
```

You'll find that using qualified names is okay for one-shot uses. But you'd likely get annoyed if you had to write `graphics.Rectangle` again and again. Also, your code would get messy and difficult to read. In such cases, you can import the member instead.

Importing a Package Member

To import a specific member into the current file, put an `import` statement at the beginning of your file before any class or interface definitions but after the `package` statement, if there is one. Here's how you would import the `Circle` class from the `graphics` package created in the previous section:

```
import graphics.Circle;
```

Now you can refer to the `Circle` class by its simple name:

```
Circle myCircle = new Circle();
```

This approach works well if you use just a few members from the `graphics` package. But if you use many classes and interfaces from a package, you can import the entire package.

Importing an Entire Package

To import all the classes and interfaces contained in a particular package, use the `import` statement with the asterisk (*) wildcard character:

```
import graphics.*;
```

Now you can refer to any class or interface in the `graphics` package by its short name:

```
Circle myCircle = new Circle();
Rectangle myRectangle = new Rectangle();
```

The asterisk in the `import` statement can be used only to specify all the classes within a package, as shown here. It cannot be used to match a subset of the classes in a package. For example, the following does not match all the classes in the `graphics` package that begin with A:

```
import graphics.A*;    // does not work
```

Instead, it generates a compiler error. With the `import` statement, you can import only a single package member or an entire package.

For your convenience, the Java runtime system automatically imports three entire packages:

- The default package (the package with no name)
- The `java.lang` package
- The current package

Disambiguating a Name

If by some chance a member in one package shares the same name with a member in another package and both packages are imported, you must refer to each member by its qualified name. For example, the previous example defined a class named `Rectangle` in the `graphics` package. The `java.awt` package also contains a `Rectangle` class. If both `graphics` and `java.awt` have been imported, the following is ambiguous:

```
Rectangle rect;
```

In such a situation, you have to be more specific and use the member's qualified name to indicate exactly which `Rectangle` class you want:

```
graphics.Rectangle rect;
```

Managing Source and Class Files

Many implementations of the Java platform rely on hierarchical file systems to manage source and class files, although *The Java Language Specification* does not require this. The strategy is as follows.

You put the source code for a class or an interface in a text file whose name is the simple name of the class or the interface and whose extension is `.java`. Then you put the source file in a directory whose name reflects the name of the package to which the class or the interface belongs. For example, the source code for the `Rectangle` class would be in a file named

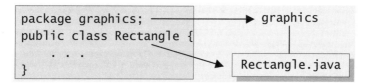

Figure 71 The source code for the Rectangle class is in the file Rectangle.java, which is located in a folder named graphics.

Rectangle.java, and the file would be in a directory named graphics. The graphics directory might be anywhere on the file system. Figure 71 shows how this works.

The qualified name of the package member and the path name to the file are parallel, assuming the UNIX file name separator slash (/):

class name	graphics.Rectangle
pathname to file	graphics/Rectangle.java

As you may recall, by convention a company uses its reversed Internet domain name in its package names. The fictional company whose Internet domain name is taranis.com would precede all its package names with com.taranis. Each component of the package name corresponds to a subdirectory. So if Taranis had a graphics package that contained a Rectangle.java source file, it would be contained in a series of subdirectories, as shown in Figure 72.

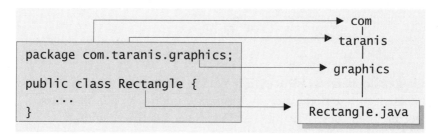

Figure 72 By convention, companies use their Internet domain names in reverse in their package names.

When you compile a source file, the compiler creates a different output file for each class and interface defined in it. The base name of the output file is the name of the class or the interface, and its extension is .class, as shown in Figur e73.

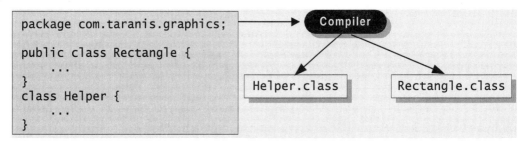

Figure 73   The compiler creates a separate .class file for every class.

Like a .java file, a .class file should also be in a series of directories that reflect the package name. However, it does not have to be in the same directory as its source. You could arrange your source and class directories separately, as in Figure 74.

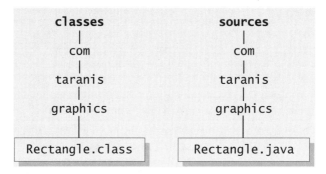

Figure 74   An example of how to arrange your source code and class files separately.

By doing this, you can give the classes directory to other programmers without revealing your sources.

Why all the bother about directories and file names? You need to manage your source and class files in this manner so that the compiler and the interpreter can find all the classes and interfaces your program uses. When the compiler encounters a new class as it's compiling your program, it must be able to find the class so as to resolve names, do type checking, and so on. Similarly, when the interpreter encounters a new class as it's running your program, it must be able to find the class to invoke its methods, and so on. Both the compiler and the interpreter search for classes in each directory or ZIP file listed in your class path.

Definition: A *class path* is an ordered list of directories or ZIP files in which to search for class files.

Each directory listed in the class path is a top-level directory in which package directories appear. From the top-level directory, the compiler and the interpreter can construct the rest of the path, based on the package and the class name for the class. For example, the class path entry for the directory structure shown in the previous diagram would include `classes` but not `com` or any of the directories below `com`. Both the compiler and the interpreter construct the path name to a `.class` file with its full package name.

By default, the compiler and the interpreter search the current directory and the ZIP file containing the Java platform class files. In other words, the current directory and the Java platform class files are automatically in your class path. Most, if not all, classes can be found in these two locations. So it's likely that you don't have to worry about your class path. In some cases, however, you might have to set your class path. Refer to the <u>Path Help</u> (page 540) for more information.

Summary of Creating and Using Packages

To create a package, you put a class or an interface in it. To put a class or an interface into a package, you put a `package` statement as the first statement in the source file for the class or the interface. The path name of the source and class file of a class or an interface mirrors the name of the package.

To use a class or an interface that's in a different package, you have three choices: You can use the fully qualified name of the class or the interface, you can import the class or the interface, or you can import the entire package of which the class or the interface is a member.

You might have to set your class path so that the compiler and the interpreter can find the source and class files for your classes and interfaces.

Questions and Exercises: Creating and Using Packages

Questions

1. Assume that you have written some classes. Belatedly, you decide that they should be split into three packages, as listed in Table 43. Furthermore, assume that the classes are currently in the default package (they have no `package` statements).

Table 43   Package Names and Class Names

Package Name	Class Name
`mygame.server`	`Server`
`mygame.shared`	`Utilities`
`mygame.client`	`Client`

    a. What line of code will you need to add to each source file to put each class in the right package?

    b. To adhere to the directory structure described in <u>Managing Source and Class Files</u> (page 238), you will need to create some subdirectories in your development directory and to put source files in the correct subdirectories. What subdirectories must you create? Which subdirectory does each source file go in?

    c. Do you think you'll need to make any other changes to the source files to make them compile correctly? If so, what?

Exercises

1. Download the source files pointed to by this page:

   ```
   http://java.sun.com/docs/books/tutorial/books/3e/exercises/
   packages.html
   ```

   a. Implement the changes you proposed in question 1, using the source files you just downloaded.

   b. Compile the revised source files. (*Hint:* If you're invoking the compiler from the command line (as opposed to using a builder), invoke the compiler from the directory that contains the `mygame` directory you just created.)

Answers

You can find answers to these Questions and Exercises online:

```
http://java.sun.com/docs/books/tutorial/java/interpack/QandE/
packages-answers.html
```

Code Samples

This chapter contains no complete examples.

The section <u>Common Problems and Their Solutions</u> (page 391) contains solutions to common problems *Tutorial* readers have encountered.

Handling Errors
Using Exceptions

IF there's a golden rule of programming, it's this: Errors occur in software programs. However, what really matters is what happens *after* the error occurs. How is the error handled? Who handles it? Can the program recover, or should it print error messages and exit? The Java™ programming language uses *exceptions* for error handling. This chapter describes how you can use exceptions in your programs to handle errors.

What Is an Exception?

The term *exception* is shorthand for the phrase "exceptional event."

Definition: An *exception* is an event that disrupts the normal flow of instructions during the execution of a program.

When an error occurs within a method, the method creates an object and hands it off to the runtime system. The object, called an *exception object*,[1] contains information about the error, including its type and the state of the program when the error occurred. Creating an exception object and handing it to the runtime system is called *throwing an exception*.

After a method throws an exception, the runtime system attempts to find something to handle it. The set of possible "somethings" to handle the exception is the ordered list of methods that had been called to get to the method where the error occurred. The list of methods is known as the *call stack* (Figure 75).

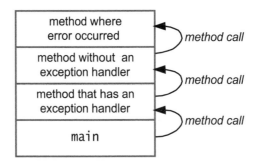

Figure 75 The call stack.

The runtime system searches the call stack for a method that contains a block of code that can handle the exception. This block of code is called an *exception handler*. The search begins with the method in which the error occurred and proceeds through the call stack in the

---

[1]   Exception objects inherit from the `Throwable` class.

reverse order that the methods were called. When an appropriate handler is found, the run-time system passes the exception to the handler. An exception handler is considered appro-priate if the type of the exception object thrown is the same as the type that can be handled by the handler. The exception handler chosen is said to *catch the exception*. If the runtime system exhaustively searches all the methods on the call stack without finding an appropriate exception handler, the runtime system (and, consequently, the program) terminates (Figure 76).

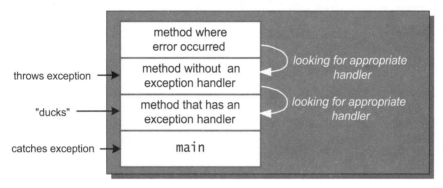

Figure 76 When an error occurs, the runtime system searches the call stack for an appropriate error handler.

Using exceptions to manage errors has some advantages over traditional error-management techniques. You can learn more in the section <u>Advantages of Exceptions</u> (page 260).

The Catch or Specify Requirement

The Java runtime system requires that a method must either catch or specify all checked exceptions that can be thrown by that method. This requirement has several components that need further description: "catch," "specify," "checked exceptions," and "exceptions that can be thrown by that method."

Catch

A method can catch an exception by providing an exception handler for that type of exception. The section <u>Catching and Handling Exceptions</u> (page 246) introduces an example program, talks about catching exceptions, and shows you how to write an exception handler for it.

Specify

A method specifies that it can throw exceptions by using the throws clause in the method declaration. The section <u>Specifying the Exceptions Thrown by a Method</u> (page 255) talks about specifying exceptions that a method throws and shows you how to do it.

..cked exceptions

There are two kinds of exceptions: runtime exceptions and nonruntime exceptions. Runtime exceptions occur within the Java runtime system: arithmetic exceptions (such as dividing by zero), pointer exceptions (such as trying to access an object's members through a `null` reference), and indexing exceptions (such as trying to access an array element with an index that is too large or too small). A method does not have to catch or specify runtime exceptions, although it may.

Nonruntime exceptions are exceptions that occur in code outside of the Java runtime system. For example, exceptions that occur during I/O are nonruntime exceptions. The compiler ensures that nonruntime exceptions are caught or specified; thus, they are also called *checked exceptions*.

Some consider the fact that you do not have to catch or specify runtime exceptions a loophole in the exception-handling mechanism. Many programmers are tempted to use runtime exceptions instead of checked exceptions so that they don't have to catch or specify them. In general, this is not recommended. The section Runtime Exceptions— The Controversy (page 260) talks about when it's appropriate to use runtime exceptions.

Exceptions that can be thrown by a method

The exceptions that a method can throw include

- Any exception thrown directly by the method with the `throw` statement
- Any exception thrown indirectly by calling another method that throws an exception

Catching and Handling Exceptions

This section shows you how to use the three components of an exception handler—the `try`, `catch`, and `finally` blocks—to write an exception handler. The last part of this section walks through the example and analyzes what occurs during various scenarios.

The following example defines and implements a class named `ListOfNumbers`.[1] Upon construction, `ListOfNumbers` creates a `Vector` that contains ten `Integer` elements with sequential values 0 through 9. The `ListOfNumbers` class also defines a method named `writeList` that writes the list of numbers into a text file called `OutFile.txt`. This example uses output classes defined in `java.io`, which are covered in Chapter 9, I/O: Reading and Writing (page 313).

```
// Note: This class won't compile by design!
import java.io.*;
import java.util.Vector;
```

---

[1] `ListOfNumbers.java` is included on the CD and is available online. See Code Samples (page 268).

```
public class ListOfNumbers {
    private Vector victor;
    private static final int SIZE = 10;

    public ListOfNumbers () {
        victor = new Vector(SIZE);
        for (int i = 0; i < SIZE; i++) {
            victor.addElement(new Integer(i));
        }
    }

    public void writeList() {
        PrintWriter out = new PrintWriter(new FileWriter("OutFile.txt"));

        for (int i = 0; i < SIZE; i++) {
            out.println("Value at: " + i + " = " + victor.elementAt(i));
        }

        out.close();
    }
}
```

The first line in boldface is a call to a constructor. The constructor initializes an output stream on a file. If the file cannot be opened, the constructor throws an IOException. The second line in boldface type is a call to the Vector class's elementAt method, which throws an ArrayIndexOutOfBoundsException if the value of its argument is too small (less than zero) or too large (larger than the number of elements currently contained by the Vector).

If you try to compile the ListOfNumbers class, the compiler prints an error message about the exception thrown by the FileWriter constructor. However, it does *not* display an error message about the exception thrown by elementAt. The reason is that the exception thrown by the constructor, IOException, is a checked exception and the one thrown by the elementAt method, ArrayIndexOutOfBoundsException, is a runtime exception. The Java platform requires only that a program deal with checked exceptions, so you get only one error message.

Now that you're familiar with the ListOfNumbers class and where the exceptions can be thrown within it, you're ready to read about how to write exception handlers to catch and handle those exceptions.

The try Block

The first step in constructing an exception handler is to enclose the statements that might throw an exception within a try block. In general, a try block looks like this.

```
try {
    statements
}
```

The segment of code labeled *statements* contains one or more legal statements that might throw an exception.

To construct an exception handler for the writeList method from the ListOfNumbers class, you need to enclose the exception-throwing statements of the writeList method within a try block. There is more than one way to do this. You can put each statement that might throw an exception within its own try block and provide separate exception handlers for each. Or, you can put all the writeList statements within a single try block and associate multiple handlers with it. The following listing uses one try block for the entire method because the code in question is very short:

```
PrintWriter out = null;

try {
    System.out.println("Entered try statement");
    out = new PrintWriter(new FileWriter("OutFile.txt"));
    for (int i = 0; i < size; i++) {
        out.println("Value at: " + i + " = " + victor.elementAt(i));
    }
}
```

If an exception occurs within the try block, that exception is handled by an exception handler associated with it. To associate an exception handler with a try block, put a catch statement after it. The next section shows you how.

The catch Block(s)

You associate exception handlers with a try block by providing one or more catch blocks directly after the try. No code can be between the end of the try and the beginning of the first catch statement:

```
try {
    ...
} catch (ExceptionType name) {
    ...
} catch (ExceptionType name) {
    ...
} ...
```

Each catch block is an exception handler and handles the type of exception indicated by its argument. The argument type, *ExceptionType*, declares the type of exception that the handler can handle and must be the name of a class that inherits from the <u>Throwable</u>[1] class. The handler can refer to the exception with *name*.

The catch block contains a series of statements. These statements are executed if and when the exception handler is invoked. The runtime system invokes the exception handler when the handler is the first one in the call stack whose *ExceptionType* matches the type of the exception thrown. The system considers it a match if the thrown object can legally be assigned to the exception handler's argument.

Here are two exception handlers for writeList method—one for each of the two types of exceptions that can be thrown within the try block:

```
try {
    ...
} catch (ArrayIndexOutOfBoundsException e) {
    System.err.println("Caught ArrayIndexOutOfBoundsException: "
                        + e.getMessage());
} catch (IOException e) {
    System.err.println("Caught IOException: " + e.getMessage());
}
```

The handlers shown print an error message. Although simple, this might be the behavior you want. The exception gets caught, the user is notified, and the program continues to execute. However, exception handlers can do more. They can do error recovery, prompt the user to make a decision, or decide to exit the program.

The finally Block

The final step in setting up an exception handler is to clean up before allowing control to be passed to a different part of the program. You do this by enclosing the clean up code within a finally block. The finally block is optional and provides a mechanism to clean up regardless of what happens within the try block. Use the finally block to close files or to release other system resources.

The try block of the writeList method that you've been working with here opens a Print-Writer. The program should close that stream before exiting the writeList method. This poses a somewhat complicated problem because writeList's try block can exit in one of three ways.

1. The new FileWriter statement fails and throws an IOException.
2. The victor.elementAt(i) statement fails and throws an ArrayIndexOutOfBounds-Exception.
3. Everything succeeds and the try block exits normally.

---

[1] http://java.sun.com/j2se/1.3/docs/api/java/lang/Throwable.html

The runtime system always executes the statements within the `finally` block regardless of what happens within the `try` block. So it's the perfect place to perform cleanup.

The following `finally` block for the `writeList` method cleans up and closes the `Print-Writer`:

```
finally {
    if (out != null) {
        System.out.println("Closing PrintWriter");
        out.close();
    } else {
        System.out.println("PrintWriter not open");
    }
}
```

In the `writeList` example, you could provide for cleanup without the intervention of a `finally` statement. For example, you could put the code to close the `PrintWriter` at the end of the `try` block and again within the exception handler for `ArrayIndexOutOfBoundsException`, as shown here:

```
try {
    ...
    out.close();        // don't do this; it duplicates code
} catch (ArrayIndexOutOfBoundsException e) {
    out.close();        // don't do this; it duplicates code
    System.err.println("Caught ArrayIndexOutOfBoundsException: "
                        + e.getMessage());
} catch (IOException e) {
    System.err.println("Caught IOException: " + e.getMessage());
}
```

However, this duplicates code, thus making the code difficult to read and error prone if you later modify it. For example, if you add to the `try` block code that can throw a new type of exception, you have to remember to close the `PrintWriter` within the new exception handler.

Putting It All Together

The previous sections describe how to construct the `try`, `catch`, and `finally` code blocks for the `writeList` example. Next, we walk you through the code and investigate what happens during three scenarios.

When all the components are put together, the `writeList` method looks like this:

```
public void writeList() {
    PrintWriter out = null;
```

```
    try {
        System.out.println("Entering try statement");
        out = new PrintWriter(new FileWriter("OutFile.txt"));
        for (int i = 0; i < size; i++) {
            out.println("Value at: " + i + " = " + victor.elementAt(i));
        }
    } catch (ArrayIndexOutOfBoundsException e) {
        System.err.println("Caught ArrayIndexOutOfBoundsException: "
                            + e.getMessage());
    } catch (IOException e) {
        System.err.println("Caught IOException: " + e.getMessage());
    } finally {
        if (out != null) {
            System.out.println("Closing PrintWriter");
            out.close();
        } else {
            System.out.println("PrintWriter not open");
        }
    }
}
```

As mentioned previously, the `try` block in this method has three exit possibilities.

1. The `new FileWriter` statement fails and throws an `IOException`.
2. The `victor.elementAt(i)` statement fails and throws an `ArrayIndexOutOfBounds-Exception`.
3. Everything succeeds and the `try` statement exits normally.

Let's look at what happens in the `writeList` method during each of these exit possibilities.

Scenario 1: An IOException Occurs

The statement that creates a `FileWriter` can fail for a number of reasons. For example, the constructor for `FileWriter` throws an `IOException` if the user doesn't have write permission on the file or directory, or the file system is full, or the directory for the file doesn't exist.

When `FileWriter` throws an `IOException`, the runtime system immediately stops executing the `try` block. The runtime system then starts searching at the top of the method call stack for an appropriate exception handler. In this example, when the `IOException` occurs, the `FileWriter` constructor is at the top of the call stack. However, the `FileWriter` constructor doesn't have an appropriate exception handler, so the runtime system checks the next method in the method call stack—the `writeList` method. The `writeList` method has two exception handlers: one for `ArrayIndexOutOfBoundsException` and one for `IOException`.

The runtime system checks writeList's handlers in the order in which they appear after the try statement. The argument to the first exception handler is ArrayIndexOutOfBoundsException. Since this does not match the type of exception that was thrown, IOException, the runtime system continues its search for an appropriate exception handler.

Next, the runtime system checks writeList's second exception handler. This handler handles IOExceptions (since it takes IOException as an argument). Now that the runtime has found an appropriate handler, the code in that catch clause is executed.

After the exception handler has executed, the runtime system passes control to the finally block. In this scenario, the PrintWriter was never opened and doesn't need to be closed. After the finally block has completed executing, the program continues with the first statement after the finally block.

Here's the complete output that you see from the ListOfNumbers program when an IOException is thrown:

```
Entering try statement
Caught IOException: OutFile.txt
PrintWriter not open
```

The boldface code in the following listing shows the statements that get executed during this scenario:

```
public void writeList() {
    PrintWriter out = null;

    try {
        System.out.println("Entering try statement");
        out = new PrintWriter(new FileWriter("OutFile.txt"));
        for (int i = 0; i < size; i++) {
            out.println("Value at: " + i + " = " + victor.elementAt(i));
        }
    } catch (ArrayIndexOutOfBoundsException e) {
        System.err.println("Caught ArrayIndexOutOfBoundsException: "
                            + e.getMessage());
    } catch (IOException e) {
        System.err.println("Caught IOException: " + e.getMessage());
    } finally {
        if (out != null) {
            System.out.println("Closing PrintWriter");
            out.close();
        } else {
            System.out.println("PrintWriter not open");
        }
    }
}
```

Scenario 2: An ArrayIndexOutOfBoundsException Occurs

In this scenario, the argument passed to the Vector's elementAt method is out of bounds. The argument is either less than 0 or is larger than the size of the array. Because of how the code is written, this is impossible, but suppose that a bug is introduced into the code when someone modifies it.

As in scenario 1, when the exception occurs, the runtime system stops executing the try block and attempts to locate an exception handler for an ArrayIndexOutOfBoundsException. The runtime system searches for an appropriate exception handler. It finds the catch statement in the writeList method, which handles exceptions of the type ArrayIndexOutOfBoundsException. Because the type of the thrown exception matches the type of the exception handler, the runtime system executes this exception handler.

After the exception handler has run, the runtime system passes control to the finally block. In this particular scenario, the PrintWriter was open, so the finally statement closes it. After the finally block has completed executing, the program continues with the first statement after the finally block.

Following is the complete output that you see from the ListOfNumbers program when an ArrayIndexOutOfBoundsException is thrown:

```
Entering try statement
Caught ArrayIndexOutOfBoundsException: 10 >= 10
Closing PrintWriter
```

The boldface code in the following listing shows the statements that get executed during this scenario:

```
public void writeList() {
    PrintWriter out = null;

    try {
        System.out.println("Entering try statement");
        out = new PrintWriter(new FileWriter("OutFile.txt"));

        for (int i = 0; i < size; i++) {
            out.println("Value at: " + i + " = " + victor.elementAt(i));
        }
    } catch (ArrayIndexOutOfBoundsException e) {
        System.err.println("Caught ArrayIndexOutOfBoundsException: "
                            + e.getMessage());
    } catch (IOException e) {
        System.err.println("Caught IOException: " + e.getMessage());
    } finally {
        if (out != null) {
            System.out.println("Closing PrintWriter");
            out.close();
```

```
        } else {
            System.out.println("PrintWriter not open");
        }
    }
}
```

Scenario 3: The try Block Exits Normally

In this scenario, all the statements within the scope of the `try` block execute successfully and throw no exceptions. Execution falls off the end of the `try` block, and the runtime system passes control to the `finally` block. Because everything was successful, the `PrintWriter` is open when control reaches the `finally` block, which closes the `PrintWriter`. Again, after the `finally` block has completed executing, the program continues with the first statement after the `finally` block.

Here is the output from the `ListOfNumbers` program when no exceptions are thrown:

```
Entering try statement
Closing PrintWriter
```

The boldface code in the following listing shows the statements that get executed during this scenario:

```
public void writeList() {
    PrintWriter out = null;

    try {
        System.out.println("Entering try statement");
        out = new PrintWriter(new FileWriter("OutFile.txt"));
        for (int i = 0; i < size; i++) {
            out.println("Value at: " + i + " = " + victor.elementAt(i));
        }
    } catch (ArrayIndexOutOfBoundsException e) {
        System.err.println("Caught ArrayIndexOutOfBoundsException: "
                            + e.getMessage());
    } catch (IOException e) {
        System.err.println("Caught IOException: " + e.getMessage());
    } finally {
        if (out != null) {
            System.out.println("Closing PrintWriter");
            out.close();
        } else {
            System.out.println("PrintWriter not open");
        }
    }
}
```

Specifying the Exceptions Thrown by a Method

The previous section showed you how to write an exception handler for the writeList method in the ListOfNumbers class. Sometimes, it's appropriate for your code to catch exceptions that can occur within it. In other cases, however, it's better to let a method farther up the call stack handle the exception. For example, if you were providing the ListOfNumbers class as part of a package of classes, you probably couldn't anticipate the needs of all the users of your package. In this case, it's better to *not* catch the exception and to allow a method farther up the call stack to handle it.

If the writeList method doesn't catch the checked exceptions that can occur within it, the writeList method must specify that it can throw these exceptions. Let's modify the original writeList method to specify the exceptions that it can throw instead of catching them. To remind you, here's the original version of the writeList method that won't compile:

```
// Note: This method won't compile by design!
public void writeList() {
    PrintWriter out = new PrintWriter(new FileWriter("OutFile.txt"));
    for (int i = 0; i < size; i++) {
        out.println("Value at: " + i + " = " + victor.elementAt(i));
    }
    out.close();
}
```

To specify that writeList can throw two exceptions, you add a throws clause to the method declaration for the writeList method. The throws clause comprises the throws keyword followed by a comma-separated list of all the exceptions thrown by that method. The clause goes after the method name and argument list and before the brace that defines the scope of the method. Here's an example:

```
public void writeList() throws IOException,
                               ArrayIndexOutOfBoundsException {
```

Remember that ArrayIndexOutOfBoundsException is a runtime exception, so you don't have to specify it in the throws clause, although you can. You could just write this:

```
public void writeList() throws IOException {
```

How to Throw Exceptions

Before you can catch an exception, some code somewhere must throw one. Any code can throw an exception: your code, code from a package written by someone else (such as the packages that come with the Java platform), or the Java runtime environment. Regardless of what throws the exception, it's always thrown with the `throw` statement.

As you have probably noticed, the Java platform provides numerous exception classes. All these classes are descendants of the `Throwable` class. And all allow programs to differentiate among the various types of exceptions that can occur during the execution of a program.

You also can create your own exception classes to represent problems that can occur within the classes that you write. Indeed, if you are a package developer, you might have to create your own set of exception classes so as to allow your users to differentiate an error that can occur in your package from errors that occur in the Java platform or other packages.

The throw Statement

All methods use the `throw` statement to throw an exception. The `throw` statement requires a single argument: a *throwable* object. Throwable objects are instances of any subclass of the `Throwable`[1] class. Here's an example of a `throw` statement:

```
throw someThrowableObject;
```

Let's look at the `throw` statement in context. The following pop method is taken from a class that implements a common stack object. The method removes the top element from the stack and returns the object:

```
public Object pop() throws EmptyStackException {
    Object obj;

    if (size == 0) {
        throw new EmptyStackException();
    }

    obj = objectAt(size - 1);
    setObjectAt(size - 1, null);
    size--;
    return obj;
}
```

The pop method checks whether any elements are on the stack. If the stack is empty (its size is equal to 0), pop instantiates a new `EmptyStackException` object (a member of `java.util`) and throws it. Later sections in this chapter explain how you can create your own exception classes. For now, all you need to remember is that you can throw only objects that inherit from the `java.lang.Throwable` class.

---

[1]   http://java.sun.com/j2se/1.3/docs/api/java/lang/Throwable.html *look @ this class*

Note that the declaration of the pop method contains a throws clause. EmptyStackExcep-tion is a checked exception, and the pop method makes no effort to catch it. Hence, the method must use the throws clause to declare that it can throw that type of exception.

The Throwable Class and Its Subclasses

The objects that inherit from the Throwable class include direct descendants (objects that inherit directly from the Throwable class) and indirect descendants (objects that inherit from children or grandchildren of the Throwable class). Figure 77 illustrates the class hierarchy of the Throwable class and its most significant subclasses. As you can see, Throwable has two direct descendants: Error and Exception.

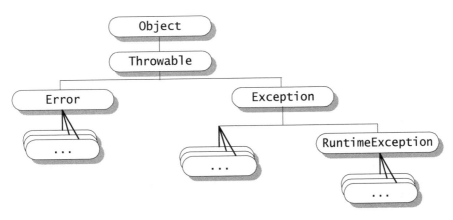

Figure 77 The Throwable class and its most significant subclasses.

Errors

When a dynamic linking failure or other "hard" failure in the Java Virtual Machine occurs, the virtual machine throws an Error. Typical programs should not catch Errors. Also, it's unlikely that typical programs will ever throw Errors.

Exceptions

Most programs throw and catch objects that derive from the Exception class. An Exception indicates that a problem occurred, but it is not a serious system problem. Most programs you write will throw and catch Exceptions (as opposed to Errors).

The Exception class has many descendants defined in the Java platform. These descendants indicate various types of exceptions that can occur. For example, IllegalAccessException signals that a particular method could not be found, and NegativeArraySizeException indicates that a program attempted to create an array with a negative size.

One `Exception` subclass has special meaning: `RuntimeException`. `RuntimeException`s are exceptions that occur within the Java Virtual Machine during runtime. An example of a runtime exception is `NullPointerException`, which occurs when a method tries to access a member of an object through a null reference. The section <u>Runtime Exceptions—The Controversy</u> (page 260) discusses why typical programs shouldn't throw runtime exceptions or subclass `RuntimeException`.

Creating Your Own Exception Classes

When faced with choosing the type of exception to throw, you can either use one written by someone else—the Java platform provides a lot of exception classes that you can use—or you can write one of your own. You should write your own exception classes if you answer yes to any of the following questions. Otherwise, you can probably use someone else's.

- Do you need an exception type that isn't represented by those in the Java platform?
- Would it help your users if they could differentiate your exceptions from those thrown by classes written by other vendors?
- Does your code throw more than one related exception?
- If you use someone else's exceptions, will your users have access to those exceptions? A similar question is, Should your package be independent and self-contained?

Suppose you are writing a linked list class that you're planning to distribute as freeware. Your linked list class supports the following methods, among others:

`objectAt(int n)`
Returns the object in the *n*th position in the list. Throws an exception if the argument is less than 0 or larger than the number of objects currently in the list.

`firstObject()`
Returns the first object in the list. Throws an exception if the list contains no objects.

`indexOf(Object o)`
Searches the list for the specified `Object` and returns its position in the list. Throws an exception if the object passed into the method is not in the list.

The linked list class can throw multiple exceptions, and it would be convenient to be able to catch all exceptions thrown by the linked list with one exception handler. Also, if you plan to distribute your linked list in a package, all related code should be packaged together. Thus, the linked list should provide its own set of exception classes.

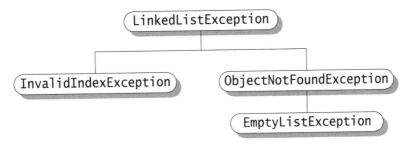

Figure 78 A possible class hierarchy for the exceptions thrown by a linked list.

Figure 78 illustrates one possible class hierarchy for the exceptions thrown by the linked list.

LinkedListException is the parent class of all the possible exceptions that can be thrown by the linked list class. Users of the linked list class can write a single exception handler to handle all linked list exceptions with a catch statement like this:

```
catch (LinkedListException) {
    . . .
}
```

Alternatively, users could write more specialized handlers for each subclass of LinkedList-Exception.

Choosing a Superclass

Any Exception subclass can be used as the parent class of LinkedListException. However, a quick perusal of those subclasses shows that they are inappropriate because they are either too specialized or completely unrelated to LinkedListException. Therefore, the parent class of LinkedListException should be Exception.

Most applets and applications that you write will throw objects that are Exceptions. Errors are reserved for serious, hard errors in the system, such as those that prevent the Java Virtual Machine from running. These are not errors in your program.

Note: For readable code, it's good practice to append the string Exception to the names of all classes that inherit (directly or indirectly) from the Exception class.

Runtime Exceptions—The Controversy

Because the Java programming language does not require methods to catch or to specify runtime exceptions, programmers can be tempted to write code that throws only runtime exceptions or to make all their exception subclasses inherit from `RuntimeException`. Both of these shortcuts allow programmers to write code without bothering with all the nagging errors from the compiler and without bothering to specify or to catch any exceptions. Although this may seem convenient to the programmer, it sidesteps the intent of the catch or specify requirement and can cause problems for programmers using your classes.

Why did the designers decide to force a method to specify all uncaught checked exceptions that can be thrown within its scope? Any exception that can be thrown by a method is part of the method's public programming interface. Callers of a method must know about the exceptions that a method can throw, in order to intelligently and consciously decide what to do about them. These exceptions are as much a part of that method's programming interface as its parameters and return value.

Your next question might be, Well, then, if it's so good to document a method's API, including the exceptions it can throw, why not specify runtime exceptions, too? Runtime exceptions represent problems that are detected by the runtime system. Such problems include arithmetic exceptions (such as dividing by zero), pointer exceptions (such as trying to access an object through a null reference), and indexing exceptions (such as attempting to access an array element through an index that is too large or too small). Runtime exceptions can occur anywhere in a program and in a typical program can be very numerous. The cost of checking for runtime exceptions can exceed the benefit of catching or specifying them. Thus, the compiler does not require that you catch or specify runtime exceptions, although you can.

What do you gain if you throw a `RuntimeException` or create a subclass of `RuntimeException` just because you don't want to deal with specifying it? Simply, you get the ability to throw an exception without specifying that you do so. In other words, it is a way to avoid documenting the exceptions that a method can throw. When is this good? Well, when is it ever good to avoid documenting a method's behavior? The answer is, hardly ever. So, generally speaking, do not throw a `RuntimeException` or create a subclass of `RuntimeException` simply because you don't want to be bothered with specifying the exceptions that your methods can throw.

Advantages of Exceptions

Now that you've read about what exceptions are and how to use them, it's time to learn the advantages of using exceptions in your programs.

Advantage 1: Separating Error-Handling Code from "Regular" Code

Exceptions provide the means to separate the details of what to do when something out of the ordinary happens from the main logic of a program. In traditional programming, error detection, reporting, and handling often lead to confusing spaghetti code. For example, consider the following pseudocode method that reads an entire file into memory:

```
readFile {
    open the file;
    determine its size;
    allocate that much memory;
    read the file into memory;
    close the file;
}
```

At first glance, this function seems simple enough, but it ignores all these potential errors.

- What happens if the file can't be opened?
- What happens if the length of the file can't be determined?
- What happens if enough memory can't be allocated?
- What happens if the read fails?
- What happens if the file can't be closed?

To handle these cases, the readFile function must have more code to do error detection, reporting, and handling. The function might look like this:

```
errorCodeType readFile {
    initialize errorCode = 0;
    open the file;
    if (theFileIsOpen) {
        determine the length of the file;
        if (gotTheFileLength) {
            allocate that much memory;
            if (gotEnoughMemory) {
                read the file into memory;
                if (readFailed) {
                    errorCode = -1;
                }
            } else {
                errorCode = -2;
            }
        } else {
            errorCode = -3;
        }
```

```
            close the file;
            if (theFileDidntClose && errorCode == 0) {
                errorCode = -4;
            } else {
                errorCode = errorCode and -4;
            }
        } else {
            errorCode = -5;
        }
        return errorCode;
    }
```

There's so much error detection, reporting, and returning here that the original seven lines of code are lost in the clutter. Worse yet, the logical flow of the code also has been lost, thus making it difficult to tell whether the code is doing the right thing: Is the file *really* being closed if the function fails to allocate enough memory? It's even more difficult to ensure that the code continues to do the right thing after you modify the function 3 months after writing it. Many programmers "solve" this problem by simply ignoring it—errors are "reported" when their programs crash.

Exceptions enable you to write the main flow of your code and to deal with the exceptional cases elsewhere. If the readFile function used exceptions instead of traditional error-management techniques, it would look more like this:

```
readFile {
    try {
        open the file;
        determine its size;
        allocate that much memory;
        read the file into memory;
        close the file;
    } catch (fileOpenFailed) {
        doSomething;
    } catch (sizeDeterminationFailed) {
        doSomething;
    } catch (memoryAllocationFailed) {
        doSomething;
    } catch (readFailed) {
        doSomething;
    } catch (fileCloseFailed) {
        doSomething;
    }
}
```

Note that exceptions don't spare you the effort of doing the work of detecting, reporting, and handling errors.

Advantage 2: Propagating Errors Up the Call Stack

A second advantage of exceptions is the ability to propagate error reporting up the call stack of methods. Suppose that the `readFile` method is the fourth method in a series of nested method calls made by the main program: `method1` calls `method2`, which calls `method3`, which finally calls `readFile`:

```
method1 {
    call method2;
}
method2 {
    call method3;
}
method3 {
    call readFile;
}
```

Suppose also that `method1` is the only method interested in the errors that might occur within `readFile`. Traditional error-notification techniques force `method2` and `method3` to propagate the error codes returned by `readFile` up the call stack until the error codes finally reach `method1`—the only method that is interested in them:

```
method1 {
    errorCodeType error;
    error = call method2;
    if (error)
        doErrorProcessing;
    else
        proceed;
}
errorCodeType method2 {
    errorCodeType error;
    error = call method3;
    if (error)
        return error;
    else
        proceed;
}
errorCodeType method3 {
    errorCodeType error;
    error = call readFile;
    if (error)
        return error;
    else
        proceed;
}
```

Recall that the Java runtime environment searches backward through the call stack to find any methods that are interested in handling a particular exception. A method can "duck" any exceptions thrown within it, thereby allowing a method farther up the call stack to catch it. Hence, only the methods that care about errors have to worry about detecting errors:

```
method1 {
    try {
        call method2;
    } catch (exception) {
        doErrorProcessing;
    }
}
method2 throws exception {
    call method3;
}
method3 throws exception {
    call readFile;
}
```

However, as the pseudocode shows, ducking an exception requires some effort on the part of the middleman methods. Any checked exceptions that can be thrown within a method must be specified in the `throws` clause of the method.

Advantage 3: Grouping and Differentiating Error Types

Because all exceptions thrown within a program are objects, grouping or categorizing of exceptions is a natural outcome of the class hierarchy. An example of a group of related exception classes in the Java platform are those defined in `java.io`: `IOException` and its descendants. `IOException` is the most general and represents any type of error that can occur when performing I/O. Its descendants represent more specific errors. For example, `FileNotFoundException` means that a file could not be located on disk.

A method can write specific handlers that can handle a very specific exception. The `File-NotFoundException` class has no descendants, so the following handler can handle only one type of exception:

```
catch (FileNotFoundException e) {
    ...
}
```

A method can catch an exception based on its group or general type by specifying any of the exception's superclasses in the `catch` statement. For example, to catch all I/O exceptions, regardless of their specific type, an exception handler specifies an `IOException` argument:

```
catch (IOException e) {
    ...
}
```

This handler will catch all I/O exceptions, including `FileNotFoundException`, `EOFException`, and so on. You can find the details on what occurred by querying the argument passed to the exception handler. For example, to print the stack trace:

```
catch (IOException e) {
    e.printStackTrace();            // output goes to Sytem.err
    e.printStackTrace(System.out);  // send trace to stdout
}
```

You could even set up an exception handler that handles any `Exception` with this handler:

```
catch (Exception e) {    // a (too) general exception handler
    ...
}
```

The `Exception` class is close to the top of the `Throwable` class hierarchy. Therefore, this handler will catch many other exceptions in addition to those that the handler is intended to catch. In general, your exception handlers should be as specific as possible. Handlers that catch most or all exceptions make error recovery unnecessarily inefficient. The reason is that the first thing a handler must do is determine what type of exception occurred before it can decide on the best recovery strategy. In effect, by not catching specific errors, the handler must accommodate any possibility. Exception handlers that are too general can make code *more* error prone by catching and handling exceptions that weren't anticipated by the programmer and for which the handler was not intended.

As we've shown, you can create groups of exceptions and handle exceptions in a general fashion, or you can use the specific exception type to differentiate exceptions and handle exceptions in an exact fashion.

Summary of Exceptions

A program can use exceptions to indicate that an error occurred. To throw an exception, you use the `throw` statement and provide it with an exception object—a descendant of `Throwable`—to provide information about the specific error that occurred. A method that throws an uncaught, checked exception must include a `throws` clause in its declaration.

A program can catch exceptions by using a combination of the `try`, `catch`, and `finally` statements. The `try` statement identifies a block of code in which an exception can occur. The `catch` statement identifies a block of code, known as an exception handler, that can handle a particular type of exception. The `finally` statement identifies a block of code that cleans up regardless of whether an exception occurred within the `try` block. A `try` statement must be accompanied by at least one `catch` statement or a `finally` statement and may have multiple `catch` statements.

The class of the exception object indicates the type of the exception thrown. The exception object can contain further information about the error, including an error message.

Questions and Exercises

Questions

1. Is the following code legal?
```
try {
    ...
} finally {
    ...
}
```

2. What exception types can be caught by the following handler?
```
catch (Exception e) {
    ...
}
```

What is wrong with using this type of exception handler?

3. Match each situation in the first column with an item in the second column: an "error," "checked exception," "runtime exception," or "no exception."

a. `int[] A;` `A[0] = 0;`	1. error
b. The Java VM starts running your program, but the VM can't find `rt.jar`. (The Java platform classes reside in `classes.zip` or `rt.jar`.)	2. checked exception
c. A program is reading a stream and reaches the end of stream marker.	3. runtime exception
d. Before closing the stream and after reaching the end of stream marker, a program tries to read the stream again.	4. no exception

[handwritten margin notes: "Why is this a runtime exception because no setup of array} int [ ] A; A = new int[1];"]

4. What exceptions can be caught by the following handler?

```
...
} catch (Exception e) {
    ...
} catch (ArithmeticException a) {
    ...
}
```

Is there anything wrong with this exception handler as written? Will this code compile?

Exercises

1. Add a `readList` method to `ListOfNumbers.java`. This method should read in `int` values from a file, print each value, and append them to the end of the vector. You should catch all appropriate errors. You will also need a text file containing numbers to read in.

2. Modify the following `cat` method so that it will compile:

```
public static void cat(File named) {
    RandomAccessFile input = null;
    String line = null;

    try {
        input = new RandomAccessFile(named, "r");
        while ((line = input.readLine()) != null) {
            System.out.println(line);
        }
        return;
    } finally {
        if (input != null) {
            input.close();
        }
    }
}
```

Answers

You can find answers to these Questions and Exercises online:

http://java.sun.com/docs/books/tutorial/essential/exceptions/QandE/answers.html

Code Samples

Table 44 lists the code samples used in this chapter and where you can find the code online and on the CD that accompanies this book.

Table 44   Code Samples in Handling Errors Using Exceptions

Code Sample	CD Location	Online Location
ListOfNumbers.java (page 246)	JavaTutorial/essential/ exceptions/example-1dot1/ ListOfNumbers.java	http://java.sun.com/docs/ books/tutorial/essential/ exceptions/example-1dot1/ ListOfNumbers.java
ListOfNumbersWO-Handler.java[a] (page 246)	JavaTutorial/essential/ exceptions/example-1dot1/ ListOfNumbersWOHandler.java	http://java.sun.com/docs/ books/tutorial/essential/ exceptions/example-1dot1/ ListOfNumbersWOHandler.java

a. This version of ListOfNumbers.java does not have a handler and will not compile, by design.

Note: The section Common Problems and Their Solutions (page 391) contains solutions to common problems *Tutorial* readers have encountered.

Threads: Doing Two or More Tasks at Once

T HE following is a snapshot of three copies of an applet that animates different sorting algorithms (Figure 79). No, this chapter is not about sorting algorithms. But these applets do provide a visual aid to understanding a powerful capability of the Java™ platform— threads.

Figure 79 You can see all three applets in action online at `http://java.sun.com/docs/ books/tutorial/essential/threads/index.html` or on the CD. Open this page in your browser and click each applet to start them running simultaneously.

These three applets run side by side at the same time. If you look at these applets in a browser, you can see each applet working its way through the data, sorting it, with shorter lines on top and longer lines on bottom. While the applets are sorting, also notice that you can scroll the page or bring up one of your browser's panels. All this is due to *threads*.

A *thread*—sometimes called an *execution context* or a *lightweight process*—is a single sequential flow of control within a program. You use threads to isolate tasks. When you run one of these sorting applets, it creates a thread that performs the sort operation. Each thread is a sequential flow of control within the same program (the browser). Each sort operation runs independently from the others but at the same time.

What Is a Thread?

All programmers are familiar with writing sequential programs. You've probably written a program that displays "Hello World!" or sorts a list of names or computes a list of prime numbers. These are sequential programs. That is, each has a beginning, an execution sequence, and an end. At any given time during the runtime of the program, there is a single point of execution.

A thread is similar to the sequential programs described previously. A single thread also has a beginning, a sequence, and an end. At any given time during the runtime of the thread, there is a single point of execution. However, a thread itself is not a program; a thread cannot run on its own. Rather, it runs within a program. Figure 80 shows this relationship.

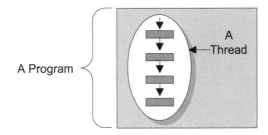

Figure 80 A thread is not a program; a thread runs *within* a program.

Definition: A *thread* is a single sequential flow of control within a program.

The real hoopla surrounding threads is not about a single sequential thread. Rather, it's about the use of multiple threads running at the same time and performing different tasks in a single program. This use is illustrated in Figure 81.

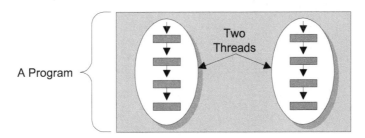

Figure 81 Two threads running concurrently in a single program.

A Web browser is an example of a multithreaded application. Within a typical browser, you can scroll a page while it's downloading an applet or an image, play animation and sound concurrently, print a page in the background while you download a new page, or watch three sorting algorithms race to the finish.

Some texts call a thread a *lightweight process*. A thread is similar to a real process in that both have a single sequential flow of control. However, a thread is considered lightweight because it runs within the context of a full-blown program and takes advantage of the resources allocated for that program and the program's environment.

As a sequential flow of control, a thread must carve out some of its own resources within a running program. For example, a thread must have its own execution stack and program counter. The code running within the thread works only within that context. Some other texts use *execution context* as a synonym for thread.

Thread programming can be tricky, so if you think you might need to implement threads, consider using high-level thread API. For example, if your program must perform a task repeatedly, consider using the `java.util.Timer` class introduced in version 1.3 of the Java platform. The `Timer` class is also useful for performing a task after a delay. Examples of its use are in the section Using the Timer and TimerTask Classes (page 273).

If you're writing a program with a graphical user interface (GUI), you might want to use the `javax.swing.Timer` class (added in version 1.2) instead of `java.util.Timer`. Another utility class, `SwingWorker`, helps you with another common job: performing a task in a background thread, optionally updating the GUI when the task completes. You can find information about both the Swing `Timer` class and the `SwingWorker` class in the section Threads and Swing (page 378) in Chapter 10.

Basic support for threads in all versions of the Java platform is in the class `java.lang.Thread`.[1] It provides a thread API and provides all the generic behavior for threads.[2] These behaviors include starting, sleeping, running, yielding, and having a priority. To implement a thread using the `Thread` class, you need to provide it with a `run` method that performs the thread's task. The section Customizing a Thread's run Method (page 277) tells you how to do this.

The first section in this chapter discusses practical aspects of using timers to implement threads. If you're using version 1.3 or a compatible release and want to put a thread in your program, the first section might be all you need. Subsequent sections go on to discuss the low-level thread API and explain threads through examples that use that API.

---

[1] http://java.sun.com/j2se/1.3/docs/api/java/lang/Thread.html

[2] The actual implementation of concurrent operation is provided by a system-specific implementation. For most programming needs, the underlying implementation doesn't matter.

Using the Timer and TimerTask Classes

In version 1.3, support for timers was added to the java.util package. The Timer[1] class in that package schedules instances of a class called TimerTask.[2] Here's an example of using a timer to perform a task after a delay, Reminder.java.[3]

```java
import java.util.Timer;
import java.util.TimerTask;

/**
 * Simple demo that uses java.util.Timer to schedule a task to execute
 * once 5 seconds have passed.
 */

public class Reminder {
    Timer timer;

    public Reminder(int seconds) {
        timer = new Timer();
        timer.schedule(new RemindTask(), seconds*1000);
    }

    class RemindTask extends TimerTask {
        public void run() {
            System.out.println("Time's up!");
            timer.cancel(); //Terminate the timer thread
        }
    }

    public static void main(String args[]) {
        new Reminder(5);
        System.out.println("Task scheduled.");
    }
}
```

When you run the example, you first see this:

```
Task scheduled.
```

Five seconds later, you see this:

```
Time's up!
```

---

[1] http://java.sun.com/j2se/1.3/docs/api/java/util/Timer.html
[2] http://java.sun.com/j2se/1.3/docs/api/java/util/TimerTask.html
[3] Reminder.java is included on the CD and is available online. See Code Samples (page 310).

This simple program illustrates the basic parts of implementing and scheduling a task to be executed by a timer thread.

- Implement a custom subclass of `TimerTask`. The `run` method contains the code that performs the task. In this example, the subclass is named `RemindTask`.

- Create a thread by instantiating the `Timer` class.

- Instantiate the timer task object (`new RemindTask()`).

- Schedule the timer task for execution. This example uses the `schedule` method, with the timer task as the first argument and the delay in milliseconds (`5000`) as the second argument. Another way of scheduling a task is to specify the time when the task should execute. For example, the following code schedules a task for execution at 11:01 P.M.:

```
//Get the Date corresponding to 11:01:00 pm today.
Calendar calendar = Calendar.getInstance();
calendar.set(Calendar.HOUR_OF_DAY, 23);
calendar.set(Calendar.MINUTE, 1);
calendar.set(Calendar.SECOND, 0);
Date time = calendar.getTime();

timer = new Timer();
timer.schedule(new RemindTask(), time);
```

Stopping Timer Threads

By default, a program keeps running as long as its timer threads are running. You can terminate a timer thread in four ways.

- Invoke `cancel` on the timer. You can do this from anywhere in the program, such as from a timer task's `run` method.

- Make the timer's thread a "daemon" by creating the timer like this: `new Timer(true)`. If the only threads left in the program are daemon threads, the program exits.

- After all the timer's scheduled tasks have finished executing, remove all references to the `Timer` object. Eventually, the timer's thread will terminate.

- Invoke the `System.exit` method, which makes the entire program (and all its threads) exit.

The `Reminder` example uses the first scheme, invoking the `cancel` method from the timer task's `run` method. Making the timer thread a daemon wouldn't work, because the program needs to keep running until the timer's task executes.

Sometimes, timer threads aren't the only threads that can prevent a program from exiting when expected. For example, if you use the AWT at all—even if only to make beeps—the AWT automatically creates a nondaemon thread that keeps the program alive. The following modification of Reminder adds beeping, which requires us to also add a call to the System.exit method to make the program exit. Significant changes are in boldface. You can find the source code in ReminderBeep.java.[1]

```
...
public class ReminderBeep {
    ...
    public ReminderBeep(int seconds) {
        toolkit = Toolkit.getDefaultToolkit();
        timer = new Timer();
        timer.schedule(new RemindTask(), seconds*1000);
    }

    class RemindTask extends TimerTask {
        public void run() {
            System.out.println("Time's up!");
            toolkit.beep();
            //timer.cancel(); //Not necessary because we call System.exit
            System.exit(0);   //Stops the AWT thread (and everything else)
        }
    }
    ...
}
```

Performing a Task Repeatedly

Here's an example of using a timer to perform a task once per second.

```
public class AnnoyingBeep {
    Toolkit toolkit;
    Timer timer;

    public AnnoyingBeep() {
        toolkit = Toolkit.getDefaultToolkit();
        timer = new Timer();
        timer.schedule(new RemindTask(),
                        0,          //initial delay
                        1*1000);    //subsequent rate
    }

    class RemindTask extends TimerTask {
        int numWarningBeeps = 3;
        public void run() {
            if (numWarningBeeps > 0) {
                toolkit.beep();
```

---

[1] ReminderBeep.java is included on the CD and is available online. See <u>Code Samples</u> (page 310).

```
                System.out.println("Beep!");
                numWarningBeeps--;
            } else {
                toolkit.beep();
                System.out.println("Time's up!");
                //timer.cancel(); //Not necessary
                                  //because we call System.exit
                System.exit(0);   //Stops the AWT thread
                                  //(and everything else)
            }
        }
    }
    ...
}
```

You can find the entire program in AnnoyingBeep.java.[1] When you execute it, you see the following output (our comments about timing are shown in italics):

```
Task scheduled.
Beep!
Beep!         //one second after the first beep
Beep!         //one second after the second beep
Time's up!    //one second after the third beep
```

The AnnoyingBeep program uses a three-argument version of the schedule method to specify that its task should execute once a second, beginning immediately. Here are all the Timer methods you can use to schedule repeated executions of tasks:

- schedule(TimerTask *task*, long *delay*, long *period*)
- schedule(TimerTask *task*, Date *time*, long *period*)
- scheduleAtFixedRate(TimerTask *task*, long *delay*, long *period*)
- scheduleAtFixedRate(TimerTask *task*, Date *firstTime*, long *period*)

When scheduling a task for repeated execution, you should use one of the schedule methods when smoothness is important and a scheduleAtFixedRate method when time synchronization is more important. For example, the AnnoyingBeep program uses the schedule method, which means that the annoying beeps will all be at least 1 second apart. If one beep is late for any reason, all subsequent beeps will be delayed. If we decide that the Annoying-Beep program should exit exactly 3 seconds after the first beep—even if it means that two beeps might occur close together if a beep is delayed for any reason—we should use the scheduleAtFixedRate method instead.

---

[1] AnnoyingBeep.java is included on the CD and is available online. See <u>Code Samples</u> (page 310).

More Information about Timers

The timer tasks we've shown have been very simple. They do almost nothing and refer only to data that either can be safely accessed from multiple threads or is private to the timer task. As long as your timer task uses only API designed to be thread-safe—such as the methods in the `Timer` class—implementing timers is relatively straightforward. However, if your timer implementation depends on shared resources, such as data used by other places in your program, you need to be careful. You can find out more later in this chapter in the section Synchronizing Threads (page 291).

For further information about timers, see

- The API documentation for `Timer`[1] and `TimerTask`.[2]
- "Using Timers in Swing Applications," an article in the online magazine *The Swing Connection*. You can read this article online at: `http://java.sun.com/products/jfc/tsc/articles/timer/`
- The May 30, 2000, edition of the *Java Developer Connection* "Tech Tips," which you can find online at: `http://developer.java.sun.com/developer/TechTips/`

Customizing a Thread's run Method

The `run` method gives a thread something to do. Its code implements the thread's running behavior. A thread's `run` method can do anything that can be encoded in statements: compute a list of prime numbers, sort some data, perform some animation.

The `Thread` class implements a generic thread that, by default, does nothing. That is, the implementation of its `run` method is empty. This is not particularly useful, so there are two techniques for providing a `run` method for a thread:

- Subclassing `Thread` and overriding `run`
- Implementing the `Runnable` interface[3]

The `Runnable` interface is discussed later in this chapter in the section Implementing the Runnable Interface (page 279).

---

[1] http://java.sun.com/j2se/1.3/docs/api/java/util/Timer.html
[2] http://java.sun.com/j2se/1.3/docs/api/java/util/TimerTask.html
[3] http://java.sun.com/j2se/1.3/docs/api/java/lang/Runnable.html

Subclassing Thread and Overriding run

The first way to customize a thread is to subclass Thread (itself a Runnable object) and to override its empty run method so that it does something. Let's look at the SimpleThread class, the first of two classes in this example, which does just that:

```
public class SimpleThread extends Thread {

    public SimpleThread(String str) {
        super(str);
    }

    public void run() {
        for (int i = 0; i < 10; i++) {
            System.out.println(i + " " + getName());
            try {
                sleep((int)(Math.random() * 1000));
            } catch (InterruptedException e) {}
        }
        System.out.println("DONE! " + getName());
    }
}
```

The first method in the SimpleThread class is a constructor that takes a String as its only argument. This constructor is implemented by calling a superclass constructor that sets the Thread's name, which is used later in the program.

The next method in the SimpleThread class is the run method. This method, the heart of any Thread, defines what the Thread does when it's running. The run method of the Simple-Thread class overrides the empty method implementation in the Thread class and contains a for loop that iterates ten times. In each iteration, the method displays the iteration number and the name of the Thread. Then the method sleeps for a random interval of up to 1 second. After the loop has finished, the run method prints DONE! and the name of the thread. That's it for the SimpleThread class. Let's put it to use in TwoThreadsDemo.

The TwoThreadsDemo class contains a main method that creates two SimpleThread threads: Jamaica and Fiji. (If you can't decide where to go on vacation, use this program to decide.)

```
public class TwoThreadsDemo {
    public static void main (String[] args) {
        new SimpleThread("Jamaica").start();
        new SimpleThread("Fiji").start();
    }
}
```

The main method starts each thread immediately following its construction by calling the start method, which in turn calls the run method. Compile and run the program and watch your vacation fate unfold. You should see output similar to this:

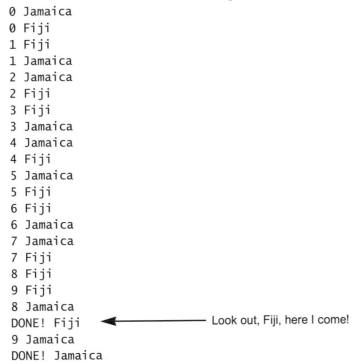

```
0 Jamaica
0 Fiji
1 Fiji
1 Jamaica
2 Jamaica
2 Fiji
3 Fiji
3 Jamaica
4 Jamaica
4 Fiji
5 Jamaica
5 Fiji
6 Fiji
6 Jamaica
7 Jamaica
7 Fiji
8 Fiji
9 Fiji
8 Jamaica
DONE! Fiji      ◄──────────── Look out, Fiji, here I come!
9 Jamaica
DONE! Jamaica
```

Note how the output from each thread is intermingled with the output from the other. The reason is that both SimpleThread threads are running concurrently. So both run methods are running, and both threads are displaying their output at the same time. When the loop completes, the thread stops running and dies.

Now let's look at another example, the Clock applet, that uses the other technique for providing a run method to a Thread.

Implementing the Runnable Interface

The following Clock applet displays the current time and updates its display every second. If you bring up the online version of this section in an HTML browser, you can scroll the page and perform other tasks while the clock updates. The reason is that the code that updates the clock's display runs within its own thread.

11:21:16 AM

http://java.sun.com/docs/books/tutorial/essential/threads/clock.html

The Clock applet uses a technique different from SimpleThread's for providing the run method for its thread. Instead of subclassing Thread, Clock implements the Runnable interface and therefore implements the run method defined in it. Clock then creates a thread with itself as the Thread's target. When created in this way, the Thread gets its run method from its target. The code that accomplishes this is shown in boldface:

```java
import java.awt.Graphics;
import java.util.*;
import java.text.DateFormat;
import java.applet.Applet;

public class Clock extends Applet implements Runnable {
    private Thread clockThread = null;
    public void start() {
        if (clockThread == null) {
            clockThread = new Thread(this, "Clock");
            clockThread.start();
        }
    }
    public void run() {
        Thread myThread = Thread.currentThread();
        while (clockThread == myThread) {
            repaint();
            try {
                Thread.sleep(1000);
            } catch (InterruptedException e) {
                //the VM doesn't want us to sleep anymore,
                //so get back to work
            }
        }
    }
    public void paint(Graphics g) {
        //get the time and convert it to a date
        Calendar cal = Calendar.getInstance();
        Date date = cal.getTime();
        //format it and display it
        DateFormat dateFormatter = DateFormat.getTimeInstance();
        g.drawString(dateFormatter.format(date), 5, 10);
    }
    //overrides Applet's stop method, not Thread's
    public void stop() {
        clockThread = null;
    }
}
```

The Clock applet's run method loops until the browser asks it to stop. During each iteration of the loop, the clock repaints its display. The paint method figures out what time it is, formats it in a localized way, and displays it. You'll see more of the Clock applet in the section The Life Cycle of a Thread (page 281), which uses it to teach you about the life of a thread.

Deciding to Use the Runnable Interface

You have now seen two ways to provide the run method.

1. Subclass the Thread class defined in the java.lang package and override the run method. See the SimpleThread class described in the section Subclassing Thread and Overriding run (page 278).

2. Provide a class that implements the Runnable interface (also defined in the java.lang package) and therefore implements the run method. In this case, a Runnable object provides the run method to the thread. See the Clock applet in the previous section.

There are good reasons for choosing either of these options over the other. However, for most cases, including that of the Clock applet, the following rule of thumb will guide you to the better option.

Rule of Thumb: If your class *must* subclass another class (the most common example being Applet), you should use Runnable as described in option 2.

To run in a browser, the Clock class has to be a subclass of the Applet class. Also, the Clock applet needs a thread so that it can continuously update its display without taking over the process in which it is running. (Some browsers might create a new thread for each applet so as to prevent a misbehaved applet from taking over the main browser thread. However, you should not count on this when writing your applets; your applets should create their own threads when doing computer-intensive work.) But because the Java programming language does not support multiple-class inheritance, the Clock class cannot be a subclass of both Thread and Applet. Thus, the Clock class must use the Runnable interface to provide its threaded behavior.

The Life Cycle of a Thread

Now that you've seen how to give a thread something to do, we'll review some details that were glossed over in the previous section. In particular, we look at how to create and start a thread, some of the special things it can do while it's running, and how to stop it.

Figure 82 shows the states that a thread can be in during its life and illustrates which method calls cause a transition to another state. This figure is not a complete finite state diagram but rather an overview of the more interesting and common facets of a thread's life. The remainder of this section uses the Clock applet previously introduced to discuss a thread's life cycle in terms of its state.

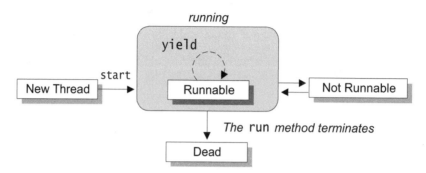

Figure 82 Possible states of a thread.

Creating a Thread

The application in which an applet is running calls the applet's start method when the user visits the applet's page. The Clock applet creates a Thread, clockThread, in its start method with the code shown here in boldface:

```
public void start() {
    if (clockThread == null) {
        clockThread = new Thread(this, "Clock");
        clockThread.start();
    }
}
```

After the statement in boldface has been executed, clockThread is in the New Thread state. A thread in this state is merely an empty Thread object; no system resources have been allocated for it yet. When a thread is in this state, you can only start the thread. Calling any method besides start when a thread is in this state makes no sense and causes an IllegalThreadStateException. In fact, the runtime system throws an IllegalThreadStateException whenever a method is called on a thread and that thread's state does not allow for that method call.

Note that the Clock instance is the first argument to the thread constructor. The first argument to this thread constructor must implement the Runnable interface and becomes the thread's target. The clock thread gets its run method from its target Runnable object—in this case, the Clock instance. The second argument is just a name for the thread.

Starting a Thread

Now consider the next line of code in Clock's start method, shown here in boldface:

```
public void start() {
    if (clockThread == null) {
        clockThread = new Thread(this, "Clock");
        clockThread.start();
    }
}
```

The start method creates the system resources necessary to run the thread, schedules the thread to run, and calls the thread's run method. ClockThread's run method is the one defined in the Clock class.

After the start method has returned, the thread is "running." Yet it's somewhat more complex than that. As Figure 82 shows, a thread that has been started is in the Runnable state. Many computers have a single processor, thus making it impossible to run all "running" threads at the same time. The Java runtime environment must implement a scheduling scheme that shares the processor among all "running" threads. (See the section <u>Understanding Thread Priority</u> (page 286) for more information about scheduling.) So at any given time, a "running" thread may be waiting for its turn in the CPU.

Here's another look at Clock's run method:

```
public void run() {
    Thread myThread = Thread.currentThread();
    while (clockThread == myThread) {
        repaint();
        try {
            Thread.sleep(1000);
        } catch (InterruptedException e) {
            //the VM doesn't want us to sleep anymore,
            //so get back to work
        }
    }
}
```

Clock's run method loops while the condition clockThread == myThread is true. This exit condition is explained in more detail in the section <u>Stopping a Thread</u> (page 285). For now, however, know that it allows the thread, and thus the applet, to exit gracefully.

Within the loop, the applet repaints itself and then tells the thread to sleep for 1 second (1,000 milliseconds). An applet's `repaint` method ultimately calls the applet's `paint` method, which does the update of the applet's display area. The `Clock` `paint` method gets the current time, formats, and displays it:

```
public void paint(Graphics g) {
    //get the time and convert it to a date
    Calendar cal = Calendar.getInstance();
    Date date = cal.getTime();
    //format it and display it
    DateFormat dateFormatter = DateFormat.getTimeInstance();
    g.drawString(dateFormatter.format(date), 5, 10);
}
```

Making a Thread Not Runnable

A thread becomes Not Runnable when one of these events occurs:

- Its `sleep` method is invoked.
- The thread calls the `wait` method to wait for a specific condition to be satisfied.
- The thread is blocking on I/O.

The `clockThread` in the `Clock` applet becomes Not Runnable when the `run` method calls `sleep` on the current thread:

```
public void run() {
    Thread myThread = Thread.currentThread();
    while (clockThread == myThread) {
        repaint();
        try {
            Thread.sleep(1000);
        } catch (InterruptedException e) {
            //the VM doesn't want us to sleep anymore,
            //so get back to work
        }
    }
}
```

During the second that the `clockThread` is asleep, the thread does not run, even if the processor becomes available. After the second has elapsed, the thread becomes Runnable again; if the processor becomes available, the thread begins running again.

For each entrance into the Not Runnable state, a specific and distinct exit returns the thread to the Runnable state. An exit works only for its corresponding entrance. For example, if a thread has been put to sleep, the specified number of milliseconds must elapse before the thread becomes Runnable again. The following list describes the exit for every entrance into the Not Runnable state.

- If a thread has been put to sleep, the specified number of milliseconds must elapse.
- If a thread is waiting for a condition, another object must notify the waiting thread of a change in condition by calling `notify` or `notifyAll`. More information is available in the section <u>Synchronizing Threads</u> (page 291).
- If a thread is blocked on I/O, the I/O must complete.

Stopping a Thread

A program doesn't stop a thread like it stops an applet (by calling a method). Rather, a thread arranges for its own death by having a `run` method that terminates naturally. For example, the `while` loop in this `run` method is a finite loop: It will iterate 100 times and then exit:

```
public void run() {
    int i = 0;
    while (i < 100) {
        i++;
        System.out.println("i = " + i);
    }
}
```

A thread with this `run` method dies naturally when the loop completes and the `run` method exits.

Let's look at how the `Clock` applet thread arranges for its own death. You might want to use this technique with your applets. Recall `Clock`'s `run` method:

```
public void run() {
    Thread myThread = Thread.currentThread();
    while (clockThread == myThread) {
        repaint();
        try {
            Thread.sleep(1000);
        } catch (InterruptedException e) {
            //the VM doesn't want us to sleep anymore,
            //so get back to work
        }
    }
}
```

The exit condition for this `run` method is the exit condition for the `while` loop because there is no code after the `while` loop:

```
while (clockThread == myThread) {
```

This condition indicates that the loop will exit when the currently executing thread is not equal to clockThread. When would this ever be the case?

When you leave the page, the application in which the applet is running calls the applet's stop method. This method then sets clockThread to null, thereby telling the main loop in the run method to terminate:

```
public void stop() {      //applets' stop method
    clockThread = null;
}
```

If you revisit the page, the start method is called again and the clock starts up again with a new thread. Even if you stop and start the applet faster than one iteration of the loop, the clockThread thread will be different from myThread, and the loop will still terminate.

The isAlive Method

A final word about thread state: The API for the Thread class includes a method called isAlive. The isAlive method returns true if the thread has been started and not stopped. If the isAlive method returns false, you know that the thread either is a New Thread or is Dead. If the isAlive method returns true, you know that the thread is either Runnable or Not Runnable. You cannot differentiate between a New Thread and a Dead thread. Nor can you differentiate between a Runnable thread and a Not Runnable thread.

Understanding Thread Priority

As mentioned briefly in the previous section, most computer configurations have a single CPU. Hence, threads run one at a time in such a way as to provide an illusion of concurrency. Execution of multiple threads on a single CPU in some order is called *scheduling*. The Java runtime environment supports a very simple, deterministic scheduling algorithm called *fixed-priority scheduling*. This algorithm schedules threads on the basis of their *priority* relative to other Runnable threads.

When a thread is created, it inherits its priority from the thread that created it. You also can modify a thread's priority at any time after its creation by using the setPriority method. Thread priorities are integers ranging between MIN_PRIORITY and MAX_PRIORITY (constants defined in the Thread class). The higher the integer, the higher the priority. At any given time, when multiple threads are ready to be executed, the runtime system chooses for execution the Runnable thread that has the highest priority. Only when that thread stops, yields, or becomes Not Runnable will a lower-priority thread start executing. If two threads of the same priority are waiting for the CPU, the scheduler arbitrarily chooses one of them to run. The chosen thread runs until one of the following conditions is true:

- A higher-priority thread becomes Runnable.
- It yields or its run method exits.
- On systems that support time slicing, its time allotment has expired.

Then the second thread is given a chance to run, and so on, until the interpreter exits.

The Java runtime environment's thread-scheduling algorithm is also *preemptive*. If at any time a thread with a priority higher than that of all other Runnable threads becomes Runnable, the runtime system chooses the new higher-priority thread for execution. This new thread is said to *preempt* the other threads.

Rule of Thumb: At any given time, the highest-priority thread is running. However, this is not guaranteed. The thread scheduler may choose to run a lower-priority thread to avoid starvation. For this reason, use thread priority only to affect scheduling policy for efficiency purposes. Do not rely on it for algorithm correctness.

The 400,000-Micron Thread Race

The applet shown in Figure 83, called RaceApplet,[1] animates a race between two "runner" threads of different priorities. Clicking the mouse on the applet starts the two runners. Runner 2 has a priority of 2; runner 3 has a priority of 3.

Try This: Go to the online version of this section and run the applet. Note that this applet may not work as intended in browsers that have security restrictions regarding setting a thread's priority. If this is true for your browser, try running this applet in an applet viewer instead.

```
2  ────────────────────
3  ────────────────────
```

Figure 83 A snapshot of RaceApplet with runners of different priorities.

The runners are implemented by a Thread subclass called Runner.[2] Here is the run method for the Runner class, which simply counts from 1 to 400,000:

---

[1] RaceApplet.java is included on the CD and is available online. See Code Samples (page 310).
[2] Runner.java is included on the CD and is available online. See Code Samples (page 310).

```
public int tick = 1;
public void run() {
    while (tick < 400000) {
        tick++;
    }
}
```

This applet has a third thread, which handles the drawing. The drawing thread's `run` method loops until the applet stops. During each iteration of the loop, the thread draws a line for each runner, whose length is computed from the runner's `tick` variable; the thread then sleeps for 10 milliseconds. The drawing thread has a thread priority of 4—higher than that of either runner. Thus, whenever the drawing thread wakes up after 10 milliseconds, it becomes the highest-priority thread, preempting whichever runner is currently running, and draws the lines. You can see the lines inch their way across the page.

This is not a fair race, because one runner has a higher priority than the other. Each time the drawing thread yields the CPU by going to sleep for 10 milliseconds, the scheduler chooses the highest-priority Runnable thread to run; in this case, it's always runner 3.

Figure 84 is another snapshot of the applet, one that implements a fair race, in which both runners have the same priority and an equal chance of being chosen to run.

Try This: Go to the online version of this section and run the applet.[1]

Figure 84 A snapshot of `RaceApplet` with runners of the same priority.

In this race, each time the drawing thread yields the CPU by going to sleep, there are two Runnable threads of equal priority—the runners—waiting for the CPU. The scheduler must choose one of the threads to run. In this case, the scheduler arbitrarily chooses one.

Selfish Threads

The Runner class used in the previous races implements "socially impaired" thread behavior. Recall the `run` method from the Runner class used in the races:

---

[1]   http://java.sun.com/docs/books/tutorial/essential/threads/priority.html

```
public int tick = 1;
public void run() {
    while (tick < 400000) {
        tick++;
    }
}
```

The `while` loop in the `run` method is in a tight loop. Once the scheduler chooses a thread with this thread body for execution, the thread never voluntarily relinquishes control of the CPU; it just continues to run until the `while` loop terminates naturally or until the thread is preempted by a higher-priority thread. This thread is called a *selfish thread*.

In some cases, having selfish threads doesn't cause any problems, because a higher-priority thread preempts the selfish one, just as the drawing thread in `RaceApplet` preempts the selfish runners. However, in other cases, threads with CPU-greedy `run` methods can take over the CPU and cause other threads to wait for a long time, even forever, before getting a chance to run.

Time Slicing

Some systems, such as Win32, fight selfish-thread behavior with a strategy known as *time slicing*. Time slicing comes into play when multiple Runnable threads of equal priority are the highest-priority threads competing for the CPU. For example, a standalone program based on `RaceApplet` creates two equal-priority selfish threads that have this `run` method:[1]

```
public void run() {
    while (tick < 400000) {
        tick++;
        if ((tick % 50000) == 0) {
            System.out.println("Thread #" + num + ", tick = " + tick);
        }
    }
}
```

This `run` method contains a tight loop that increments the integer `tick`. Every 50,000 ticks prints out the thread's identifier and its `tick` count.

When running this program on a time-sliced system, you will see messages from both threads intermingled, like this:

```
Thread #1, tick = 50000
Thread #0, tick = 50000
Thread #0, tick = 100000
```

---

[1] `RaceDemo.java` is included on the CD and is available online. See Code Samples (page 310).

```
Thread #1, tick = 100000
Thread #1, tick = 150000
Thread #1, tick = 200000
Thread #0, tick = 150000
Thread #0, tick = 200000
Thread #1, tick = 250000
Thread #0, tick = 250000
Thread #0, tick = 300000
Thread #1, tick = 300000
Thread #1, tick = 350000
Thread #0, tick = 350000
Thread #0, tick = 400000
Thread #1, tick = 400000
```

This output is produced because a time-sliced system divides the CPU into time slots and gives each equal-and-highest priority thread a time slot in which to run. The time-sliced system iterates through the equal-and-highest priority threads, allowing each one a bit of time to run, until one or more finishes or until a higher-priority thread preempts them. Note that time slicing makes no guarantees as to how often or in what order threads are scheduled to run.

When running this program on a system that is not time sliced, you will see messages from one thread finish printing before the other thread ever gets a chance to print one message. The output will look like this:

```
Thread #0, tick = 50000
Thread #0, tick = 100000
Thread #0, tick = 150000
Thread #0, tick = 200000
Thread #0, tick = 250000
Thread #0, tick = 300000
Thread #0, tick = 350000
Thread #0, tick = 400000
Thread #1, tick = 50000
Thread #1, tick = 100000
Thread #1, tick = 150000
Thread #1, tick = 200000
Thread #1, tick = 250000
Thread #1, tick = 300000
Thread #1, tick = 350000
Thread #1, tick = 400000
```

The reason is that a system that is not time sliced chooses one of the equal-and-highest priority threads to run and allows that thread to run until it relinquishes the CPU (by sleeping, yielding, or finishing its job) or until a higher-priority preempts it.

Purity Tip: The Java platform does not implement (and therefore does not guarantee) time slicing. However, some platforms do support time slicing. Your programs should not rely on time slicing, as it may produce different results on different systems.

As you can imagine, writing CPU-intensive code can have negative repercussions on other threads running in the same process. In general, try to write well-behaved threads that voluntarily relinquish the CPU periodically and give other threads an opportunity to run.

A thread can voluntarily yield the CPU by calling the yield method. The yield method gives other threads of the same priority a chance to run. If no equal-priority threads are Runnable, the yield is ignored.

Summarizing Thread Priority

- Most computers have only one CPU, so threads must share the CPU with other threads. The execution of multiple threads on a single CPU, in some order, is called *scheduling*. The Java platform supports a simple, deterministic scheduling algorithm called fixed-priority scheduling.
- Each thread has a numeric priority between MIN_PRIORITY and MAX_PRIORITY (constants defined in the Thread class). At any given time, when multiple threads are ready to be executed, the highest-priority thread is chosen for execution. Only when that thread stops or is suspended will a lower-priority thread start executing.
- Scheduling of the CPU is fully preemptive. If a thread with a priority higher than that of the currently executing thread needs to execute, the higher-priority thread is immediately scheduled.
- The Java platform does not directly time slice. However, the system implementation of threads underlying the Thread class may support time slicing. Do not write code that relies on time slicing.
- A given thread may, at any time, give up its right to execute by calling the yield method. Threads can yield the CPU only to other threads of the same priority. Attempts to yield to a lower-priority thread are ignored.
- When all the Runnable threads in the system have the same priority, the scheduler arbitrarily chooses one of them to run.

Synchronizing Threads

The examples in this chapter so far have contained independent, asynchronous threads. Each thread contained all the data and methods required for its execution and didn't require any outside resources or methods. Also, the threads in those examples ran at their own pace without concern for the state or activities of any other concurrently running threads.

However, in many interesting situations, separate, concurrently running threads do share data and must consider the state and activities of other threads. In one such set of programming situations, called producer/consumer scenarios, the producer generates a stream of data that a consumer uses.

For example, imagine an application in which one thread (the producer) writes data to a file while a second thread (the consumer) reads data from the same file. Or, as you type characters on the keyboard, the producer thread places mouse events in an event queue and the consumer thread reads the events from the same queue. Both of these examples use concurrent threads that share a common resource: The first shares a file, and the second shares an event queue. Because the threads share a common resource, they must be synchronized.

This section teaches you about thread synchronization through a simple producer/consumer example.

Producer/Consumer Example

The `Producer.java` generates an integer between 0 and 9 (inclusive), stores it in a Cubby-Hole object, and prints the generated number.[1] To make the synchronization problem more interesting, the `Producer` sleeps for a random amount of time between 0 and 100 milliseconds before repeating the number-generating cycle:

```
public class Producer extends Thread {
    private CubbyHole cubbyhole;
    private int number;

    public Producer(CubbyHole c, int number) {
        cubbyhole = c;
        this.number = number;
    }

    public void run() {
        for (int i = 0; i < 10; i++) {
            cubbyhole.put(i);
            System.out.println("Producer #" + this.number + " put: " + i);
            try {
                sleep((int)(Math.random() * 100));
            } catch (InterruptedException e) { }
        }
    }
}
```

---

[1] `Producer.java`, `Cubbyhole.java`, and `Consumer.java` are included on the CD and are available online. See Code Samples (page 310).

The Consumer.java, being ravenous, consumes all integers from the CubbyHole (the exact same object into which the Producer put the integers) as quickly as they become available:

```java
public class Consumer extends Thread {
    private CubbyHole cubbyhole;
    private int number;

    public Consumer(CubbyHole c, int number) {
        cubbyhole = c;
        this.number = number;
    }

    public void run() {
        int value = 0;
        for (int i = 0; i < 10; i++) {
            value = cubbyhole.get();
            System.out.println("Consumer #" + this.number
                                + " got: " + value);
        }
    }
}
```

The Producer and Consumer in this example share data through a common CubbyHole object. Also, although the Consumer ideally will get each value produced once and only once, neither the Producer nor the Consumer makes any effort whatsoever to ensure that that happens. The synchronization between these two threads occurs at a lower level, within the get and put methods of the CubbyHole object. However, assume for a moment that these two threads make no arrangements for synchronization, and let's discuss the potential problems that might arise from this.

One problem arises when the Producer is quicker than the Consumer and generates two numbers before the Consumer has a chance to consume the first one. In this situation, the Consumer misses a number. Part of the output might look like this:

```
        . . .
Consumer #1 got: 3
Producer #1 put: 4  ◄──────────────  Consumer missed 4
Producer #1 put: 5
Consumer #1 got: 5

        . . .
```

Another problem might arise when the Consumer is quicker than the Producer and consumes the same value twice. In this situation, the Consumer might produce output that looks like this:

```
    . . .
Producer #1 put: 4  ◄──────────── Consumer got 4 twice
Consumer #1 got: 4
Consumer #1 got: 4
Producer #1 put: 5

    . . .
```

Either way, the result is wrong because the Consumer should get each integer produced by the Producer exactly once. A problem such as this is called a *race condition*. Race conditions arise from multiple, asynchronously executing threads trying to access a single object at the same time and getting the wrong result.

Race conditions in the producer/consumer example are prevented by having the storage of a new integer into the CubbyHole by the Producer be synchronized with the retrieval of an integer from the CubbyHole by the Consumer. The activities of the Producer and the Consumer must be synchronized in two ways. First, the two threads must not simultaneously access the CubbyHole. A thread can prevent this from happening by locking an object. When an object is locked by one thread and another thread tries to call a synchronized method on the same object, the second thread will block until the object is unlocked.

Second, the two threads must do some simple coordination. That is, the Producer must have a way to indicate to the Consumer that the value is ready, and the Consumer must have a way to indicate that the value has been retrieved. The Thread class provides a collection of methods—wait, notify, and notifyAll—to help threads wait for a condition and notify other threads when that condition changes.

Locking an Object

Within a program, the code segments that access the same object from separate, concurrent threads are called *critical sections*. A critical section can be a block or a method and is identified with the synchronized keyword. The Java platform then associates a lock with every object that has synchronized code.

In the producer/consumer example, the put and get methods of CubbyHole.java are the critical sections. The Consumer should not access the CubbyHole when the Producer is changing it, and the Producer should not modify it when the Consumer is getting the value. So put and get in the CubbyHole class should be marked with the synchronized keyword.

Here's a code skeleton for the CubbyHole class:

```
public class CubbyHole {
    private int contents;
    private boolean available = false;

    public synchronized int get() {
        ...
    }

    public synchronized void put(int value) {
        ...
    }
}
```

The method declarations for both put and get contain the synchronized keyword, so the system associates a unique lock with every instance of CubbyHole. Whenever control enters a synchronized method, the thread that called the method locks the object whose method has been called. Other threads cannot call a synchronized method on the same object until the object is unlocked.

Thus, when it calls CubbyHole's put method, the Producer locks the CubbyHole, thereby preventing the Consumer from calling the CubbyHole's get method:

```
public synchronized void put(int value) {
    //CubbyHole locked by the Producer
    ...
    //CubbyHole unlocked by the Producer
}
```

When the put method returns, the Producer unlocks the CubbyHole.

Similarly, when the Consumer calls CubbyHole's get method, it locks the CubbyHole, thereby preventing the Producer from calling put:

```
public synchronized int get() {
    //CubbyHole locked by the Consumer
    ...
    //CubbyHole unlocked by the Consumer
}
```

The acquisition and release of a lock is done automatically and atomically by the Java runtime environment. This ensures that race conditions cannot occur in the underlying implementation of the threads, thus ensuring data integrity.

Synchronization isn't the whole story. The two threads must also be able to notify each other when they've done their jobs. Learn more about that after a brief foray into reentrant locks.

The same thread can call a synchronized method on an object for which it already holds the lock, thereby reacquiring the lock. The Java runtime environment allows a thread to reacquire a lock because the locks are *reentrant*. Reentrant locks are important because they eliminate the possibility of a single thread's deadlocking itself on a lock that it already holds.

Consider this class:

```
public class Reentrant {
    public synchronized void a() {
        b();
        System.out.println("here I am, in a()");
    }
    public synchronized void b() {
        System.out.println("here I am, in b()");
    }
}
```

Reentrant contains two synchronized methods: a and b. The first, a, calls the other, b. When control enters method a, the current thread acquires the lock for the Reentrant object. Now a calls b; because b is also synchronized, the thread attempts to acquire the same lock again. Because the Java platform supports reentrant locks, this works. In platforms that don't support reentrant locks, this sequence of method calls causes deadlock. The current thread can acquire the Reentrant object's lock again, and both a and b execute to conclusion, as is evidenced by the output:

```
here I am, in b()
here I am, in a()
```

Using the notifyAll and wait Methods

Let's investigate how the code in CubbyHole's put and get methods helps the Producer and the Consumer coordinate their activities. The CubbyHole stores its value in a private member variable called contents. CubbyHole has another private member variable, available, that is a boolean. The available variable is true when the value has been put but not yet gotten and is false when the value has been gotten but not yet put. Here's one possible implementation for the put and get methods:

```
public synchronized int get() {      //won't work!
    if (available == true) {
        available = false;
        return contents;
    }
}
public synchronized int put(int value) {      //won't work!
    if (available == false) {
```

```
            available = true;
            contents = value;
        }
    }
```

As implemented, these two methods won't work. Look at the get method. What happens if the Producer hasn't put anything in the CubbyHole and available isn't true? The get method does nothing. Similarly, if the Producer calls put before the Consumer got the value, put doesn't do anything.

You really want the Consumer to *wait* until the Producer puts something in the CubbyHole and the Producer to *notify* the Consumer when it's done so. Similarly, the Producer should *wait* until the Consumer takes a value (and notifies the Producer of its activities) before replacing it with a new value. The two threads must coordinate more fully and can use Object's wait and notifyAll methods to do so.

Here are the new get and put implementations that wait on and notify each other of their activities:

```
public synchronized int get() {
    while (available == false) {
        try {
            //wait for Producer to put value
            wait();
        } catch (InterruptedException e) { }
    }
    available = false;
    //notify Producer that value has been retrieved
    notifyAll();
    return contents;
}

public synchronized void put(int value) {
    while (available == true) {
        try {
            //wait for Consumer to get value
            wait();
        } catch (InterruptedException e) { }
    }
    contents = value;
    available = true;
    //notify Consumer that value has been set
    notifyAll();
}
```

The code in the get method loops until the Producer has produced a new value. Each time through the loop, get calls the wait method. The wait method relinquishes the lock held by the Consumer on the CubbyHole (thereby allowing the Producer to get the lock and update the CubbyHole) and then waits for notification from the Producer. When it puts something in the CubbyHole, the Producer notifies the Consumer by calling notifyAll. The Consumer then comes out of the wait state, available is now true, the loop exits, and the get method returns the value in the CubbyHole.

The put method works in a similar fashion. It waits for the Consumer thread to consume the current value before allowing the Producer to produce a new one.

The notifyAll method wakes up all threads waiting on the object in question (in this case, the CubbyHole). The awakened threads compete for the lock. One thread gets it, and the others go back to waiting. The Object class also defines the notify method, which arbitrarily wakes up one of the threads waiting on this object.

The Object class contains three versions of the wait method:

wait()	Waits indefinitely for notification. (This method was used in the producer/consumer example.)
wait(long *timeout*)	Waits for notification or until the timeout period has elapsed. The *timeout* argument is specified in milliseconds.
wait(long *timeout*, int *nanos*)	Waits for notification or until *timeout* milliseconds plus *nanos* nanoseconds have elapsed.

Note: Besides using these timed wait methods to synchronize threads, you also can use them in place of sleep. Both wait and sleep delay for the requested amount of time. You can easily wake up wait with a notify, but a sleeping thread cannot be awakened prematurely. This doesn't matter too much for threads that don't sleep for long, but it could be important for threads that sleep for minutes at a time.

Running the Producer/Consumer Example

Here's a small standalone application, called ProducerConsumerDemo,[1] that creates a Cub-byHole object, a Producer, and a Consumer and then starts both the Producer and the Consumer:

---

[1] ProducerConsumerDemo.java is included on the CD and is available online. See Code Samples (page 310).

```
public class ProducerConsumerDemo {
    public static void main(String[] args) {
        CubbyHole c = new CubbyHole();
        Producer p1 = new Producer(c, 1);
        Consumer c1 = new Consumer(c, 1);

        p1.start();
        c1.start();
    }
}
```

Here's the output of `ProducerConsumerDemo`:

```
Producer #1 put: 0
Consumer #1 got: 0
Producer #1 put: 1
Consumer #1 got: 1
Producer #1 put: 2
Consumer #1 got: 2
Producer #1 put: 3
Consumer #1 got: 3
Producer #1 put: 4
Consumer #1 got: 4
Producer #1 put: 5
Consumer #1 got: 5
Producer #1 put: 6
Consumer #1 got: 6
Producer #1 put: 7
Consumer #1 got: 7
Producer #1 put: 8
Consumer #1 got: 8
Producer #1 put: 9
Consumer #1 got: 9
```

Avoiding Starvation and Deadlock

If you write a program in which several concurrent threads are competing for resources, you must take precautions to ensure fairness. A system is fair when each thread gets enough access to limited resources to make reasonable progress. A fair system prevents *starvation* and *deadlock*. Starvation occurs when one or more threads in your program are blocked from gaining access to a resource and, as a result, cannot make progress. Deadlock, the ultimate form of starvation, occurs when two or more threads are waiting on a condition that cannot be satisfied. Deadlock most often occurs when two (or more) threads are each waiting for the other(s) to do something.

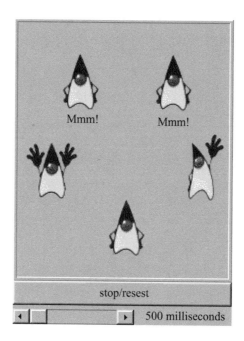

http://java.sun.com/docs/books/tutorial/essential/threads/deadlock.html

The story of the dining philosophers is often used to illustrate various problems that can occur when many synchronized threads are competing for limited resources. The story goes like this. Five philosophers are sitting at a round table. In front of each philosopher is a bowl of rice. Between each pair of philosophers is one chopstick. Before taking a bite of rice, an individual philosopher must have two chopsticks: one taken from the left and one taken from the right. The philosophers must find a way to share chopsticks so that they all get to eat.

The dining philosophers algorithm implemented by the following applet works like this. Duke always reaches for the chopstick on his right first. If the chopstick is there, Duke takes it and raises his right hand. Next, Duke tries for the left chopstick. If the chopstick is available, Duke picks it up and raises his other hand. Now that Duke has both chopsticks, he takes a bite of rice and says, "Mmm!" He then puts both chopsticks down, thereby allowing either of his two neighbors to get the chopsticks. Duke then starts all over again by trying for the right chopstick. Between each attempt to grab a chopstick, Duke pauses for a random period of time.

The slider at the bottom of the applet controls the amount of time that each philosopher waits before attempting to pick up a chopstick. When the slider is set to 0, the philosophers don't wait—they just grab—and the applet often ends up in deadlock—that is, all the philosophers are frozen with their right hands in the air. Why? Because each immediately has one chopstick and is waiting on a condition that cannot be satisfied. That is, each is waiting for the chopstick on the left, which is held by the philosopher to the left.

When you move the slider so that the waiting period is longer, the applet may proceed for a while without deadlocking. However, deadlock is always possible with this particular implementation of the dining philosophers problem because it is possible for all five philosophers to be holding their right chopsticks. Rather than rely on luck to prevent deadlock, you must either explicitly prevent it or detect it.

For most programmers, the better choice is to prevent deadlock rather than to try to detect it. The simplest approach to preventing deadlock is to impose ordering on the condition variables. In the dining philosopher applet, no ordering is imposed on the condition variables because the philosophers and the chopsticks are arranged in a circle. All chopsticks are equal.

However, you can change the rules in the applet by numbering the chopsticks 1 through 5 and insisting that the philosophers pick up first the chopstick that has the lower number. The philosopher who is sitting between chopsticks 1 and 2 and the philosopher who is sitting between chopsticks 1 and 5 must now reach for the same chopstick first (chopstick 1) rather than picking up the one on the right. Whoever gets chopstick 1 first is then free to take another chopstick. Whoever doesn't get chopstick 1 must now wait for the first philosopher to release it. Deadlock is not possible.

Grouping Threads

Every thread is a member of a *thread group*. A thread group provides a mechanism for collecting multiple threads into a single object and manipulating those threads all at once rather than individually. For example, you can interrupt all the threads within a group with a single method call. Thread groups are implemented by the `ThreadGroup`[1] class in the `java.lang` package.

The runtime system puts a thread into a thread group during thread construction. When you create a thread, you can either allow the runtime system to figure out the appropriate thread group, or you can explicitly set the new thread's group. The thread is a permanent member of whatever thread group it joins on its creation. You cannot move a thread to a new group after the thread has been created.

---

[1] http://java.sun.com/j2se/1.3/docs/api/java/lang/ThreadGroup.html

The Thread Group

If you create a new thread without specifying its group in the constructor, the runtime system automatically places the new thread in the same group as the thread that created it (called the *current thread group* and the *current thread*, respectively). When an application first starts up, the Java runtime environment creates a ThreadGroup named main. Thus, all new threads that a program creates become members of the main thread group unless the program explicitly creates other groups and puts threads in them.

> **Note:** If you create a thread within an applet, the new thread's group may be something other than main, depending on the browser or the viewer in which the applet is running. Refer to the sections Threads in AWT Applets (page 449) and Threads in Swing Applets (page 459) in Chapter 11 for information.

Many programmers ignore thread groups altogether and allow the runtime system to handle all the details regarding thread groups. However, if your program creates a lot of threads that should be manipulated as a group or if you are implementing a custom security manager, you will likely want more control over thread groups. Continue reading for more details.

Creating a Thread Explicitly in a Group

To put a new thread in a thread group other than the default, you must specify the thread group explicitly when you create it. The Thread class has three constructors that set a new thread's group:

```
public Thread(ThreadGroup group, Runnable target)
public Thread(ThreadGroup group, String name)
public Thread(ThreadGroup group, Runnable target, String name)
```

Each constructor creates a new thread, initializes it based on the Runnable and String parameters, and makes the new thread a member of the specified group. For example, the following code sample creates a thread group (myThreadGroup) and then creates a thread (myThread) in that group:

```
ThreadGroup myThreadGroup = new ThreadGroup("My Group of Threads");
Thread myThread = new Thread(myThreadGroup, "a thread for my group");
```

The ThreadGroup passed into a Thread constructor can be any group: one created by your program, by the Java runtime environment, or by the browser in which an applet is running.

Getting a Thread's Group

To find out what group a thread is in, call its `getThreadGroup` method:

```
theGroup = myThread.getThreadGroup();
```

Once you've obtained a thread's `ThreadGroup`, you can query the group for information, such as what other threads are in the group. You also can modify the threads in that group by using a single method invocation.

Using the ThreadGroup Class

The `ThreadGroup` class manages groups of threads for programs. A `ThreadGroup` can contain any number of threads and can contain other `ThreadGroups`. The threads in a group are generally related, such as by who created them, what function they perform, or when they should be started and stopped.

The topmost thread group in an application is the thread group named `main`. A program can create threads and groups in the `main` group or in its subgroups. The result is a hierarchy of threads and groups, as shown in Figure 85.

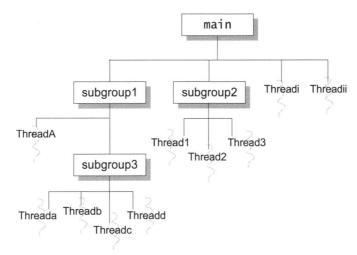

Figure 85 Thread groups can be nested, thereby creating a hierarchy of groups and threads.

The `ThreadGroup` class has several categories of methods, discussed in the following sections.

- Collection Management Methods (page 304): Methods that manage the collection of threads and subgroups contained in the thread group
- Methods That Operate on the Group Object (page 304): Methods that set or get attributes of the ThreadGroup object
- Methods That Operate on All Threads within a Group (page 306): A set of methods that perform an operation on all the threads and subgroups within the group
- Access Restriction Methods (page 306): Methods that allow the security manager to restrict access to threads, based on group membership; allowed by ThreadGroup and Thread

Collection Management Methods

The ThreadGroup provides a set of methods that manage the threads and subgroups within the group and that allow other objects to query the ThreadGroup for information about its contents. For example, you can call ThreadGroup's activeCount method to learn the number of active threads currently in the group. This method can be used with the enumerate method to get an array filled with references to all the active threads in a ThreadGroup. For example, the listCurrentThreads method in the following example fills an array with all the active threads in the current thread group and prints their names:

```
public class EnumerateDemo {
    public void listCurrentThreads() {
        ThreadGroup currentGroup =
            Thread.currentThread().getThreadGroup();
        int numThreads = currentGroup.activeCount();
        Thread[] listOfThreads = new Thread[numThreads];

        currentGroup.enumerate(listOfThreads);
        for (int i = 0; i < numThreads; i++) {
            System.out.println("Thread #" + i + " = "
                                + listOfThreads[i].getName());
        }
    }
}
```

Other collection management methods provided by the ThreadGroup class include active-GroupCount, which returns an estimate of the number of active threads in the group, and list, which prints information about this thread group to the standard output.

Methods That Operate on the Group Object

The ThreadGroup class supports several attributes that are set and retrieved from the group as a whole. These attributes include the maximum priority that any thread within the group can have, whether the group is a daemon group, the name of the group, and the parent of the group.

The methods that get and set ThreadGroup attributes operate at the group level. They inspect or change the attribute on the ThreadGroup object, but they do not affect any of the threads within the group. Following are the ThreadGroup methods that operate at the group level:

- getMaxPriority and setMaxPriority
- getDaemon and setDaemon
- getName
- getParent and parentOf
- toString

When you use setMaxPriority to change a group's maximum priority, you are changing only the attribute on the group object; you are not changing the priority of any of the threads within it. Consider the following program that creates a group and a thread within that group:

```java
public class MaxPriorityDemo {
    public static void main(String[] args) {

        ThreadGroup groupNORM = new ThreadGroup(
                            "A group with normal priority");
        Thread priorityMAX = new Thread(groupNORM,
                            "A thread with maximum priority");

        // set Thread's priority to max (10)
        priorityMAX.setPriority(Thread.MAX_PRIORITY);

        // set ThreadGroup's max priority to normal (5)
        groupNORM.setMaxPriority(Thread.NORM_PRIORITY);

        System.out.println("Group's maximum priority = "
                            + groupNORM.getMaxPriority());
        System.out.println("Thread's priority = "
                            + priorityMAX.getPriority());
    }
}
```

When the ThreadGroup groupNORM is created, the thread inherits its maximum priority attribute from its parent thread group. In this case, the parent group priority is the maximum (MAX_PRIORITY) allowed by the Java runtime environment. Next, the program sets the priority of the priorityMAX thread to the maximum allowed by the Java runtime environment. Then the program lowers the group's maximum to the normal priority (NORM_PRIORITY). The setMaxPriority method does not affect the priority of the priorityMAX thread, so at this point, the `priorityMAX` thread has a priority of `MAX_PRIORITY`, which is greater than the maximum priority of its group. Here is the output from the program:

```
Group's maximum priority = 5
Thread's priority = 10
```

As you can see, a thread can have a priority higher than the maximum allowed by its group as long as the thread's priority is set before the group's maximum priority is lowered. A thread group's maximum priority is used to limit a thread's priority when the thread is first created within a group or when you use `setPriority` to change the thread's priority. Note that the `setMaxPriority` method *does* change the maximum priority of all its descendant-thread groups.

Similarly, a group's daemon status applies only to the group object. Changing a group's daemon status does not affect the daemon status of any thread in the group. Furthermore, a group's daemon status does not in any way determine the daemon status of its threads—you can put any thread within a daemon thread group. The daemon status of a thread group simply indicates that the group will be destroyed when all its threads have been terminated.

Methods That Operate on All Threads within a Group

The `ThreadGroup` class has a method for interrupting all the threads within it: `interrupt`. The `ThreadGroup`'s `interrupt` method calls the `interrupt` method on every thread in the group and its subgroups.

The `resume`, `stop`, and `suspend` methods operate on all threads in the group. However, these methods have been deprecated. Refer to <u>Deprecated Thread Methods</u> (page 527).

Access Restriction Methods

The `ThreadGroup` class itself does not impose any access restrictions, such as allowing threads from one group to inspect or to modify threads in a different group. Rather, the `Thread` and the `ThreadGroup` classes cooperate with security managers (subclasses of the `java.lang.SecurityManager` class), which can impose access restrictions based on thread group membership.

The `Thread` and the `ThreadGroup` classes both have a method, `checkAccess`, that calls the current security manager's `checkAccess` method. The security manager decides whether to allow the access based on the group membership of the threads involved. If access is not allowed, the `checkAccess` method throws a `SecurityException`. Otherwise, `checkAccess` simply returns.

Following is a list of `ThreadGroup` methods that call `ThreadGroup`'s `checkAccess` method before performing the action of the method. These are called *regulated accesses*. A regulated access must be approved by the security manager before it can be completed.

- `ThreadGroup(ThreadGroup `*`parent`*`, String `*`name`*`)`
- `setDaemon(boolean `*`isDaemon`*`)`
- `setMaxPriority(int `*`maxPriority`*`)`
- `destroy()`

Here are the `Thread` class constructors and methods that call `checkAccess` before proceeding:

- Constructors that specify a thread group
- `setPriority(int `*`priority`*`)`
- `setName(String `*`name`*`)`
- `setDaemon(boolean `*`isDaemon`*`)`

By default, a standalone application does not have a security manager. No restrictions are imposed, and any thread can inspect or modify any other thread, regardless of the group in which they are located. You can define and implement your own access restrictions for thread groups by subclassing `SecurityManager`, overriding the appropriate methods, and installing the `SecurityManager` as the current security manager in your application.

The HotJava™ Web browser is an example of an application that implements its own security manager. HotJava needs to ensure that applets are well behaved and don't attempt any negative interactions with other applets, such as lowering the priority of another applet's threads, that are running at the same time. HotJava's security manager does not allow threads in different groups to modify one another. Note that access restrictions based on thread groups may vary among browsers, and thus applets may behave differently in different browsers.

Summary of Threads

This chapter provided a great deal of information about using threads in the Java platform. This section summarizes where you can find various classes, methods, and language features that participate in the threads story.

Package Support of Threads

<u>java.lang.Thread</u>[1]

In the Java platform, threads are objects that derive from java.lang's Thread class. The Thread class defines and implements threads. You can subclass the Thread class to provide your own thread implementations.

<u>java.lang.Runnable</u>[2]

The java.lang package also defines the Runnable interface, which allows any class to provide the body (the run method) for a thread.

<u>java.lang.Object</u>[3]

The root class, Object, defines three methods you can use to synchronize methods around a condition variable: wait, notify, and notifyAll.

<u>java.lang.ThreadGroup</u>[4]

All threads belong to a thread group, which typically contains related threads. The ThreadGroup class in the java.lang package implements groups of threads.

Language Support of Threads

The Java programming language has two keywords related to the synchronization of threads: volatile and synchronized. Both of these language features help ensure the integrity of data that is shared between two concurrently running threads. The section <u>Synchronizing Threads</u> (page 291) discusses thread synchronization issues.

Runtime Support of Threads

The Java runtime environment contains the scheduler, which is responsible for running all the existing threads. The scheduler uses a fixed-priority scheduling algorithm, which boils down to the following simple rule of thumb.

Rule of Thumb: At any given time, the highest-priority thread is running. However, this is not guaranteed. The thread scheduler may choose to run a lower-priority thread to avoid starvation. For this reason, use priority only to affect scheduling policy for efficiency purposes. Do not rely on thread priority for algorithm correctness.

---

[1] http://java.sun.com/j2se/1.3/docs/api/java/lang/Thread.html
[2] http://java.sun.com/j2se/1.3/docs/api/java/lang/Runnable.html
[3] http://java.sun.com/j2se/1.3/docs/api/java/lang/Object.html
[4] http://java.sun.com/j2se/1.3/docs/api/java/lang/ThreadGroup.html

Questions and Exercises

Questions

1. What method in `Timer` or `TimerTask` can you use to determine when the task was most recently scheduled to execute? (*Hint:* You can find the answer by looking at the API documentation for `Timer` and `TimerTask`. Remember that these classes were introduced in version 1.3 of the Java platform.)

2. What is the effect of calling the `start` method on a `Thread` object?

3. What are the two ways you can provide the implementation for a thread's `run` method?

Exercises

1. Convert `AnnoyingBeep.java`[1] so that the initial delay is 5 seconds, instead of 0.

2. Convert `AnnoyingBeep.java` to use the `scheduleAtFixedRate` method instead of `schedule` to schedule the task. Change the implementation of the `run` method so that if the `run` method is called too late for a warning beep (say, more than 5 milliseconds after it was scheduled to run), nothing happens—no beep and string are generated. (*Hint:* Remember your answer to question 1.)

3. Change the `main` program of `TwoThreadsDemo.java`[2] so that it creates a third thread, named "Bora Bora." Compile and run the program again. Note that you will also need `SimpleThread.java`.[3] Does this change your vacation destiny?

4. Compile and run `RaceDemo.java`[4] and `SelfishRunner.java`[5] on your computer. Do you have a time-sliced system?

5. Well-behaved threads voluntarily relinquish the CPU periodically and give other threads an opportunity to run. Rewrite the `SelfishRunner` class to be a `PoliteRunner`. Be sure to modify the main program in `RaceDemo.java` to create `PoliteRunners` instead of `SelfishRunners`.

Answers

You can find answers to these Questions and Exercises online:

```
http://java.sun.com/docs/books/tutorial/essential/threads/QandE/
answers.html
```

---

[1] `AnnoyingBeep.java` is included on the CD and is available online. See Code Samples (page 310).

[2] `TwoThreadsDemo.java` is included on the CD and is available online. See Code Samples (page 310).

[3] `SimpleThread.java` is included on the CD and is available online. See Code Samples (page 310).

[4] `RaceDemo.java` is included on the CD and is available online. See Code Samples (page 310).

[5] `SelfishRunnerDemo.java` is included on the CD and is available online. See Code Samples (page 310).

Code Samples

Table 45 lists the code samples used in this chapter and where you can find the code online and on the CD that accompanies this book.

Table 45   Code Samples in Threads: Doing Two or More Tasks at Once

Code Sample	CD Location	Online Location
Reminder.java (page 273)	JavaTutorial/essential/ threads/example-1dot3/ Reminder.java	http://java.sun.com/docs/ books/tutorial/essential/ threads/example-1dot3/ Reminder.java
ReminderBeep.java (page 275)	JavaTutorial/essential/ threads/example-1dot3/Remind-erBeep.java	http://java.sun.com/docs/ books/tutorial/essential/ threads/example-1dot3/Remind-erBeep.java
AnnoyingBeep.java (page 276), (page 309)	JavaTutorial/essential/ threads/example-1dot3/Annoy-ingBeep.java	http://java.sun.com/docs/ books/tutorial/essential/ threads/example-1dot3/Annoy-ingBeep.java
RaceApplet.java (page 287)	JavaTutorial/essential/ threads/example-swing/RaceAp-plet.java	http://java.sun.com/docs/ books/tutorial/essential/ threads/example-swing/RaceAp-plet.java
Runner.java (page 287)	JavaTutorial/essential/ threads/example-swing/Run-ner.java	http://java.sun.com/docs/ books/tutorial/essential/ threads/example-swing/Run-ner.java
RaceDemo.java (page 289), (page 309)	JavaTutorial/essential/ threads/example/RaceDemo.java	http://java.sun.com/docs/ books/tutorial/essential/ threads/example/RaceDemo.java
Producer.java (page 292)	JavaTutorial/essential/ threads/example/Producer.java	http://java.sun.com/docs/ books/tutorial/essential/ threads/example/Producer.java
Cubbyhole.java (page 292)	JavaTutorial/essential/ threads/example/Cubbyhole.java	http://java.sun.com/docs/ books/tutorial/essential/ threads/example/Cubbyhole.java
Consumer.java (page 292)	JavaTutorial/essential/ threads/example/Consumer.java	http://java.sun.com/docs/ books/tutorial/essential/ threads/example/Consumer.java
ProducerConsumer-Demo.java (page 298)	JavaTutorial/essential/ threads/example/ProducerCon-sumerDemo.java	http://java.sun.com/docs/ books/tutorial/essential/ threads/example/ProducerCon-sumerDemo.java

Table 45   Code Samples in Threads: Doing Two or More Tasks at Once

TwoThreads- Demo.java (page 309)	JavaTutorial/essential/ threads/example/TwoThreads- Demo.java	http://java.sun.com/docs/ books/tutorial/essential/ threads/example/TwoThreads- Demo.java
SimpleThread.java (page 309)	JavaTutorial/essential/ threads/example/SimpleTh- read.java	http://java.sun.com/docs/ books/tutorial/essential/ threads/example/SimpleTh- read.java
SelfishRunner.java (page 309)	JavaTutorial/essential/ threads/example/SelfishRun- ner.java	http://java.sun.com/docs/ books/tutorial/essential/ threads/example/SelfishRun- ner.java

Note: The section <u>Common Problems and Their Solutions</u> (page 391) contains solutions to common problems Tutorial readers have encountered.

I/O: Reading and Writing

OFTEN a program needs to bring in information from an external source or to send out information to an external destination. The information can be anywhere: in a file, on disk, somewhere on the network, in memory, or in another program. Also, the information can be of any type: objects, characters, images, or sounds. This chapter covers the Java™ platform classes that your programs can use to read and to write data.

Overview of I/O Streams

To bring in information, a program opens a *stream* on an information source (a file, memory, a socket) and reads the information sequentially, as shown in Figure 86.

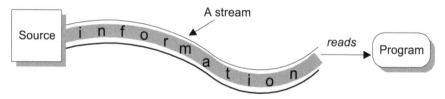

Figure 86 Reading information into a program.

Similarly, a program can send information to an external destination by opening a stream to a destination and writing the information out sequentially, as in Figure 87.

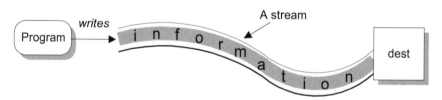

Figure 87 Writing information out of a program.

No matter where the data is coming from or going to and no matter what its type, the algorithms for sequentially reading and writing data are shown in Table 46.

Table 46

Reading	Writing
open a stream while more information read information close the stream	open a stream while more information write information close the stream

The java.io package contains a collection of stream classes that support these algorithms. To use these classes, a program needs to import the java.io package. The stream classes are divided into two class hierarchies, based on the data type (either characters or bytes) on which they operate, as show in Figure 88.

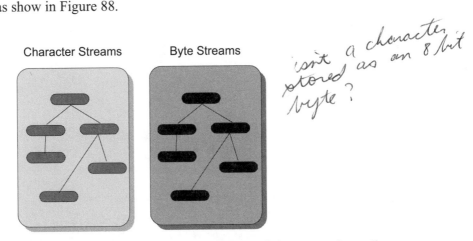

isn't a character stored as an 8 bit byte?

Figure 88 The java.io package contains two independent hierarchies of classes: one for reading and writing bytes and the other for reading and writing characters.

Character Streams

Reader[1] and Writer[2] are the abstract superclasses for character streams. Reader provides the API and partial implementation for *readers*—streams that read 16-bit characters—and Writer provides the API and partial implementation for *writers*—streams that write 16-bit characters. Subclasses of Reader and Writer implement specialized streams (Figure 89).

---

[1] http://java.sun.com/j2se/1.3/docs/api/java/io/Reader.html
[2] http://java.sun.com/j2se/1.3/docs/api/java/io/Writer.html

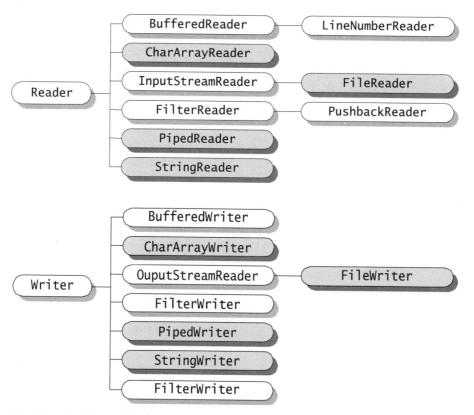

Figure 89 The class hierarchies for readers and writers in java.io. Subclasses of Reader and Writer implement specialized streams and are divided into two categories: those that read from or write to data sinks (shaded) and those that perform some sort of processing (unshaded).

Most programs should use readers and writers to read and write textual information. The reason is that they can handle any character in the Unicode character set, whereas the byte streams are limited to ISO-Latin-1 8-bit bytes.

Byte Streams

To read and write 8-bit bytes, programs should use the byte streams, descendants of <u>Input-Stream</u>[1] and <u>OutputStream</u>.[2] InputStream and OutputStream provide the API and partial

---

[1] http://java.sun.com/j2se/1.3/docs/api/java/io/InputStream.html
[2] http://java.sun.com/j2se/1.3/docs/api/java/io/OutputStream.html

implementation for *input streams* (streams that read 8-bit bytes) and *output streams* (streams that write 8-bit bytes) (Figure 90). These streams are typically used to read and write binary data, such as images and sounds. Two of the byte stream classes, `ObjectInputStream` and `ObjectOutputStream`, are used for object serialization. These classes are covered in the section <u>Object Serialization</u> (page 334).

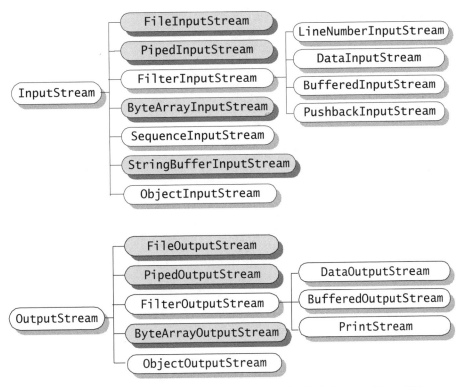

Figure 90 The class hierarchies for byte streams in `java.io`. Subclasses of `InputStream` and `OutputStream` are divided into two categories: data sink streams (shaded) and processing streams (unshaded).

Understanding the I/O Superclasses

`Reader` and `InputStream` define similar APIs but for different data types. For example, `Reader` contains these methods for reading characters and arrays of characters:

```
int read()
int read(char cbuf[])
int read(char cbuf[], int offset, int length)
```

`InputStream` defines the same methods but for reading bytes and arrays of bytes:

```
int read()
int read(byte cbuf[])
int read(byte cbuf[], int offset, int length)
```

Also, both `Reader` and `InputStream` provide methods for marking a location in the stream, skipping input, and resetting the current position.

`Writer` and `OutputStream` are similarly parallel. `Writer` defines these methods for writing characters and arrays of characters:

```
int write(int c)
int write(char cbuf[])
int write(char cbuf[], int offset, int length)
```

And `OutputStream` defines the same methods for bytes:

```
int write(int c)
int write(byte cbuf[])
int write(byte cbuf[], int offset, int length)
```

All the streams—readers, writers, input streams, and output streams—are automatically opened when created. You should close any stream explicitly by calling its `close` method. Or, the garbage collector can implicitly close it, which occurs when the object is no longer referenced.

Security Consideration: Some I/O operations are subject to approval by the current security manager. The example programs in this chapter are standalone applications, which have no security manager. This code might not work in an applet, depending on the browser or the viewer in which it is running. See the online tutorial at `http://java.sun.com/docs/books/tutorial/applet/practical/security.html` for information about the security restrictions placed on applets.

Using the Streams

Table 47 lists `java.io`'s streams and describes what they do. Note that many times, `java.io` contains character streams and byte streams that perform the same type of I/O but for different data types.

Table 47   I/O Streams

Type of I/O	Streams	Description
Memory	CharArrayReader CharArrayWriter ByteArrayInputStream ByteArrayOutputStream	Use these streams to read from and write to memory. You create these streams on an existing array and then use the read and write methods to read from or write to the array.
	StringReader StringWriter StringBufferInputStream	Use StringReader to read characters from a String in memory. Use StringWriter to write to a String. StringWriter collects the characters written to it in a StringBuffer, which can then be converted to a String. StringBufferInputStream is similar to StringReader, except that it reads bytes from a StringBuffer.
Pipe	PipedReader PipedWriter PipedInputStream PipedOutputStream	Implement the input and output components of a pipe. Pipes are used to channel the output from one thread into the input of another. See PipedReader and PipedWriter in action in the section How to Use Pipe Streams (page 322).
File	FileReader FileWriter FileInputStream FileOutputStream	Collectively called file streams, these streams are used to read from or write to a file on the native file system. The section How to Use File Streams (page 320) has an example that uses FileReader and FileWriter to copy the contents of one file into another.
Concatenation	*N/A* SequenceInputStream	Concatenates multiple input streams into one input stream. The section How to Concatenate Files (page 325) has a short example of this class.
Object Serialization	*N/A* ObjectInputStream ObjectOutputStream	Used to serialize objects. See the section Object Serialization (page 334).
Data Conversion	*N/A* DataInputStream DataOutputStream	Read or write primitive data types in a machine-independent format. The section How to Use DataInputStream and DataOutputStream (page 328) shows an example of using these two streams.
Counting	LineNumberReader LineNumberInputStream	Keeps track of line numbers while reading.
Peeking Ahead	PushbackReader PushbackInputStream	These input streams each have a pushback buffer. When reading data from a stream, it is sometimes useful to peek at the next few bytes or characters in the stream to decide what to do next.
Printing	PrintWriter PrintStream	Contain convenient printing methods. These are the easiest streams to write to, so you will often see other writable streams wrapped in one of these.

Table 47   I/O Streams

Type of I/O	Streams	Description

Buffering	`BufferedReader`
	`BufferedWriter`
	
	`BufferedInputStream`
	`BufferedOutputStream`
		Buffer data while reading or writing, thereby reducing the number of accesses required on the original data source. Buffered streams are typically more efficient than similar nonbuffered streams and are often used with other streams.

Filtering	`FilterReader`
	`FilterWriter`
	
	`FilterInputStream`
	`FilterOutputStream`
		These abstract classes define the interface for filter streams, which filter data as it's being read or written. The section Working with Filter Streams (page 327) shows you how to use filter streams and how to implement your own.

Converting between Bytes and Characters	`InputStreamReader` `OutputStreamWriter`	A reader and writer pair that forms the bridge between byte streams and character streams. An `InputStreamReader` reads bytes from an Input-Stream and converts them to characters, using the default character encoding or a character encoding specified by name. An `OutputStreamWriter` converts characters to bytes, using the default character encoding or a character encoding specified by name and then writes those bytes to an OutputStream. You can get the name of the default character encoding by calling `System.getProperty("file.encoding")`.

The next several sections provide examples on how to use several of these streams.

How to Use File Streams

File streams are perhaps the easiest streams to understand. The file streams—`FileReader`,[1] `FileWriter`,[2] `FileInputStream`,[3] and `FileOutputStream`[4]—each read or write from a file on the native file system. You can create a file stream from a file name in the form of a string, a `File`[5] object, or a `FileDescriptor`[6] object.

---

[1] http://java.sun.com/j2se/1.3/docs/api/java/io/FileReader.html
[2] http://java.sun.com/j2se/1.3/docs/api/java/io/FileWriter.html
[3] http://java.sun.com/j2se/1.3/docs/api/java/io/FileInputStream.html
[4] http://java.sun.com/j2se/1.3/docs/api/java/io/FileOutputStream.html
[5] http://java.sun.com/j2se/1.3/docs/api/java/io/File.html
[6] http://java.sun.com/j2se/1.3/docs/api/java/io/FileDescriptor.html

The following program, Copy,[1] uses `FileReader` and `FileWriter` to copy the contents of a file named `farrago.txt` into a file called `outagain.txt`:

```java
import java.io.*;
public class Copy {
    public static void main(String[] args) throws IOException {
        File inputFile = new File("farrago.txt");
        File outputFile = new File("outagain.txt");

        FileReader in = new FileReader(inputFile);
        FileWriter out = new FileWriter(outputFile);
        int c;

        while ((c = in.read()) != -1) {
            out.write(c);
        }
        in.close();
        out.close();
    }
}
```

This program is very simple. It opens a file reader on `farrago.txt` and opens a file writer on `outagain.txt`. The program reads characters from the reader as long as there's more input in the input file and writes those characters to the writer. When the input runs out, the program closes both the reader and the writer.

Here is the code that the Copy program uses to create a file reader:

```java
File inputFile = new File("farrago.txt");
FileReader in = new FileReader(inputFile);
```

This code creates a `File` object that represents the named file on the native file system. `File` is a utility class provided by `java.io`. The Copy program uses this object only to construct a file reader on a file. However, the program could use `inputFile` to get information, such as its full path name, about the file.

After you've run the program, you should find an exact copy of `farrago.txt` in a file named `outagain.txt` in the same directory. Here is the content of the file:

```
So she went into the garden to cut a cabbage-leaf, to
make an apple-pie; and at the same time a great
she-bear, coming up the street, pops its head into the
shop. 'What! no soap?' So he died, and she very
```

---

[1] Copy.java and the text file `farrago.txt` are included on the CD and are available online. See Code Samples (page 348).

```
imprudently married the barber; and there were
present the Picninnies, and the Joblillies, and the
Garyalies, and the grand Panjandrum himself, with the
little round button at top, and they all fell to playing
the game of catch as catch can, till the gun powder ran
out at the heels of their boots.
                        - Samuel Foote 1720-1777
```

Remember that `FileReader` and `FileWriter` read and write 16-bit characters. However, most native file systems are based on 8-bit bytes. These streams encode the characters as they read or write according to the default character-encoding scheme. You can find out the default character encoding by using `System.getProperty("file.encoding")`. To specify an encoding other than the default, you should construct an `OutputStreamWriter` on a `FileOutputStream` and specify the encoding. For information about encoding characters, see the "Writing Global Programs" section of the Internationalization chapter; this chapter is included in *The Java Tutorial Continued* book and online.[1]

Another version of this program, `CopyBytes.java`,[2] uses `FileInputStream` and `FileOutputStream` instead of `FileReader` and `FileWriter`. This program is available on this book's CD and online.

How to Use Pipe Streams

Pipes are used to channel the output from one thread into the input of another. `PipedReader`[3] and `PipedWriter`[4] (and their input and output stream counterparts `PipedInputStream`[5] and `PipedOutputStream`[6]) implement the input and output components of a pipe. Why are pipes useful?

Consider a class that implements various string manipulation utilities, such as sorting and reversing text. It would be nice if the output of one of these methods could be used as the input for another so that you could string a series of method calls together to perform a higher-order function. For example, you could reverse each word in a list, sort the words, and then reverse each word again to create a list of rhyming words.

---

[1] http://java.sun.com/docs/books/tutorial/i18n/index.html
[2] `CopyBytes.java` is included on the CD and is available online. See Code Samples (page 348).
[3] http://java.sun.com/j2se/1.3/docs/api/java/io/PipedReader.html
[4] http://java.sun.com/j2se/1.3/docs/api/java/io/PipedWriter.html
[5] http://java.sun.com/j2se/1.3/docs/api/java/io/PipedInputStream.html
[6] http://java.sun.com/j2se/1.3/docs/api/java/io/PipedOutputStream.html

Without pipe streams, a program would have to store the results somewhere (such as in a file or in memory) between each step, as shown in Figure 91.

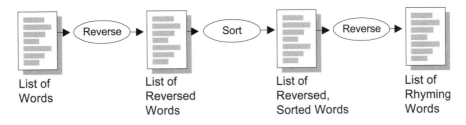

List of
Words

List of
Reversed
Words

List of
Reversed,
Sorted Words

List of
Rhyming
Words

Figure 91 Without a pipe, a program must store intermediate results.

With pipe streams, the output from one method is the input for the next method, as shown in Figure 92.

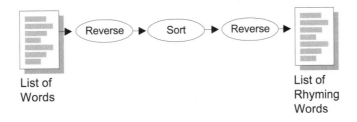

List of
Words

List of
Rhyming
Words

Figure 92 With a pipe, a program can pipe information directly from one thread to another.

Let's look at a program, called RhymingWords,[1] that implements what's represented in Figure 92. This program uses PipedReader and PipedWriter to connect the input and output of its reverse and sort methods to create a list of rhyming words. Several classes make up this program.

First, let's look at the calling sequence of the reverse and sort methods from the main method:

```
FileReader words = new FileReader("words.txt");
Reader rhymingWords = reverse(sort(reverse(words)));
```

---

[1] RhymingWords.java is included on the CD and is available online. The other files you need for this example are words.txt, ReverseThread.java, and SortThread.java. See <u>Code Samples</u> (page 348).

The innermost call to `reverse` takes a `FileReader`, which is opened on the file `words.txt`, which contains a list of words.[1] The return value of `reverse` is passed to `sort`, whose return value is then passed to another call to `reverse`.

Let's look at the `reverse` method; the `sort` method is similar, and you will understand it once you understand `reverse`.

```
public static Reader reverse(Reader src) throws IOException {
    BufferedReader in = new BufferedReader(source);

    PipedWriter pipeOut = new PipedWriter();
    PipedReader pipeIn = new PipedReader(pipeOut);
    PrintWriter out = new PrintWriter(pipeOut);

    new ReverseThread(out, in).start();

    return pipeIn;
}
```

The statements in boldface create both ends of a pipe—a `PipedWriter` and a `Piped-Reader`—and connect them by constructing the `PipedReader` "on" the `PipedWriter`. Whatever is written to the `PipedWriter` can be read from the `PipedReader`. The connection forms a pipe, as illustrated in Figure 93.

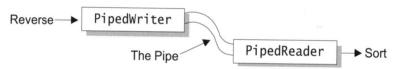

Figure 93 Using `PipedWriter` and `PipedReader` to form a pipe.

The `reverse` method starts a `ReverseThread` that writes its output to the `PipedWriter` and returns the `PipedReader` to the caller. The caller then arranges for a sorting thread to read from it. The `sort` method is exactly the same, except that it creates and starts a `Sort-Thread`.[2]

How to Wrap a Stream

The `reverse` method contains some other interesting code; in particular, these two statements:

---

[1] The file `words.txt` is included on the CD and is available online. See <u>Code Samples</u> (page 348).

[2] `WriteReverseThread.java` and `SortThread.java` are included on the CD and are available online. See <u>Code Samples</u> (page 348).

```
BufferedReader in = new BufferedReader(source);
...
PrintWriter out = new PrintWriter(pipeOut);
```

This code opens a `BufferedReader` on source, which is another reader of a different type. This essentially "wraps" source in a `BufferedReader`. The program reads from the `BufferedReader`, which in turn reads from source. The program does this so that it can use `BufferedReader`'s convenient `readLine` method. Similarly, the `PipedWriter` is wrapped in a `PrintWriter` so that the program can use `PrintWriter`'s convenient `println` method. You will often see streams wrapped in this way so as to combine the various features of the many streams.

How to Concatenate Files

`SequenceInputStream`[1] creates a single input stream from multiple input sources. This example program, `Concatenate`,[2] uses `SequenceInputStream` to implement a concatenation utility that sequentially concatenates files together in the order in which they are listed on the command line.

The following is the controlling class of the `Concatenate` utility:

```java
import java.io.*;

public class Concatenate {
    public static void main(String[] args) throws IOException {
        ListOfFiles mylist = new ListOfFiles(args);

        SequenceInputStream s = new SequenceInputStream(mylist);
        int c;

        while ((c = s.read()) != -1) {
            System.out.write(c);
        }
        s.close();
    }
}
```

First, the `Concatenate` utility creates a `ListOfFiles` object named `mylist`, which is initialized from the command line arguments entered by the user. The `mylist` object is an enumeration that `SequenceInputStream` uses to obtain a new `InputStream` whenever it needs one.

```java
import java.util.*;
```

---

[1] http://java.sun.com/j2se/1.3/docs/api/java/io/SequenceInputStream.html
[2] `Concatenate.java` is included on the CD and is available online. See Code Samples (page 348).

```
import java.io.*;

public class ListOfFiles implements Enumeration {

    private String[] listOfFiles;
    private int current = 0;

    public ListOfFiles(String[] listOfFiles) {
        this.listOfFiles = listOfFiles;
    }

    public boolean hasMoreElements() {
        if (current < listOfFiles.length) {
            return true;
        } else {
            return false;
        }
    }

    public Object nextElement() {
        InputStream in = null;

        if (!hasMoreElements()) {
            throw new NoSuchElementException("No more files.");
        } else {
            String nextElement = listOfFiles[current];
            current++;
            try {
                in = new FileInputStream(nextElement);
            } catch (FileNotFoundException e) {
                System.out.println("ListOfFiles: Can't open " +
                                        nextElement);
            }
        }
        return in;
    }
}
```

(handwritten annotation: constructor)

(handwritten annotation: method)

ListOfFiles implements the Enumeration[1] interface. You'll see how this comes into play as you walk through the rest of the program.

After creating the SequenceInputStream, the main method reads from that stream one byte at a time. When it needs an InputStream from a new source, such as for the first byte read or when it runs off the end of the current input stream, the SequenceInputStream calls next-Element on the Enumeration object to get the next InputStream. ListOfFiles creates FileInputStream objects lazily. This means that whenever SequenceInputStream calls

---

[1] http://java.sun.com/j2se/1.3/docs/api/java/util/Enumeration.html

nextElement, ListOfFiles opens a FileInputStream on the next file name in the list and returns the stream. When the ListOfFiles object runs out of files to read (it has no more elements), nextElement returns null, and the call to SequenceInputStream's read method returns −1 to indicate the end of input.

Try This: Run Concatenate on the farrago.txt and words.txt files; both are text files used as input to other examples in this chapter.

Working with Filter Streams

The java.io package provides a set of abstract classes that define and partially implement *filter streams*. A filter stream filters data as it's being read from or written to the stream. The filter streams are <u>FileReader</u>,[1] <u>FileWriter</u>,[2] <u>FileInputStream</u>,[3] and <u>FileOutputStream</u>.[4]

A filter stream is constructed on another stream (the *underlying* stream). The read method in a readable filter stream reads input from the underlying stream, filters it, and passes on the filtered data to the caller. The write method in a writable filter stream filters the data and then writes it to the underlying stream. The filtering done by the streams depends on the stream. Some streams buffer the data, some count data as it goes by, and others convert data to another form.

Most filter streams provided by the java.io package are subclasses of FilterInputStream and FilterOutputStream and are listed here:

- DataInputStream and DataOutputStream
- BufferedInputStream and BufferedOutputStream
- LineNumberInputStream
- PushbackInputStream
- PrintStream (This is an output stream.)

The java.io package contains only one subclass of FilterReader: PushbackReader. So this section focuses on filter byte streams.

This section shows you how to use filter streams by presenting an example that uses a DataInputStream and a DataOutputStream. This section also covers how to subclass FilterInputStream and FilterOutputStream to create your own filter streams.

---

[1] http://java.sun.com/j2se/1.3/docs/api/java/io/FileReader.html
[2] http://java.sun.com/j2se/1.3/docs/api/java/io/FileWriter.html
[3] http://java.sun.com/j2se/1.3/docs/api/java/io/FileInputStream.html
[4] http://java.sun.com/j2se/1.3/docs/api/java/io/FileOutputStream.html

Using Filter Streams

To use a filter input or output stream, attach the filter stream to another input or output stream when you create it. For example, you can attach a `DataInputStream` to the standard input stream, as in the following code:

```
DataInputStream in = new DataInputStream(System.in);
String input;

while ((input = in.readLine()) != null) {
    ... //do something interesting here
}
```

You might do this so that you can use the more convenient read methods, such as `readLine`, implemented by `DataInputStream`.

How to Use DataInputStream and DataOutputStream

This section features an example, `DataIODemo`,[1] that reads and writes tabular data (invoices for merchandise). The tabular data is formatted in columns and separated by tabs. The columns contain the sales price, the number of units ordered, and a description of the item. Conceptually, the data looks like this, although it is read and written in binary form and is non-ASCII:

```
19.99   12      Java T-shirt
9.99    8       Java Mug
```

`DataOutputStream`, like other filter output streams, must be attached to another `Output-Stream`. In this case, it's attached to a `FileOutputStream` that is set up to write to a file named `invoice1.txt`:

```
DataOutputStream out = new DataOutputStream(new
                            FileOutputStream("invoice1.txt"));
```

Next, `DataIODemo` uses `DataOutputStream`'s specialized write methods to write the invoice data contained within arrays in the program according to the type of data being written:

```
for (int i = 0; i < prices.length; i++) {
    out.writeDouble(prices[i]);
    out.writeChar('\t');
    out.writeInt(units[i]);
    out.writeChar('\t');
```

---

[1] `DataIODemo.java` is included on the CD and is available online. See <u>Code Samples</u> (page 348).

```
        out.writeChars(descs[i]);
        out.writeChar('\n');
    }
    out.close();
```

Next, DataIODemo opens a DataInputStream on the file just written:

```
DataInputStream in = new DataInputStream(new
                        FileInputStream("invoice1.txt"));
```

DataInputStream also must be attached to another InputStream, in this case, a FileInput-Stream set up to read the file just written, invoice1. Then DataIODemo just reads the data back in, using DataInputStream's specialized read methods:

```
try {
    while (true) {
        price = in.readDouble();
        in.readChar();          //throws out the tab
        unit = in.readInt();
        in.readChar();          //throws out the tab
        char chr;
        desc = new StringBuffer(20);
        char lineSep = System.getProperty("line.separator").charAt(0);

        while ((chr = in.readChar() != lineSep) {
            desc.append(chr);
        }

        System.out.println("You've ordered " + unit +  " units of "
                            + desc + " at $" + price);
        total = total + unit * price;
    }
} catch (EOFException e) { }
System.out.println("For a TOTAL of: $" + total);
in.close();
```

When all the data has been read, DataIODemo displays a statement summarizing the order and the total amount owed and then closes the stream.

Note the loop that DataIODemo uses to read the data from the DataInputStream. Normally, when data is read, you see loops like this:

```
while ((input = in.read()) != null) {
    ...
}
```

The `read` method returns a value, `null`, which indicates that the end of the file has been reached. Many of the `DataInputStream` read methods can't do this, because any value that could be returned to indicate the end of file may also be a legitimate value read from the stream. For example, suppose that you want to use –1 to indicate end of file. Well, you can't, because –1 is a legitimate value that can be read from the input stream, using `readDouble`, `readInt`, or one of the other methods that reads numbers. So `DataInputStream`'s read methods throw an `EOFException` instead. When the `EOFException` occurs, the `while (true)` terminates.

When you run the `DataIODemo` program, you should see the following output:

```
You've ordered 12 units of Java T-shirt at $19.99
You've ordered 8 units of Java Mug at $9.99
You've ordered 13 units of Duke Juggling Dolls at $15.99
You've ordered 29 units of Java Pin at $3.99
You've ordered 50 units of Java Key Chain at $4.99
For a TOTAL of: $892.88
```

How to Write Your Own Filter Streams

Following are the steps to take when you are writing your own filtered input and output streams:

1. Create a subclass of `FilterInputStream` and `FilterOutputStream`. Input and output streams often come in pairs, so it's likely that you will need to create both input and output versions of your filter stream.
2. Override the `read` and `write` methods, and any others, if you need to.
3. Provide any new methods.
4. Make sure that the input and output streams work together.

This section shows you how to implement your own filter streams, presenting an example that implements a matched pair of filter input and output streams.

Both the input and the output streams use a checksum class to compute a checksum on the data written to or read from the stream. The checksum is used to determine whether the data read by the input stream matches that written by the output stream.

Four classes and one interface make up this example program:

- The filtered input and output stream subclasses: `CheckedOutputStream` and `Checked-InputStream`
- The `Checksum` interface and the `Adler32` class, which compute a checksum for the streams
- The `CheckedIODemo` class to define the `main` method for the program

Except for CheckedIODemo, the classes in this example are based on classes, which are now members of the java.util.zip package, written by David Connelly.

The CheckedOutputStream Class. The CheckedOutputStream[1] class, a subclass of FilterOutputStream, computes a checksum on data as it is being written to the stream. When creating a CheckedOutputStream, you must use its only constructor:

```
public CheckedOutputStream(OutputStream out, Checksum cksum) {
    super(out);
    this.cksum = cksum;
}
```

This constructor takes an OutputStream argument and a Checksum argument. The Output-Stream argument is the output stream that this CheckedOutputStream should filter. The Checksum argument is an object that can compute a checksum. CheckedOutputStream initializes itself by calling its superclass constructor and initializing a private variable, cksum, with the Checksum object. The CheckedOutputStream uses cksum to update the checksum each time data is written to the stream.

CheckedOutputStream needs to override FilterOutputStream's write methods so that each time the write method is called, the checksum is updated. FilterOutputStream defines three versions of the write method. CheckedOutputStream overrides all three of these methods with the following code:

```
public void write(int b) throws IOException {
    out.write(b);
    cksum.update(b);
}

public void write(byte[] b) throws IOException {
    out.write(b, 0, b.length);
    cksum.update(b, 0, b.length);
}

public void write(byte[] b, int off, int len) throws IOException {
    out.write(b, off, len);
    cksum.update(b, off, len);
}
```

The implementations of these three write methods are straightforward: Write the data to the output stream that this filter stream is attached to, and then update the checksum.

---

[1] CheckedOutputStream.java is included on the CD and is available online. See <u>Code Samples</u> (page 348).

The CheckedInputStream Class. The class CheckedInputStream[1] is similar to the CheckedOutputStream class. A subclass of FilterInputStream, it computes a checksum on data as it is read from the stream. When creating a CheckedInputStream, you must use its only constructor:

```
public CheckedInputStream(InputStream in, Checksum cksum) {
    super(in);
    this.cksum = cksum;
}
```

This constructor is similar to CheckedOutputStream's.

Just as CheckedOutputStream needed to override FilterOutputStream's write methods, CheckedInputStream must override FilterInputStream's read methods. This is to ensure that each time the read method is called, the checksum is updated. As with FilterOutput-Stream, FilterInputStream defines three versions of the read method. CheckedInput-Stream overrides all of them by using the following code:

```
public int read() throws IOException {
    int b = in.read();
    if (b != -1) {
        cksum.update(b);
    }
    return b;
}

public int read(byte[] b) throws IOException {
    int len;
    len = in.read(b, 0, b.length);
    if (len != -1) {
        cksum.update(b, 0, b.length);
    }
    return len;
}

public int read(byte[] b, int off, int len) throws IOException {
    len = in.read(b, off, len);
    if (len != -1) {
        cksum.update(b, off, len);
    }
    return len;
}
```

---

[1] CheckedInputStream.java is included on the CD and is available online. See Code Samples (page 348).

The implementations of these three read methods are straightforward: Read the data from the input stream to which this filter stream is attached. If any data was read, update the checksum.

The Checksum Interface and the Adler32 Class. The interface Checksum.java[1] defines four methods for checksum objects to implement. These methods reset, update, and return the checksum value. You could write a Checksum class that computes a specific type of checksum, such as the CRC-32 checksum.[2] Note that inherent in the checksum is the notion of state. The checksum object doesn't just compute a checksum in one pass. Rather, the checksum is updated each time information is read from or written to the stream for which this object computes a checksum. If you want to reuse a checksum object, you must reset it.

For this example, we implemented the checksum Adler32,[3] which is almost as reliable as a CRC-32 checksum but can be computed more quickly.

A Program for Testing. The last class in the example, CheckedIODemo,[4] contains the main method for the program:

```
import java.io.*;

public class CheckedIODemo {
    public static void main(String[] args) throws IOException {

        Adler32 inChecker = new Adler32();
        Adler32 outChecker = new Adler32();
        CheckedInputStream in = null;
        CheckedOutputStream out = null;
        try {
            in = new CheckedInputStream(
                    new FileInputStream("farrago.txt"),
                    inChecker);
            out = new CheckedOutputStream(
                    new FileOutputStream("outagain.txt"),
                    outChecker);
        } catch (FileNotFoundException e) {
            System.err.println("CheckedIODemo: " + e);
            System.exit(-1);
        } catch (IOException e) {
            System.err.println("CheckedIODemo: " + e);
```

---

[1] Checksum.java is included on the CD and is available online. See <u>Code Samples</u> (page 348).
[2] You can find more CRC-32 information here: http://www.freesoft.org/CIE/RFC/1510/78.htm
[3] Adler32.java is included on the CD and is available online. See <u>Code Samples</u> (page 348).
[4] CheckedIODemo.java is included on the CD and is available online. See <u>Code Samples</u> (page 348).

```
            System.exit(-1);
        }

        int c;

        while ((c = in.read()) != -1) {
            out.write(c);
        }

        System.out.println("Input stream check sum: "
                            + inChecker.getValue());
        System.out.println("Output stream check sum: "
                            + outChecker.getValue());

        in.close();
        out.close();
    }
}
```

The `main` method creates two `Adler32` checksum objects, one each for `CheckedOutput-Stream` and `CheckedInputStream`. This example requires two checksum objects because the checksum objects are updated during calls to `read` and `write`, and those calls occur concurrently.

Next, `main` opens a `CheckedInputStream` on a small text file named `farrago.txt` and a `CheckedOutputStream` on an output file named `outagain.txt`, which doesn't exist until you run the program for the first time. The `main` method reads the text from the `CheckedInputStream` and simply copies it to the `CheckedOutputStream`. The `read` and `write` methods use the `Adler32` checksum objects to compute a checksum during reading and writing. After the input file has been completely read and the output file has been completely written, the program prints out the checksum for both the input and output streams (which should match) and then closes them both.

When you run `CheckedIODemo`, you should see this (or similar) output:

```
Input stream check sum: 736868089
Output stream check sum: 736868089
```

Object Serialization

Two streams in `java.io`—`ObjectInputStream` and `ObjectOutputStream`—are run-of-the-mill byte streams and work like the other input and output streams. However, they are special in that they can read and write objects.

The key to writing an object is to represent its state in a serialized form sufficient to reconstruct the object as it is read. Thus, reading and writing objects is a process called *object serialization*. Object serialization is essential to building all but the most transient applications. You can use object serialization in the following ways:

- Remote method invocation (RMI)—communication between objects via sockets.

  The client and server programs in <u>Putting It All Together</u>,[1] use RMI to communicate. You can see object serialization used in that example to pass various objects back and forth between the client and the server. Refer to the online version of this tutorial to read about the example's use of RMI and object serialization.

- Lightweight persistence—the archival of an object for use in a later invocation of the same program.

You need to know about object serialization from two points of view. First, you need to know how to serialize objects by writing them to an `ObjectOutputStream` and reading them in again, using an `ObjectInputStream`. The next section, <u>Serializing Objects</u> (page 335), shows you how. Second, you will want to know how to write a class so that its instances can be serialized. You can read how to do this in the section after that, <u>Providing Object Serialization for Your Classes</u> (page 336).

Serializing Objects

Reconstructing an object from a stream requires that the object first be written to a stream. So let's start there.

How to Write to an ObjectOutputStream

Writing objects to a stream is a straightforward process. For example, the following gets the current time in milliseconds by constructing a `Date` object and then serializes that object:

```
FileOutputStream out = new FileOutputStream("theTime");
ObjectOutputStream s = new ObjectOutputStream(out);
s.writeObject("Today");
s.writeObject(new Date());
s.flush();
```

`ObjectOutputStream` must be constructed on another stream. This code constructs an `ObjectOutputStream` on a `FileOutputStream`, thereby serializing the object to a file named `theTime`. Next, the string `Today` and a `Date` object are written to the stream with the `writeObject` method of `ObjectOutputStream`.

---

[1] http://java.sun.com/docs/books/tutorial/together/index.html

Thus, the `writeObject` method serializes the specified object, traverses its references to other objects recursively, and writes them all. In this way, relationships between objects are maintained.

`ObjectOutputStream` implements the `DataOutput` interface that defines many methods for writing primitive data types, such as `writeInt`, `writeFloat`, or `writeUTF`. You can use these methods to write primitive data types to an `ObjectOutputStream`.

The `writeObject` method throws a `NotSerializableException` if it's given an object that is not serializable. An object is serializable only if its class implements the `Serializable` interface.

How to Read from an ObjectOutputStream

Once you've written objects and primitive data types to a stream, you'll likely want to read them out again and reconstruct the objects. This is also straightforward. Here's code that reads in the `String` and the `Date` objects that were written to the file named `theTime` in the previous example:

```
FileInputStream in = new FileInputStream("theTime");
ObjectInputStream s = new ObjectInputStream(in);
String today = (String)s.readObject();
Date date = (Date)s.readObject();
```

Like `ObjectOutputStream`, `ObjectInputStream` must be constructed on another stream. In this example, the objects were archived in a file, so the code constructs an `ObjectInput-Stream` on a `FileInputStream`. Next, the code uses `ObjectInputStream`'s `readObject` method to read the `String` and the `Date` objects from the file. The objects must be read from the stream in the same order in which they were written. Note that the return value from `readObject` is an object that is cast to and assigned to a specific type.

The `readObject` method deserializes the next object in the stream and traverses its references to other objects recursively to deserialize all objects that are reachable from it. In this way, it maintains the relationships between the objects.

`ObjectInputStream` implements the `DataInput` interface that defines methods for reading primitive data types. The methods in `DataInput` parallel those defined in `DataOutput` for writing primitive data types. They include such methods as `readInt`, `readFloat`, and `readUTF`. Use these methods to read primitive data types from an `ObjectInputStream`.

Providing Object Serialization for Your Classes

An object is serializable only if its class implements the `Serializable` interface. Thus, if you want to serialize the instances of one of your classes, the class must implement the

Serializable interface. The good news is that Serializable is an empty interface. That is, it doesn't contain any method declarations; its purpose is simply to identify classes whose objects are serializable.

Implementing the Serializable Interface

Here's the complete definition of the Serializable interface:

```
package java.io;
public interface Serializable {
    //there's nothing in here!
};
```

Making instances of your classes serializable is easy. You just add the implements Serializable clause to your class declaration, like this:

```
public class MySerializableClass implements Serializable {
    ...
}
```

You don't have to write any methods. You can serialize instances of this class with the defaultWriteObject method of ObjectOutputStream. This method automatically writes out everything required to reconstruct an instance of the class, including the following:

- Class of the object
- Class signature
- Values of all non-transient and non-static members, including members that refer to other objects

You can deserialize any instance of the class with the defaultReadObject method in ObjectInputStream.

For many classes, the default behavior is good enough. However, default serialization can be slow, and a class might want more explicit control over the serialization.

Customizing Serialization

You can customize serialization for your classes by providing two methods for it: writeObject and readObject. The writeObject method controls what information is saved and is typically used to append additional information to the stream. The readObject method either reads the information written by the corresponding writeObject method or can be used to update the state of the object after it has been restored.

The `writeObject` method must be declared exactly as shown in the following example and should call the stream's `defaultWriteObject` as the first thing it does to perform default serialization. Any special arrangements can be handled afterward:

```
private void writeObject(ObjectOutputStream s) throws IOException {
    s.defaultWriteObject();
    //customized serialization code
}
```

The `readObject` method must read in everything written by `writeObject` in the same order in which it was written. Also, the `readObject` method can perform calculations or update the state of the object. Here's the `readObject` method that corresponds to the `writeObject` method just shown:

```
private void readObject(ObjectInputStream s) throws IOException {
    s.defaultReadObject();
    //customized deserialization code
    ...
    //followed by code to update the object, if necessary
}
```

The `readObject` method must be declared exactly as shown.

The `writeObject` and `readObject` methods are responsible for serializing only the immediate class. Any serialization required by the superclasses is handled automatically. However, a class that needs to explicitly coordinate with its superclasses to serialize itself can do so by implementing the `Externalizable` interface.

Implementing the Externalizable Interface

For complete, explicit control of the serialization process, a class must implement the `Externalizable` interface. For `Externalizable` objects, only the identity of the object's class is automatically saved by the stream. The class is responsible for writing and reading its contents, and it must coordinate with its superclasses to do so.

Here's the complete definition of the `Externalizable` interface that extends `Serializable`:

```
package java.io;
public interface Externalizable extends Serializable {
    public void writeExternal(ObjectOutput out) throws IOException;
    public void readExternal(ObjectInput in) throws IOException,
                             java.lang.ClassNotFoundException;
}
```

The following holds for an `Externalizable` class:

- It must implement the `java.io.Externalizable` interface.
- It must implement a `writeExternal` method to save the state of the object. Also, it must explicitly coordinate with its supertype to save its state.
- It must implement a `readExternal` method to read the data written by the `writeExternal` method from the stream and restore the state of the object. It must explicitly coordinate with the supertype to restore its state.
- If an externally defined format is being written, the `writeExternal` and `readExternal` methods are solely responsible for that format.

The `writeExternal` and `readExternal` methods are public and carry the risk that a client may be able to write or read information in the object other than by using its methods and variables. These methods must be used only when the information held by the object is not sensitive or when exposing that information would not present a security risk.

Protecting Sensitive Information

When developing a class that provides controlled access to resources, you must take care to protect sensitive information and functions. During deserialization, the private state of the object is restored. For example, a file descriptor contains a handle that provides access to an operating system resource. Being able to forge a file descriptor would allow some forms of illegal access, because restoring state is done from a stream. Therefore, the serializing runtime must take the conservative approach and not trust the stream to contain only valid representations of objects. To avoid compromising a class, you must provide either that the sensitive state of an object must not be restored from the stream or that it must be reverified by the class.

Several techniques are available to protect sensitive data in classes. The easiest is to mark as `private transient` variables that contain sensitive data. Transient and static variables are not serialized or deserialized. Marking the variables will prevent the state from appearing in the stream and from being restored during deserialization. Because writing and reading (of private variables) cannot be superseded outside of the class, the class's transient variables are safe.

Particularly sensitive classes should not be serialized. To accomplish this, the object should not implement either the `Serializable` or the `Externalizable` interface.

Some classes may find it beneficial to allow writing and reading but to specifically handle and revalidate the state as it is deserialized. The class should implement `writeObject` and `readObject` methods to save and restore only the appropriate state. If access should be denied, throwing a `NotSerializableException` will prevent further access.

Working with Random Access Files

The input and output streams in this chapter so far have been *sequential access streams—streams* whose contents must be read or written sequentially. Although such streams are still incredibly useful, they are a consequence of sequential media, such as paper and magnetic tape. A *random access file*, on the other hand, permits nonsequential, or random, access to a file's contents.

So why might you need random access files? Consider the archive format called ZIP. A ZIP archive contains files and is typically compressed to save space. It also contains a dir-entry at the end that indicates where the various files contained within the ZIP archive begin. This is shown in Figure 94.

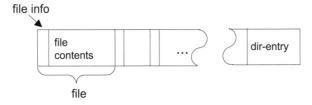

Figure 94 A ZIP archive.

Suppose you want to extract a specific file from a ZIP archive. If you use a sequential access stream, you have to

1. Open the ZIP archive.
2. Search through the ZIP archive until you locate the file you want to extract.
3. Extract the file.
4. Close the ZIP archive.

Using this algorithm, you will have to read, on average, half of the ZIP archive before finding the file that you want to extract. You can extract the same file from the ZIP archive more efficiently by using the seek feature of a random access file and following these steps:

1. Open the ZIP archive.
2. Seek to the dir-entry and locate the entry for the file you want to extract from the ZIP archive.
3. Seek (backward) within the ZIP archive to the position of the file to extract.
4. Extract the file.
5. Close the ZIP archive.

This algorithm is more efficient because you read only the dir-entry and the file that you want to extract.

The `RandomAccessFile`[1] class in the `java.io` package implements a random access file. Unlike the input and output stream classes in `java.io`, `RandomAccessFile` is used for both reading and writing files. You create a `RandomAccessFile` object with different arguments, depending on whether you intend to read or to write.

`RandomAccessFile` is somewhat disconnected from the input and output streams in `java.io`; that is, it doesn't inherit from `InputStream` or `OutputStream`. This has some disadvantages in that you can't apply the same filters to `RandomAccessFiles` that you can to streams. However, `RandomAccessFile` does implement the `DataInput`[2] and the `DataOutput`[3] interfaces, so if you design a filter that works for either `DataInput` or `DataOutput`, it will work on some sequential access files (the ones that implement `DataInput` or `DataOutput`) and on any `RandomAccessFile`.

Using Random Access Files

The `RandomAccessFile` class implements both the `DataInput` and the `DataOutput` interfaces and therefore can be used for both reading and writing. `RandomAccessFile` is similar to `FileInputStream` and `FileOutputStream` in that you specify a file on the native file system to open when you create it. You can do this with a file name or a `File`[4] object. When you create a `RandomAccessFile`, you must indicate whether you will be just reading the file or also writing to it. (You have to be able to read a file in order to write to it.) The following code creates a `RandomAccessFile` to read the file named `farrago.txt`:

```
new RandomAccessFile("farrago.txt", "r");
```

This statement opens the same file for both reading and writing:

```
new RandomAccessFile("farrago.txt", "rw");
```

After the file has been opened, you can use the `read` or `write` methods defined in the `DataInput` and `DataOutput` interfaces to perform I/O on the file.

`RandomAccessFile` supports the notion of a *file pointer*. The file pointer indicates the current location in the file, as illustrated in Figure 95. When the file is first created, the file

---

[1] http://java.sun.com/j2se/1.3/docs/api/java/io/RandomAccessFile.html

[2] http://java.sun.com/j2se/1.3/docs/api/java/io/DataInput.html

[3] http://java.sun.com/j2se/1.3/docs/api/java/io/DataOutput.html

[4] http://java.sun.com/j2se/1.3/docs/api/java/io/File.html

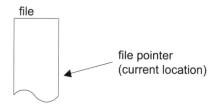

Figure 95   A ZIP file has the notion of a current file pointer.

pointer is set to 0, indicating the beginning of the file. Calls to the `read` or `write` methods adjust the file pointer by the number of bytes read or written.

In addition to the normal file I/O methods for reading and writing that implicitly move the file pointer when the operation occurs, `RandomAccessFile` contains three methods for explicitly manipulating the file pointer:

- `int skipBytes(int)`—Moves the file pointer forward the specified number of bytes
- `void seek(long)`—Positions the file pointer just before the specified byte
- `long getFilePointer()`—Returns the current byte location of the file pointer

Writing Filters for Random Access Files

Let's rewrite the example from the section <u>How to Write Your Own Filter Streams</u> (page 330) so that it works on `RandomAccessFiles`. Because `RandomAccessFile` implements the `DataInput` and the `DataOutput` interfaces, a side benefit is that the filtered stream will also work with other `DataInput` and `DataOutput` streams, including some sequential access streams, such as `DataInputStream` and `DataOutputStream`.

The example `CheckedIODemo` from the section <u>How to Write Your Own Filter Streams</u> (page 330) implements two filter streams that compute a checksum as data is read from or written to the stream. Those streams are `CheckedInputStream` and `CheckedOutputStream`.

In the new example, `CheckedDataOutput` is a rewrite of `CheckedOutputStream`—it computes a checksum for data written to the stream. However, it operates on `DataOutput` objects instead of on `OutputStream` objects. Similarly, `CheckedDataInput` modifies `CheckedInputStream` so that it now works on `DataInput` objects instead of on `InputStream` objects. All the example code is available in the example directory on this book's CD and online; see <u>Code Samples</u> (page 348).

CheckedDataOutput versus CheckedOutputStream

Let's look at how CheckedDataOutput differs from CheckedOutputStream. The first difference in these two classes is that CheckedDataOutput does *not* extend FilterOutputStream. Instead, it implements the DataOutput interface:

```
public class CheckedDataOutput implements DataOutput
```

Note: To keep the example code simple, in the sources on the CD, we did not require that the CheckedDataOutput class be declared to implement DataOutput, because the DataOutput interface specifies a lot of methods. However, the CheckedDataOutput class in the example does implement several of DataOutput's methods, to illustrate how it should work.

Next, CheckedDataOutput declares a private variable to hold a DataOutput object:

```
private DataOutput out;
```

This is the object to which data will be written.

The constructor for CheckedDataOutput differs from CheckedOutputStream's constructor in that CheckedDataOutput is created on a DataOutput object rather than on an Output-Stream:

```
public CheckedDataOutput(DataOutput out, Checksum cksum) {
    this.cksum = cksum;
    this.out = out;
}
```

This constructor does not call super(out) like the CheckedOutputStream constructor did, because CheckedDataOutput extends from Object rather than from a stream class.

Those are the only modifications made to CheckedOutputStream to create a filter that works on DataOutput objects.

CheckedDataInput versus CheckedInputStream

CheckedDataInput requires the same changes as CheckedDataOutput, as follows:

- CheckedDataInput does not derive from FilterInputStream. Instead, it implements the DataInput interface.
- CheckedDataInput declares a private variable to hold a DataInput object, which it wraps.
- The constructor for CheckedDataInput requires a DataInput object rather than an InputStream.

In addition to these changes, the read methods are changed. CheckedInputStream from the original example implements two read methods: one for reading a single byte and one for reading a byte array. The DataInput interface has methods that implement the same functionality, but they have different names and different method signatures. Thus, the read methods in the CheckedDataInput class have new names and method signatures:

```java
public byte readByte() throws IOException {
    byte b = in.readByte();
    cksum.update(b);
    return b;
}

public void readFully(byte[] b) throws IOException {
    in.readFully(b, 0, b.length);
    cksum.update(b, 0, b.length);
}

public void readFully(byte[] b, int off, int len) throws IOException {
    in.readFully(b, off, len);
    cksum.update(b, off, len);
}
```

Also, the DataInput interface declares many other methods that we don't implement for this example.

The Main Programs

Finally, this example has two main programs to test the new filters:

- CheckedDIDemo, which runs the filters on sequential access files (DataInputStream and DataOutputStream objects)
- CheckedRAFDemo, which runs the filters on random access files (RandomAccessFile objects)

These two main programs differ only in the type of object on which they open the checksum filters. CheckedDIDemo creates a DataInputStream and a DataOutputStream and uses the checksum filter on them, as in the following code:

```java
in = new CheckedDataInput(new DataInputStream(
        new FileInputStream("farrago.txt")), inChecker);
out = new CheckedDataOutput(new DataOutputStream(
        new FileOutputStream("outagain.txt")), outChecker);
```

CheckedRAFDemo creates two RandomAccessFile objects: one for reading and one for writing. It uses the checksum filter on them as follows:

```
in = new CheckedDataInput(
        new RandomAccessFile("farrago.txt", "r"), inChecker);
out = new CheckedDataOutput(
        new RandomAccessFile("outagain.txt", "rw"), outChecker);
```

When you run either of these programs, you should see the following output:

```
Input stream check sum: 736868089
Output stream check sum: 736868089
```

And the Rest . . .

In addition to the classes and interfaces discussed in this chapter, java.io contains the following classes and interfaces:

File
> Represents a file on the native file system. You can create a File object for a file on the native file system and then query the object for information about that file, such as its full path name.

FileDescriptor
> Represents a file handle (or descriptor) to an open file or an open socket. You will not typically use this class.

StreamTokenizer
> Breaks the contents of a stream into tokens. Tokens are the smallest unit recognized by a text-parsing algorithm (such as words, symbols, and so on). A StreamTokenizer object can be used to parse any text file. For example, you could use it to parse a source file into variable names, operators, and so on, or to parse an HTML file into HTML tags.

FilenameFilter
> Used by the list method in the File class to determine which files in a directory to list. The FilenameFilter accepts or rejects files, based on their names. You could use FilenameFilter to implement simple regular expression style file search patterns, such as foo*.

You also can find some other input and output streams in the java.util.zip package, including these:

CheckedInputStream and CheckedOutputStream
> An input and output stream pair that maintains a checksum as the data is being read or written.

DeflaterOutputStream and InflaterInputStream
> Compresses or uncompresses the data as it is being read or written.

GZIPInputStream and **GZIPOutputStream**
Reads and writes compressed data in the GZIP format.

ZipInputStream and **ZipOutputStream**
Reads and writes compressed data in the ZIP format.

Summary of Reading and Writing

The java.io package contains many classes that your programs can use to read and write data. Most of the classes implement sequential access streams. The sequential access streams can be divided into two groups: those that read and write bytes and those that read and write Unicode characters. Each sequential access stream has a speciality, such as reading from or writing to a file, filtering data as its read or written, or serializing an object.

One class, RandomAccessFile, implements random input/output access to a file. An object of this type maintains a file pointer, which indicates the current location from which data will be read or to which data will be written.

In addition to the I/O classes in java.io, the java.util.zip package contains other useful I/O classes.

Questions and Exercises

Questions

1. What class would you use to read a few pieces of data that are at known positions near the end of a large file?

2. What class in the java.util.zip package gives you access to the entries in a ZIP archive and allows you to read those entries through a stream?

3. How would you append data to the end of a file? Show the constructor for the class you would use and explain your answer.

4. Suppose you wanted to write code that reads from a file one word at a time. The code needs to peek ahead to find where the words are separated by whitespace. What input stream could you use to accomplish this?

5. How can you improve the performance of the following code? Explain your answer and show the new line(s) of code.

```
int i;
URL url = new URL("http://java.sun.com/");
URLConnection javaSite = url.openConnection();
InputStream input = javaSite.getInputStream();
InputStreamReader reader = new InputStreamReader(input);
while ((i = reader.read()) != -1) {
    System.out.print(i);
}
```

Exercises

1. Modify the program discussed in the section <u>How to Use Pipe Streams</u> (page 322) so that it uses input streams and output streams in place of readers and writers.

2. Implement a pair of classes, one `Reader` and one `Writer`, that count the number of times a particular character, such as `e`, is read or written. The character can be specified when the stream is created. Write a program to test your classes. You can use `far-rago.txt`[1] as the input file.

3. The file `datafile`[2] begins with a single `long` that tells you the offset of a single `int` piece of data within the same file. Using the `RandomAccessFile` class, write a program that gets the `int` piece of data. What is the `int` data?

4. In this exercise, you'll implement object serialization for the `Card2` class.[3]

   a. Rename the class `Card3` and make it serializable.

   b. Create a program named `CardWriter` that creates a `Card3` instance, displays its value, and serializes it into a file named `card.out`. Here is an example of what `CardWriter` might display:

      ```
      Card to write is: Ace of Spades
      ```

   c. Create a program named `CardReader` that reads the `Card3` object from `card.out` and displays its value. For example:

      ```
      Card read is: Ace of Spades
      ```

Answers

You can find answers to these Questions and Exercises online:

```
http://java.sun.com/docs/books/tutorial/essential/io/QandE/answers.html
```

---

[1] `farrago.txt` is included on the CD and is available online. See <u>Code Samples</u> (page 348).
[2] `datafile` is included on the CD and is available online. See <u>Code Samples</u> (page 348).
[3] `Card2.java` is included on the CD and is available online. See <u>Code Samples</u> (page 348).

Code Samples

Table 48 lists the code samples used in this chapter and where you can find the code online and on the CD that accompanies this book.

Table 48   Code Samples in I/O: Reading and Writing

Code Sample	CD Location	Online Location
Copy.java (page 321)	JavaTutorial/essential/io/ example-1dot1/Copy.java	http://java.sun.com/docs/ books/tutorial/essential/io/ example-1dot1/Copy.java
farrago.txt (page 321) and (page 347)	JavaTutorial/essential/io/ example-1dot1/farrago.txt	http://java.sun.com/docs/ books/tutorial/essential/io/ example-1dot1/farrago.txt
CopyBytes.java (page 322)	JavaTutorial/essential/io/ example/CopyBytes.java	http://java.sun.com/docs/ books/tutorial/essential/io/ example/CopyBytes.java
RhymingWords.java[a] (page 323)	JavaTutorial/essential/io/ example/RhymingWords.java	http://java.sun.com/docs/ books/tutorial/essential/io/ example/RhymingWords.java
words.txt (page 324)	JavaTutorial/essential/io/ example/words.txt	http://java.sun.com/docs/ books/tutorial/essential/io/ example/words.txt
WriteReverse-Thread.java (page 324)	JavaTutorial/essential/io/ example/ReverseThread.java	http://java.sun.com/docs/ books/tutorial/essential/io/ example/ReverseThread.java
SortThread.java (page 324)	JavaTutorial/essential/io/ example-1dot1/SortThread.java	http://java.sun.com/docs/ books/tutorial/essential/io/ example-1dot1/SortThread.java
Concatenate.java (page 325)	JavaTutorial/essential/io/ example/Concatenate.java	http://java.sun.com/docs/ books/tutorial/essential/io/ example/Concatenate.java
DataIODemo.java (page 328)	JavaTutorial/essential/io/ example/DataIODemo.java	http://java.sun.com/docs/ books/tutorial/essential/io/ example/DataIODemo.java
CheckedOutput-Stream.java (page 331)	JavaTutorial/essential/ io/example/ CheckedOutputStream.java	http://java.sun.com/docs/ books/tutorial/essential/io/ example/ CheckedOutputStream.java

Table 48   Code Samples in I/O: Reading and Writing

CheckedInput- Stream.java (page 332)	JavaTutorial/essential/ io/example/ CheckedInputStream.java	http://java.sun.com/docs/ books/tutorial/essential/io/ example/ CheckedInputStream.java
Checksum.java (page 333)	JavaTutorial/essential/io/ example/Checksum.java	http://java.sun.com/docs/ books/tutorial/essential/io/ example/Checksum.java
Adler32.java (page 333)	JavaTutorial/essential/io/ example/Adler32.java	http://java.sun.com/docs/ books/tutorial/essential/io/ example/Adler32.java
CheckedIODemo.java (page 333)	JavaTutorial/essential/io/ example/CheckedIODemo.java	http://java.sun.com/docs/ books/tutorial/essential/io/ example/CheckedIODemo.java
datafile (page 347)	JavaTutorial/essential/io/ example/datafile	http://java.sun.com/docs/ books/tutorial/essential/io/ example/datafile
Card2.java (page 347)	JavaTutorial/essential/io/ example/Card2.java	http://java.sun.com/docs/ books/tutorial/essential/io/ example/Card2.java

a. The RhymingWords program uses the following four files: RhymingWords.java, words.txt, WriteReverse-Thread.java, and SortThread.java.

Note: The section <u>Common Problems and Their Solutions</u> (page 391) contains solutions to common problems Tutorial readers have encountered.

User Interfaces That Swing

UP to this point, most of the programs we've written haven't been anything pretty to look at. More important, our programs haven't enabled user interaction. We have come to expect software programs to have buttons and text areas and things for us to interact with.

User interface is a broad term that refers to all sorts of communication between a program and its users. This chapter is built around several progressively complicated examples that demonstrate how to create user interfaces using components in the `javax.swing` package. We cover many standard graphical user interface (GUI)[1] components that the Java™ 2 platform provides, such as buttons, labels, and text areas. The handling of events is also discussed, as are layout management and accessibility. The chapter ends with a visual index of Swing components and a handy reference to where you can find more information.

Note: "Swing" was the code name of the project that developed the new components. Although it's an unofficial name, it's frequently used to refer to the new components and related API. It's immortalized in the package names for the Swing API, which begin with `javax.swing`.

---

[1] The acronym for graphical user interface, GUI, is pronounced "gooey."

Overview of the Swing API

The Swing package is part of the Java™ Foundation Classes (JFC) in the Java platform. The JFC encompasses a group of features to help people build GUIs; Swing provides all the components from buttons to split panes and tables.

The Swing package was first available as an add-on to JDK 1.1. Prior to the introduction of the Swing package, the Abstract Window Toolkit (AWT) components provided all the UI components in the JDK 1.0 and 1.1 platforms. Although the Java 2 Platform still supports the AWT components, we strongly encourage you to use Swing components instead. You can identify Swing components because their names start with J. The AWT button class, for example, is named `Button`, whereas the Swing button class is named `JButton`. In addition, the AWT components are in the `java.awt` package, whereas the Swing components are in the `javax.swing` package.

As a rule, programs should not use "heavyweight" AWT components alongside Swing components. Heavyweight components include all the ready-to-use AWT components, such as `Menu` and `ScrollPane`, and all components that inherit from the AWT `Canvas` and `Panel` classes. When Swing components (and all other "lightweight" components) overlap with heavyweight components, the heavyweight component is always painted on top.[1]

Compiling and Running Swing Programs

To compile and run your Swing programs, we recommend that you either use the latest release of the Java 2 Platform downloaded from `http://java.sun.com` or use the Java 2 Platform v 1.3 included on this book's CD. You can run Swing applets in any browser that has the appropriate version of Java™ Plug-in installed.[2] Swing applets are covered in Appendix B, Internet-Ready Applets (page 407).

Your First Swing Program

This is the first of several sections that teach Swing basics by looking at example code. This section examines the code for a simple program, `HelloWorldSwing`.[3] The examples in the following sections will become progressively more difficult as we introduce and explain more features.

Here's a snapshot of the `HelloWorldSwing` program (Figure 96).

Figure 96 The `HelloWorldSwing` application.

And here's the code for `HelloWorldSwing`:

---

[1] To learn more about the differences between Swing components and AWT components, see the section "Converting to Swing" in the book *The JFC Swing Tutorial*. This section is also available on this book's CD and online at http://java.sun.com/docs/books/tutorial/uiswing/converting/index.html.

[2] The Java Plug-in is included as part of the JRE 1.3 Win32 release. For more information about the Plug-in on other platforms, see http://java.sun.com/products/plugin/index.html

[3] `HelloWorldSwing.java` is included on the CD and is available online. See Code Samples (page 390).

```
import javax.swing.*;

public class HelloWorldSwing {
    public static void main(String[] args) {
        JFrame frame = new JFrame("HelloWorldSwing");
        final JLabel label = new JLabel("Hello World");
        frame.getContentPane().add(label);

        frame.setDefaultCloseOperation(JFrame.EXIT_ON_CLOSE);
        frame.pack();
        frame.setVisible(true);
    }
}
```

This is one of the simplest Swing applications you can write. It doesn't do much, but the code demonstrates the basic code in every Swing program:

- Import the pertinent packages.
- Set up a top-level container.

The first line imports the main Swing package:

```
import javax.swing.*;
```

This is the only package that HelloWorldSwing needs. However, most Swing programs also need to import two AWT packages:

```
import java.awt.*;
import java.awt.event.*;
```

These packages are required because Swing components use the AWT infrastructure, including the AWT event model. The event model governs how a component reacts to events, such as button clicks and mouse motion. You'll learn more about events in <u>Handling Events</u> (page 358).

Every program with a Swing GUI must contain at least one top-level Swing container. A top-level Swing container provides the support that Swing components need to perform their painting and event handling. There are three top-level Swing containers: JFrame, JDialog, and (for applets) JApplet. Each JFrame object implements a single main window, and each JDialog implements a secondary window (a window that's dependent on another window). Each JApplet object implements an applet's display area within a browser window.[1]

---

[1] Swing applets are covered in Appendix B.

The HelloWorldSwing example has only one top-level container, a JFrame. A frame, implemented as an instance of the JFrame class, is a window that has decorations, such as a border, a title, and buttons for iconifying and closing the window. Applications with a GUI typically use at least one frame.

Here is the code that sets up and shows the frame:

```
JFrame frame = new JFrame("HelloWorldSwing");
...
frame.pack();
frame.setVisible(true);
```

HelloWorldSwing also has one component, a label that reads "Hello World." These two lines of code construct and then add the component to the frame:

```
final JLabel label = new JLabel("Hello World");
frame.getContentPane().add(label);
```

To close the window when the close button ⊠ is clicked, we include this code in our HelloWorldSwing program:

```
frame.setDefaultCloseOperation(JFrame.EXIT_ON_CLOSE);
```

JFrame provides the setDefaultCloseOperation method to configure the default action for when the user clicks the close button. For single-window applications, most likely you want the application to exit. The EXIT_ON_CLOSE constant lets you specify this, as of version 1.3 of the Java 2 Platform. If you're using an earlier version of the platform, you implement an event listener to exit when the window closes:[1]

```
frame.addWindowListener(new WindowAdapter() {
    public void windowClosing(WindowEvent e) {
        System.exit(0);
    }
});
```

The next example will go into more details on event listeners.

---

[1] To learn about your other options for window-closing events, see the chapter "How to Write a Window Listener" in the book *The JFC Swing Tutorial*. This chapter is also available on this book's CD and online at: http://java.sun.com/docs/books/tutorial/uiswing/events/windowlistener.html

Example Two: SwingApplication

Let's look at another simple program, SwingApplication.[1] Each time the user clicks the button (JButton), the label (JLabel) is updated.

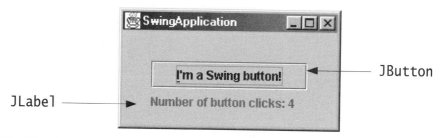

Figure 97   The simple GUI of SwingApplication presents a JButton and a JLabel.

Look and Feel

Figure 98 shows three views of a GUI that uses Swing components. Each picture shows the same program but with a different look and feel.

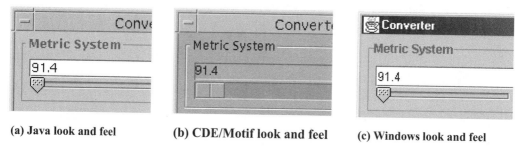

(a) Java look and feel   (b) CDE/Motif look and feel   (c) Windows look and feel

Figure 98   Three samples of look and feel.

Swing allows you to specify which look and feel your program uses—Java look and feel, CDE/Motif look and feel, Windows look and feel, and so on. The code in boldface type in the following snippet shows you how SwingApplication specifies its look and feel:

```
public static void main(String[] args) {
    try {
        UIManager.setLookAndFeel(
            UIManager.getCrossPlatformLookAndFeelClassName());
```

---

[1] SwingApplication.java is included on the CD and is available online. See <u>Code Samples</u> (page 390).

```
    } catch (Exception e) { }
    ...// Create and show the GUI...
}
```

The preceding code essentially says, "I don't care whether the user has chosen a look and feel—use the cross-platform look and feel (the Java look and feel)."

Setting Up Buttons and Labels

Like most GUIs, the SwingApplication GUI contains a button and a label. (Unlike most GUIs, that's about all that SwingApplication contains.) Here's the code that initializes the button:

```
JButton button = new JButton("I'm a Swing button!");
button.setMnemonic('i');
button.addActionListener(...create an action listener...);
```

The first line creates the button. The second sets the letter "i" as the mnemonic that the user can use to simulate a click of the button. For example, in the Java look and feel, typing Alt-i results in a button click. The third line registers an event handler for the button click, as discussed later in this section.

Here's the code that initializes and manipulates the label:

```
...// where instance variables are declared:
private static String labelPrefix = "Number of button clicks: ";
private int numClicks = 0;

...// in GUI initialization code:
final JLabel label = new JLabel(labelPrefix + "0       ");
...
label.setLabelFor(button);

...// in the event handler for button clicks:
label.setText(labelPrefix + numClicks);
```

The preceding code is pretty straightforward, except for the line that invokes the setLabelFor method. That code exists solely to hint to assistive technologies that the label describes the button.[1]

---

[1] Assistive technologies enable people with permanent or temporary disabilities to use computers. For more information, see the section "How to Support Assistive Technologies" in the book *The JFC Swing Tutorial*. This section is also available on this book's CD and online at: http://java.sun.com/docs/books/tutorial/uiswing/misc/access.html

Now that you know how to set up buttons, you also know how to set up check boxes and radio buttons, as they all inherit from the `AbstractButton` class. Check boxes are similar to radio buttons, but by convention their selection models are different. Any number of check boxes in a group—none, some, or all—can be selected. On the other hand, only one button can be selected from a group of radio buttons. Figure 99 shows pictures of two programs that use radio buttons and check boxes.

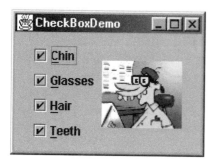
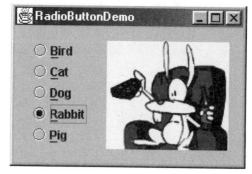

Figure 99　　As you'd expect, the `CheckBoxDemo` application shows the use of check boxes, and the `RadioButtonDemo` application shows the use of radio buttons. Both programs are available on this book's CD and online.

You'll get a chance to take a closer look at radio buttons in the section Example Five: Vote-Dialog (page 368).

Handling Events

Every time the user types a character or pushes a mouse button, an event occurs. Any object can be notified of the event. All the object has to do is implement the appropriate interface and be registered as an *event listener* on the appropriate *event source.*

How to Implement an Event Handler

Every event handler requires three pieces of code:

1. In the declaration for the event handler class, one line of code specifies that the class either implements a listener interface or extends a class that implements a listener interface. For example:

   ```
   public class MyClass implements ActionListener {
   ```

2. Another line of code registers an instance of the event handler class as a listener on one or more components. For example:

   ```
   someComponent.addActionListener(instanceOfMyClass);
   ```

3. In the event handler class, a few lines of code implement the methods in the listener interface. For example:

```
public void actionPerformed(ActionEvent e) {
    ...//code that reacts to the action...
}
```

Event handlers can be instances of any class. Often an event handler that has only a few lines of code is implemented using an *anonymous inner class*—an unnamed class defined inside of another class. Anonymous inner classes can be confusing at first, but once you're used to them, they make the code clearer by keeping the implementation of an event handler close to where the event handler is registered.

`SwingApplication` has two event handlers. One handles window closing (window events); the other handles button clicks (action events). We've already seen the window-closing code. Here is the code that handles button clicks in the `SwingApplication`:

```
button.addActionListener(new ActionListener() {
    public void actionPerformed(ActionEvent e) {
        numClicks++;
        label.setText(labelPrefix + numClicks);
    }
});
```

In general, to detect when the user clicks an on-screen button (or does the keyboard equivalent), a program must have an object that implements the `ActionListener` interface. The program must register this object as an action listener on the button (the event source), using the `addActionListener` method. When the user clicks the on-screen button, the button fires an action event. This results in the invocation of the action listener's `actionPerformed` method (the only method in the `ActionListener` interface). The single argument to the method is an `ActionEvent` object that gives information about the event and its source.

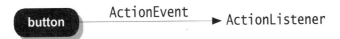

Figure 100 When the user clicks a button, the button's action listeners are notified.

Swing components can generate many kinds of events. Table 49 lists a few examples.

Table 49   Examples of Events and Their Associated Event Listeners

Act that Results in the Event	Listener Type
User clicks a button, presses Return while typing in a text field, or chooses a menu item	`ActionListener`
User closes a frame (main window)	`WindowListener`
User presses a mouse button while the cursor is over a component	`MouseListener`
User moves the mouse over a component	`MouseMotionListener`
Component becomes visible	`ComponentListener`
Component gets the keyboard focus	`FocusListener`
Table or list selection changes	`ListSelectionListener`

To learn more about how to detect events from a particular component, refer to each component's how-to section in the "Creating a GUI with JFC Swing" trail. This trail is also available on the CD or online at: `http://java.sun.com/docs/books/tutorial/uiswing/components/index.html`.

Note: Event-handling code executes in an single thread, the *event-dispatching thread*. This ensures that each event handler finishes execution before the next one executes. For instance, the `actionPerformed` method in the preceding example executes in the event-dispatching thread. Painting code also executes in the event-dispatching thread. Therefore, while the `actionPerformed` method is executing, the program's GUI is frozen—it won't repaint or respond to mouse clicks. See the section Threads and Swing (page 378) for more information.

Adding Borders Around Components

If you take another look at the snapshot of `SwingApplication` (Figure 97 on page 356), you'll notice that there is extra space surrounding the `JPanel` on all four edges. Here is the code that adds a border to the panel:

```
pane.setBorder(BorderFactory.createEmptyBorder(
                         30, //top
                         30, //left
                         10, //bottom
                         30) //right
                     );
```

This border simply provides some empty space around the panel's contents—30 extra pixels on the top, left, and right, and 10 extra pixels on the bottom. Borders are a feature that JPanel inherits from the JComponent class.

Example Three: CelsiusConverter

Our next example, CelsiusConverter,[1] does something that's somewhat useful: It is a simple conversion tool. The user enters a temperature in degrees Celsius and clicks the Convert... button, and a label displays the equivalent in degrees Fahrenheit.

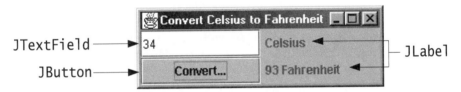

Figure 101 The CelsiusConverter GUI.

Let's examine the code to see how CelsiusConverter parses the number entered in the JTextField. First, here's the code that sets up the JTextField:

```
JTextField tempCelsius = null;
...
tempCelsius = new JTextField(5);
```

The integer argument passed in the JTextField constructor, 5 in the example, indicates the number of columns in the field. This number is used along with metrics provided by the current font to calculate the field's preferred width. This number does not limit how many character the user can enter.

We want to handle the button-click event, so we add an event listener to the button.

---

[1] CelsiusConverter.java is included on the CD and is available online. See <u>Code Samples</u> (page 390).

```
JButton convertTemp;
...
convertTemp.addActionListener(this);
...
public void actionPerformed(ActionEvent event) {
    // Parse degrees Celsius as a double and convert to Fahrenheit.
    int tempFahr = (int)((Double.parseDouble(tempCelsius.getText()))
                         * 1.8 + 32);
    fahrenheitLabel.setText(tempFahr + " Fahrenheit");
}
```

The getText method is called on the text field, tempCelsius, to retrieve the data within it. Next, the parseDouble method parses the text as a double before converting the temperature and casting the result to an integer. Finally, the setText method is called on the fahrenheitLabel to display the converted temperature. All this code is found in the event handler for the button, as the conversion happens only once the button is clicked.

Note: You can make a JButton be the default button. At most one button in a top-level container can be the default button. The default button typically has a highlighted appearance and acts clicked whenever the top-level container has the keyboard focus and the user presses the Return or Enter key. The exact implementation depends on the look and feel. You set the default button by invoking the setDefaultButton method on a top-level container's root pane:

```
//In the constructor for a JDialog subclass:
getRootPane().setDefaultButton(setButton);
```

Adding HTML

You can use HTML to specify the text on some Swing components, such as buttons and labels. We can spice up the CelsiusConverter program by adding HTML text to the fahrenheitLabel and adding an image to the convertTemp button.

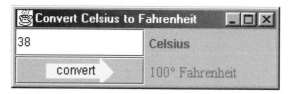

Figure 102 The improved CelsiusConverter2[1] application with colored fonts on the Fahrenheit label and a graphic on the button.

---

[1] CelsiusConverter2.java is included on the CD and is available online. See <u>Code Samples</u> (page 390).

First, let's look at how we specify the HTML tags for the `fahrenheitLabel`. As you can see from this code, the temperature (`tempFahr`) is displayed one of three different colors, depending on how hot or cold the converted temperature is:

```
// Set fahrenheitLabel to new value and font color based on temperature.
if (tempFahr <= 32) {
    fahrenheitLabel.setText("<html><font color=blue>" + tempFahr
                         + "&#176  Fahrenheit </font></html>");

} else if (tempFahr <= 80) {
    fahrenheitLabel.setText("<html><font color=green>" + tempFahr
                         + "&#176  Fahrenheit </font></html>");
} else {
    fahrenheitLabel.setText("<html><font color=red>" + tempFahr
                         + "&#176  Fahrenheit </font></html>");
}
```

To add HTML code to the label, simply put the <HTML> tag at the beginning of a string, and then use any valid HTML code in the remainder of the string. Using HTML can be useful for varying the text font or color within a button and for adding line breaks. To display the degree symbol, we use the HTML code "&#176".

Note: If the string is to be all one size and color, you don't have to use HTML. You can call the `setFont` method to specify the font of any component. For more information, see the API documentation on the CD or online at: `http://java.sun.com/j2se/1.3/docs/api/javax/swing/JComponent.html#setFont(java.awt.Font)`.

Warning: Don't use HTML in buttons unless you're absolutely sure that the program is running in a release that supports this feature. In releases that don't support HTML text, such as Swing 1.1, putting HTML in a button results in one ugly-looking button whose label starts (not surprisingly) with <HTML>.

Adding an Icon

Some Swing components can be decorated with an *icon*—a fixed-size image. A Swing icon is an object that adheres to the `Icon` interface. Swing provides a particularly useful implementation of the `Icon` interface: `ImageIcon`. `ImageIcon` paints an icon from a GIF or a JPEG image. Here's the code that adds the arrow graphic to the `convertTemp` button:

```
ImageIcon icon = new ImageIcon("images/convert.gif",
                               "Convert temperature");
...
convertTemp = new JButton(icon);
```

The first argument of the ImageIcon constructor specifies the file to load, relative to the directory containing the application's class file. The second argument provides a description of the icon that assistive technologies can use.

Example Four: LunarPhases

This next example, LunarPhases.java,[1] is a more complicated example of how to use images in your application. As an added bonus, you'll also see how to implement combo boxes. Here are two pictures of the LunarPhases application:

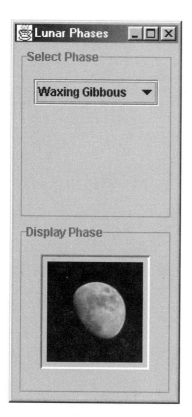 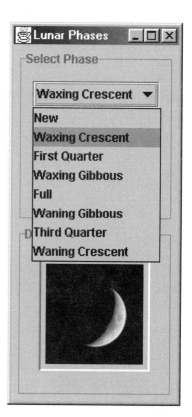

Figure 103 Two screenshots of the LunarPhases application.

---

[1] LunarPhases.java is included on the CD and is available online. See <u>Code Samples</u> (page 390).

In this program, the user chooses the lunar phase from the combo box, and the selected phase of the moon is shown in the lower panel. This is the first example we've seen that uses multiple panels to group components. Let's take a quick look at how we set up these panels.

`LunarPhases` has three panels, as shown in Figure 104.

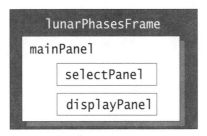

Figure 104 A depiction of the main panel and two subpanels in `LunarPhases.java`.

In the following code in the `LunarPhases` constructor, we construct all three panels and add the two subpanels (`selectPanel` and `displayPanel`) to `mainPanel`.

```
// Create the phase selection and display panels.
selectPanel = new JPanel();
displayPanel = new JPanel();

// Add various widgets to the subpanels.
addWidgets();

// Create the main panel to contain the two subpanels.
mainPanel = new JPanel();
mainPanel.setLayout(new GridLayout(2,1,5,5));
mainPanel.setBorder(BorderFactory.createEmptyBorder(5,5,5,5));

// Add the select and display panels to the main panel.
mainPanel.add(selectPanel);
mainPanel.add(displayPanel);
```

When we add the subpanels to the main panel, how can we make sure that they're added in the right place? By default, each container has a *layout manager*—an object that performs layout management for the components within the container. *Layout management* is the process of determining the size and the position of components. The default layout manager for the containers we've looked at is `FlowLayout`. With `FlowLayout`, the components are simply positioned in the container from left to right in the order they are added.

In the previous code snippet, we use a layout manager called `GridLayout` to position the components within. Layout is further discussed in the section <u>Layout Management</u> (page 375).

Compound Borders

In previous examples, we've added a simple border to add a buffer of space around components. In this example, both subpanels, `selectPanel` and `displayPanel`, have a *compound*
border. This compound border consists of a titled border (an outlined border with a title) and
an empty border (to add extra space), as shown in Figure 105.

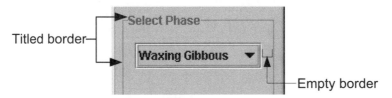

Titled border—

Empty border

Figure 105 The compound border used in `selectPanel`.

The code for the `selectPanel` border follows.

```
// Add border around the select panel
selectPanel.setBorder(BorderFactory.createCompoundBorder(
                    BorderFactory.createTitledBorder("Select Phase"),
                    BorderFactory.createEmptyBorder(5,5,5,5)));
```

The `displayPanel` sets its own border in the same way.

Combo Boxes

A combo box enables user choice. A combo box can be either editable or uneditable, but by
default it is uneditable. An uneditable combo box looks like a button until the user interacts
with it. When the user clicks it, the combo box displays a menu of items.

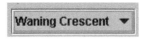

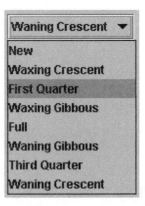

Figure 106 Two pictures of a combo box; the combo box on the right has been one dropped-down.

Use an uneditable combo box to display one-of-many choices when space is limited, when the number of choices is large, or when the menu items are computed at runtime. The following code in LunarPhases.java creates an uneditable combo box, phaseChoices, and sets it up:

```
JComboBox phaseChoices = null;
...
// Create combo box with lunar phase choices
String[] phases = { "New", "Waxing Crescent", "First Quarter",
                    "Waxing Gibbous", "Full", "Waning Gibbous",
                    "Third Quarter", "Waning Crescent" };
phaseChoices = new JComboBox(phases);
phaseChoices.setSelectedIndex(START_INDEX);
```

The code initializes the combo box with an array of strings, phases. You can also put icons in a combo box or initialize the combo box with a vector.[1] In the last line of code, the setSelectedIndex method specifies which phase of the moon should be shown when the program starts.

Handling Events on a Combo Box

The combo box fires an action event when the user selects an item from the combo box's menu. The following code from LunarPhases registers and implements an action listener on the combo box:

```
phaseChoices.addActionListener(this);
...
public void actionPerformed(ActionEvent event) {
    if ("comboBoxChanged".equals(event.getActionCommand())) {
        // update the icon to display the new phase
        phaseIconLabel.setIcon(images[phaseChoices.getSelectedIndex()]);
    }
}
```

This action listener gets the newly selected item from the combo box, uses that item to compute the name of an image file, and updates a label to display the image.

---

[1] To put other types of objects in a combo box or to customize how the items in a combo box look, you need to write a custom renderer. An editable combo box would need a custom editor, in addition. Refer to the section "Providing a Custom Renderer" in the book *The JFC Swing Tutorial*. This section is also available on this book's CD and online at: http://java.sun.com/docs/books/tutorial/uiswing/components/combobox.html#renderer

Multiple Images

In the CelsiusConverter program, we saw how to add a single ImageIcon to a button. The LunarPhases uses eight images. Only one image of the eight is used at a time, so we have a choice as to whether we load all the images up front or load the images as they are needed (known as "lazy image loading"). In this example, the images are all loaded up front when the class is constructed.

```
final static int NUM_IMAGES = 8;
final static int START_INDEX = 3;

ImageIcon[] images = new ImageIcon[NUM_IMAGES];
...

// Create the widgets to select and display the phases of the moon.
private void addWidgets() {
    // Get the images and put them into an array of ImageIcon.
    for (int i = 0; i < NUM_IMAGES; i++) {
        String imageName = "images/image" + i + ".jpg";
        URL iconURL = ClassLoader.getSystemResource(imageName);

        ImageIcon icon = new ImageIcon(iconURL);
        images[i] = icon;
    }
}
```

Note the use of getSystemResource, a method in ClassLoader that searches the classpath to find the image file names so that we don't have to specify the fully qualified path name.

Example Five: VoteDialog

The last example in this chapter is VoteDialog.java.[1] The main purpose of this example is to illustrate the use of dialogs, but we'll also explain how to set up radio buttons.

In this program, the user casts a vote by selecting a radio button and clicking the Vote button. After the button is clicked, a dialog appears with an informational message or a follow-up question. You can close the dialog either by clicking a button in the dialog or explicitly by clicking the close button.

---

[1]   VoteDialog.java is included on the CD and is available online. See Code Samples (page 390).

Here's a picture of the VoteDialog application (Figure 107).

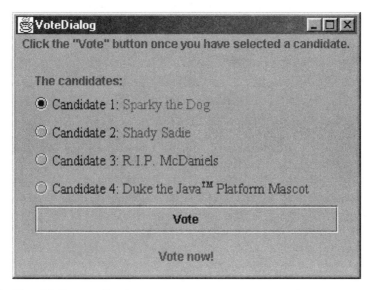

Figure 107 The VoteDialog application.

Radio Buttons

This application has one action listener that listens to clicks on the Vote button. Each time the action listener receives an event, the application determines which radio button was selected and displays the appropriate dialog. For each group of radio buttons, you need to create a ButtonGroup instance and add each radio button to it. The ButtonGroup takes care of unselecting the previously selected button when the user selects another button in the group. You should generally initialize a group of radio buttons so that one is selected. However, the API doesn't enforce this rule; a group of radio buttons can have no initial selection. Once the user has made a selection, exactly one button is selected from then on.

Here is the code from VoteDialog.java in which we create the ButtonGroup instance and add four radio buttons to it. The setActionCommand method associates a specific dialog with each radio button item. We use the setSelected method to specify the default selected radio button.

```
final int numButtons = 4;
JRadioButton[] radioButtons = new JRadioButton[numButtons];

final ButtonGroup group = new ButtonGroup();
...
```

```java
final String defaultMessageCommand = "default";
final String yesNoCommand = "yesno";
final String yeahNahCommand = "yeahnah";
final String yncCommand = "ync";

radioButtons[0] = new JRadioButton("<html>Candidate 1:
    <font color=red>Sparky the Dog</font></html>");
radioButtons[0].setActionCommand(defaultMessageCommand);

radioButtons[1] = new JRadioButton("<html>Candidate 2:
    <font color=green>Shady Sadie</font></html>");
radioButtons[1].setActionCommand(yesNoCommand);

radioButtons[2] = new JRadioButton("<html>Candidate 3:
    <font color=blue>R.I.P. McDaniels</font></html>");
radioButtons[2].setActionCommand(yeahNahCommand);

radioButtons[3] = new JRadioButton("<html>Candidate 4:
    <font color=maroon>Duke the Java<font size=-2><sup>TM</sup>
    </font size> Platform Mascot</font></html>");
radioButtons[3].setActionCommand(yncCommand);

for (int i = 0; i < numButtons; i++) {
    group.add(radioButtons[i]);
}

// Select the first button by default.
radioButtons[0].setSelected(true);
```

Note the use of HTML code on the radio buttons. This feature was added to the version 1.3 of the Java 2 platform.

Dialogs

In our previous examples, our top-level container has always been a JFrame. Several classes support *dialogs*—windows that are more limited than frames. To create simple, standard dialogs, you use the JOptionPane[1] class. The dialogs that JOptionPane provides are *modal*. When a modal dialog is visible, it blocks user input to all other windows in the program.

---

[1] API documentation for this class is available on this book's CD and online at http://java.sun.com/j2se/1.3/docs/api/javax/swing/JOptionPane.html

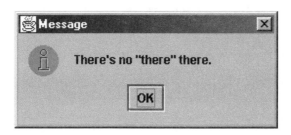

Figure 108 A simple dialog.

The code for simple dialogs can be minimal. For example, Figure 108 shows an instructive dialog.

Here is the code that creates and shows that dialog:

```
JOptionPane.showMessageDialog(frame, "There's no \"there\" there.");
```

Every dialog is dependent on a frame. When that frame is destroyed, so are its dependent dialogs. When the frame is iconified, its dependent dialogs disappear from the screen. When the frame is deiconified, its dependent dialogs return to the screen. The AWT automatically provides this behavior.

JOptionPane Features

Using JOptionPane, you can create and customize several kinds of dialogs. JOptionPane provides support for laying out standard dialogs, providing icons, specifying the dialog's title and text, and customizing the button text. Other features allow you to customize the components the dialog displays and to specify where the dialog should appear on-screen.

JOptionPane's icon support lets you easily specify which icon the dialog displays. You can use a custom icon, no icon at all, or any one of four standard JOptionPane icons (question, information, warning, and error). Each look and feel has its own versions of the four standard icons. The following figure shows the icons used in the Java look and feel.

question   information   warning   error

Figure 109 Icons provided by JOptionPane (Java look and feel shown).

Creating and Showing Simple Dialogs

For most simple modal dialogs, you can use either the showMessageDialog or the showOptionDialog method. The showMessageDialog method displays a simple, one-button dialog. The show-OptionDialog method displays a customized dialog—it can display a variety of buttons with customized button text and can contain a standard text message or a collection of components.

showMessageDialog

Displays a modal dialog with one button, which is labeled OK (or the localized equivalent). You can easily specify the message, icon, and title that the dialog displays. Table 50 shows an example of the use of showMessageDialog in VoteDialog.java.

Table 50   Examples Using showMessageDialog

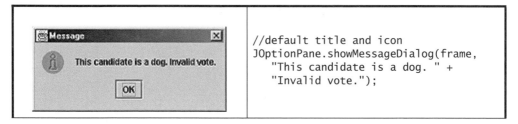

![Message dialog: This candidate is a dog. Invalid vote. OK]	`//default title and icon`
	`JOptionPane.showMessageDialog(frame,`
	`   "This candidate is a dog. " +`
	`   "Invalid vote.");`

showOptionDialog

Displays a modal dialog with the specified buttons, icons, message, title, and so on. You can use this method to change the text that appears on the buttons of standard dialogs. You can also perform many other kinds of customization. Table 51 shows an example that uses showOptionDialog.

Table 51   An Example Using showOptionDialog

![A Follow-up Question dialog: Duke is a cartoon mascot. Do you still want to cast your vote? Yes! / No, I'll pass / Well, if I must]	`Object[] options = {"Yes!",`
	`                     "No, I'll pass",`
	`                     "Well, if I must"};`
	`int n = JOptionPane.showOptionDialog(frame,`
	`   "Duke is a cartoon mascot. \n"`
	`   + "Do you still want to cast your vote?",`
	`   "A Follow-up Question",`
	`   JOptionPane.YES_NO_CANCEL_OPTION,`
	`   JOptionPane.QUESTION_MESSAGE,`
	`   null,`
	`   options,`
	`   options[2]);`

The arguments to all the show*Xxx*Dialog methods and JOptionPane constructors are standardized, although the number of arguments for each method and constructor varies. The following list describes each argument.

Component parentComponent

The first argument to each show*Xxx*Dialog method is always the parent component, which must be a frame, a component inside a frame, or null. If you specify a frame, the dialog will appear over the center of the frame and will depend on that frame. If you specify a component inside a frame, the dialog will appear over the center of that component and will depend on that component's frame. If you specify null, the look and feel picks an appropriate position for the dialog—generally the center of the screen—and the dialog doesn't depend on any visible frame.

The JOptionPane constructors do not include this argument. Instead, you specify the parent frame when you create the JDialog that contains the JOptionPane, and you use the JDialog setLocationRelativeTo method to set the dialog's position.

Object message

This required argument specifies what the dialog should display in its main area. Generally you specify a string, which results in the dialog's displaying a label with the specified text.

String title

This is the title of the dialog.

int optionType

This specifies the set of buttons that appears at the bottom of the dialog. You can choose one of the following four standard sets: DEFAULT_OPTION, YES_NO_OPTION, YES_NO_CANCEL_OPTION, OK_CANCEL_OPTION.

int messageType

This argument determines the icon displayed in the dialog. Choose from one of the following values: PLAIN_MESSAGE (no icon), ERROR_MESSAGE, INFORMATION_MESSAGE, WARNING_MESSAGE, QUESTION_MESSAGE.

Icon icon

This specifies the custom icon to display in the dialog.

Object[] options

This further specifies the option buttons to appear at the button of the dialog. Generally, you specify an array of strings for the buttons.

Object initialValue

This specifies the default value to be selected. You can either let the default icon be used or specify the icon, using the messageType or the icon argument. By default, a dialog created with showMessageDialog displays the information icon, and a dialog created with showConfirmDialog displays the question icon. To specify that the dialog display a standard icon or no icon, specify the message type. To specify a custom icon, use the icon argument.

Getting User Input from a Dialog

As the code snippets in Tables 50 and 51 show, the showMessageDialog and showOption-Dialog methods return an integer indicating the user's choice. The values for this integer are YES_OPTION, NO_OPTION, CANCEL_OPTION, OK_OPTION, and CLOSED_OPTION. Each option, except for CLOSED_OPTION, corresponds to the button the user clicked. When CLOSED_OPTION is returned, it indicates that the user closed the dialog window explicitly rather than by choosing a button inside the option pane. The following code detects whether the yes or no button was selected or the dialog was closed and then sets the frame's label with the appropriate text.

```
// yes/no dialog
} else if (command == yesNoCommand) {
    int n = JOptionPane.showConfirmDialog(
                        frame, "This candidate is a convicted felon. \n
                             Do you still want to vote for her?",
                        "A Follow-up Question",
                        JOptionPane.YES_NO_OPTION);
    if (n == JOptionPane.YES_OPTION) {
        setLabel("OK. Keep an eye on your wallet.");
    } else if (n == JOptionPane.NO_OPTION) {
        setLabel("Whew! Good choice.");
    } else {
        setLabel("It is your civic duty to cast your vote.");
    }
...
```

Even if you change the strings that the standard dialog buttons display, the return value is still one of the predefined integers. For example, a YES_NO_OPTION dialog always returns one of the following values: YES_OPTION, NO_OPTION, or CLOSED_OPTION.

You can get more information on dialogs in the section "How to Make Dialogs" in the book *The JFC Swing Tutorial*. This section is also available on this book's CD and online at: http://java.sun.com/docs/books/tutorial/uiswing/components/dialog.html

Now that we've finished our progress through the examples in this chapter, it's time to look at two important topics: Layout Management (page 375) and Threads and Swing (page 378).

Layout Management

Figure 110 shows the GUIs of five programs, each of which displays five buttons. The buttons are identical, and the code for the programs is almost identical. So why do the GUIs look so different? Because they use different layout managers to control the size and the position of the buttons.

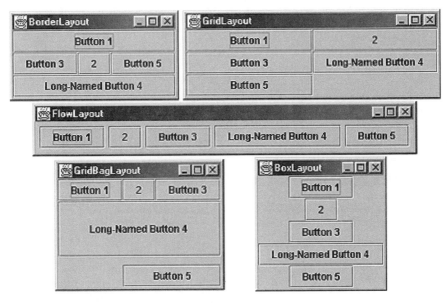

Figure 110 Five examples of layout management.

The Java platform supplies five commonly used layout managers: BorderLayout, BoxLayout, FlowLayout, GridBagLayout, and GridLayout.

Using Layout Managers

By default, every container has a layout manager. All JPanel objects use a FlowLayout by default, whereas content panes (the main containers in JApplet, JDialog, and JFrame objects) use BorderLayout by default. As a rule, the only time you have to think about layout managers is when you create a JPanel or add components to a content pane. If you don't like the default layout manager that a panel or content pane uses, you can change it to a different one. Just invoke the container's setLayout method. For example, here's the code that makes a panel use BorderLayout:

```
JPanel pane = new JPanel();
pane.setLayout(new BorderLayout());
```

When you add components to a panel or a content pane, the arguments you specify to the add method depend on the layout manager that the panel or content pane is using. So be sure to check the API documentation for the layout manager for details.

Here's a quick summary of the various layout managers and where to find about them.

BorderLayout

BorderLayout is the default layout manager for every content pane. The content pane is the main container in all frames, applets, and dialogs. A BorderLayout has five areas available to hold components: north, south, east, west, and center. All extra space is placed in the center area.

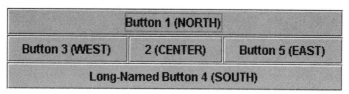

The Java Tutorial:
```
http://java.sun.com/docs/books/tutorial/uiswing/layout/border.html
```

API documentation:
```
http://java.sun.com/j2se/1.3/docs/api/java/awt/BorderLayout.html
```

BoxLayout

The BoxLayout class puts components in a single row or column. This class respects the components' requested maximum sizes and also lets you align components.

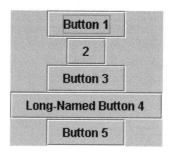

The Java Tutorial:
```
http://java.sun.com/docs/books/tutorial/uiswing/layout/box.html
```

API documentation:
```
http://java.sun.com/j2se/1.3/docs/api/javax/swing/BoxLayout.html
```

FlowLayout

FlowLayout is the default layout manager for every JPanel. This layout manager simply lays out components from left to right, starting new rows, if necessary.

The Java Tutorial:
    http://java.sun.com/docs/books/tutorial/uiswing/layout/flow.html

API documentation:
    http://java.sun.com/j2se/1.3/docs/api/java/awt/FlowLayout.html

GridLayout

GridLayout simply makes a bunch of components equal in size and displays them in the requested number of rows and columns.

Button 1	2
Button 3	Long-Named Button 4
Button 5	

The Java Tutorial:
    http://java.sun.com/docs/books/tutorial/uiswing/layout/grid.html

API documentation:
    http://java.sun.com/j2se/1.3/docs/api/java/awt/GridLayout.html

GridBagLayout

GridBagLayout is the most sophisticated, flexible layout manager the Java platform provides. This layout manager aligns components by placing them within a grid of cells, allowing some components to span more than one cell. The rows in the grid aren't necessarily all the same height; similarly, grid columns can have different widths.

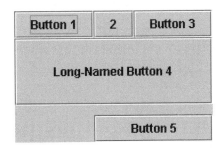

The Java Tutorial:
    http://java.sun.com/docs/books/tutorial/uiswing/layout/gridbag.html

API documentation:
    http://java.sun.com/j2se/1.3/docs/api/java/awt/GridBagLayout.html

Threads and Swing

If your program creates and refers to its GUI the correct way, you might not need to worry about threads.[1] If your program is an applet, it's safe to construct its GUI in the init method. You're also safe if your program is an application with the following common pattern:

```
//Thread-safe example
public class MyApplication {
    public static void main(String[] args) {
        JFrame f = new JFrame(...);
        ...//Add components to the frame here...
        f.pack();
        f.setVisible(true);
        //Don't do any more GUI work here.
    }

    ...
    //All manipulation of the GUI -- setText, getText, etc.
    //is performed in event handlers such as actionPerformed().
    ...
}
```

However, if your program creates threads to perform tasks that affect the GUI or if it manipulates an already visible GUI in response to anything but a standard event, read on.

The Single-Thread Rule

Swing components can be accessed by only one thread at a time, generally the event-dispatching thread. Thus, the single-thread rule is as follows.

Rule: Once a Swing component has been realized, all code that might affect or depend on the state of that component should be executed in the event-dispatching thread.

This rule might sound scary, but for many simple programs, you don't have to worry about threads.

Before we go into detail about how to write Swing code, let's define the term *realized. Realized* means that the component has been painted on-screen or that it is ready to be painted. A Swing component that's a top-level window is realized by having one of these methods invoked on it: setVisible(true), show, or pack. Once a window is realized, all the compo-

---

[1] For general information on threads, see Chapter 8, <u>Threads: Doing Two or More Tasks at Once</u> (page 269).

nents it contains are realized. Another way to realize a component is to add it to a container that's already realized. You'll see examples of realizing components later.

Note: The show method does the same thing as setVisible(true).

Exceptions to the Rule

The rule that all code that might affect a realized Swing component must run in the event-dispatching thread has a few exceptions.

A few methods are thread safe.

In the Swing API documentation, thread-safe methods are marked with this text:

> This method is thread safe, although most Swing methods are not.

An application's GUI can often be constructed and shown in the main thread.

As long as no Swing or other components have been realized in the current runtime environment, it's fine to construct and show a GUI in the main thread of an application. To help you see why, here's an analysis of the thread safety of the thread-safe example. To refresh your memory, here are the important lines from the example:

```
public static void main(String[] args) {
    JFrame f = new JFrame(...);
    ...//Add components to the frame here...
    f.pack();
    f.setVisible(true);
    //Don't do any more GUI work here.
}
```

1. The example constructs the GUI in the main thread. In general, you can construct (but not show) a GUI in any thread, as long as you don't make any calls that refer to or affect already realized components.

2. The components in the GUI are realized by the pack call.

3. Immediately afterward, the components in the GUI are shown with the setVisible (or show) call. Technically the setVisible call is unsafe, because the components have already been realized by the pack call. However, because the program doesn't already have a visible GUI, it's exceedingly unlikely that a paint request will occur before set-Visible returns.

4. The main thread executes no GUI code after the setVisible call. This means that all GUI work moves from the main thread to the event-dispatching thread, and the example is, in practice, thread safe.

An applet's GUI can be constructed and shown in the `init` method.

Existing browsers don't paint an applet until after its `init` and `start` methods have been called. Thus constructing the GUI in the applet's `init` method is safe, as long as you never call `show()` or `setVisible(true)` on the applet object.

These `JComponent` methods are safe to call from any thread: `repaint` and `revalidate`.

These methods queue requests to be executed on the event-dispatching thread.

Listener lists can be modified from any thread.

It's always safe to call the add*ListenerType*Listener and remove*ListenerType*Listener methods. The add/remove operations have no effect on an event dispatch that's under way.

How to Execute Code in the Event-Dispatching Thread

Most postinitialization GUI work naturally occurs in the event-dispatching thread. Once the GUI is visible, most programs are driven by events, such as button actions or mouse clicks, which are always handled in the event-dispatching thread.

However, some programs need to perform nonevent-driven GUI work after the GUI is visible. Here are two examples.

Programs that must perform a lengthy initialization operation before they can be used

This kind of program should generally show some GUI while the initialization is occurring and then update or change the GUI. The initialization should *not* occur in the event-dispatching thread; otherwise, repainting and event dispatching would stop. However, after initialization, the GUI update or change *should* occur in the event-dispatching thread, for thread-safety reasons.

Programs whose GUI must be updated as the result of nonstandard events

For example, suppose that a server program can get requests from other programs that might be running on different machines. These requests can come at any time, and they result in one of the server's methods being invoked in a possibly unknown thread. How can that method update the GUI? By executing the GUI-update code in the event-dispatching thread.

The `SwingUtilities`[1] class provides two methods to help you run code in the event-dispatching thread:

`invokeLater`

Requests that some code be executed in the event-dispatching thread. This method returns immediately, without waiting for the code to execute.

---

[1] API documentation for this class is available on the CD that accompanies this book and online at: http://java.sun.com/products/jdk/1.2/docs/api/javax/swing/SwingUtilities.html

invokeAndWait

Acts like `invokeLater`, except that this method waits for the code to execute. As a rule, you should use `invokeLater` rather than this method.

For more information on deploying threads in your Swing programs, see the section "How to Use Threads" in the book *The JFC Swing Tutorial*. This section is also available on this book's CD and online at:

```
http://java.sun.com/docs/books/tutorial/uiswing/misc/threads.html
```

Visual Index to Swing Components

Now that you've gotten a taste of how to build your own Swing programs, this section gives a quick, visual reference of the Swing components so you can find more information online and on the CD. The components are broken down into six categories: top-level containers, general-purpose containers, special-purpose containers, basic controls, uneditable information displays, and editable displays of formatted information.

Table 52   Top-Level Containers: The components at the top of any Swing containment hierarchy

Component	URLs

Applet
 	
	The Java Tutorial:
	`http://java.sun.com/docs/books/tutorial/uiswing/`
	`components/applet.html`
	
	API Documentation:
	`http://java.sun.com/j2se/1.3/docs/api/javax/swing/`
	`JApplet.html`

Dialog
 	
	The Java Tutorial:
	`http://java.sun.com/docs/books/tutorial/uiswing/`
	`components/dialog.html`
	
	API Documentation:
	`http://java.sun.com/j2se/1.3/docs/api/javax/swing/`
	`JDialog.html`

Frame
 	
	The Java Tutorial:
	`http://java.sun.com/docs/books/tutorial/uiswing/`
	`components/frame.html`
	
	API Documentation:
	`http://java.sun.com/j2se/1.3/docs/api/javax/swing/`
	`JFrame.html`

Table 53   General-Purpose Containers: Intermediate containers that can be used under many different circumstances

Component	URLs

Panels
 	
	The Java Tutorial:
	`http://java.sun.com/docs/books/tutorial/`
	`uiswing/components/panel.html`
	
	API Documentation:
	`http://java.sun.com/j2se/1.3/docs/api/javax/`
	`swing/JPanel.html`

Scroll Pane
 	
	The Java Tutorial:
	`http://java.sun.com/docs/books/tutorial/`
	`uiswing/components/scrollpane.html`
	
	API Documentation:
	`http://java.sun.com/j2se/1.3/docs/api/javax/`
	`swing/JScrollPane.html`

Split Pane
 	
	The Java Tutorial:
	`http://java.sun.com/docs/books/tutorial/`
	`uiswing/components/splitpane.html`
	
	API Documentation:
	`http://java.sun.com/j2se/1.3/docs/api/javax/`
	`swing/JSplitPane.html`

Tabbed Pane
 	
	The Java Tutorial:
	`http://java.sun.com/docs/books/tutorial/`
	`uiswing/components/tabbedpane.html`
	
	API Documentation:
	`http://java.sun.com/j2se/1.3/docs/api/javax/`
	`swing/JTabbedPane.html`

Tool Bar
 	
	The Java Tutorial:
	`http://java.sun.com/docs/books/tutorial/`
	`uiswing/components/toolbar.html`
	
	API Documentation:
	`http://java.sun.com/j2se/1.3/docs/api/javax/`
	`swing/JToolBar.html`

Table 54   Special-Purpose Containers: Intermediate containers that play specific roles in the UI

Components	URLs

Internal Frames
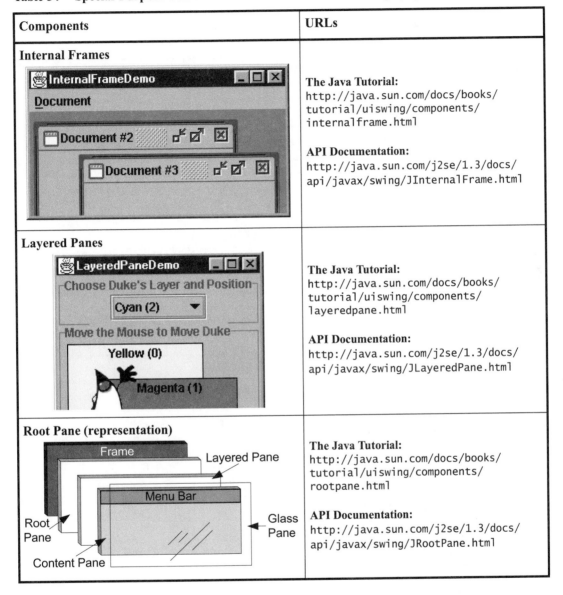
	The Java Tutorial:
	`http://java.sun.com/docs/books/`
	`tutorial/uiswing/components/`
	`internalframe.html`
	
	API Documentation:
	`http://java.sun.com/j2se/1.3/docs/`
	`api/javax/swing/JInternalFrame.html`

Layered Panes	**The Java Tutorial:**
	`http://java.sun.com/docs/books/`
	`tutorial/uiswing/components/`
	`layeredpane.html`
	
	API Documentation:
	`http://java.sun.com/j2se/1.3/docs/`
	`api/javax/swing/JLayeredPane.html`

Root Pane (representation)	**The Java Tutorial:**
	`http://java.sun.com/docs/books/`
	`tutorial/uiswing/components/`
	`rootpane.html`
	
	API Documentation:
	`http://java.sun.com/j2se/1.3/docs/`
	`api/javax/swing/JRootPane.html`

Table 55   Basic Controls: Atomic components that exist primarily to get input from the user and that generally also show simple state

Components	URLs

Buttons
 	
☑ Check 1
⦿ Radio 2
OK
	The Java Tutorial:
	`http://java.sun.com/docs/books/tutorial/`
	`uiswing/components/button.html`
	
	API Documentation:
	`http://java.sun.com/j2se/1.3/docs/api/javax/`
	`swing/JButton.html`

Combo Box
 	
Monday ▼
Monday
Tuesday
Wednesday
Thursday
Friday
	The Java Tutorial:
	`http://java.sun.com/docs/books/tutorial/`
	`uiswing/components/combobox.html`
	
	API Documentation:
	`http://java.sun.com/j2se/1.3/docs/api/javax/`
	`swing/JComboBox.html`

List
 	
January ▲
February
March
April ▼
	The Java Tutorial:
	`http://java.sun.com/docs/books/tutorial/`
	`uiswing/components/list.html`
	
	API Documentation:
	`http://java.sun.com/j2se/1.3/docs/api/javax/`
	`swing/JList.html`

Menu
 	
Theme Help
☑ **metal** ctrl-m
☑ **Organic** ctrl-o
☐ **metal2** ctrl-2
	The Java Tutorial:
	`http://java.sun.com/docs/books/tutorial/`
	`uiswing/components/menu.html`
	
	API Documentation:
	`http://java.sun.com/j2se/1.3/docs/api/javax/`
	`swing/JMenu.html`

Slider
 	
L   R
	The Java Tutorial:
	`http://java.sun.com/docs/books/tutorial/`
	`uiswing/components/slider.html`
	
	API Documentation:
	`http://java.sun.com/j2se/1.3/docs/api/javax/`
	`swing/JSlider.html`

Table 55   Basic Controls: Atomic components that exist primarily to get input from the user and that generally also show simple state

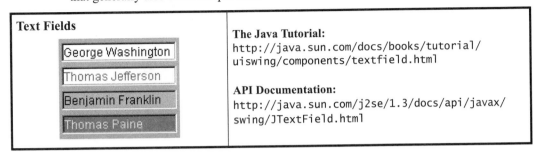

Text Fields	The Java Tutorial:
	`http://java.sun.com/docs/books/tutorial/`
	`uiswing/components/textfield.html`
	
	API Documentation:
	`http://java.sun.com/j2se/1.3/docs/api/javax/`
	`swing/JTextField.html`

Table 56   Uneditable Information Displays: Atomic components that exist solely to give the user information

Components	URLs

Label	**The Java Tutorial:**
	`http://java.sun.com/docs/books/tutorial/uiswing/`
	`components/label.html`
	
	API Documentation:
	`http://java.sun.com/j2se/1.3/docs/api/javax/swing/`
	`JLabel.html`

Progress Bar	**The Java Tutorial:**
	`http://java.sun.com/docs/books/tutorial/uiswing/`
	`components/progress.html`
	
	API Documentation:
	`http://java.sun.com/j2se/1.3/docs/api/javax/swing/`
	`JProgressBar.html`

Tool Tip	**The Java Tutorial:**
	`http://java.sun.com/docs/books/tutorial/uiswing/`
	`components/tooltip.html`
	
	API Documentation:
	`http://java.sun.com/j2se/1.3/docs/api/javax/swing/`
	`JToolTip.html`

Table 57   **Editable Displays of Formatted Information:** Atomic components that display highly formatted information that (if you choose) can be edited by the user

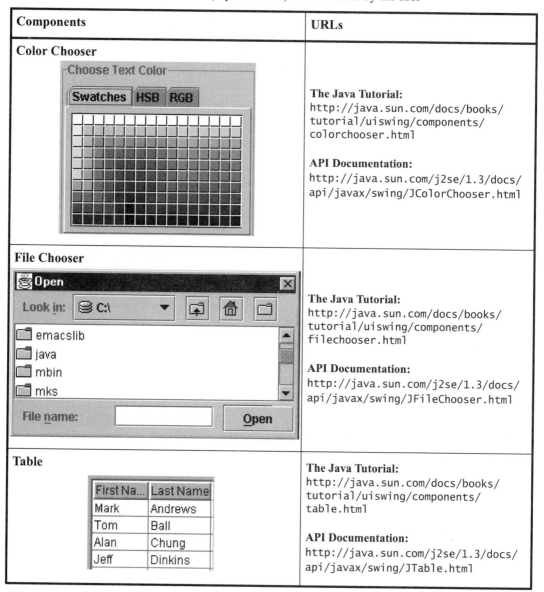

Components	URLs

Color Chooser	**The Java Tutorial:**
	`http://java.sun.com/docs/books/`
	`tutorial/uiswing/components/`
	`colorchooser.html`
	
	API Documentation:
	`http://java.sun.com/j2se/1.3/docs/`
	`api/javax/swing/JColorChooser.html`

File Chooser	**The Java Tutorial:**
	`http://java.sun.com/docs/books/`
	`tutorial/uiswing/components/`
	`filechooser.html`
	
	API Documentation:
	`http://java.sun.com/j2se/1.3/docs/`
	`api/javax/swing/JFileChooser.html`

Table	**The Java Tutorial:**
	`http://java.sun.com/docs/books/`
	`tutorial/uiswing/components/`
	`table.html`
	
	API Documentation:
	`http://java.sun.com/j2se/1.3/docs/`
	`api/javax/swing/JTable.html`

Table 57   Editable Displays of Formatted Information: Atomic components that display highly formatted information that (if you choose) can be edited by the user

Text		**The Java Tutorial:**
		`http://java.sun.com/docs/books/`
		`tutorial/uiswing/components/`
		`generaltext.html`
		
		API Documentation:
		`http://java.sun.com/j2se/1.3/docs/`
		`api/javax/swing/text/`
		`JTextComponent.html`

	With *styled text*, you can have multiple fonts, styles, colors, and **extras** such as embedded pictures and components.	

Tree		**The Java Tutorial:**
		`http://java.sun.com/docs/books/`
		`tutorial/uiswing/components/`
		`tree.html`
		
		API Documentation:
		`http://java.sun.com/j2se/1.3/docs/`
		`api/javax/swing/JTree.html`

	The Java Series
	  Books for Java Programmers
	  Books for Java Implementers
	    The Java Virtual Machine Specification
	    The Java Language Specification	

Summary

This discussion glossed over many details and left some things unexplained, but you should have some understanding now of what you can build with Swing components. You should now have a general understanding of the following:

- How to set up the containment hierarchy of each Swing component. To add a component to a container, you use some form of the add method.
- How to implement many standard GUI components, such as buttons, labels, combo boxes, and radio buttons, which you combine to create your program's GUI.
- How to change the layout of components by using layout managers.
- How to handle events and accommodate threads in Swing programs. Recall that the event-handling mechanism is based on the AWT event-handling model in which you register event listeners upon the components which generate events.

For more complete information on Swing, see the book *The JFC Swing Tutorial* or the online tutorial: `http://java.sun.com/docs/books/tutorial/uiswing/index.html`

Questions and Exercises

Questions

Use the API documentation to answer these questions.

1. Show the code that creates a label displaying the following text, with the italics and boldface as shown in this screenshot:

2. Use the API documentation or online tutorial, if necessary, to answer the following questions:

   a. Assume that you have a Swing label that tends to have more horizontal space than it needs to display its text. What code would you use to make the text within a label (`JLabel`) be centered instead of left-aligned?

   b. What method do you use to enable and disable such components as Swing buttons?

   c. How do you add a component to the rightmost (east) cell in a container that uses `BorderLayout`?

3. Is the following code thread-safe? If so, why? If not, what can you do to make it thread-safe?

```
JLabel label;

Container createGUI() {
    ...
    //create a JPanel; add components to it, including label
    ...
    return panel;
}

public static void main(String[] args) {
    JFrame f = new JFrame("A Frame");
    f.setContentPane(createGUI());
    f.pack();
    f.setVisible(true);
    String labelText = findTextFromSomewhere();
    label.setText(labelText);
}
```

Exercises

You'll need to work on these exercises in order, as they build upon each other. *Hint:* Your answer to question 2 will be useful.

1. Write an application called `SwingApp1` that has two buttons and one label, arranged as shown in the following screenshot:

   Hint: You can use the content pane's default `BorderLayout` to manage the buttons and label.

2. Copy `SwingApp1.java` to `SwingApp2.java`, and modify `SwingApp2` so that the Stop button is initially disabled. Implement and register one or two action listeners so that when the user clicks either button, the clicked button is disabled, the other button is enabled, and the label is updated appropriately. Your application should look like this:

3. Copy `SwingApp2.java` to `SwingApp3.java`, and modify `SwingApp3` so that its Start button brings up a dialog that looks like this:

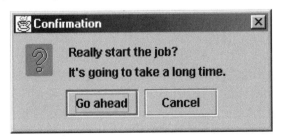

   If the user chooses the Go ahead button, the Start button should do exactly what it did in `SwingApp2`. If the user does anything else, the application should update the label to report the cancellation and leave the buttons in their existing state.

Answers

You can find answers to these Questions and Exercises online:

`http://java.sun.com/docs/books/tutorial/uiswing/QandE/answers.html`

Code Samples

Table 58 lists the code samples used in this chapter and where you can find the code online and on the CD that accompanies this book.

Table 58   Code Samples in User Interfaces That Swing

Code Sample (where discussed)	CD Location	Online Location
HelloWorldSwing.java (page 354)	JavaTutorial/uiswing/ mini/example-1dot3/ HelloWorldSwing.java	http://java.sun.com/docs/books/ tutorial/uiswing/mini/example-1dot3/HelloWorldSwing.java
SwingApplication.java (page 356)	JavaTutorial/uiswing/ mini/example-1dot3/ SwingApplication.java	http://java.sun.com/docs/books/ tutorial/uiswing/mini/example-1dot3/SwingApplication.java
CelsiusConverter.java (page 361)	JavaTutorial/uiswing/ mini/example-1dot3/ CelsiusConverter.java	http://java.sun.com/docs/books/ tutorial/uiswing/mini/example-1dot3/CelsiusConverter.java
CelsiusConverter2.java (page 362)	JavaTutorial/uiswing/ mini/example-1dot3/ CelsiusConverter2.java	http://java.sun.com/docs/books/ tutorial/uiswing/mini/example-1dot3/CelsiusConverter2.java
LunarPhases.java (page 364)	JavaTutorial/uiswing/ mini/example-1dot3/ LunarPhases.java	http://java.sun.com/docs/books/ tutorial/uiswing/mini/example-1dot3/LunarPhases.java
VoteDialog.java (page 368)	JavaTutorial/uiswing/ mini/example-1dot3/ VoteDialog.java	http://java.sun.com/docs/books/ tutorial/uiswing/mini/example-1dot3/VoteDialog.java

Note: The section <u>Common Problems and Their Solutions</u> (page 391) contains solutions to common problems Tutorial readers have encountered.

Common Problems and Their Solutions

T HIS appendix covers some common problems that you might encounter when learning the Java™ programming language. A list of possible solutions follows each problem.

Getting Started Problems

If you're having trouble compiling your source code or running your application or applet, this section might help you find and fix your problem. If nothing in this section helps, refer to the documentation for the compiler or the interpreter you're using.

Some of the problems that first-time programmers experience are the result of incorrectly installed development environments. If you can't compile even a single program, double-check that you installed your development environment correctly and that your path has been updated so that the operating system can find your development environment.

You can find installation instructions for the Java 2 Software Development Kit (SDK) in the README.txt file at the top of the SDK release. You can also find these instructions on the Java 2 SDK Web site.[1]

Another common problem results from using a text editor that saves files in 8.3 format or with a TXT suffix. Most development tools are picky about file names. Save yourself some trouble: Avoid editors that don't give you full control over file names.

One problem that vexes beginners and experts alike results from incorrectly setting the CLASSPATH environment variable. Do *not* set CLASSPATH unless you are sure of what you're doing.

Compiler Problems

Can't Run the Compiler

If you can't get the compiler to run at all, it's because the operating system can't find it. You probably need to either specify the full path to the compiler or set your path environment variable so that it contains the SDK's bin directory.

Platform-Specific Details: Setting the Path

UNIX:

If you use the C shell (csh), you can set the path by adding the following line to your startup file (~/.cshrc):

```
set path=($path /usr/local/JDK1.3/bin)
```

Then load the startup file and use the which command to verify that the path is set correctly:

```
% source ~/.cshrc
% which javac
```

Win32:

Open the C:\AUTOEXEC.BAT file and edit the PATH statement with the system editor. (Open the system editor from the Start menu, select Run, and type sysedit in the text-box.) Ensure that no other versions of the SDK are in the path, and then add the SDK to the end of the path. Here's an example of a PATH statement:

```
PATH C:\WINDOWS;C:\WINDOWS\COMMAND;C:\JDK1.3\BIN
```

---

[1]   http://java.sun.com/products/index.html

Note that after installing both the SDK software and documentation, the SDK directory will have the following structure.

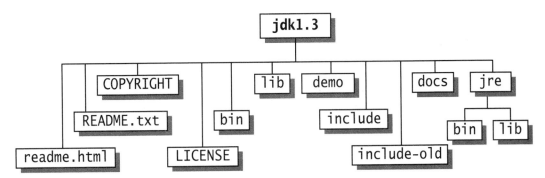

Figure 111   The SDK installed directory tree.

Can't Find the File

If the compiler can't find the file you're trying to compile, try these solutions.

- Make sure that the file is named exactly *Class*.java, where *Class* is the name of the class in the file you're trying to compile.
- Make sure that you're invoking the compiler from the directory in which the .java file is located.
- Make sure that you invoked the compiler rather than the interpreter. The compiler is named javac; the interpreter is named java.

Note: A source file's name must exactly match the name of the class that the file contains, including the same capitalization. Be sure that the full .java suffix follows the class name.

Changes Didn't Take Effect

If you changed your program and recompiled it but the changes didn't take effect, try these solutions.

- Make sure that the program compiled cleanly. If the program couldn't compile, the old class files might still exist.
- If your program compiled successfully, make sure that you're specifying the new class files and not a backup copy of the old files. Delete the old class files, if necessary, to avoid confusion.
- Make sure that the tool you're using hasn't cached the old class files. Usually, you can empty a cache by quitting the tool and then restarting it. If you are trying to view

changes made to an applet in a browser, try clicking `Shift` and the `Reload` or `Refresh` button. If this doesn't work, try explicitly clearing the cache on your browser.

Syntax Errors

If you mistype part of a program, the compiler may issue a *syntax* error. The message usually displays the name of the file in which the error occurred, the line number on which the error was detected, a description of the error (to the best abilities of the compiler), the code on that line, and the position of the error within the code. Here's an error caused by the omission of a semicolon (`;`) at the end of a statement:

```
testing.java:14: ';' expected.
System.out.println("Counted " + count + " chars.")
                                                    ^

1 error
```

Sometimes, the compiler can't guess your intent, so it prints one or more confusing error messages for one mistake. For example, the following code snippet omits a semicolon (`;`) from the line in boldface:

```
while (in.read() != -1)
    count++
System.out.println("Counted " + count + " chars.");
```

When processing this code, the compiler issues two error messages:

```
testing.java:13: Invalid type expression.
        count++
              ^

testing.java:14: Invalid declaration.
    System.out.println("Counted " + count + "chars.");
          ^
2 errors
```

The compiler issues two error messages because after it processes `count++`, the compiler's state indicates that it's in the middle of an expression. Without the semicolon, the compiler has no way of knowing that the statement is complete.

If you see any compiler errors, your program did not successfully compile, and the compiler did not create or update your `.class` file. Carefully verify the program, fix the errors, and try again.

Semantic Errors

In addition to verifying that your program is syntactically correct, the compiler checks for basic correctness. For example, it warns you each time you use a variable that has not been initialized:

```
testing.java:13: Variable count may not have been initialized.
        count++
^
testing.java:14: Variable count may not have been initialized.
System.out.println("Counted " + count + " chars.");
                                        ^
2 errors
```

Again, your program did not successfully compile, and the compiler did not create a `.class` file. Fix the error and try again.

Interpreter Problems

Can't Find the Class

If the interpreter says that it can't find the class you just compiled, try these solutions:

- Make sure that you specified the *class* name—not the class *file* name—to the interpreter. For example, the following command doesn't work: `java HelloWorldApp.class`. Instead, use `java HelloWorldApp`. (Notice that you shouldn't add `.class`!)
- Unset the `CLASSPATH` environment variable if it's set. See the section Path Help in Appendix E (page 540) for information about `CLASSPATH`.
- Make sure that you're invoking the interpreter from the directory in which the `.class` file is located.
- Make sure that you invoked the interpreter rather than the compiler. The compiler is named `javac`; the interpreter is named `java`.

The main Method Is Not Defined

If the interpreter tells you that the `main` method is not defined, try these solutions.

- Make sure that the program you tried to execute is an application and not just an applet. Most applets don't have `main` methods, because applets are designed to be executed in browsers.
- If the program should be an application, make sure that it has a `main` method.

- Make sure that the program's `main` method is defined exactly as described in the section <u>The main Method</u> in Chapter 1 (page 34). For example, make sure that you specify the `main` method as `public`.

General Programming Problems

Problem: The compiler complains that it can't find a class.

- Make sure that you've imported the class or its package.
- If the `CLASSPATH` environment variable is set, unset it.
- Make sure that you're spelling the class name exactly the same way as it is declared. Case matters!
- If your classes are in packages, make sure that they appear in the correct subdirectory, as outlined in <u>Managing Source and Class Files</u> (page 238).
- Also, some programmers use different names for the class name and the `.java` filename. Make sure that you're using the class name and not the filename. In fact, make the names the same, and you won't run into this problem.

Problem: The interpreter says that it can't find one of my classes.

- Make sure that you specified the *class* name—not the class *file* name—to the interpreter.
- If the `CLASSPATH` environment variable is set, unset it.
- If your classes are in packages, make sure that they appear in the correct subdirectory, as outlined in the section <u>Managing Source and Class Files</u> (page 238).
- Make sure that you're invoking the interpreter from the directory in which the `.class` file is located.

Problem: My program doesn't work! What's wrong with it?

The following is a list of common programming mistakes novice Java programmers make. Confirm that one of these errors isn't what's holding you back.

- Did you forget to use `break` after each `case` statement in a `switch` statement?
- Did you use the assignment operator = when you intended to use the comparison operator ==?
- Are the termination conditions on your loops correct? Make sure that you're not terminating loops one iteration too early or too late. That is, make sure that you are using < or <= and > or >= as appropriate for your situation.

- Remember that array indices begin at 0, so iterating over an array looks like this:

  ```
  for (int i = 0; i < array.length; i++)
  ```

- Are you comparing floating-point numbers using ==? Remember that floats are approximations of the real thing. The greater than and less than (> and <) operators are more appropriate when conditional logic is performed on floating-point numbers.

- Are you having trouble with encapsulation, inheritance, or other object-oriented programming and design concepts? Review the information in Chapter 2, Object-Oriented Programming Concepts (page 45).

- Make sure that blocks of statements are enclosed in braces {}. The following code looks right because of indentation, but it doesn't do what the indents imply, because the braces are missing:

  ```
  for (int i = 0; i < arrayOfInts.length; i++)
      arrayOfInts[i] = i;
      System.out.println("[i] = " + arrayOfInts[i]);
  ```

- Are you using the correct conditional operator? Make sure that you understand && and || and are using them appropriately.

- Do you use the negation operator ! a lot? Try to express conditions without it. Doing so is less confusing and error prone.

- Are you using a do-while? If so, do you know that the loop executes one more time than a similar while loop?

- Are you trying to change the value of an argument from a method? Arguments in Java are passed by value and can't be changed in a method.

- Did you inadvertently add an extra semicolon (;), thereby terminating a statement prematurely? Note the extra semicolon at the end of this for statement:

  ```
  for (int i = 0; i < arrayOfInts.length; i++) ;
      arrayOfInts[i] = i;
  ```

Note: To help you debug your programs, add lines with System.out.println to print out error messages or the values of variables:

```
System.out.println("The value of a is: " + a);
```

Applet Problems

This section covers some common problems that you might encounter when writing applets. A list of possible solutions follows each problem.

Problem: Applet Viewer says that there's no <APPLET> tag on my HTML page, but it is there.

- Check whether you have a closing applet tag: </APPLET>.
- Check whether you entered the correct URL for the page.

Problem: I recompiled my applet, but my browser won't show the new version, even though I told it to reload it.

- In many browsers, reloading isn't reliable. This is why we recommend that you use the SDK Applet Viewer, invoking it anew each time you change the applet.
- In some browsers, using Shift-Reload might reload the applet.
- If the applet has an archive file, make sure that you updated the archive.
- If you get an old version of the applet no matter what you do, make sure that you don't have an old copy of the applet in a directory in your CLASSPATH. See the section Path Help in Appendix E (page 540) for information.

Problem: The light gray background of my applet causes the applet to flicker when it is drawn on a page of a different color.

- You need to set the background color of the applet so that it works well with the page color.
- You might need to implement double buffering. See the "2D Graphics" trail in *The Java Tutorial* online at http://java.sun.com/docs/books/tutorial/2d/images/doublebuffering.html. (Note that Swing painting is double-buffered by default.)

Problem: The applet getImage method doesn't work.

- Make sure that you're calling getImage from the init method or a method that's called after init. The getImage method does not work when it's called from a constructor.

Problem: I've copied my applet's class file onto my HTTP server, but the applet doesn't work.

- Does your applet define more than one class? If so, make sure that the class file (*ClassName*.class) for each class is on the HTTP server. Even if all the classes are defined in one source file, the compiler produces one class file per class or interface. If you use inner classes, be sure to copy their class files as well.
- Did you copy all the data files for your applet—image and sound files, for example—to the server?

- Make sure that all the applet's class and data files can be read by everyone and that the directories they're in can be read and searched by everyone.

- Make sure that the class and data files are in the correct directory, relative to the document. If you specify a code base, make sure that the class and data files are under the code base directory and that the directory name has the proper capitalization. Similarly, if your applet's classes are in a package, make sure the class files are in the right directory under the code base.

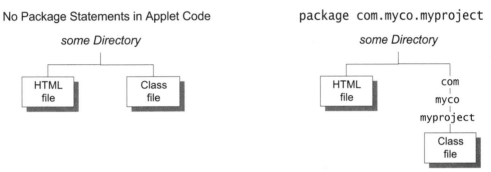

- Make sure the applet's class and data files weren't garbled during the transfer. One common source of trouble is using the ASCII mode of FTP (rather than the binary ("BIN") mode) to transfer files. Make sure that you transfer your files in binary mode by typing `bin` at the command line.

Problem: When I restart my applet, it seems to show up twice—or at least the components it contains show up twice.

- Your applet's `init` method is being called twice. This isn't supposed to happen, although the Applet Viewer lets you do it. One solution is to implement the applet's `destroy` method so that it calls `removeAll`, which `Applet` inherits from `Container`.

User Interface Problems

Swing Components

This section discusses problems that you might encounter while using Swing components.

Problem: I can't make HTML tags work in my labels, buttons, and so on.

- Make sure that your program is running in a release that supports HTML text in the desired component. (If you are using Java 2 SDK versions 1.2 or 1.3, you do not need to worry.)

- `JCheckBox` and `JRadioButton` don't support HTML yet. We don't know when that support will be added.
- If you can't guarantee that your program will be executed only with a release that supports HTML text in the desired component, *don't use that feature!*

Problem: Certain areas of the content pane look weird when they're repainted.

- If you set the content pane, make sure that it's opaque. `JPanel` and `JDesktopPane` make good content panes because they're opaque by default.
- If one or more of your components performs custom painting, make sure that you implemented it correctly. See *The Java Tutorial* online at `http://java.sun.com/docs/books/tutorial/uiswing/painting/index.html` for help.
- You might have a thread safety problem. See the next entry.

Problem: My program is exhibiting weird symptoms that sometimes seem to be related to timing.

- Make sure that your code is thread-safe. See <u>Threads and Swing</u> (page 378) for details.

Problem: The scroll bar policies don't seem to be working as advertised.

- Some Swing releases contain bugs in the implementations for the policies `VERTICAL_SCROLLBAR_AS_NEEDED` and `HORIZONTAL_SCROLLBAR_AS_NEEDED`. If feasible for your project, use the most recent release of Swing.
- If the scroll pane's client can change size dynamically, the program should set the client's preferred size and then call `revalidate` on the client.
- Make sure that you specified the policy you intended for the orientation you intended.

Problem: My scroll pane has no scroll bars.

- If you want a scroll bar to appear all the time, specify one of the following scroll bar policies: `VERTICAL_SCROLLBAR_ALWAYS` or `HORIZONTAL_SCROLLBAR_ALWAYS`.
- If you want the scroll bars to appear as needed and you want to force the scroll bars to be needed when the scroll pane is created, you have two choices: (1) either set the preferred size of the scroll pane or its container, or (2) implement a scroll-savvy class and return a value smaller than the component's standard preferred size from the `getPreferredScrollableViewportSize` method. Refer to the section "Sizing a Scroll Pane" in *The Java Tutorial* online at `http://java.sun.com/docs/books/tutorial/uiswing/components/scrollpane.html#sizing`

Problem: The divider in my split pane won't move!

- You need to set the minimum size of at least one of the components in the split pane. Refer to the section "Positioning the Divider and Restricting Its Range" in *The Java Tutorial* online at `http://java.sun.com/docs/books/tutorial/uiswing/components/splitpane.html#divider`.

Problem: The `setDividerLocation` method doesn't work.

- Some releases of Swing have a bug whereby a call to `setDividerLocation` doesn't work unless the split pane is already on screen. For information and possible workarounds, see bug #4101306 and bug #4182558 in the *Bug Parade* at the Java Developer's Connection at `http://developer.java.sun.com/`.

Problem: The borders on nested split panes look too wide.

- If you nest split panes, the borders accumulate. The border of the inner split panes display next to the border of the outer split pane, causing borders that look extra wide. The problem is particularly noticeable when nesting many split panes. The workaround is to set the border to `null` on any split pane that is placed within another split pane. For information, see bug #4131528 in the *Bug Parade* at the Java Developer's Connection online at `http://developer.java.sun.com/`.

Problem: The buttons in my tool bar are too big.

- Try reducing the margin for the buttons. For example:
  ```
  button.setMargin(new Insets(0,0,0,0));
  ```

Problem: The components in my layered pane aren't layered correctly. In fact, the layers seem to be inverted—the lower the depth, the higher the component.

- This can happen if you use an `int` instead of an `Integer` when adding components to a layered pane. To see what happens, make the following change to `LayeredPaneDemo`.

Change this:	to this:
`layeredPane.add(label, new Integer(i));`	`layeredPane.add(label, i);`

Problem: The method call `colorChooser.setPreviewPanel(null)` does not remove the color chooser's preview panel as expected.

- A `null` argument specifies the default preview panel. To remove the preview panel, specify a standard panel with no size, like this:
  ```
  colorChooser.setPreviewPanel(new JPanel());
  ```

Layout

Problem: How do I specify a component's exact size?

- First, make sure that you really need to set the component's exact size. Each Swing component has a different preferred size, depending on the font it uses and the look and feel. Therefore, it often doesn't make sense to specify a Swing component's exact size.

- If the component isn't controlled by a layout manager, you can set its size by invoking the `setSize` or the `setBounds` method on it. Otherwise, you need to provide size hints and then make sure that you're using a layout manager that respects the size hints.

- If you extend a Swing component class, you can give size hints by overriding the component's `getMinimumSize`, `getPreferredSize`, and `getMaximumSize` methods. What's nice about this approach is that each get*Xxxx*Size method can get the component's default size hints by invoking `super.get`*Xxxx*`Size()`. Then it can adjust the size, if necessary, before returning it.

- Another way to give size hints is to invoke the component's `setMinimumSize`, `setPreferredSize`, and `setMaximumSize` methods.

If you specify new size hints for a component that's already visible, you then need to invoke the `revalidate` method on it, to make sure that its containment hierarchy is laid out again. Then invoke the `repaint` method.

Note: No matter how you specify your component's size, be sure that your component's container uses a layout manager that respects the requested size of the component. The `FlowLayout` and `GridBagLayout` managers use the component's preferred size (the latter depending on the constraints that you set), but `BorderLayout` and `GridLayout` usually don't. The `BoxLayout` manager generally uses a component's preferred size (although components can be larger) and is the only layout manager that respects the component's maximum size.

Problem: My custom component is being sized too small.

- Does the component implement the `getPreferredSize` and the `getMinimumSize` methods? If so, do they return the correct values?

- Are you using a layout manager that can use as much space as is available? See the section <u>Using Layout Managers</u> (page 375) for some tips on choosing a layout manager and specifying that it use the maximum available space for a particular component.

Event Handling

This section discusses problems that you might encounter while handling events.

Problem: I'm trying to handle certain events from a component, but the component isn't generating the events it should.

- First, make sure that you registered the correct kind of listener to detect the events. See whether another kind of listener might detect the kind of events you need.
- Make sure that you registered the listener on the correct object.
- Did you implement the event handler correctly? For example, if you extended an adapter class, make sure that you used the correct method signature. Make sure that each event-handling method is `public void`, that the name is spelled correctly, and that the argument is of the correct type.
- If you still think that the component isn't generating the events it should, check the Java Developer Connection[1] to see whether this is a known bug.

Problem: My combo box isn't generating low-level events, such as focus events.

- Combo boxes are compound components—components implemented using multiple components. For this reason, combo boxes don't fire the low-level events that simple components fire.

Problem: The document for an editor pane (or text pane) isn't firing document events.

- The document instance for an editor pane or text pane might change when loading text from a URL. Thus, your listeners might be listening for events on an unused document. For example, if you load an editor pane or text pane with HTML that was previously loaded with plain text, the document will change to an `HTMLDocument` instance. If your program dynamically loads text into an editor pane or a text pane, make sure that the code adjusts for possible changes to the document (reregister document listeners on the new document, and so on).

Swing Graphics

Problem: I don't know where to put my painting code.

- Painting code belongs in the `paintComponent` method of any component descended from `JComponent`. See "Overview of Custom Painting" in *The Java Tutorial* online at: `http://java.sun.com/docs/books/tutorial/uiswing/painting/overview.html`.

---

[1] You can find the *Java Developer Connection* online at http://developer.java.sun.com

Problem: The stuff I paint does not show up.

- Check whether your component is showing up at all. The section <u>Swing Components</u> (page 399) in this appendix should help you with this problem.

- Check whether your component is obscured by another component. For example, you shouldn't put painting code in a JFrame or a JDialog subclass, because it will be covered by the applet's frame or content pane.

Problem: The background of my applet shows up, but the stuff in the foreground does not show up.

- Did you make the mistake of performing painting directly in a JApplet subclass? If so, your contents will be covered by the content pane that is automatically created for every JApplet instance. Instead, create another class that performs the painting and then add that class to the JApplet's content pane. For more information on how painting in Swing works see *The Java Tutorial* online at `http://java.sun.com/docs/ books/tutorial/uiswing/overview/draw.html`.

Problem: My component's foreground shows up, but its background is invisible. The result is that one or more components directly behind my component are unexpectedly visible.

- Make sure that your component is opaque. JPanels, for example, are opaque by default. To make other components, such as JLabels, opaque, you must invoke `setOpaque(true)` on them.

- If your custom component extends JPanel or a more specialized JComponent descendant, you can paint the background by invoking `super.paintComponent` before painting the contents of your component.

- You can paint the background yourself, using this code at the top of a custom component's `paintComponent` method:
  ```
  g.setColor(getBackground());
  g.fillRect(0, 0, getWidth(), getHeight());
  g.setColor(getForeground());
  ```

Problem: I used `setBackground` to set my component's background color, but it seemed to have no effect.

- Most likely, your component isn't painting its background either because it's not opaque or your custom painting code doesn't paint the background. If you set the background color for a JLabel, for example, you must also invoke `setOpaque(true)` on the label to make the label's background be painted. For more help, see the preceding problem.

Problem: I'm using the exact same code as a tutorial example, but it doesn't work. Why?

- Is the code executed in the exact same method as the tutorial example? For example, if the tutorial example has the code in the example's `paintComponent` method, this method might be the only place where the code is guaranteed to work.

Problem: How do I paint thick lines? Patterns?

- The Java 2D API provides extensive support for implementing line widths and styles, as well as patterns for use in filling and stroking shapes. See the "2D Graphics" trail for more information on using the Java 2D API.[1]

Swing Conversion

For information on converting your programs to Swing, see the book *The JFC/Swing Tutorial* or the online tutorial at `http://java/sun/com/docs/books/tutorial/uiswing/converting`.

Problem: I'm seeing weird problems that are either intermittent or dependent on timing.

- Does your main thread modify the GUI after it's visible? If so, either move the code so that it executes before the GUI is shown, or execute the GUI-modifying code in the event-dispatching thread.

- Does your program have multiple threads or query/modify the GUI in response to messages from other programs? If so, you should ensure that all GUI-related code is executed in the event-dispatching thread.

- If your program is an applet that implements the `stop` and `start` methods, make sure that any GUI work performed by those methods is executed in the event-dispatching thread.

- The preceding suggestions assume that your problem is caused by code that isn't thread safe. See the section <u>Threads and Swing</u> (page 378) for information about thread safety for information about API you can use to help make your programs thread safe.

Problem: My applet/dialog/frame is blank.

- Does the applet/dialog/frame perform custom drawing? If so, you need to move the custom drawing code out of the `JApplet/JDialog/JFrame` subclass and into a custom component that you add to the content pane.

- Do you either set the applet/frame/dialog's content pane or add components to the existing content pane? See <u>Your First Swing Program</u> (page 353) for more information.

---

[1] The 2D trail is available in the book *The Java Tutorial Continued* and online at http://java.sun.com/docs/books/tutorial/2d/index.html.

Problem: In the Swing version of my program, the list/text component is missing its scroll bars.

- Swing list and text components don't have automatic scroll bars. Instead, you need to add the list or text component to a scroll pane.

Problem: Although I'm using the same grid bag layout code as before, one scrollable component is tiny.

- Make sure that you set constraints on the scroll pane rather than on its client.

Problem: I'm not getting the kinds of events I expected for the Swing component I'm using.

- Read both the conversion tips and how-to section for the component you're using. Chances are, the relevant event details are covered in those sections.

- If you think that the problem might be a bug, search the bug database at the Java Developer Connection at `http://developer.java.sun.com/`.

Internet-Ready Applets

$\mathbf{W}$ HEN the Java™ technology was first introduced, much of the surrounding hype focused on applets because they allow programs to be downloaded to a browser and to run on the fly over the Internet. It's important to keep in mind that applets are just another way of delivering a program. Newer ways of delivering programs are continually being invented, one example is Java WebStart.[1]

Applets can run in any browser with a Java Virtual Machine. However, the major browsers haven't kept up with the latest releases of the Java 2 Platform. To ensure that most users can run your applets, you have two options:

- You can create applets that use the JDK 1.1 API.[2] Most Netscape Navigator and Internet Explorer browsers in use will run applets written to the 1.1 API.

- You can use the Java Plug-in solution, which installs as an extension to either Internet Explorer or Netscape Navigator browsers.[3] The Java Plug-in does not replace or modify the browser's underlying Java runtime; rather, Java Plug-in allows a Web author to specify the use of Sun Microsystems' Java runtime environment (JRE) for a given Web page.

Although the Java Plug-in can guarantee the use of the appropriate virtual machine, it is a hefty download, about 6MB. The plug-in is recommended for use on internal corporate intranets but not for distributing applets on the Internet. For this reason, this appendix presents the information you need to write applets that use the JDK 1.1 API.

This appendix starts by telling you how applets work. The next section covers sound, applet parameters, the <APPLET> tag, interapplet communication, and browser requests.

---

[1] You can learn more about Java WebStart at: http://java.sun.com/products/javawebstart/
[2] JDK 1.1 is an earlier release of the Java SDK.
[3] The Plug-in is now included in Sun Microsystems' release of the Java Runtime Environment (JRE).   **407**

The appendix then discusses factors to consider when writing the graphical user interface (GUI) for your applet and security restrictions on applets. The next section describes the characteristics of a high-quality applet and includes a checklist of annoying behaviors to avoid in your applet. If you're interested in running applets that use the Java 2 SDK, read the last section, <u>Swing-Based Applets</u> (page 457), which has information on running and writing applets that use Swing GUI components.

Overview of Applets

This section discusses the parts of an applet. If you haven't yet compiled an applet and included it in an HTML page, you might want to follow the step-by-step instructions found in the chapter Getting Started (page 1).

Every applet is implemented by creating a subclass of the Applet class. Figure 112 shows the inheritance hierarchy of the Applet class. This hierarchy determines much of what an applet can do and how it does it, as you'll see on the next few pages.

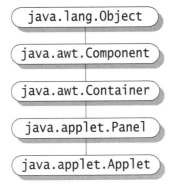

Figure 112   The Applet class inherits much of its functionality from its superclasses.

A Simple Applet

Following is the source code for an applet called Simple.[1] The Simple applet displays a descriptive string whenever it encounters a *milestone*—a major event in an applet's life cycle, such as when the user first visits the page that contains the applet. The following pages build on the Simple applet to illustrate concepts that are common to many applets.

```
import java.applet.Applet;
import java.awt.Graphics;

public class Simple extends Applet {
```

---

[1]   Simple.java is included on the CD and is available online. See Code Samples (page 463).

```
StringBuffer buffer;

public void init() {
    buffer = new StringBuffer();
    addItem("initializing... ");
}

public void start() {
    addItem("starting... ");
}

public void stop() {
    addItem("stopping... ");
}

public void destroy() {
    addItem("preparing for unloading...");
}

void addItem(String newWord) {
    System.out.println(newWord);
    buffer.append(newWord);
    repaint();
}

public void paint(Graphics g) {
    //Draw a Rectangle around the applet's display area.
    g.drawRect(0, 0,
                getSize().width - 1,
                getSize().height - 1);

    //Draw the current string inside the rectangle.
    g.drawString(buffer.toString(), 5, 15);
}
}
```

The Life Cycle of an Applet

Here is a picture of the Simple applet.

initializing... starting...

http://java.sun.com/docs/books/tutorial/applet/overview/lifeCycle.html

Loading the Applet

The initializing... starting... text you see in the previous applet is the result of the applet's being loaded. When an applet is loaded, here's what happens.

- An instance of the applet's controlling class (an `Applet` subclass) is created.
- The applet *initializes* itself.
- The applet *starts* running.

Note: Some browsers let you load *serialized applets*—applets that have been saved while running. When a serialized applet is loaded, it doesn't initialize itself; it simply *starts* running.

Leaving and Returning to the Applet's Page

When the user leaves the page—for example, to go to another page—the applet has the option of *stopping* itself. When the user returns to the page, the applet can *start* itself again. The same sequence occurs when the user iconifies and then deiconifies the window that contains the applet. (Alternative terms for "iconify" are *miniaturize, minimize,* and *close.*)

Try This: Visit the online version of this tutorial at this URL: `http://java.sun.com/docs/books/tutorial/applet/overview/lifeCycle.html`. Leave and then return to this page. You'll see `stopping...` added to the applet output, as the applet is given the chance to stop itself. You'll also see `starting...` when the applet is told to start itself again. Next, iconify the window that contains the online version of this section, and then open it again. Many window systems provide a title bar button that lets you iconify the window. You should see `stopping...` then `preparing for unloading...`, `initializing...`, and `starting...` added to the applet output. Note that the exact text displayed will depend on your browser and platform.

Reloading the Applet

Some browsers let the user reload applets, a process that consists of unloading the applet and then loading it again. Before an applet is unloaded, it's given the chance to *stop* itself and then to perform a *final cleanup* so that the applet can release any resources it holds. After that, the applet is unloaded and then loaded again.

Try This: Try to reload the applet. (Shift-Reload in Netscape Navigator or Shift-Refresh in Internet Explorer might reload the applet.) Look at the standard output in the lower-left-hand corner of the browser to see what happens. You should see `stopping...` and `preparing for unloading...` when the applet is unloaded. You can't see this in the applet GUI, because the applet is unloaded before the text can be displayed. When the applet is reloaded, you should see `initializing...` and `starting...`, just like when you loaded the applet for the first time. However, the only way to make sure the browser reloaded the applet is to change the applet and look for a change in a visible way; for example, change the string to make sure you unloaded the applet.

Quitting the Browser

When the user quits the browser, the applet has the chance to *stop* itself and to do *final cleanup* before the browser exits.

Summary

An applet can react to milestones in the following ways.

- It can *initialize* itself.
- It can *start* running.
- It can *stop* running.
- It can perform a *final cleanup*, in preparation for being unloaded.

The next section describes the four applet methods that correspond to these four reactions.

Methods for Milestones

The Simple applet, like every other applet, contains a subclass of the Applet class. The Simple class overrides four Applet methods so that it can respond to major events:

```
public class Simple extends Applet {
    . . .
    public void init() { . . . }
    public void start() { . . . }
    public void stop() { . . . }
    public void destroy() { . . . }
    . . .
}
```

init

> To *initialize* the applet each time it is loaded or reloaded

start

> To *start* the applet's execution, such as when the applet is loaded or when the user revisits a page that contains the applet

stop

> To *stop* the applet's execution, such as when the user leaves the applet's page or quits the browser

destroy

> To perform a *final cleanup* in preparation for unloading

Not every applet needs to override every one of these methods. Some simple applets override none of them. For example, the HelloWorld applet discussed in the chapter Getting Started (page 1) doesn't override any of these methods, because it doesn't do anything except draw itself. It just displays a string once, using its `paint` method. (The `paint` method is described in the next section.)

The `init` method is useful for one-time initialization that doesn't take very long. In general, this method should contain the code that you would normally put into a constructor. An applet usually shouldn't have constructors, because it isn't guaranteed to have a full environment until its `init` method is called. For example, the `Applet` image-loading methods simply don't work inside a constructor. The `init` method, on the other hand, is a great place to call the image-loading methods, because the methods return quickly.

Note: When a browser loads a serialized applet, it does not invoke the applet's `init` method. The reason: The `init` method was presumably executed before the applet was serialized. See the section Object Serialization (page 334) for more information.

Every applet that does something after initialization (except in direct response to user actions) must override the `start` method. The `start` method either performs the applet's work or, more likely, starts up one or more threads to perform the work. You can read more about threads later in this appendix in the section Threads in AWT Applets (page 449).[1] The next section talks more about handling the events that represent user actions.

Most applets that override `start` should also override the `stop` method, which should suspend the applet's execution so that it doesn't take up system resources when the user isn't viewing the applet's page. For example, an applet that displays animation should stop drawing the animation when the user isn't viewing it in the current browser window.

Many applets don't need to override the `destroy` method, because their `stop` methods (called before `destroy`) do everything necessary to shut down the applet's execution. However, `destroy` is available for applets that need to release additional resources.

The `init`, `start`, `stop`, and `destroy` methods are discussed and used throughout this tutorial. For more information, you can also refer to the Applet API documentation for JDK 1.1.[2]

Methods for Drawing and Event Handling

The `Simple` applet defines its on-screen appearance by overriding the `paint` method:

---

[1] Threads are also covered in the chapter Threads: Doing Two or More Tasks at Once (page 269).

[2] http://java.sun.com/products/jdk/1.1/api/java.applet.Applet.html

```
class Simple extends Applet {
    . . .
    public void paint(Graphics g) { . . . }
    . . .
}
```

The paint method is one of two display methods that applets can override:

paint

The basic display method. Many applets implement the paint method to draw the applet's representation within a browser window.

update

A method that you can use with paint to improve drawing performance.

Applets inherit their paint and update methods from the Applet class, which inherits them from the Abstract Window Toolkit (AWT) Component class. Applets inherit event-related functionality and methods from the Component class. The architecture of the event system is discussed in the section <u>Handling Events</u> (page 358) in Chapter 10. The Component class defines several methods, such as addMouseListener and addKeyListener, that register objects to be automatically notified about various kinds of events. To be registered, an object must implement the appropriate interface.

For example, for an object to be registered as a mouse listener on an applet, that object must implement the MouseListener interface. Once registered, that listener object will be notified every time the user clicks in the applet's drawing area. This notification comes in the form of calling the listener's mouseClicked method. The listener can be the Applet object itself or any other object. The only requirement is that the object implement the correct listener interface.

Adding the following boldface code to the Simple applet registers it as a mouse listener and makes it respond to mouse clicks:[1]

```
import java.awt.event.MouseListener;
import java.awt.event.MouseEvent;
. . .
public class Simple extends Applet
                implements MouseListener {
    . . .
    public void init() {
        addMouseListener(this);
        . . .
    }
    . . .
```

---

[1] SimpleClick.java is included on the CD and is available online. See <u>Code Samples</u> (page 463).

```
    public void mouseClicked(MouseEvent event) {
        addItem("click!... ");
    }
    . . .
}
```

Note: To keep the example simple, we've left out a few empty method definitions.

Following is the resulting output from the applet. When you click within its rectangle, it displays the word `click!...`.

initializing... starting... click!... click!...

http://java.sun.com/docs/books/tutorial/applet/overview/componentMethods.html

Methods for Adding UI Components

The `Simple` applet's display code (implemented in its `paint` method) is flawed: It doesn't support scrolling. Once the text it displays reaches the end of the display rectangle, you can't see any new text.

Here's an example of the problem:

initializing... starting... stopping... starting... stopping... starting... stopp

The simplest cure for this problem is to use a premade user interface (UI) component that has the correct behavior. The Java platform supplies many UI components, including buttons, text fields, and menus. Remember that if you're designing an applet to run on most Web browsers without the Java Plug-in, you'll want to build an applet with AWT components. The section <u>AWT Components</u> (page 419) gives an overview of the major AWT components. Chapter 10 gave an overview of the Swing UI components, and the last section in this appendix will discuss how to make Swing applets.

Methods for Using UI Components in Applets

Because the `Applet` class inherits from the AWT `Container` class, it's easy to add components to applets. Here are some of the `Container` methods an applet can use:

add
    Adds the specified `Component` to the applet.

remove
    Removes the specified `Component` from the applet.

setLayout

Sets the applet's layout manager, which controls the positions and sizes of the components in the applet.

Adding an Uneditable Text Field to the Simple Applet

Using the TextField class, you can add a scrolling, uneditable text field to the Simple applet.[1] The changes are in boldface in the following code:

```
//Importing java.awt.Graphics is no longer necessary
//since this applet no longer implements the paint method.
. . .
import java.awt.TextField;
public class Simple extends Applet {

    //Instead of using a StringBuffer, use a TextField:
    TextField field;

    public void init() {
        //Create the text field and make it uneditable.
        field = new TextField();
        field.setEditable(false);

        //Set the layout manager so that the text field will
        //be as wide as possible.
        setLayout(new java.awt.GridLayout(1,0));
        //Add the text field to the applet.
        add(field);

        addItem("initializing... ");
    }
    . . .
    void addItem(String newWord) {
        //This used to append the string to the StringBuffer;
        //now it appends it to the TextField.
        String t = field.getText();
        System.out.println(newWord);
        field.setText(t + newWord);
    }

    //The paint method is no longer necessary,
    //since the TextField paints itself automatically.
```

The revised init method creates an uneditable text field, a TextField instance. This method also sets the applet's layout manager to one that makes the text field as wide as pos-

---

[1] ScrollingSimple.java is included on the CD and is available online. See Code Samples (page 463).

sible and then adds the text field to the applet. You can read about layout managers in the section <u>Layout Management</u> (page 375) in Chapter 10.

Following is the output of the resulting applet. By dragging the mouse, you can scroll backward or forward to see all the messages that have been displayed.

initializing... starting... stopping... starting... stopping... starting... stopp

http://java.sun.com/docs/books/tutorial/applet/overview/containerMethods.html

What Applets Can and Cannot Do

When you write an applet, you can, in theory, use any of the API in the Java platform. In practice, however, applets are limited in a couple of ways.

- An applet can use only the API supported by the browser in which it runs. For example, unless a browser supports the API defined in JDK 1.1, no applet that uses 1.1 API can run in that browser.
- An untrusted applet can't perform operations that might pose a security threat. For example, an untrusted applet cannot read or write files on the computer on which it is executing. See the section <u>Security Restrictions</u> (page 442) for more information.

Despite these restrictions, applets have access to a wide range of functionality. For example, applets can communicate with certain other applets running in the same browser. Applets can also request that the browser display a particular URL. See the section <u>Taking Advantage of the Applet API</u> (page 423) for information about the API that's reserved just for applets. See the section <u>Practical Considerations of Writing Applets</u> (page 442) for information about the other API applets commonly use.

Test Driving an Applet

Once you've written some code for your applet, you'll want to run your applet to test it. To run an applet, you first need to add the applet to an HTML page, using the <APPLET> tag. You then specify the URL of the HTML page to your Java-enabled browser.

Note: Because you can't always rely on browsers to reload your applet's classes, you might want to use a quick-starting tool, such as the Applet Viewer, for most of your applet testing. Every time you change your applet, restart the Applet Viewer to make sure that it loads all the latest classes.

Here's the simplest form of the <APPLET> tag:

```
<APPLET CODE="AppletSubclass.class" WIDTH=anInt HEIGHT=anInt>
</APPLET>
```

This tag tells the browser to load the applet whose `Applet` subclass is named *AppletSubclass*. Figure 113 shows where the applet class file must be, relative to the HTML document that contains the `<APPLET>` tag. As Figure 113 shows, unless the applet is declared to be in a package, its class file should be in the same directory as the HTML file that has the `<APPLET>` tag.

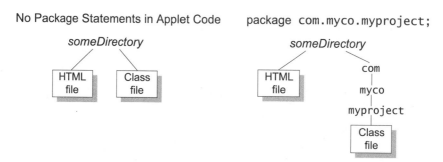

Figure 113   An applet's class files live under the same directory as the HTML file that includes the applet.

When it encounters an `<APPLET>` tag, a Java-enabled browser reserves a display area of the specified width and height for the applet, loads the bytecodes for the specified `Applet` subclass, creates an instance of the subclass, and then calls the instance's `init` and `start` methods.

The `<APPLET>` tag has many options that you can use to customize your applet's execution. For example, you can put your applet's files into an archive. You can also specify parameters to be passed to the applet. These options are described in the section Using the <APPLET> Tag (page 438).

Summary

This section gave you lots of information—almost everything you need to know to start writing an applet based on the 1.0 and 1.1 JDK. So let's review the big picture: To write an applet, you must create a subclass of the `java.applet` `Applet` class. In your `Applet` subclass, you must implement at least one of the following methods: `init`, `start`, and `paint`. The methods `init` and `start`, along with `stop` and `destroy`, are called when major events (milestones) occur in the applet's life cycle. The `paint` method is called when the applet needs to draw itself to the screen.

The `Applet` class extends the `Panel` class, which extends the `Container` class, which extends the `Component` class. From `Component`, an applet inherits the ability to draw and to handle events. From `Container`, an applet inherits the ability to include other components and to have a layout manager control the size and the position of those components. From `Applet`, an applet inherits several capabilities, including the ability to respond to milestones. The next section tells you more about what the `Applet` class provides.

You include applets in HTML pages by using the `<APPLET>` tag. When a browser user visits a page that contains an applet, the following sequence occurs.

1. The browser finds the class file (which contains Java bytecodes) for the applet's `Applet` subclass.

2. The browser brings the `Applet` subclass bytecodes over the network to the user's computer.

3. The browser creates an instance of the `Applet` subclass. (When we refer to an *applet*, we're generally referring to this instance.)

4. The browser calls the applet's `init` method. This method performs any initialization that is required.

5. The browser calls the applet's `start` method. This method often starts a thread to perform the applet's duties.

An applet's `Applet` subclass is its main, controlling class, but applets can use other classes as well. These other classes can be either local to the browser (provided as part of the Java platform) or custom classes that you supply. When the applet tries to use a class for the first time, the browser tries to find the class on the host that is running the browser and applet. If the browser cannot find the class there, it looks for the class in the same place from which the applet's `Applet` subclass came. When the browser finds the class, it loads the bytecodes for the class (over the network, if necessary) and continues executing the applet.

Loading executable code over the network is a classic security risk. For Java applets, some of this risk is reduced because the Java language is designed to be safe—for example, it doesn't allow pointers to random memory. In addition, browsers enforce security by imposing restrictions on untrusted applets.

AWT Components

We discussed Swing components in Chapter 10. In this section, we introduce the older AWT components, which you can use in Internet-ready applets.[1] The program in Figure 114 illus-

---

[1] By "Internet ready," we mean that the applets will run in most Web browsers without the Java Plug-in installed. These applets are based on the 1.0 and 1.1 JDKs (an earlier version of the Java 2 Platform).

trates the graphical UI (GUI) components that the AWT provides. With the exception of menus, every AWT component is implemented with a subclass of the AWT Component[1] class.

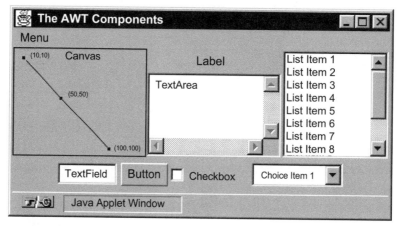

Figure 114   Snapshot of the an applet that uses all the AWT GUI components.

> **Note:** Remember that programs should not use "heavyweight" AWT components alongside Swing components. Heavyweight components include all the ready-to-use AWT components and all components that inherit from the AWT Canvas and Panel classes. When Swing components (and all other "lightweight" components) overlap with heavyweight components, the heavyweight component is always painted on top.

AWT Basic Controls

The Button, Checkbox, Choice, List, MenuItem, and TextField classes provide basic controls. These are the most common ways that users give instructions to programs. When a user activates one of these controls—by clicking a button or by pressing Return in a text field, for example—it posts an *action event*. See the documentation for each class for examples of handling action events.

Other Ways of Getting User Input

When the basic controls aren't appropriate, you can sometimes use the Scrollbar and the TextArea classes to get user input. The Scrollbar class is used for both slider and scroll bar

---

[1]   http://java.sun.com/products/jdk/1.1/docs/api/java.awt.Component.html

functionality. Scroll bars are automatically included in lists and text areas (as shown in the example program) and in ScrollPane.

The TextArea class provides an area to display or to allow editing of several lines of text. As you can see from the example program in Figure 114, text areas automatically include scroll-bars.

Creating Custom Components

The Canvas class lets you write custom components. With your Canvas subclass, you can draw custom graphics to the screen—in a paint program, image processor, or game, for example—and implement any kind of event handling.

Labels

A Label object displays an unselectable line of text.

Containers

The AWT provides three types of containers, all implemented as subclasses of the Container[1] class, which is a Component subclass. The Window subclasses— Dialog, FileDialog, and Frame—provide windows to contain components. A Panel groups components within an area of an existing window. A ScrollPane is similar to a panel but has a more specialized purpose: to display a potentially large component in a limited amount of space, generally using scroll bars to control which part of the component is displayed.

Frames create normal, full-fledged windows, as opposed to the windows that Dialogs create, which are dependent on Frames and can be modal. When you select the File dialog... item in the menu, the program creates a FileDialog object, which is a Dialog that can be either an Open or a Save dialog.

Browser Note: Some browsers might not implement the FileDialog class if they never allow applets to read or to write files on the local file system. Instead of seeing a file dialog, you'll see an error message in the standard output or error stream. See the section Displaying Diagnostics to the Standard Output and Standard Error Streams (page 446) for information about applets' standard output.

Figure 115 shows a picture of the FileDialog window that the Applet Viewer brings up.

---

[1] http://java.sun.com/products/jdk/1.1/docs/api/java.awt.Container.html

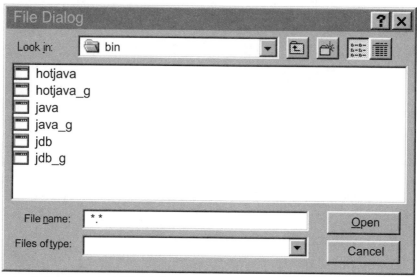

Figure 115 A window from the `FileDialog` applet.

The example program uses a `Panel` to group the label and the text area, another `Panel` to group them with a canvas, and a third `Panel` to group the text field, button, check box, and pop-up list of choices. All these `Panel`s are grouped by a `Frame` object, which presents the window they're displayed in. The `Frame` also holds a menu and a list.

Other AWT Classes

In addition to components, the AWT contains a variety of classes related to drawing and event handling. This section discusses the AWT classes that are in the `java.awt` and `java.awt.event` packages. The AWT contains three other packages—`java.awt.datatransfer`, `java.awt.image`, and `java.awt.peer`—that most programs don't have to use. The classes and the interfaces in those packages are discussed as needed elsewhere in this appendix.

As you learned in the previous section, components are grouped into containers. What the previous section didn't tell you is that each container uses a *layout manager* to control the on-screen size and position of the components it contains. The `java.awt` package supplies several layout manager classes. You learned all about layout managers in the section <u>Layout Management</u> (page 375) in Chapter 10.

The `java.awt` package supplies several classes to represent sizes and shapes. One is the `Dimension` class, which specifies the size of a rectangular area. Another is the `Insets` class, which is usually used to specify how much padding should exist between the outside edges of a container and the container's display area. Shape classes include `Point`, `Rectangle`, and `Polygon`.

The Color class is useful for representing and manipulating colors. It defines constants for commonly used colors, for example, Color.black. Although it generally uses colors in RGB (red-green-blue) format, it also understands HSB (hue-saturation-brightness) format.

The Image class provides a way to represent image data. Applets can get Image objects for GIF and JPEG images by using the Applet getImage methods. Programs that are not applets get images by using a different helper class: Toolkit. The Toolkit class provides a platform-independent interface to the platform-dependent implementation of the AWT. Although that sounds impressive, most programs don't deal with Toolkit objects directly, except to get images. Images are loaded asynchronously—you can have a valid Image object even if the image data hasn't been loaded yet or doesn't exist. Using a MediaTracker object, you can keep track of the status of the image loading. MediaTracker currently works only with images, but it might eventually work with other media types, such as sounds.

To control the look of the text your program draws, use Font and FontMetrics objects. The Font class lets you get basic information about fonts and create objects representing various fonts. With a FontMetrics object, you can get detailed information about the size characteristics of a particular font. You can set the font a component uses by using the Component and Graphics setFont methods.

Finally, the Graphics class and various types from the java.awt.event package are crucial to the AWT drawing and event-handling system. A Graphics object represents a drawing context—without a Graphics object, no program can draw itself to the screen. The java.awt.event package defines classes such as MouseEvent, which represents user input made with a mouse or a similar device.

Taking Advantage of the Applet API

The applet API lets you take advantage of the close relationship that applets have with Web browsers. The API is provided by the java.applet package—mainly by the Applet[1] class and the AppletContext[2] interface. Thanks to the applet API, applets can:

- Be notified by the browser of milestones
- Load data files specified relative to the URL of the applet or the page in which it is running
- Display short status strings
- Make the browser display a document
- Find other applets running in the same page

---

[1] http://java.sun.com/products/jdk/1.1/api/java.applet.Applet.html
[2] http://java.sun.com/products/jdk/1.1/api/java.applet.AppletContext.html

- Play sounds
- Get parameters specified by the user in the <APPLET> tag

Finding and Loading Data Files

Whenever an applet needs to load some data from a file that's specified with a *relative URL* (a URL that doesn't completely specify the file's location), the applet usually uses either the code base or the document base to form the complete URL. The *code base*, returned by the Applet getCodeBase method, is a URL that specifies the directory from which the applet's classes were loaded. The *document base*, returned by the Applet getDocumentBase method, specifies the directory of the HTML page that contains the applet.

Unless the <APPLET> tag specifies a code base, both the code base and the document base refer to the same directory on the same server. For example, in Figure 116, the code base and the document base would both specify the someDirectory directory.

Data that the applet always needs or needs to rely on as a backup is usually specified relative to the code base. Data that the applet user specifies, often by using parameters, is usually specified relative to the document base.

Note: For security reasons, browsers limit the URLs from which untrusted applets can read. For example, most browsers don't allow untrusted applets to use ".." to access directories above the code base or the document base. Also, because untrusted applets can't read files except those on the applet's originating host, the document base isn't generally useful if the document and the untrusted applet are on different servers.

The Applet class defines convenient forms of image-loading and sound-loading methods that let you specify images and sounds relative to a base URL. For example, assume that an applet is set up with one of the directory structures shown in Figure 116.

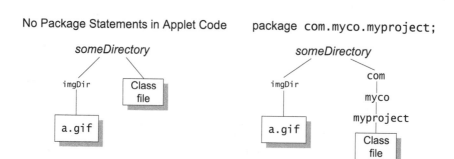

Figure 116 This applet's image file is in the imgDir directory, relative to the code base.

To create an `Image` object using the `a.gif` image file under `imgDir`, the applet can use the following code:

```
Image image = getImage(getCodeBase(), "imgDir/a.gif");
```

Displaying Short Status Strings

Most browsers allow applets to display a short status string. This string typically appears on the status line of the window containing the applet. In full-fledged Web browsers, all applets on the page, as well as the browser itself, generally share the same status line.

You should never put crucial information in the status line. If many users might need the information, it should instead be displayed within the applet area. If only a few, sophisticated users might need the information, consider displaying it on the standard output. See the section <u>Displaying Diagnostics to the Standard Output and Standard Error Streams</u> (page 446) for details.

The status line is not usually very prominent, and it can be overwritten by other applets or by the browser. For these reasons, use the status line only for incidental, transitory information. For example, an applet that loads several image files might display the name of the image file it is currently loading.

Applets display status lines with the `showStatus` method. Here's an example of its use:

```
showStatus("MyApplet: Loading image file " + filename);
```

Note: Please don't put scrolling text in the status line. Browser users find such status line abuse highly annoying!

Displaying Documents in the Browser

Have you ever wanted an applet to display formatted HTML text? Here's the easy way to do it: Ask the browser to display the text for you.

With the `AppletContext` `showDocument` methods, an applet can tell the browser which URL to show and in which browser window. (By the way, the JDK Applet Viewer ignores these methods, because it can't display documents.) Here are the two forms of `showDocument`:

```
showDocument(java.net.URL url)
showDocument(java.net.URL url, String targetWindow)
```

The one-argument form of showDocument simply tells the browser to display the document at the specified URL, without specifying the window in which to display the document.

Terminology Note: In this discussion, *frame* does not refer to a Frame object but rather to an HTML frame within a browser window.

The two-argument form of showDocument lets you specify the window or the HTML frame in which to display the document. The second argument can have any one of the following values:

"_blank"
Displays the document in a new, nameless window.

"*windowName*"
Displays the document in a window named *windowName*. This window is created if necessary.

"_self"
Displays the document in the window and frame that contain the applet.

"_parent"
Displays the document in the applet's window but in the parent frame of the applet's frame. If the applet frame has no parent frame, this acts the same as "_self".

"_top"
Displays the document in the applet's window but in the top-level frame. If the applet's frame is the top-level frame, this acts the same as "_self".

The following applet lets you try every option of both forms of showDocument. The applet brings up a window that lets you type in a URL and choose any of the showDocument options. When you press Return or click the Show document button, the applet calls show-Document.[1]

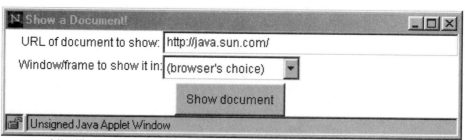

http://java.sun.com/docs/books/tutorial/applet/appletsonly/browser.html

---

[1] ShowDocument.java is included on the CD and is available online. See Code Samples (page 463).

Following is the applet code that calls showDocument.

```
.../In an Applet subclass:
urlWindow = new URLWindow(getAppletContext());
. . .


class URLWindow extends Frame {
    . . .
    public URLWindow(AppletContext appletContext) {
        . . .
        this.appletContext = appletContext;
        . . .
    }

    public void actionPerformed(ActionEvent event) {
        String urlString = /* user-entered string */;
        URL url = null;
        try {
            url = new URL(urlString);
        } catch (MalformedURLException e) {
            .../Inform the user and return...
        }

        if (url != null) {
            if (/* user doesn't want to specify window */) {
                appletContext.showDocument(url);
            } else {
                appletContext.showDocument(url,
                /* user-specified window */);
            }
        }
    }
}
```

Sending Messages to Other Applets

Applets can find other applets and send messages to them, with the following security restrictions.

- Many browsers require that the applets originate from the same server.
- Many browsers also require that the applets originate from the same directory on the server (that is, the same code base).
- The Java platform API requires that the applets be running on the same page, in the same browser window.

Note: Some browsers let applets invoke methods on other applets—even applets on different pages in the same browser—as long as all the applets come from the same code base. This method of interapplet communication isn't supported by the Java API, so it's possible that it will not be supported by all browsers.

An applet can find another applet either by looking it up by name (using the `AppletContext` `getApplet` method) or by finding all the applets on the page (using the `AppletContext` `getApplets` method). Both methods, if successful, give the caller one or more `Applet` objects. Once it finds an `Applet` object, the caller can invoke methods on the object.

Finding an Applet by Name: The getApplet Method

The `getApplet` method looks through all the applets on the current page to see whether one has the specified name. If so, `getApplet` returns the applet's `Applet` object.

By default, an applet has no name. For an applet to have a name, you must specify one in the HTML code that adds the applet to a page. You can do this by specifying either:

- A NAME attribute within the applet's `<APPLET>` tag; for example:

```
<APPLET CODEBASE="example/" CODE="Sender.class"
        WIDTH=450 HEIGHT=200
        NAME="buddy">
. . .
</APPLET>
```

- A NAME parameter with a `<PARAM>` tag; for example:

```
<APPLET CODEBASE="example/" CODE="Receiver.class"
        WIDTH=450 HEIGHT=35>
<PARAM NAME="name" VALUE="old pal">
. . .
</APPLET>
```

Browser Note: Although at least one Java-enabled browser conducts a case-sensitive search, the expected behavior is for the `getApplet` method to perform a case-*in*sensitive search. For example, `getApplet("old pal")` and `getApplet("OLD PAL")` should both find an applet named "Old Pal".

Following are two applets that illustrate lookup by name. The first applet, the `Sender`, looks up the second, the `Receiver`.[1] When it finds the `Receiver`, the `Sender` sends a message to

---

[1]   `Sender.java` and `Receiver.java` are included on the CD and available online. See <u>Code Samples</u> (page 463).

the `Receiver` by invoking one of the `Receiver`'s methods (passing the `Sender`'s name as an argument). The `Receiver` reacts to this method call by changing its leftmost text string to `Received message from sender-name!`

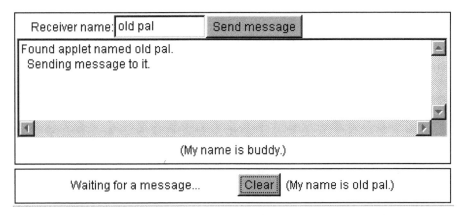

http://java.sun.com/docs/books/tutorial/applet/appletsonly/iac.html

---

Try This: Visit the page that contains these applets: `http://java.sun.com/docs/books/tutorial/applet/appletsonly/iac.html`. Click the Send message button of the top applet (the Sender). Some status information will appear in the `Sender`'s window, and the `Receiver` will confirm, with its own status string, that it received a message. After you've read the `Receiver`'s status string, click its Clear button to reset it. In the `Sender`'s text field labeled `Receiver name:`, type **buddy** and press Return. Because **buddy** is the `Sender`'s own name, it will find an applet named **buddy**, but it won't send it a message, as it isn't a `Receiver` instance.

The code the `Sender` uses to look up and to communicate with the `Receiver` is listed next. Code that you can use in your own applet is in boldface.

```
Applet receiver = null;
String receiverName = nameField.getText(); //Name to search for
receiver = getAppletContext().getApplet(receiverName);
```

The `Sender` goes on to make sure that the `Receiver` was found and that it's an instance of the correct class (`Receiver`). If all goes well, the `Sender` sends a message to the `Receiver`:

```
if (receiver != null) {
    //Use the instanceof operator to make sure the applet
    //we found is a Receiver object.
    if (!(receiver instanceof Receiver)) {
        status.append("Found applet named "
                    + receiverName + ", "
                    + "but it's not a Receiver object."
                    + newline);
    } else {
        status.append("Found applet named "
                    + receiverName + newline
                    + "  Sending message to it.);
                    + newline);
        //Cast the receiver to be a Receiver object
        //(instead of just an Applet object) so that the
        //compiler will let us call a Receiver method.
        ((Receiver)receiver).processRequestFrom(myName);
    }
}
```

From an applet's point of view, its name is stored in a parameter called NAME. It can get the value of the parameter by using the Applet getParameter method. For example, Sender gets its own name with the following code:

```
myName = getParameter("NAME");
```

For more information on using getParameter, see the section <u>Writing the Code to Support Parameters</u> (page 436).

The example applets in this section perform one-way communication—from the Sender to the Receiver. If you want your receiver to be able to send messages to the sender, just have the sender give a reference to itself (this) to the receiver. For example:

```
((Receiver)receiver).startCommunicating(this);
```

Finding All the Applets on a Page: The getApplets Method

The getApplets method returns a list (an <u>Enumeration</u>,[1] to be precise) of all the applets on the page. For security reasons, getApplets returns only those applets that originated from the same host as the applet that is calling getApplets. Following is an applet that simply lists all the applets it can find on its page:[2]

---

[1] http://java.sun.com/products/jdk/1.1/api/java.util.Enumeration.html
[2] GetApplets.java is included on the CD and is available online. See <u>Code Samples</u> (page 463).

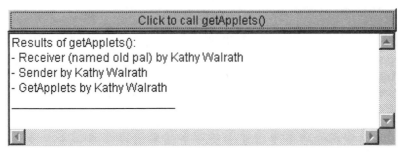

http://java.sun.com/docs/books/tutorial/applet/appletsonly/iac.html

The following code contains the relevant parts of the method that calls `getApplets`:

```
public void printApplets() {
    //Enumeration will contain all applets on this page
    //(including this one) that we can send messages to.
    Enumeration e = getAppletContext().getApplets();
    . . .
    while (e.hasMoreElements()) {
        Applet applet = (Applet)e.nextElement();
        String info = applet.getAppletInfo();
        if (info != null) {
            textArea.append("- " + info + newline);
        } else {
            textArea.append("- "
                            + applet.getClass().getName()
                            + newline);
        }
    }
    . . .
}
```

Playing Sounds

In the applet package (`java.applet`), the `Applet` class and the `AudioClip` interface provide basic support for playing sounds. In JDK 1.1, the API supports only one sound format: 8-bit, μ law, 8,000Hz, one-channel, Sun .au files. You can create these on a Sun workstation by using the `audiotool` application. You can convert files from other sound formats by using an audio format conversion program.

Note: Support for sound has improved in the recent releases of the Java 2 Platform. See the "Sound" chapter in the book, *The Java Tutorial Continued*. This chapter is also available on the CD or online at `http://java.sun.com/docs/books/tutorial/sound/index.html`

Sound-Related Methods

Following are the sound-related `Applet` methods:

AudioClip getAudioClip(URL)

AudioClip getAudioClip(URL, String)
　　Return an object that implements the `AudioClip` interface.

void play(URL)

void play(URL, String)
　　Play the `AudioClip` corresponding to the specified URL.

The two-argument form of each method takes a base URL, which is usually returned by either `getCodeBase` or `getDocumentBase`, and the location of the sound file relative to the base URL. You should use the code base for sounds that are integral to the applet. The document base is for sounds specified by the applet user, such as through applet parameters.

The `AudioClip` interface defines the following methods:

void loop()
　　Starts playing the clip repeatedly.

void play()
　　Plays the clip once.

void stop()
　　Stops the clip. Works with both looping and one-time sounds.

An Example: SoundExample

Here is an applet called `SoundExample`[1] that illustrates a few things about sound:

http://java.sun.com/docs/books/tutorial/applet/appletsonly/sound.html

The `SoundExample` applet provides an architecture for loading and playing multiple sounds in an applet. For this reason, it is more complex than necessary. Essentially, the sound loading and playing code boils down to this:

---

[1]　`SoundExample.java` is included on the CD and is available online. See Code Samples (page 463).

```
AudioClip onceClip, loopClip;
onceClip = applet.getAudioClip(getCodeBase(), "bark.au");
loopClip = applet.getAudioClip(getCodeBase(), "train.au");
onceClip.play();//Play it once.
onceClip.stop();//Cut off the sound.
loopClip.loop();//Start the sound loop.
loopClip.stop();//Stop the sound loop.
```

Because nothing is more annoying than an applet that continues to make noise after you've left its page, the `SoundExample` applet stops playing the continuously looping sound when the user leaves the page and resumes playing it when the user comes back. The applet does this by implementing its `stop` and `start` methods, as shown:

```
public void stop() {
    onceClip.stop();        //Cut short the one-time sound.
    if (looping) {
        loopClip.stop();    //Stop the sound loop.
    }
}

public void start() {
    if (looping) {
        loopClip.loop();    //Restart the sound loop.
    }
}
```

This example is discussed in more detail in the section <u>Using a Thread to Perform a One-Time Task</u> (page 452).

Defining and Using Applet Parameters

Parameters are to applets what command line arguments are to UNIX applications. Parameters allow the user to customize the program's operation. By defining parameters, you can increase your applet's flexibility, making your applet work in multiple situations without your having to recode and recompile it.

Deciding Which Parameters to Support

As you implement parameters, you should ask four questions:

1. What should the applet allow the user to configure?
2. What should the parameters be named?
3. What kind of value should each parameter take?
4. What should the default value of each parameter be?

What Should the Applet Allow the User to Configure? Which   parameters   your applet should support depends on what your applet does and on how flexible you want it to be. Applets that display images might have parameters to specify the image locations. Similarly, applets that play sounds might have parameters to specify the sounds.

Besides parameters that specify resource locations, such as image and sound files, applets sometimes provide parameters for specifying details of the applet's appearance or operation. For example, an animation applet might let the user specify the number of images shown per second. Or, an applet might let the user change the strings that the applet displays. Anything is possible.

What Should the Parameters Be Named? Once you decide what parameters your applet will support, you need to determine their names. Here are some typical parameter names:

SOURCE or **SRC**
> For a data file such as an image file.

***XXX*SOURCE** (for example, **IMAGESOURCE**)
> Used in applets that let the user specify more than one type of data file.

***XXX*S**
> For a parameter that takes a list of *XXX*s, where *XXX* might be IMAGE, again.

NAME
> Used *only* for an applet's name. Applet names are used for interapplet communication, as described in the section <u>Sending Messages to Other Applets</u> (page 427).

Clarity of names is more important than keeping the name length short. Do *not* use names of <APPLET> tag attributes, which are documented in the section <u>The <APPLET> Tag</u> in Appendix E (page 537).

Note: Although this tutorial usually uses all uppercase letters to refer to parameter names, parameter names actually are case insensitive. For example, IMAGESOURCE and imageSource both refer to the same parameter. Parameter *values*, on the other hand, are case sensitive unless you take steps to interpret them otherwise, such as by using the String toLowerCase method before interpreting the parameter's value.

What Kind of Value Should Each Parameter Take? Parameter values are all strings. Regardless of whether the user puts quotation marks around a parameter value, that value is passed to your applet as a string. However, your applet can interpret the string in many ways, typically as one of the following types:

- A URL
- An integer
- A floating-point number
- A Boolean value—typically `true`/`false` or yes/no
- A string—for example, the string to use as a window title
- A list of any of the preceding

What Should the Default Value of Each Parameter Be? Applets should attempt to provide useful default values for each parameter so that the applet will execute even if the user doesn't specify a parameter or specifies it incorrectly. For example, an animation applet should provide a reasonable setting for the number of images it displays per second. In this way, if the user doesn't specify the relevant parameter, the applet will still work well.

Take the `AppletButton` as an example.[1] Its GUI is simple: a button and a label that displays status. When the user clicks the button, the applet brings up a window. The `AppletButton` class is flexible because it defines parameters that let the user specify any or all of the following:

- The type of window to bring up
- The window's title
- The window's height
- The window's width
- The label of the button that brings up the window

Here's what a typical <APPLET> tag for `AppletButton` looks like:

```
<APPLET CODE="AppletButton.class" WIDTH=350 HEIGHT=60>
<PARAM NAME="windowClass" VALUE="BorderWindow">
<PARAM NAME="windowTitle" VALUE="BorderLayout">
<PARAM NAME="buttonText"
       VALUE="Click here to see a BorderLayout in action">
</APPLET>
```

When the user doesn't specify a value for a parameter, `AppletButton` uses a reasonable default value. For example, if the user doesn't specify the window's title, `AppletButton` uses the window's type as the title.

---

[1] `AppletButton.java` is included on the CD and is available online. See <u>Code Samples</u> (page 463).

Writing the Code to Support Parameters

Applets use the `Applet` `getParameter` method to get user-specified values for applet parameters. The `getParameter` method is declared as follows:

```
String getParameter(String name)
```

Your applet might need to convert the string that `getParameter` returns into another form, such as an integer. The `java.lang` package provides classes, such as `Integer`, that cast strings to primitive types. The following example from the `AppletButton` class converts a parameter's value into an integer:

```
int requestedWidth = 0;
. . .
String windowWidthString = getParameter("WINDOWWIDTH");
if (windowWidthString != null) {
    try {
        requestedWidth = Integer.parseInt(windowWidthString);
    } catch (NumberFormatException e) {
        //Use default width.
    }
}
```

Note that if the user doesn't specify a value for the `WINDOWWIDTH` parameter, this code uses a default value of `0`, which the applet interprets as "use the window's natural size." It's important to supply default values wherever possible.

Besides using the `getParameter` method to get values of applet-specific parameters, you also can use `getParameter` to get the values of attributes of the applet's <APPLET> tag. For example, by specifying `"HEIGHT"` to the `getParameter` method, an applet could read the height that the user specified in the <APPLET> tag. See the section <u>The <APPLET> Tag</u> in Appendix E (page 537) for a complete list of <APPLET> tag attributes.

Following is the `AppletButton` code that gets the applet's parameters:

```
String windowClass;
String buttonText;
String windowTitle;
int requestedWidth = 0;
int requestedHeight = 0;
. . .
public void init() {
    windowClass = getParameter("WINDOWCLASS");
    if (windowClass == null) {
        windowClass = "TestWindow";
    }
```

```
buttonText = getParameter("BUTTONTEXT");
if (buttonText == null) {
    buttonText = "Click here to bring up a " + windowClass;
}

windowTitle = getParameter("WINDOWTITLE");
if (windowTitle == null) {
    windowTitle = windowClass;
}

String windowWidthString = getParameter("WINDOWWIDTH");
if (windowWidthString != null) {
    try {
        requestedWidth = Integer.parseInt(windowWidthString);
    } catch (NumberFormatException e) {
        //Use default width.
    }
}

String windowHeightString = getParameter("WINDOWHEIGHT");
if (windowHeightString != null) {
    try {
        requestedHeight =
            Integer.parseInt(windowHeightString);
    } catch (NumberFormatException e) {
        //Use default height.
    }
}
```

Giving Information about Parameters

Now that you've provided all those nice parameters to the user, you need to help the user set the parameter values correctly. Of course, your applet's documentation should describe each parameter and give the user examples and hints for setting them. Your job doesn't stop there, though. You also should implement the `getParameterInfo` method so that it returns information about your applet's parameters. Browsers can use this information to help the user set your applet's parameter values.

The following code is an example of implementing the `getParameterInfo` method. This example is from the `Animator` applet, a wonderfully flexible applet that provides 13 parameters for users to customize their animation:[1]

```
public String[][] getParameterInfo() {
    String[][] info = {
        // Parameter Name   Kind of Value Description
```

---

[1]　`Animator.java` is included on the CD and is available online. See <u>Code Samples</u> (page 463).

```
            {"imagesource",   "URL",          "a directory"},
            {"startup",       "URL",          "displayed at startup"},
            {"background",    "URL",          "displayed as background"},
            {"startimage",    "int",          "start index"},
            {"endimage",      "int",          "end index"},
            {"namepattern",   "URL",          "used to generate " +
                                              "indexed names"},
            {"pause",         "int",          "milliseconds"},
            {"pauses",        "ints",         "milliseconds"},
            {"repeat",        "boolean",      "repeat or not"},
            {"positions",     "coordinates",  "path"},
            {"soundsource",   "URL",          "audio directory"},
            {"soundtrack",    "URL",          "background music"},
            {"sounds",        "URLs",         "audio samples"},
        };
        return info;
    }
```

As you can see, the getParameterInfo method must return an array of three-String arrays. In each three-String array, the first string is the parameter name. The second string hints as to what general kind of value the applet needs for the parameter. The third string describes the meaning of the parameter.

Using the <APPLET> Tag

This section starts by showing you the <APPLET> tag's simplest form. This section then discusses some of the most common additions to that simple form: the <PARAM> tag, alternative HTML code and text, the CODEBASE attribute, and the ARCHIVE attribute. For a detailed description of the <APPLET> tag, refer to the section The <APPLET> Tag in Appendix E (page 537).

You've already have seen the simplest form of the <APPLET> tag:

```
<APPLET CODE="AppletSubclass.class" WIDTH=numPixels HEIGHT=numPixels>
</APPLET>
```

This tag tells the browser to load the applet whose Applet subclass is named *AppletSubclass*, displaying it in an area of the specified width and height.

Note: The World Wide Web Consortium (W3C) has deprecated the <APPLET> tag in the HTML 4.01 Specification in favor of the <OBJECT> tag. The <OBJECT> element is an all-purpose tag to include generic objects—whether they're applets or a new media type—in Web pages. At present, not all browsers support the <OBJECT> tag, but we mention it here for your future reference. Read the specification for more information:

```
http://www.w3.org/TR/REC-html40/struct/objects.html
```

To run in the Java Plug-in, the <APPLET> tag must be converted to <OBJECT> and <EMBED> tags. For more information on converting <APPLET> and <EMBED> tags, visit: `http://java.sun.com/products/plugin/` and search for the text "HTML Converter."

Specifying Parameters

Some applets let the user customize the applet's configuration with parameters. For example, `AppletButton` allows the user to set the button's text by specifying the value of a parameter named BUTTONTEXT.

The user specifies the value of a parameter, using a <PARAM> tag. The <PARAM> tags should appear just after the <APPLET> tag for the applet they affect:

```
<APPLET CODE="AppletSubclass.class" WIDTH=numPixels HEIGHT=numPixels>
<PARAM NAME=parameter1Name VALUE=aValue>
<PARAM NAME=parameter2Name VALUE=anotherValue>
</APPLET>
```

Here's an example of the <PARAM> tag in use:

```
<APPLET CODE="Animator.class" WIDTH=460 HEIGHT=160>
<PARAM NAME="imageSource" VALUE="images/Beans">
<PARAM NAME="backgroundColor" VALUE="0xc0c0c0">
<PARAM NAME="endImage" VALUE=10>
<PARAM NAME="soundSource" VALUE="audio">
<PARAM NAME="soundtrack" VALUE="spacemusic.au">
<PARAM NAME="sounds"
    VALUE="1.au|2.au|3.au|4.au|5.au|6.au|7.au|8au|9.au|0.au">
<PARAM NAME="pause" VALUE=200>
 . . .
</APPLET>
```

Specifying Alternative HTML Code and Text

Note the ellipsis points (. . .) in the previous HTML example. What did the example leave out? It omitted *alternative HTML code*—HTML code interpreted only by browsers that don't understand the <APPLET> tag. Alternative HTML code is any text that appears between the <APPLET> and the </APPLET> tags, after any <PARAM> tags. Browsers with a Java Virtual Machine ignore alternative HTML code.

To specify alternative text to Java-enabled browsers and other browsers that understand the <APPLET> tag, use the ALT attribute. If it can't display an applet for some reason, the browser can display the applet's ALT text.

We use alternative HTML code throughout the online version of this tutorial to tell readers about the applets they're missing. Often, the alternative HTML code includes one or more pictures of the applet. Here's the complete HTML code for the `Animator` example shown previously:

```
<APPLET CODE="Animator.class" WIDTH=460 HEIGHT=160
 ALT="If you could run this applet, you'd see some animation">
<PARAM NAME="imageSource" VALUE="images/Beans">
<PARAM NAME="backgroundColor" VALUE="0xc0c0c0">
<PARAM NAME="endImage" VALUE=10>
<PARAM NAME="soundSource" VALUE="audio">
<PARAM NAME="soundtrack" VALUE="spacemusic.au">
<PARAM NAME="sounds"
    VALUE="1.au|2.au|3.au|4.au|5.au|6.au|7.au|8au|9.au|0.au">
<PARAM NAME="pause" VALUE=200>
Your browser is completely ignoring the &lt;APPLET&gt; tag!
</APPLET>
```

A browser that doesn't understand the `<APPLET>` tag ignores everything in the previous HTML code except the line that begins with `Your browser is`. A browser that *does* understand the `<APPLET>` tag ignores everything on that line. If it can't run the applet, the applet-savvy browser might display the text listed after the `ALT` tag.

Specifying the Applet Directory

By default, a browser looks for an applet's class and archive files in the same directory as the HTML file that has the `<APPLET>` tag. (If the applet's class is in a package, the browser uses the package name to construct a directory path underneath the HTML file's directory.) Sometimes, it's useful to put the applet's files somewhere else. You can use the `CODEBASE` attribute to tell the browser in which directory the applet's files are located:

```
<APPLET CODE="AppletSubclass.class" CODEBASE="aURL"
       WIDTH=anInt HEIGHT=anInt>
</APPLET>
```

If *aURL* is a relative URL, it's interpreted relative to the HTML document's location. By making *aURL* an absolute URL, you can load an applet from just about anywhere—even from another HTTP server.

This tutorial uses `CODEBASE="someDirectory/"` frequently, because we group the examples for each section in subdirectories. For example, here's the `<APPLET>` tag that includes the `Simple` applet in the section The Life Cycle of an Applet (page 410):

```
<APPLET CODE="Simple.class" CODEBASE="example/"
       WIDTH=500 HEIGHT=20>
</APPLET>
```

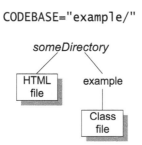

Figure 117   The location of an applet's class file when `CODEBASE = "example/"`.

Figure 117 shows the location of the class file, relative to the HTML file, when `CODEBASE` is set to `"example/"`. Figure 118 shows where the applet class can be if you specify an absolute URL for the value of `CODEBASE`.

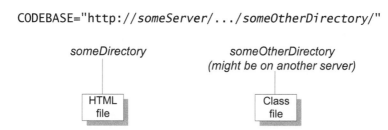

Figure 118   The directory hierarchy when `CODEBASE` is set to an absolute URL.

Combining an Applet's Files into a Single File

If your applet has more than one file, you should consider providing an archive file that bundles the applet's files into a single file. Whether archive files make sense for your applet depends on several factors, including your applet's size, performance considerations, and the environment you expect your users to have.

Archive files reduce your applet's total download time. Much of the time saved comes from reducing the number of HTTP connections that the browser must make. Each HTTP connection can take several seconds to start. This means that for a multifile applet, connection time can dwarf transfer time. You can further reduce transfer time by compressing the files in your archive file.

If you specify one or more archive files, the browser looks for them in the same directory that it would search for the applet class file. The browser then looks for the applet's class files in the archive files. If a file isn't in the archive, the browser generally tries to load it just as it would if the archive file weren't present.

The standard Java archive format, called JAR (Java ARchive), was introduced in JDK 1.1 and is based on the ZIP file format.[1] You specify JAR files by using the ARCHIVE attribute of the <APPLET> tag. You can specify multiple archive files by separating them with commas:

```
<APPLET CODE="AppletSubclass.class" ARCHIVE="file1, file2"
        WIDTH=anInt HEIGHT=anInt>
</APPLET>
```

Platform-Specific Details: Creating a JAR File

You can create JAR files by using the JDK `jar` tool. Some examples of creating JAR files follow.

To create a JAR file named `file.jar` that includes compressed versions of all the class and GIF files in the current directory:

```
jar cvf file.zip *.class *.gif
```

To create a JAR file for an applet whose classes are in a package named `com.mycompany.myproject`:

Solaris:

```
jar cvf file.zip com/mycompany/myproject/*.class *.gif
```

Win32:
```
jar cvf file.zip com\mycompany\myproject\*.class *.gif
```

For detailed descriptions of other <APPLET> attributes, see the section <u>The <APPLET> Tag</u> in Appendix E (page 537).

Practical Considerations of Writing Applets

We have already discussed the applet-specific API in this appendix. However, most applets rely on a lot of API that isn't specific to applets. This section gives you hints about using the Java platform API, covering the areas that are affected by applets' close relationships with browsers.

Security Restrictions

One of the main goals of the Java platform is to make users feel secure running any applet in their browsers. To achieve this goal, browsers with the Java Virtual Machine started out con-

---

[1] See the "JAR File Format" trail for the latest information about browser support for JAR and details on JAR in the Java 2 Platform. This trail is included in the book *The Java Tutorial Continued* and is also included on this book's CD and online.

servatively, restricting capabilities perhaps more than necessary. However, applets are getting more and more abilities, mainly by differentiating between trusted and untrusted applets.

How you mark an applet as trusted varies by browser. Some browsers that are written in the Java programming language implicitly and completely trust any applet loaded from a directory in the user's classpath. The reason is that an applet in the user's CLASSPATH has the same capabilities as the application that loads it.

Often, a browser uses a combination of signing and user-set preferences to indicate that classes with a certain signature are trusted. Another possibility is to have applets from certain URLs be trusted. Some browsers let the user specify certain files that any applet can read or write.

This section tells you about the security restrictions that browsers impose on untrusted applets and how they affect applet design. For more information on applet security, refer to this online FAQ: "Frequently Asked Questions—Applet Security."[1]

Most browsers impose the following restrictions

Untrusted applets cannot load libraries or define native methods.

Untrusted applets can use only their own code and the API that the browser provides. At a minimum, each browser must provide access to the API defined in the java.* packages.

An untrusted applet cannot read or write files on the host executing it.

The JDK Applet Viewer permits some user-specified exceptions to this rule, but Netscape Navigator 4.0, for example, does not. A workaround for not being able to write files is to have the applet forward data to an application on the host from which the applet came. This application can write the data files on its own host.

An untrusted applet cannot make network connections except to the host from which it came.

For example, an untrusted applet can't read a file specified by a URL unless the file is on the applet's originating host. The reason is that it would be a security breach for applets delivered across firewalls to view files published within the firewall. The workaround for this restriction is to have the applet work with an application on the host from which it came. The application can make its own connections anywhere on the network.

An untrusted applet cannot start any program on the host executing it.

Again, an applet can work with a server-side application instead.

---

[1] Available online at: http://java.sun.com/sfaq/index.html

An untrusted applet cannot get many system properties.

See the section <u>Getting System Properties</u> (page 447) for more information.

Windows that an untrusted applet brings up look different from windows that an application brings up.

Windows brought up by untrusted applets have some warning text and either a colored bar or an image. This helps the user distinguish untrusted applet windows from those of trusted applications. Figure 119 shows a window brought up by a program that can run either as an applet or as an application. In Figure 119, the window appears as it does when the program is run as an application on the Windows 95 platform. In Figure 120, the window is shown as it appears when the program runs as an applet within the Windows 95 Applet Viewer. As you can see, the applet window has a warning.

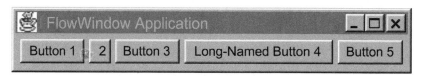

Figure 119   A window brought up by an application.

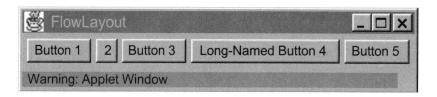

Figure 120   A window brought up by an untrusted applet.

Creating a User Interface

Most applets have a GUI. This is a natural consequence of the fact that each applet appears within a browser window. Because the `Applet` class is a subclass of the AWT `Panel` class and thus participates in the AWT event and drawing model, creating an applet's GUI is just as easy as creating an application's GUI—easier, in fact, because the applet's window (the browser window) already exists. We've already seen a selection of the most popular AWT GUI components in the section <u>AWT Components</u> (page 419).

In addition to its graphical UI, an applet can use several other UI types, depending on the kind of information it needs to give or to get. Some applets play sounds, either to give the user feedback or to provide ambiance. Applets can get configuration information from the user through parameters that the applet defines. To give text information to the user, an applet can use its GUI, display a short status string (for text that's not crucial), or display to the standard output or standard error stream (for debugging purposes).

Following are a few issues that are particular to applet GUIs.

Applets appear in preexisting browser windows.

Unlike GUI-based applications, applets don't have to create a window in which to display themselves. They *can* create a window, but they often just display themselves within the browser window.

The applet background color might not match the page color.

Each browser defines a default background color for applets—usually white or light gray. HTML pages, however, can have other background colors and can use background patterns. If the applet designer and the page designer aren't careful, the applet's different background color can cause it to stick out on the page or cause noticeable flashing when the applet is drawn.

One solution to prevent this is to define an applet parameter that specifies the applet's background color. The `Applet` subclass can use `Component`'s `setBackground` method to set its background to the user-specified color. Using the background color parameter, the page designer can choose an applet color that works well with the page colors. Parameters are described in the section <u>Defining and Using Applet Parameters</u> (page 433).

Each applet has a user-specified, predetermined size.

Because the `<APPLET>` tag requires that the applet's width and height be specified and because browsers don't usually allow applets to resize themselves, applets must make do with a fixed amount of space that might not be ideal. Some parts of the applet, such as text, might require different amounts of space on another platform. You can compensate by recommending that pages that include your applet specify a little more space than might be necessary. Then use flexible layouts that adapt well to extra space, such as the classes `GridBagLayout` and `BorderLayout`.

Applets load images using the `Applet getImage` methods.

The `Applet` class provides a convenient `getImage` form that lets you specify a base URL as one argument, followed by a second argument that specifies the image file location, relative to the base URL. See the section the section <u>Finding and Loading Data Files</u> (page 424) for information on how to get base URLs.

Applet classes and data files are loaded over the network. This process can be slow.

Classes and data files that load slowly can cause noticeable delays when the user interacts with your program. For example, an applet might have a button that the user clicks to bring up a specialized window, to play a sound, or to draw graphics. If the user clicks the button before the applet has loaded the necessary classes or data, the user will notice a long delay while the browser fetches the necessary files.

Consider using background threads to preload classes and data that the user is likely to need. You also can archive related files in order to reduce transfer time. See the sections Threads in AWT Applets (page 449) and Combining an Applet's Files into a Single File (page 441) for information on how to implement threads and archives.

An `Applet` is a `Panel`.

Because `Applet` is a subclass of the Panel[1] class, applets can contain other Components,[2] just as any `Panel` can. Applets inherit `Panel`'s default layout manager: FlowLayout.[3] As `Panel` objects (and thus `Component` objects), applets participate in the AWT drawing and event hierarchy.

Displaying Diagnostics to the Standard Output and Standard Error Streams

Displaying diagnostics to the standard output or standard error stream can be an invaluable tool when debugging an applet. You'll also see messages at the standard output or standard error stream when an uncaught exception occurs in an applet. Even when an applet catches an exception, such as a security exception, the browser sometimes puts a message in the standard output or standard error stream before forwarding the exception.

Impurity Alert! Displaying to the standard output and standard error streams has platform-dependent results and thus is not done in 100% Pure Java programs.

Where exactly the standard output and standard error streams are displayed varies, depending on how the browser is implemented, what platform it's running on, and (sometimes) how you launch the browser. For example, when you launch the Applet Viewer from a UNIX shell window, strings sent to the standard output and standard error appear in that shell window, unless you redirect the output. On the Win32 platform, when you launch the Applet Viewer from an MS-DOS prompt, the standard output and standard error streams go to the MS-DOS window. Netscape Navigator 4.0, on the other hand, displays applet standard output and standard error to the Java console.

Applets display to the standard output stream, using `System.out.print(String)` and `System.out.println(String)`. To display to the standard error stream, specify `System.err` instead of `System.out`. Here's an example of displaying to the standard output:

---

[1] http://java.sun.com/products/jdk/1.1/api/java.awt.Panel.html
[2] http://java.sun.com/products/jdk/1.1/api/java.awt.Component.html
[3] http://java.sun.com/products/jdk/1.1/api/java.awt.FlowLayout.html

```
//Where instance variables are declared:
boolean DEBUG = true;
. . .
//Later, when we want to print some status:
if (DEBUG) {
    System.out.println("Called someMethod(" + x + "," + y + ")");
}
```

Note: Displaying to the standard output and standard error streams is relatively slow. If you have a timing-related problem, printing messages to either of these streams might not be helpful.

Be sure to disable all debugging output before you release your applet. For example, if you have an applet that uses the code in the preceding example, you can turn off the applet's debugging output by setting DEBUG to `false` and recompiling the applet.

Getting System Properties

Applets find out about the current working environment by getting the values of system properties. System properties are key/value pairs that contain such information as the operating system under which the applet is running.

Untrusted applets can get some system properties but not all. This section lists the minimum set of system properties that applets can get, followed by a list of properties that untrusted applets can't get.

System Properties That Applets Can Get

Table 59 explains the system properties that even untrusted applets can get. It's possible that more properties will be added to this list.

Table 59   System Properties That Applets Can Get

Key	Meaning
`"file.separator"`	File separator (for example, `"/"`)
`"line.separator"`	Line separator (for example, `"\n"`)
`"path.separator"`	Path separator (for example, `":"`)
`"java.class.version"`	Java class version number
`"java.vendor"`	Java vendor-specific string
`"java.vendor.url"`	Java vendor URL

Table 59   System Properties That Applets Can Get

Key	Meaning
`"java.version"`	Java version number
`"os.arch"`	Operating system architecture
`"os.name"`	Operating system name
`"os.version"`	Operating system version

To get a system property, an applet uses the `System` class method `getProperty`:

```
String newline = System.getProperty("line.separator");
```

The following applet, called `GetOpenProperties`, gets the values of all the system properties listed in Table 59.[1] The `GetOpenProperties` applet's architecture is explained in the section <u>Revisiting the GetOpenProperties Applet</u> (page 453).

file.separator	\
line.separator	□□
path.separator	;
java.class.version	45.3
java.vendor	Netscape Communications Corporation
java.vendor.url	http://home.netscape.com/
java.version	1.1.5
os.name	Windows 95
os.arch	x86
os.version	4.10

http://java.sun.com/docs/books/tutorial/applet/practical/properties.html

---

[1]   `GetOpenProperties.java` is included on the CD and is available online. See <u>Code Samples</u> (page 463).

Forbidden System Properties

For security reasons, untrusted applets can't get the system properties listed in Table 60. Applets might also be forbidden from getting other system properties.

Table 60 System Properties That Untrusted Applets Can't Get.

Key	Meaning
`"java.class.path"`	Classpath
`"java.home"`	Installation directory
`"user.dir"`	User's current working directory
`"user.home"`	User's home directory
`"user.name"`	User's account name

Threads in AWT Applets

> **Note:** This section assumes that you're familiar with threads and so doesn't explain basic thread code. If you find yourself getting confused by the discussion or code in this section, read the chapter Threads: Doing Two or More Tasks at Once (page 269). If you're writing Swing applets, see section Threads in Swing Applets (page 459).

Every applet can run in multiple threads. Applet drawing methods (`paint` and `update`) are always called from a dedicated drawing and event-handling thread, the *AWT event thread*. Exactly which threads execute the milestone methods—`init`, `start`, `stop`, and `destroy`—depends on the browser that is running the applet. But no browser *ever* calls the milestone methods from the AWT event thread.

Browsers can vary in their approaches to using threads. One browser might allocate a thread for each applet on a page, using that thread for all calls to the applet's milestone methods. Another browser might allocate a thread group for each applet so that it's easy to find all the threads that belong to a particular applet. In any case, you're guaranteed that every thread created by any of an applet's milestone methods belongs to the same thread group.

Following are two `PrintThread` applets, one on top of the other:[1]

---

[1] `LamePrintThread.java` and `PrintThread.java` are included on the CD and available online. See Code Samples (page 463).

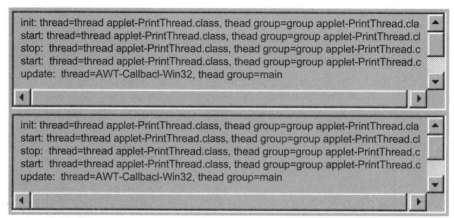

http://java.sun.com/docs/books/tutorial/applet/practical/threads.html

PrintThread is a modified version of the Simple applet, which prints the thread and thread group from which init, start, stop, destroy, and update are called. PrintThread calls repaint unnecessarily every once in a while so that you'll be able to see how its update method gets called. As usual, you need to look at the standard output to see the output for the methods, such as destroy, that are called during unloading.

So why would an applet need to create and to use its own threads? Imagine an applet that performs some time-consuming initialization in its init method—loading sound data, for example. The thread that invokes init cannot do anything else until init returns. In some browsers, this might mean that the browser cannot display the applet or anything after it until the applet has finished initializing itself. So if the applet is at the top of the page, nothing appears on the page until the applet has finished initializing itself.

Even in browsers that create a separate thread for each applet, it makes sense to put any time-consuming tasks into an applet-created thread so that the applet can perform other tasks while it waits for the time-consuming ones to be completed. When writing your threads, be careful that they don't rely on thread priorities for correct behavior. If you think you might need to specify thread priorities, see the section <u>Understanding Thread Priority</u> (page 286) in Chapter 8.

Rule of Thumb: An applet that performs a time-consuming task should create and use its own thread to perform that task.

Most applets implement the stop method, if necessary, to suspend any processing when the user leaves the applet's page. Sometimes, however, it's appropriate for an applet to continue executing. For example, if a user tells an applet to perform a complex calculation, the user might want the calculation to continue. (The user should generally be able to specify whether it should continue, though.)

Applets typically perform two kinds of time-consuming tasks: those they perform repeatedly and those they perform only once.

Using a Thread to Perform Repeated Tasks

An applet that performs the same task over and over again typically should have a thread with a while (or do-while) loop that performs the task. A typical example is an applet that performs timed animation, such as a movie player or a game. Animation applets need a thread that requests repaints at regular intervals. Another example is an applet that reads data supplied by a server-side application.

Applets typically create threads for repetitive tasks in the applet start method. Creating the thread there makes it easy for the applet to stop the thread when the user leaves the page. All you need to do is implement the stop method so that it tells the applet's thread to finish executing. When the user returns to the applet's page, the start method is called again. Then the applet can again create a thread to perform the repetitive task.

The AnimatorApplet puts its animation loop in a separate thread. Following is AnimatorApplet's implementation of the start and stop methods.

```
public void start() {
    ...//applet-specific code...
    //Start animating!
    if (animatorThread == null) {
        animatorThread = new Thread(this);
    }
    animatorThread.start();
}

public void stop() {
    animatorThread = null;
}
```

The this in new Thread(this) indicates that the applet provides the body of the thread. It does so by implementing the java.lang.Runnable interface, which requires the applet to provide a run method that forms the body of the thread.

Notice that nowhere in the AnimatorApplet class is the Thread stop method called. The reason is that calling the Thread stop method is like clubbing the thread over the head. It's a drastic way to get the thread to stop what it's doing. Instead, you can write the thread's run method in such a way that the thread exits gracefully when you tap it on the shoulder. This shoulder tap comes in the form of setting an instance variable.

In AnimatorApplet, this instance variable is called animatorThread. The start method sets it to refer to the newly created Thread object. When it needs to kill the thread, the applet sets animatorThread to null. This kills the thread *not* by making it be garbage-collected—it can't be garbage-collected while it's capable of running—but because at the top of its loop, the thread checks animatorThread, continuing or exiting depending on the value of animatorThread.

Here's the relevant code:

```
public void run() {
    . . .
    Thread currentThread = Thread.currentThread();
    while (currentThread == animatorThread) {
        ...//Display a frame of animation and then sleep.
    }
}
```

If animatorThread refers to the same thread as the currently executing thread, the thread continues executing. However, if animatorThread is null, the thread exits. If animatorThread refers to *another* thread, a race condition has occurred. That is, start has been called so soon after stop (or this thread has taken such a long time in its loop) that start has created another thread before this thread reaches the top of its while loop. Whatever the cause of the race condition, this thread should exit.

For more information about and examples of stopping threads, see the section Stopping a Thread (page 285) in Chapter 8.

Using a Thread to Perform a One-Time Task

If your applet needs to perform a task that can take a while, consider performing it in a thread. For example, anything that requires making a network connection should generally be done in a background thread. Anything with deliberate pauses should *always* be done in a background thread.

Fortunately, the AWT Image class loads GIF and JPEG images in the background, using threads that you don't need to worry about. Sound loading, unfortunately, is not guaranteed to be done in the background. In the JDK 1.1 implementation, the Applet getAudioClip methods don't return until they have loaded all the audio data. As a result, you might want to create one or more threads to load sounds.

Revisiting the GetOpenProperties Applet

The section <u>Getting System Properties</u> (page 447) has an applet that uses a thread to initialize its display. When the applet is initialized, it sets up its user interface, which consists of two columns of labels. The applet waits 3 seconds to give the user time to see the initial text in the labels. Then, one by one, the applet changes the text displayed by the labels in the right column. The applet's appearance doesn't change after that.

Because the applet's appearance doesn't change after the applet is initialized, it makes sense to put the applet's functionality in its `init` method. However, it's not good for the `init` method to execute for a long time. For this reason, the `init` method spins off a low-priority thread that performs the time-consuming part of the initialization.

Another way to implement the applet would be to have the `start` method start the thread. This would make it possible to stop the applet if the user quickly left the page. If the user returned to the page, the applet could start initialization all over again or could pick up where it left off. However, in this applet, using `init` should work just fine, because initialization shouldn't take more than a few seconds and because it's performed in a thread with very low priority that frequently yields the processor.

Here's the code that implements the thread:

```
public class GetOpenProperties extends Applet
                            implements Runnable {
    . . .
    public void init() {
        ...//Create and add a bunch of Labels...
        new Thread(this, "Loading System Properties").start();
    }

    /*
     * This method runs in a separate thread, loading
     * properties one by one.
     */
    public void run() {
        . . .
        Thread.currentThread().setPriority(Thread.MIN_PRIORITY);

        //Pause to let the reader see the default strings.
        pause(3000);

        for (int i = 0; i < numProperties; i++) {
            //Pause for dramatic effect.
            pause(250);
```

```
        ...//Look up a value; make a label show it...
        }
    }
}

synchronized void pause(int millis) {
    try {
        wait(millis);
    } catch (InterruptedException e) { }
}
```

Finishing an Applet

When is your applet finished? When it works and meets at least the minimum standards described in the following section. Some higher standards we'd like you to meet are described in the section The Perfectly Finished Applet (page 455).

Before You Ship That Applet

Stop! Before you let the whole world know about your applet, make sure that the answer to all of the following questions is yes.

1. Have you removed or disabled debugging output?

Debugging output (generally created with System.out.println), although useful to you, is generally confusing or annoying to users. It also can slow down your applet. If you need to give textual feedback to the user, try to do it inside the applet's display area or in the status area at the bottom of the window. Information on using the status area is in the section Displaying Short Status Strings (page 425).

2. Does the applet stop running when it's off-screen?

Most applets should not use CPU resources when the browser is iconified or is displaying a page that doesn't contain the applet. If your applet code doesn't launch any threads explicitly, you're probably okay.

If your applet code launches any threads, unless you have a *really good* excuse not to, you should implement the stop method so that it notifies the threads that they should stop. For an example of implementing the stop method, see the section Using a Thread to Perform Repeated Tasks (page 451).

3. If the applet does something that might get annoying—play sounds or animation, for example—does it give the user a way to stop the annoying behavior?

Be kind to your users. Give them a way to stop the applet in its tracks, without leaving the page. In an applet that otherwise doesn't respond to mouse clicks, you can do this by implementing the `mouseClicked` method so that a mouse press suspends or resumes the annoying thread. For example:

```
boolean frozen = false; //an instance variable

public void mouseClicked(MouseEvent e) {
    if (frozen) {
        frozen = false;
        start();
    } else {
        frozen = true;
        stop();
    }
}
```

The Perfectly Finished Applet

The previous section listed some rules you should follow to avoid making your applet's users want to throttle you. This section offers tips that can make dealing with your applet as pleasant as possible. Some of the tips here aren't easy to implement. Still, you should be aware of them and implement what makes sense for your applet.

1. Test your applet well.

Before you unleash your applet on the world, test it thoroughly. Once it works well in your normal browser/platform combination, run it in as many browser/platform combinations as you can find. Ask people whose computers are behind firewalls to test it. Take advantage of the Web; you can usually get other people to perform much of the testing for you.

2. Make sure that your applet follows the 100% Pure Java guidelines.

Throughout this tutorial, you can find tips on how to make programs work well on any Java platform.

3. Use parameters to make your applet as flexible as possible.

You often can define parameters that let your applet be used in a variety of situations without any rewriting. See the section Defining and Using Applet Parameters (page 433) for information.

4. If your applet has more than one file, consider providing an archive.

See the section Combining an Applet's Files into a Single File (page 441) for information.

5. Make your applet appear as soon as possible.

Applets can do several things to decrease their perceived startup time. The `Applet` sub-class can be a small one that immediately displays a status message. Some or all of the applet's files can be compressed into an archive file to decrease total download time. If some of the applet's classes or data aren't used right away, the applet can either delay loading them until they're needed or use a background thread to load them. If you can't avoid a lengthy delay in your applet's startup, consider using a small helper applet nearby to give status.

6. Make your applet adjust well to different sizes, different available fonts, and different platforms.

Applets don't always get all the screen real estate they want. Also, the amount of space required to display your applet's UI can be affected by platform/machine variances in font availability, drawing techniques, resolution, and so on.

By using layout managers wisely, you can make your applet adjust well. If your applet has a minimum required size, you can use the `getSize` method to check whether your applet is big enough. If your applet or custom components in it draw text using graphics primitives, you should check and adjust font sizes.

7. If your applet can't do its job, make it fail gracefully.

Sometimes, your applet doesn't get the resources it needs. It might get so little space that it can't present a meaningful user interface. Or it might not be able to connect to a server. Even if your applet can't adjust successfully to the lack of resources, you should at least attempt to make your applet fail gracefully. For example, you might display a visible message—either in the applet's drawing area or in a helper applet near it—that explains what happened and gives hints on how to fix the problem.

8. Be wary of using text in images.

Although using images to draw text can result in good-looking, predictably sized text, the result may be illegible on some low-resolution displays.

9. Use windows wisely.

Windows have good points and bad points. Some platforms, such as TV-based browsers, might not allow top-level windows. Also, since applet-created windows can take a while to appear, they can be disconcerting to the user. However, putting some or all of an applet's UI in a window makes sense when your applet needs more space than it can get in the browser. Using a window might also make sense in the rare case when your applet needs to remain visible even when the user changes pages.

10. Supply alternative text for your applet.

By using alternative text to explain what your users are missing, you can be kind to users who can't run your applet. You can supply alternative text as described in the section Specifying Alternative HTML Code and Text (page 439).

11. Implement the `getParameterInfo` method.

Implementing the `getParameterInfo` method now might make your applet easier to customize in the future. Browsers can use this method to help generate a GUI that allows the user to interactively set parameter values. See the section Giving Information about Parameters (page 437) for information on implementing `getParameter-Info`.

12. Implement the `getAppletInfo` method.

The `getAppletInfo` method returns a short, informative string describing an applet. Browsers and other applets can use this to give information about your applet. Here's an example of implementing `getAppletInfo`:

```
public String getAppletInfo() {
    return "GetApplets by Kathy Walrath";
}
```

Swing-Based Applets

Now that we've covered how to create applets based on the 1.1 version of the Java Platform, this section gives an overview of how to run and write Swing-based applets.

Running Swing-Based Applets

This section explains how to run applets that use Swing components. For information on *writing* Swing applets, see the section Writing Swing-Based Applets (page 458).

You can run Swing applets in any browser that has the appropriate version of Java Plug-in installed.[1] You can do this by visiting the URL for either of the preceding applets. Another alternative is to use Applet Viewer (`appletviewer`).[2] Java Plug-in supports certain versions of Netscape Navigator and Internet Explorer. See the Java Plug-in documentation on this book's CD for details.

---

[1] The Java Plug-in is included in the JRE (as of version 1.2 of the Java 2 platform).

[2] We recommend that you use Applet Viewer in version 1.2 (and higher) of the Java 2 platform. If you're using JDK 1.1 Applet Viewer, you'll need to load the Swing JAR file.

To test whether your browser can run Swing applets, go to this page in the online tutorial:

```
http://java.sun.com/docs/books/tutorial/uiswing/start/
HelloSwingApplet.html
```

You should see a box that looks like this.[1]

> You are successfully running a Swing applet!

Figure 121   A snapshot of the simple applet, `HelloSwingApplet`.

If you view the source of that Web page, you'll see that the HTML code for including the applet is rather convoluted. The good news is that you can generate the HTML code automatically from a simple <APPLET> tag. See the Java Plug-in documentation for details on downloading a free HTML converter.[2]

Writing Swing-Based Applets

This section covers the `JApplet` class, which enables applets to use Swing components. `JApplet` is a subclass of `java.applet.Applet`. If you've never written a regular applet before, we urge you to read the preceding sections in this appendix before proceeding with this section.

Any applet that contains Swing components must be implemented with a subclass of `JApplet`.[3] Here's a Swing version of one of the applets that helped make Java famous—an applet that animates our mascot, Duke, doing cartwheels.

Figure 122   One frame of the Duke tumbling applet.

---

[1] `HelloSwingApplet.java` and `HelloSwingApplet.html` are included on the CD and are available online. See <u>Code Samples</u> (page 463).

[2] The Java Plug-in documentation is online at http://java.sun.com/products/plugin/index.html

[3] API documentation for this class is available on this book's CD and online at http://java.sun.com/j2se/1.3/
docs/api/javax/swing/JApplet.html

The CD that accompanies this book includes the source code (`TumbleItem.java` and `SwingWorker.java`) and the 17 images used in this applet.[1]

JApplet Features

`JApplet` adds two major features to the functionality that it inherits from `java.applet.Applet`. First, `JApplet` provides support for assistive technologies. Second, because `JApplet` is a top-level Swing container, each Swing applet has a root pane. The most noticeable results of the root pane's presence are support for adding a menu bar and the need to use a content pane.

As described in Overview of the Swing API (page 352) in Chapter 10, each top-level container, such as `JApplet`, has a single content pane. The content pane makes Swing applets different from regular applets in the following ways:

- You add components to a Swing applet's content pane, not directly to the applet.
- You set the layout manager on a Swing applet's content pane, not directly on the applet.
- The default layout manager for a Swing applet's content pane is `BorderLayout`. This differs from the default layout manager for `Applet`, which is `FlowLayout`.
- You should not put painting code directly in a `JApplet` object. See the section Converting AWT Applets to Swing Applets (page 462) for information on converting applet painting code.

JDK 1.1 Note: If you run a Swing applet using JDK 1.1 and JFC 1.1, you might see an error message that looks like this:

```
Swing: checked access to system event queue.
```

You can often avoid this message by telling the applet not to check whether it has access to the system event queue. To do so, put the following code in the constructor for the applet class:

```
getRootPane().putClientProperty("defeatSystemEventQueueCheck",
                                Boolean.TRUE);
```

Threads in Swing Applets

Because applets inherently use multiple threads and Swing components aren't thread safe, you should take care with threads in Swing applets. It's generally considered safe to create and to manipulate Swing components directly in the `init` method. However, the other milestone methods—`start`, `stop`, and `destroy`—might cause trouble when the browser invokes

---

[1] The directory with the tumbling Duke images on the CD is: JavaTutorial/uiswing/components/example-swing/images/tumble/

them after the applet's already visible. To avoid trouble, you should make these methods thread safe.

For example, when you implement a `stop` or a `start` method, be aware that the browser doesn't call them from the event-dispatching thread. Thus, those methods shouldn't affect or query Swing components directly. Instead, they should use such techniques as using the `SwingUtilities.invokeLater` method to affect components.

For more information about using threads, see the section <u>Threads and Swing</u> (page 378) in Chapter 10 and Chapter 8, <u>Threads: Doing Two or More Tasks at Once</u> (page 269). Threads in AWT applets was covered in an earlier section, <u>Threads in AWT Applets</u> (page 449).

Using Images in a Swing Applet

Recall that the `Applet` class provides the `getImage` method for loading images into an applet. The `getImage` method creates and returns an `Image` object that represents the loaded image. Because Swing components use `Icons` rather than `Images` to refer to pictures, Swing applets tend not to use `getImage`. Instead, Swing applets usually create instances of `Image-Icon`—an icon loaded from an image file. `ImageIcon` comes with a code-saving benefit: It handles image tracking automatically.

The animation of Duke doing cartwheels requires 17 pictures, with one `ImageIcon` per picture. Because images can take a long time to load, the icons are loaded in a separate thread implemented by a `SwingWorker` object. The applet's `init` method starts the thread by creating the `SwingWorker` object. Here's the code:

```
public void init() {
    ...
    imgs = new ImageIcon[nimgs];
    final SwingWorker worker = new SwingWorker() {
        public Object construct() {
            URL baseURL = getCodeBase();
            String prefix = dir + "/T";
            //Images are numbered 1 to nimgs,
            //but fill array from 0 to nimgs-1
            for (int i = 0; i < nimgs; i++) {
                imgs[i] = new ImageIcon(getURL(baseURL, prefix
                                        + (i+1) + ".gif"));
            }
            finishLoading = true;
            return imgs;
        } ...
    };
    worker.start();
}
```

To create an `ImageIcon` and load it with an image, you specify the image file's URL to the `ImageIcon`'s constructor. The preceding applet defines a method named `getURL` to construct the URL for each image file. Here is the code:

```
protected URL getURL(URL codeBase, String filename) {
    URL url = null;
    try {
        url = new URL(codeBase, filename);
    } catch (java.net.MalformedURLException e) {
        System.out.println("Couldn't create image: " +
                            "badly specified URL");
        return null;
    }
    return url;
}
```

Providing an OBJECT/EMBED Tag for Java Plug-in

To run, an applet must be included in an HTML page. If you're using Applet Viewer to run a Swing applet, you include the applet by using an <APPLET> tag.[1] Here's the <APPLET> tag for the cartwheeling Duke applet:

```
<applet code="TumbleItem.class"
        codebase="example-swing/"
        archive="tumble.jar"
        width="600" height="95">
    <param name="maxwidth" value="120">
    <param name="nimgs" value="17">
    <param name="offset" value="-57">
    <param name="img" value="images/tumble">
Your browser is completely ignoring the &lt;APPLET&gt; tag!
</applet>
```

To make an applet work with the Java Plug-in, you need to convert the <APPLET> tag into <OBJECT> and <EMBED> tags so that an applet can be included in an HTML page. You can download a free tool that automatically generates the necessary tags from an <APPLET> tag. To download Java Plug-in and the HTML conversion tool, as well as related documentation, go to the Java Plug-in home page.[2]

---

[1] To find out about the various <APPLET> tag parameters, refer to the section Using the <APPLET> Tag (page 438).

[2] http://java.sun.com/products/plugin/index.html

Because the Java Plug-in can take a while to download and load into the browser, it's considerate to give users advance warning that a page contains an applet. You might have noticed that the tutorial's applets don't run the same page as the text that describes the applet. Instead we provide a screenshot of the applet running and a link that brings up a separate browser window in which to run the applet. We feel that this provides a better experience because users can choose whether to visit a page that contains an applet.

Converting AWT Applets to Swing Applets

This section gives you several tips for converting your AWT applets to Swing applets. First, remember that AWT programs add components directly to the `Applet` object and directly set the applet's layout manager. Swing applets, on the other hand, add components to and set the layout manager on the `JApplet`'s content pane. So to convert an applet, you must make the source code changes described in that section. Furthermore, whereas `FlowLayout` is the default layout manager for AWT applets, `BorderLayout` is the default layout manager for Swing applets. This has two repercussions:

- If you want to use a `FlowLayout`, the Swing version of your program must use `setLayout` on the content pane to specify it.
- If you specified `BorderLayout` in your AWT applet, you can remove the `setLayout` statement from the Swing version.

Don't paint directly in a `JApplet`, because it will be covered by the applet's content pane. Instead of seeing your painting, you'll just see a blank area. The solution is to have a custom component do the painting, and add it to the content pane. See the instructions for converting canvases for tips on choosing a class for the custom component and for moving the paint code to the appropriate method.

Be very aware of thread issues when converting your applet. Because the stop and start methods aren't called from the event-dispatching thread, you should use `SwingUtilities.invokeLater` in those methods whenever you make a change that might result in a call upon a component. See <u>Threads and Swing</u> (page 378) in Chapter 10 for more information.

Lastly, your applet's users will probably use Java Plug-in to run your applet. So you will need to convert the `<APPLET>` tag to an `OBJECT/EMBED` tag. An automatic HTML converter can be found at the Java Plug-in site.

For More Information

A number of resources on the Web teach the basics of HTML. A quick search on your favorite search engine will yield numerous HTML tutorials. The World Wide Web Consortium (W3C) hosts an excellent and compact tutorial, "Getting Started with HTML":

```
http://www.w3.org/MarkUp/Guide/
```

For more complete information on Swing, see *The JFC Swing Tutorial* book or the online tutorial:

```
http://java.sun.com/docs/books/tutorial/uiswing/components/applet.html
```

Code Samples

Table 61 lists the code samples used in this appendix and where you can find the code online and on the CD that accompanies this book. (Note that some of these files have 1.0 versions.You can find these versions by replacing "example-1dot1" in the path with "example.")

Table 61   Code Samples in Internet-Ready Applets

Code Sample	CD Location	Online Location
Simple.java (page 412)	JavaTutorial/applet/ overview/example-1dot1/ Simple.java	http://java.sun.com/docs/ books/tutorial/applet/ overview/example-1dot1/ Simple.java
SimpleClick.java (page 414)	JavaTutorial/applet/ overview/example-1dot1/ SimpleClick.java	http://java.sun.com/docs/ books/tutorial/applet/ overview/example-1dot1/ SimpleClick.java
ScrollingSimple.java (page 416)	JavaTutorial/applet/ overview/example/ ScrollingSimple.java	http://java.sun.com/docs/ books/tutorial/applet/ overview/example/ ScrollingSimple.java
ShowDocument.java (page 426)	JavaTutorial/applet/ appletsonly/example-1dot1/ ShowDocument.java	http://java.sun.com/docs/ books/tutorial/applet/ appletsonly/example-1dot1/ ShowDocument.java
Sender.java (page 428)	JavaTutorial/applet/ appletsonly/example-1dot1/ Sender.java	http://java.sun.com/docs/ books/tutorial/applet/ appletsonly/example-1dot1/ Sender.java

Table 61 Code Samples in Internet-Ready Applets

Receiver.java (page 428)	JavaTutorial/applet/ appletsonly/example-1dot1/ Receiver.java	http://java.sun.com/docs/ books/tutorial/applet/ appletsonly/example-1dot1/ Receiver.java
GetApplets.java (page 430)	JavaTutorial/applet/ appletsonly/example-1dot1/ GetApplets.java	http://java.sun.com/docs/ books/tutorial/applet/ appletsonly/example-1dot1/ GetApplets.java
SoundExample.java (page 432)	JavaTutorial/applet/ appletsonly/example-1dot1/ SoundExample.java	http://java.sun.com/docs/ books/tutorial/applet/ appletsonly/example-1dot1/ SoundExample.java
SoundList.java (page 432)	JavaTutorial/applet/ appletsonly/example-1dot1/ SoundList.java	http://java.sun.com/docs/ books/tutorial/applet/ appletsonly/example-1dot1/ SoundList.java
SoundLoader.java (page 432)	JavaTutorial/applet/ appletsonly/example-1dot1/ SoundLoader.java	http://java.sun.com/docs/ books/tutorial/applet/ appletsonly/example-1dot1/ SoundLoader.java
AppletButton.java (page 435)	JavaTutorial/applet/ appletsonly/example/ AppletButton.java	http://java.sun.com/docs/ books/tutorial/applet/ appletsonly/example/ AppletButton.java
Animator.java (page 437)	JavaTutorial/applet/ appletsonly/example/ Animator.java	http://java.sun.com/docs/ books/tutorial/getStarted/ example/Animator.java
GetOpenProperties.java (page 448)	JavaTutorial/applet/ practical/example/ GetOpenProperties.java	http://java.sun.com/docs/ books/tutorial/applet/ practical/example/ GetOpenProperties.java
LamePrintThread.java (page 449)	JavaTutorial/applet/ practical/example/ LamePrintThread.java	http://java.sun.com/docs/ books/tutorial/applet/ practical/example/ LamePrintThread.java
PrintThread.java (page 449)	JavaTutorial/applet/ appletsonly/example-1dot1/ PrintThread.java	http://java.sun.com/docs/ books/tutorial/applet/ practical/example-1dot1/ PrintThread.java
QuoteClientApplet.java (page 449)	JavaTutorial/applet/ practical/example-1dot1/ QuoteClientApplet.java	http://java.sun.com/docs/ books/tutorial/applet/ practical/example-1dot1/ QuoteClientApplet.java

Table 61   Code Samples in Internet-Ready Applets

HelloSwingApplet.java (page 458)	JavaTutorial/uiswing/ start/example-swing/ HelloSwingApplet.java	http://java.sun.com/docs/ books/tutorial/uiswing/ start/example-swing/ HelloSwingApplet.java
HelloSwingApplet.html (page 458)	JavaTutorial/uiswing/start/ HelloSwingApplet.html	http://java.sun.com/docs/ books/tutorial/uiswing/ start/HelloSwingApplet.html

Note: For solutions to common problems Tutorial readers have encountered, see Appendix A, <u>Common Problems and Their Solutions</u> (page 391).

Collections

THIS appendix introduces the Java Collections Framework.™ You will learn what collections are and how they'll make your job easier and your programs better. You'll learn about the core elements that comprise the Collections Framework: *interfaces*, *implementations*, and *algorithms*.

This appendix also describes the *core collection interfaces*, which are the heart and soul of the Java Collections Framework. You'll learn general guidelines for effective use of these interfaces, including when to use which interface. You'll also learn idioms for each interface to help you get the most out of the interfaces.

Introduction

A collection—sometimes called a *container*—is simply an object that groups multiple elements into a single unit. Collections are used to store, to retrieve, and to manipulate data and to transmit data from one method to another. Collections typically represent data items that form a natural group, such as a poker hand (a collection of cards), a mail folder (a collection of letters), or a telephone directory (a mapping of names to phone numbers).

If you've used the Java programming language—or just about any other programming language—you're already familiar with collections. Collection implementations in earlier versions of the Java platform included `Vector`, `Hashtable`, and `array`. Those earlier versions, however, did not contain a *Collections Framework*.

What Is a Collections Framework?

A Collections Framework is a unified architecture for representing and manipulating collections. All collections frameworks contain

- **Interfaces:** abstract data types representing collections. Interfaces allow collections to be manipulated independently of the details of their representation. In object-oriented languages, these interfaces generally form a hierarchy.

- **Implementations:** concrete implementations of the collection interfaces. In essence, these are *reusable data structures*.

- **Algorithms:** methods that perform useful computations, such as searching and sorting, on objects that implement collection interfaces. These algorithms are said to be *polymorphic;* the same method can be used on many different implementations of the appropriate collection interface. In essence, algorithms are *reusable functionality.*

The best-known examples of collections frameworks are the C++ Standard Template Library (STL) and Smalltalk's collection hierarchy.

Benefits

The Collections Framework provides the following benefits.

- **Reduces programming effort:** By providing useful data structures and algorithms, the Collections Framework frees you to concentrate on the important parts of your program rather than on the low-level plumbing required to make it work. By facilitating interoperability among unrelated APIs, the Collections Framework frees you from writing oodles of adapter objects or conversion code to connect APIs.

- **Increases program speed and quality:** The Collections Framework does this primarily by providing high-performance, high-quality implementations of useful data structures and algorithms. Also, because the various implementations of each interface are interchangeable, programs can be easily tuned by switching collection implementations. Finally, because you're freed from the drudgery of writing your own data structures, you'll have more time to devote to improving the rest of your program's quality and performance.

- **Allows interoperability among unrelated APIs:** The collection interfaces will become the vernacular by which APIs pass collections back and forth. If my network administration API furnishes a `Collection` of node names and if your GUI toolkit expects a `Collection` of column headings, our APIs will interoperate seamlessly, even though they were written independently.

- **Reduces effort to learn and to use new APIs:** Many APIs naturally take collections on input and output. In the past, each such API had a little "sub-API" devoted to manipulating its collections. There was little consistency among these ad hoc collections sub-APIs, so you had to learn each one from scratch, and it was easy to make mistakes when using them. With the advent of standard collection interfaces, the problem goes away.

- **Reduces effort to design new APIs:** This is the flip side of the previous advantage. Designers and implementers don't have to reinvent the wheel each time they create an API that relies on collections but instead just use the standard collection interfaces.

- **Fosters software reuse:** New data structures that conform to the standard collection interfaces are by nature reusable. The same goes for new algorithms that operate on objects that implement these interfaces.

Drawbacks of the Collections Framework

Historically, collections frameworks have been quite complex, which gave them a reputation for having a steep learning curve. We believe that Java's new Collections Framework breaks with this tradition, as you will learn for yourself in this appendix.

Interfaces

The *core collection interfaces* are used to manipulate collections and to pass them from one method to another. The basic purpose of these interfaces is to allow collections to be manipulated independently of the details of their representation. The core collection interfaces are the heart and soul of the Collections Framework. When you understand how to use these interfaces, you know most of what there is to know about the framework. The core collection interfaces are shown in the following figure.

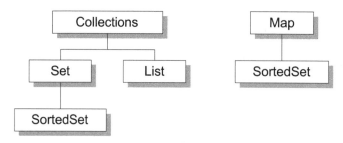

Figure 123   The core collection interfaces.

The core collection interfaces form a *hierarchy*: A Set is a special kind of Collection, a SortedSet is a special kind of Set, and so forth. Note also that the hierarchy consists of two distinct trees: A Map is not a true Collection.

To keep the number of core collection interfaces manageable, the Java 2 SDK doesn't provide separate interfaces for each variant of each collection type. (Immutable, fixed-size, and append-only variants are possible.) Instead, the modification operations in each interface are designated *optional:* A given implementation may not support some of these operations. If an unsupported operation is invoked, a collection throws an UnsupportedOperationException. Implementations are responsible for documenting which of the optional operations they support. All the Java 2 Platform's general-purpose implementations support all the optional operations.

The four basic core collection interfaces are as follows.

- The Collection interface, the root of the collection hierarchy, represents a group of objects, known as its *elements*. Some Collection implementations allow duplicate elements, and others do not. Some are ordered and others unordered. The Java 2 SDK doesn't provide any direct implementations of this interface but does provide implementations of more specific subinterfaces, such as `Set` and `List`. This interface is the least common denominator that all collections implement and is used to pass collections around and to manipulate them when maximum generality is desired. See the section <u>Collection Interface</u> (page 472).

- A `Set` is a collection that cannot contain duplicate elements. As you might expect, this interface models the mathematical *set* abstraction and is used to represent sets, such as the cards comprising a poker hand, the courses making up a student's schedule, or the processes running on a machine. See the section <u>Set Interface</u> (page 475).

- A `List` is an ordered collection (sometimes called a *sequence*). Lists can contain duplicate elements. The user of a `List` generally has precise control over where in the `List` each element is inserted. The user can access elements by their integer index (position). If you've used `Vector`, you're familiar with the general flavor of `List`. See the section <u>List Interface</u> (page 479).

- A `Map` is an object that maps keys to values. Maps cannot contain duplicate keys: Each key can map to at most one value. If you've used `Hashtable`, you're already familiar with the general flavor of `Map`. See the section <u>Map Interface</u> (page 487).

The last two core collection interfaces (`SortedSet` and `SortedMap`) are merely sorted versions of `Set` and `Map`. To understand these interfaces, you have to know how order is maintained among objects.

There are two ways to order objects: The `Comparable` interface provides automatic *natural order* on classes that implement it; the `Comparator` interface gives the programmer complete control over object ordering. Note that these are *not* core collection interfaces but rather underlying infrastructure. See the section <u>Object Ordering</u> (page 496).

The last two core collection interfaces are as follows.

- A `SortedSet` is a `Set` that maintains its elements in ascending order. Several additional operations are provided to take advantage of the ordering. Sorted sets are used for naturally ordered sets, such as word lists and membership rolls. See the section <u>SortedSet Interface</u> (page 503).

- A `SortedMap`, a `Map` that maintains its mappings in ascending key order, is the `Map` analog of `SortedSet`. Sorted maps are used for naturally ordered collections of key/value pairs, such as dictionaries and telephone directories. See the section <u>SortedMap Interface</u> (page 506).

Collection Interface

A `Collection` represents a group of objects, known as its *elements*. The primary use of the `Collection` interface is to pass around collections of objects where maximum generality is desired. For example, by convention all general-purpose collection implementations, which typically implement a subinterface of `Collection`, such as `Set` or `List`, have a constructor that takes a `Collection` argument. This constructor initializes the new `Collection` to contain all the elements in the specified `Collection`. This constructor allows the caller to create a `Collection` of a desired implementation type, initially containing all the elements in any given `Collection`, whatever its subinterface or implementation type. Suppose, for example, that you have a `Collection`, c, which may be a `List`, a `Set`, or another kind of `Collection`. The following idiom creates a new `ArrayList` (an implementation of the `List` interface), initially containing all the elements in c:

```
List l = new ArrayList(c);
```

The `Collection` interface follows:

```
public interface Collection {
    // Basic Operations
    int size();
    boolean isEmpty();
    boolean contains(Object element);
    boolean add(Object element);      // Optional
    boolean remove(Object element);   // Optional
    Iterator iterator();

    // Bulk Operations
    boolean containsAll(Collection c);
    boolean addAll(Collection c);      // Optional
    boolean removeAll(Collection c);   // Optional
    boolean retainAll(Collection c);   // Optional
    void clear();                      // Optional

    // Array Operations
    Object[] toArray();
    Object[] toArray(Object a[]);
}
```

The interface does about what you'd expect, given that a `Collection` represents a group of objects. The interface has methods to tell you how many elements are in the collection (`size`, `isEmpty`), to check whether a given object is in the collection (`contains`), to add and to remove an element from the collection (`add`, `remove`), and to provide an iterator over the collection (`iterator`).

The add method is defined generally enough so that it makes sense for both collections that allow duplicates and those that don't. It guarantees that the Collection will contain the specified element after the call completes and returns true if the Collection changes as a result of the call. Similarly, the remove method is defined to remove *a single instance* of the specified element from the Collection, assuming that it contains the element, and to return true if the Collection was modified as a result.

Iterators

The object returned by the iterator method deserves special mention. It is an Iterator, which is very similar to an Enumeration, but differs in two respects.

- Iterator allows the caller to remove elements from the underlying collection during the iteration with well-defined semantics.
- Method names have been improved.

The first point is important: There was *no* safe way to remove elements from a collection while traversing it with an Enumeration. The semantics of this operation were ill-defined and differed from implementation to implementation.

The Iterator interface follows:

```
public interface Iterator {
    boolean hasNext();
    Object next();
    void remove();     // Optional
}
```

The hasNext method is identical in function to Enumeration.hasMoreElements, and the next method is identical in function to Enumeration.nextElement. The remove method removes from the underlying Collection the last element that was returned by next. The remove method may be called only once per call to next and throws an exception if this rule is violated. Note that Iterator.remove is the *only* safe way to modify a collection during iteration; the behavior is unspecified if the underlying collection is modified in any other way while the iteration is in progress.

The following snippet shows you how to use an Iterator to filter a Collection, that is, to traverse the collection, removing every element that does not satisfy a condition:

```
static void filter(Collection c) {
    for (Iterator i = c.iterator(); i.hasNext(); )
        if (!cond(i.next()))
            i.remove();
}
```

You should keep two things in mind when looking at this simple piece of code.

- The code is *polymorphic*: It works for *any* Collection that supports element removal, regardless of implementation. That's how easy it is to write a polymorphic algorithm under the Collections Framework!

- It would have been impossible to write this using Enumeration instead of Iterator, because there's no safe way to remove an element from a collection while traversing it with an Enumeration.

Bulk Operations

The *bulk operations* perform an operation on an entire Collection in a single shot. These shorthand operations can be simulated, perhaps less efficiently, by using the basic operations described previously. The bulk operations follow.

- containsAll: Returns true if the target Collection contains all the elements in the specified Collection (c).
- addAll: Adds all the elements in the specified Collection to the target Collection.
- removeAll: Removes from the target Collection all its elements that are also contained in the specified Collection.
- retainAll: Removes from the target Collection all its elements that are *not* also contained in the specified Collection. That is, it retains in the target Collection only those elements that are also contained in the specified Collection.
- clear: Removes all elements from the Collection.

The addAll, removeAll, and retainAll methods all return true if the target Collection was modified in the process of executing the operation.

As a simple example of the power of the bulk operations, consider the following idiom to remove *all* instances of a specified element, e, from a Collection, c:

```
c.removeAll(Collections.singleton(e));
```

More specifically, suppose that you want to remove all the null elements from a Collection:

```
c.removeAll(Collections.singleton(null));
```

This idiom uses Collections.singleton, which is a static factory method that returns an immutable Set containing only the specified element.

Array Operations

The `toArray` methods are provided as a bridge between collections and older APIs that expect arrays on input. The array operations allow the contents of a `Collection` to be translated into an array. The simple form with no arguments creates a new array of `Object`. The more complex form allows the caller to provide an array or to choose the runtime type of the output array.

For example, suppose that `c` is a `Collection`. The following snippet dumps the contents of `c` into a newly allocated array of `Object` whose length is identical to the number of elements in `c`:

```
Object[] a = c.toArray();
```

Suppose that `c` is known to contain only strings. The following snippet dumps the contents of `c` into a newly allocated array of `String` whose length is identical to the number of elements in `c`:

```
String[] a = (String[]) c.toArray(new String[0]);
```

Set Interface

A `Set` is a `Collection` that cannot contain duplicate elements. `Set` models the mathematical *set* abstraction. The `Set` interface contains *no* methods other than those inherited from `Collection`. `Set` adds the restriction that duplicate elements are prohibited. `Set` also adds a stronger contract on the behavior of the `equals` and `hashCode` operations, allowing `Set` objects to be compared meaningfully, even if their implementation types differ. Two `Set` objects are equal if they contain the same elements.

The `Set` interface follows:

```
public interface Set {
    // Basic Operations
    int size();
    boolean isEmpty();
    boolean contains(Object element);
    boolean add(Object element);    // Optional
    boolean remove(Object element); // Optional
    Iterator iterator();

    // Bulk Operations
    boolean containsAll(Collection c);
    boolean addAll(Collection c);    // Optional
    boolean removeAll(Collection c); // Optional
    boolean retainAll(Collection c); // Optional
    void clear();                    // Optional
```

```
        // Array Operations
        Object[] toArray();
        Object[] toArray(Object a[]);
    }
```

The SDK contains two general-purpose Set implementations. HashSet, which stores its elements in a hash table, is the better-performing implementation. TreeSet, which stores its elements in a red-black tree,[1] guarantees the order of iteration.

Here's a simple but useful Set idiom. Suppose that you have a Collection, c, and that you want to create another Collection containing the same elements but with all duplicates eliminated. The following one-liner does the trick:

```
    Collection noDups = new HashSet(c);
```

It works by creating a Set, which by definition cannot contain duplicates, initially containing all the elements in c. It uses the standard Collection constructor described in the section <u>Collection Interface</u> (page 472).

Basic Operations

The size operation returns the number of elements in the Set (its *cardinality*). The isEmpty method does exactly what you think it does. The add method adds the specified element to the Set if it's not already present and returns a Boolean indicating whether the element was added. Similarly, the remove method removes from the Set the specified element if it's present and returns a Boolean indicating whether the element was present. The iterator method returns an Iterator over the Set.

Here's a little program that takes the words in its argument list and prints out any duplicate words, the number of distinct words, and a list of the words with duplicates eliminated:

```
    import java.util.*;

    public class FindDups {
        public static void main(String args[]) {
            Set s = new HashSet();
            for (int i=0; i<args.length; i++)
                if (!s.add(args[i]))
                    System.out.println("Duplicate: " + args[i]);

            System.out.println(s.size() + " distinct words: " + s);
        }
    }
```

---

[1] A red-black tree is a data structure, a kind of balanced binary tree generally regarded to be among the best. The red-black tree offers guaranteed log(n) performance for all basic operations (lookup, insert, delete) and empirically speaking, is just plain fast.

Now let's run the program:

```
java FindDups i came i saw i left
```

The following output is produced:

```
Duplicate: i
Duplicate: i
4 distinct words: [came, left, saw, i]
```

Note that the code always refers to the collection by its interface type (Set) rather than by its implementation type (HashSet). This is a *strongly* recommended programming practice, as it gives you the flexibility to change implementations merely by changing the constructor. If either the variables used to store a collection or the parameters used to pass it around are declared to be of the collection's implementation type rather than of its interface type, *all* such variables and parameters must be changed to change the collection's implementation type. Furthermore, there's no guarantee that the resulting program will work; if the program uses any nonstandard operations that are present in the original implementation type but not in the new one, the program will fail. Referring to collections only by their interface keeps you honest, preventing you from using any nonstandard operations.

The implementation type of the Set in the preceding example is HashSet, which makes no guarantees as to the order of the elements in the Set. If you want the program to print the word list in alphabetical order, merely change the set's implementation type from HashSet to TreeSet. Making this trivial one-line change causes the command line in the previous example to generate the following output:

```
java FindDups i came i saw i left
Duplicate word: i
Duplicate word: i
4 distinct words: [came, i, left, saw]
```

Bulk Operations

The bulk operations are particularly well suited to Sets; when applied to sets, they perform standard set-algebraic operations. Suppose that s1 and s2 are Sets. Here's what the bulk operations do:

- s1.containsAll(s2): Returns true if s2 is a *subset* of s1. (Set s2 is a subset of set s1 if set s1 contains all the elements in s2.)
- s1.addAll(s2): Transforms s1 into the *union* of s1 and s2. (The union of two sets is the set containing all the elements contained in either set.)
- s1.retainAll(s2): Transforms s1 into the *intersection* of s1 and s2. (The intersection of two sets is the set containing only the elements that are common to both sets.)

- `s1.removeAll(s2)`: Transforms `s1` into the (asymmetric) *set difference* of `s1` and `s2`. (For example, the set difference of `s1 - s2` is the set containing all the elements found in `s1` but not in `s2`.)

To calculate the union, intersection, or set difference of two sets *nondestructively* (without modifying either set), the caller must copy one set before calling the appropriate bulk operation. The resulting idioms follow:

```
Set union = new HashSet(s1);
union.addAll(s2);

Set intersection = new HashSet(s1);
intersection.retainAll(s2);

Set difference = new HashSet(s1);
difference.removeAll(s2);
```

The implementation type of the result `Set` in the preceding idioms is `HashSet`, which is, as already mentioned, the best all-around `Set` implementation in the SDK. However, any general-purpose `Set` implementation could be substituted.

Let's revisit the `FindDups` program. Suppose that you want to know which words in the argument list occur only once and which occur more than once but that you do not want any duplicates printed out repeatedly. This effect can be achieved by generating two sets, one containing every word in the argument list and the other containing only the duplicates. The words that occur only once are the set difference of these two sets, which we know how to compute. Here's how the resulting program looks:

```
import java.util.*;

public class FindDups2 {
    public static void main(String args[]) {
        Set uniques = new HashSet();
        Set dups = new HashSet();

        for (int i = 0; i < args.length; i++)
            if (!uniques.add(args[i]))
                dups.add(args[i]);

        uniques.removeAll(dups); // Destructive set-difference

        System.out.println("Unique words:    " + uniques);
        System.out.println("Duplicate words: " + dups);
    }
}
```

When run with the same argument list used earlier (i came i saw i left), this program yields the output:

```
Unique words:    [came, left, saw]
Duplicate words: [i]
```

A less common set-algebraic operation is the *symmetric set difference:* the set of elements contained in either of two specified sets but not in both. The following code calculates the symmetric set difference of two sets nondestructively:

```
Set symmetricDiff = new HashSet(s1);
symmetricDiff.addAll(s2);
Set tmp = new HashSet(s1);
tmp.retainAll(s2));
symmetricDiff.removeAll(tmp);
```

Array Operations

The array operations don't do anything special for Sets beyond what they do for any other Collection. These operations are described in the section <u>Collection Interface</u> (page 472).

List Interface

A List is an ordered Collection, sometimes called a *sequence*. Lists may contain duplicate elements. In addition to the operations inherited from Collection, the List interface includes operations for the following:

- **Positional access:** Manipulate elements based on their numerical position in the list.
- **Search:** Search for a specified object in the list and return its numerical position.
- **List iteration:** Extend Iterator semantics to take advantage of the list's sequential nature.
- **Range view:** Perform arbitrary *range operations* on the list.

The List interface follows:

```
public interface List extends Collection {
    // Positional Access
    Object get(int index);
    Object set(int index, Object element);        // Optional
    void add(int index, Object element);          // Optional
    Object remove(int index);                     // Optional
    abstract boolean addAll(int index, Collection c);//Optional
```

```
        // Search
        int indexOf(Object o);
        int lastIndexOf(Object o);
        // Iteration
        ListIterator listIterator();
        ListIterator listIterator(int index);

        // Range-view
        List subList(int from, int to);
    }
```

The Java 2 SDK contains two general-purpose List implementations: ArrayList, which is generally the better-performing implementation, and LinkedList, which offers better performance under certain circumstances. Also, Vector has been retrofitted to implement List.

Comparison to Vector

If you've used Vector, you're already familiar with the general flavor of List. (Of course, List is an interface and Vector is a concrete implementation.) List fixes several minor API deficiencies in Vector. Commonly used Vector operations, such as elementAt and setElementAt, have been given much shorter names. When you consider that these two operations are the List analog of brackets for arrays, it becomes apparent that shorter names are highly desirable. Consider the following assignment statement:

```
    a[i] = a[j].Times(a[k]);
```

The Vector equivalent is:

```
    v.setElementAt(v.elementAt(j).Times(v.elementAt(k)), i);
```

The List equivalent is:

```
    v.set(i, v.get(j).Times(v.get(k)));
```

You may already have noticed that the set method, which replaces the Vector method set-ElementAt, reverses the order of the arguments so that they match the corresponding array operation. Consider this assignment statement:

```
    beatle[5] = "Billy Preston";
```

The Vector equivalent is:

```
    beatle.setElementAt("Billy Preston", 5);
```

The List equivalent is:

```
beatle.set(5, "Billy Preston");
```

For consistency's sake, the add(int, Object) method, which replaces the method insertElementAt(Object, int), also reverses the order of the arguments.

The various range operations in Vector (indexOf, lastIndexOf(setSize) have been replaced by a single *range-view* operation (subList), which is far more powerful and consistent.

Collection Operations

The operations inherited from Collection all do about what you'd expect them to do, assuming that you're already familiar with them from Collection. If you're not familiar with them, now would be a good time to read the section Interfaces (page 470). The remove operation always removes the *first* occurrence of the specified element from the list. The add and addAll operations always append the new element(s) to the *end* of the list. Thus, the following idiom concatenates one list to another:

```
list1.addAll(list2);
```

Here's a nondestructive form of this idiom, which produces a third List consisting of the second list appended to the first:

```
List list3 = new ArrayList(list1);
list3.addAll(list2);
```

Note that the idiom, in its nondestructive form, takes advantage of ArrayList's standard Collection constructor.

Like the Set interface, List strengthens the requirements on the equals and hashCode methods so that two List objects can be compared for logical equality without regard to their implementation classes. Two List objects are equal if they contain the same elements in the same order.

Positional Access and Search Operations

The basic positional access operations (get, set, add, and remove) behave just like their longer-named counterparts in Vector (elementAt, setElementAt, insertElementAt, and removeElementAt), with one noteworthy exception. The set and the remove operations return the old value that is being overwritten or removed; the counterparts in Vector (setElementAt and removeElementAt) return nothing (void). The search operations indexOf and lastIndexOf behave exactly like the identically named operations in Vector.

The addAll(int, Collection) operation inserts all the elements of the specified Collection, starting at the specified position. The elements are inserted in the order they are returned by the specified Collection's *iterator*. This call is the positional access analog of Collection's addAll operation.

Here's a little function to swap two indexed values in a List. It should look familiar from Programming 101 (assuming you stayed awake):

```java
private static void swap(List a, int i, int j) {
    Object tmp = a.get(i);
    a.set(i, a.get(j));
    a.set(j, tmp);
}
```

Of course, there's one big difference. This is a *polymorphic* algorithm: It swaps two elements in *any* List, regardless of its implementation type. "Big deal," you say, "what's it good for?" Funny you should ask. Take a look at this:

```java
public static void shuffle(List list, Random rnd) {
    for (int i=list.size(); i>1; i--)
        swap(list, i-1, rnd.nextInt(i));
}
```

This algorithm, which is included in the Java 2 SDK's Collections class, randomly permutes the specified List, using the specified source of randomness. It's a bit subtle: It runs up the list from the bottom, repeatedly swapping a randomly selected element into the current position. Unlike most naive attempts at shuffling, it's *fair* (all permutations occur with equal likelihood, assuming an unbiased source of randomness) and *fast* (requiring exactly list.size()-1 iterations). The following short program uses this algorithm to print the words in its argument list in random order:

```java
import java.util.*;

public class Shuffle {
    public static void main(String args[]) {
        List l = new ArrayList();
        for (int i=0; i<args.length; i++)
            l.add(args[i]);
        Collections.shuffle(l, new Random());
        System.out.println(l);
    }
}
```

In fact, we can make this program even shorter and faster. The Arrays class has a static factory method, asList, that allows an array to be *viewed* as a List. This method does not copy the array; changes in the List write through to the array, and vice versa. The resulting List is not a general-purpose List implementation in that it doesn't implement the (optional) add and remove operations: Arrays are not resizable. Taking advantage of Arrays.asList and calling an alternative form of shuffle that uses a default source of randomness, you get the following tiny program, whose behavior is identical to that of the previous program:

```
import java.util.*;

public class Shuffle {
    public static void main(String args[]) {
        List l = Arrays.asList(args);
        Collections.shuffle(l);
        System.out.println(l);
    }
}
```

Iterators

As you'd expect, the Iterator returned by List's iterator operation returns the elements of the list in proper sequence. List also provides a richer iterator, called a ListIterator, that allows you to traverse the list in either direction, to modify the list during iteration, and to obtain the current position of the iterator. The ListIterator interface follows, including the three methods it inherits from Iterator:

```
public interface ListIterator extends Iterator {
    boolean hasNext();
    Object next();

    boolean hasPrevious();
    Object previous();

    int nextIndex();
    int previousIndex();

    void remove(); // Optional
    void set(Object o); // Optional
    void add(Object o); // Optional
}
```

The three methods that ListIterator inherits from Iterator (hasNext, next, and remove) are intended to do exactly the same thing in both interfaces. The hasPrevious and the previous operations are exact analogs of hasNext and next. The former operations refer to the element before the (implicit) cursor, whereas the latter refer to the element after the cursor. The previous operation moves the cursor backward, whereas next moves it forward.

Here's the standard idiom for iterating backward through a list:

```
for (ListIterator i = l.listIterator(l.size());
    l.hasPrevious(); ) {
    Foo f = (Foo) l.previous();
    ...
}
```

Note the argument to `listIterator` in the preceding idiom. The `List` interface has two forms of the `listIterator` method. The form with no arguments returns a `ListIterator` positioned at the beginning of the list; the form with an `int` argument returns a `ListIterator` positioned at the specified index. The index refers to the element that would be returned by an initial call to `next`. An initial call to `previous` would return the element whose index was `index-1`. In a list of length n, there are n+1 valid values for `index`, from 0 to n, inclusive.

Intuitively speaking, the cursor is always between two elements: the one that would be returned by a call to `previous` and the one that would be returned by a call to `next`. The n+1 valid `index` values correspond to the n+1 gaps between elements, from the gap before the first element to the gap after the last one. The following diagram shows the five possible cursor positions in a list containing four elements.

Figure 124 Five possible cursor positions in a list with four elements.

Calls to `next` and `previous` can be intermixed, but you have to be a bit careful. After a sequence of calls to `next`, the first call to `previous` returns the same element as the last call to `next`. Similarly, the first call to `next` after a sequence of calls to `previous` returns the same element as the last call to `previous`.

It should come as no surprise that the `nextIndex` method returns the index of the element that would be returned by a subsequent call to `next` and that `previousIndex` returns the index of the element that would be returned by a subsequent call to `previous`. These calls are typically used either to report the position where something was found or to record the position of the `ListIterator` so that another `ListIterator` with identical position can be created.

It should also come as no surprise that the number returned by `nextIndex` is always one greater than the number returned by `previousIndex`. This implies the behavior of the two boundary cases: A call to `previousIndex` when the cursor is before the initial element returns -1, and a call to nextIndex when the cursor is after the final element returns list.size(). To make all this concrete, here's a possible implementation of List.indexOf:

```
public int indexOf(Object o) {
    for (ListIterator i = listIterator(); i.hasNext(); ) {
        if (o==null ? i.next()==null : o.equals(i.next())) {
            return i.previousIndex();

    return -1; // Object not found **this line is online!**
}
```

Note that the indexOf method returns i.previousIndex(), although it is traversing the list in the forward direction. The reason is that i.nextIndex() would return the index of the element that we are about to examine, and we want to return the index of the element we just examined.

The Iterator interface provides the remove operation to remove from the Collection the last element returned by next. For ListIterator, this operation removes the last element returned by next or previous. The ListIterator interface provides two additional operations to modify the list: set and add. The set method overwrites the last element returned by next or previous with the specified element. The following polymorphic algorithm uses set to replace all occurrences of one specified value with another.

```
public void replace(List l, Object val, Object newVal) {
    for (ListIterator i = l.listIterator(); i.hasNext(); )
        if (val==null ? i.next()==null : val.equals(i.next()))
            i.set(newVal);
}
```

The only bit of trickiness in this example is the equality test between val and i.next. We have to special-case an old value of null in order to prevent a NullPointerException.

The add method inserts a new element into the list, immediately before the current cursor position. This method is illustrated in the following polymorphic algorithm to replace all occurrences of a specified value with the sequence of values contained in the specified list:

```
public static void replace(List l, Object val, List newVals) {
    for (ListIterator i = l.listIterator(); i.hasNext(); ) {
        if (val==null ? i.next()==null : val.equals(i.next())) {
            i.remove();
            for (Iterator j= newVals.iterator(); j.hasNext(); )
                i.add(j.next());
        }
    }
}
```

Range-View Operation

The range-view operation, subList(int fromIndex, int toIndex), returns a List *view* of the portion of this list whose indices range from fromIndex, inclusive, to toIndex, exclusive. This *half-open range* mirrors the typical for loop:

```
for (int i=fromIndex; i<toIndex; i++) {
    ...
}
```

As the term *view* implies, the returned List is backed by the List on which subList was called, so changes in the former List are reflected in the latter.

This method eliminates the need for explicit range operations (of the sort that commonly exist for arrays). Any operation that expects a List can be used as a range operation by passing a subList view instead of a whole List. For example, the following idiom removes a range of elements from a list:

```
list.subList(fromIndex, toIndex).clear();
```

Similar idioms may be constructed to search for an element in a range:

```
int i = list.subList(fromIndex, toIndex).indexOf(o);
int j = list.subList(fromIndex, toIndex).lastIndexOf(o);
```

Note that the preceding idioms return the index of the found element in the subList, not the index in the backing List.

Any polymorphic algorithm that operates on a List, such as the replace and shuffle examples, works with the List returned by subList.

Here's a polymorphic algorithm whose implementation uses subList to deal a hand from a deck. That is to say, it returns a new List (the "hand") containing the specified number of elements taken from the end of the specified List (the "deck"). The elements returned in the hand are removed from the deck:

```
public static List dealHand(List deck, int n) {
    int deckSize = deck.size();
    List handView = deck.subList(deckSize-n, deckSize);
    List hand = new ArrayList(handView);
    handView.clear();
    return hand;
}
```

Note that this algorithm removes the hand from the *end* of the deck. For many common List implementations, such as ArrayList, the performance of removing elements from the end of the list is substantially better than that of removing elements from the beginning.[1]

Although the subList operation is extremely powerful, some care must be exercised when using it. The semantics of the List returned by subList become undefined if elements are added to or removed from the backing List in any way other than via the returned List. Thus, it's highly recommended that you use the List returned by subList only as a transient object: to perform one or a sequence of range operations on the backing List. The longer you use the subList object, the greater the probability that you'll compromise it by modifying the backing List directly or through another subList object. Note that it is legal to modify a sublist of a sublist and to continue using the original sublist.

Algorithms

Most of the polymorphic algorithms in the Collections class apply specifically to List. Having all these algorithms at your disposal makes it very easy to manipulate lists. Here's a summary of these algorithms, which are described in more detail in the section Algorithms (page 515):

- sort(List): Sorts a List, using a merge sort algorithm, which provides a fast, *stable* sort. (A stable sort is one that does not reorder equal elements.)
- shuffle(List): Randomly permutes the elements in a List.
- reverse(List): Reverses the order of the elements in a List.
- fill(List, Object): Overwrites every element in a List with the specified value.
- copy(List dest, List src): Copies the source List into the destination List.
- binarySearch(List, Object): Searches for an element in an ordered List, using the binary search algorithm.

Map Interface

A Map is an object that maps keys to values. A map cannot contain duplicate keys: Each key can map to at most one value. The Map interface follows:

```
public interface Map {
    // Basic Operations
    Object put(Object key, Object value);
    Object get(Object key);
    Object remove(Object key);
```

---

[1] The literal-minded might say that this program deals from the bottom of the deck, but we prefer to think that the computer is holding the deck upside down.

```
boolean containsKey(Object key);
boolean containsValue(Object value);
int size();
boolean isEmpty();

// Bulk Operations
void putAll(Map t);
void clear();

// Collection Views
public Set keySet();
public Collection values();
public Set entrySet();

// Interface for entrySet elements
public interface Entry {
    Object getKey();
    Object getValue();
    Object setValue(Object value);
}
}
```

The Java 2 SDK contains two new general-purpose Map implementations. HashMap, which stores its entries in a hash table, is the better-performing implementation. TreeMap, which stores its entries in a red-black tree, guarantees the order of iteration. Also, Hashtable has been retrofitted to implement Map.

Comparison to Hashtable

If you've used Hashtable, you're already familiar with the general flavor of Map. (Of course, Map is an interface, whereas Hashtable is a concrete implementation.) Here are the major differences.

- Map provides Collection views instead of direct support for iteration via Enumeration objects. Collection views greatly enhance the expressiveness of the interface, as discussed later in this section.

- Map allows you to iterate over keys, values, or key-value pairs; Hashtable does not provide the third option.

- Map provides a safe way to remove entries in the midst of iteration; Hashtable does not.

Further, Map fixes a minor deficiency in the Hashtable interface. Hashtable has a method called contains, which returns true if the Hashtable contains a given *value*. Given its name, you'd expect this method to return true if the Hashtable contained a given *key*, as the key is the primary access mechanism for a Hashtable. The Map interface eliminates this source of confusion by renaming the method `containsValue`. Also, this improves the consistency of the interface: `containsValue` parallels `containsKey` nicely.

Basic Operations

The basic operations (`put`, `get`, `remove`, `containsKey`, `containsValue`, `size`, and `isEmpty`) behave exactly like their counterparts in `Hashtable`. Here's a simple program to generate a frequency table of the words found in its argument list. The frequency table maps each word to the number of times it occurs in the argument list:

```
import java.util.*;

public class Freq {
    private static final Integer ONE = new Integer(1);

    public static void main(String args[]) {
        Map m = new HashMap();

        // Initialize frequency table from command line
        for (int i=0; i<args.length; i++) {
            Integer freq = (Integer) m.get(args[i]);
            m.put(args[i], (freq==null ? ONE :
                            new Integer(freq.intValue() + 1)));
        }
        System.out.println(m.size() + " distinct words:");
        System.out.println(m);
    }
}
```

The only thing even slightly tricky about this program is the second argument of the `put` statement. That argument is a conditional expression that has the effect of setting the frequency to one if the word has never been seen before or one more than its current value if the word has already been seen. Try running this program with the command

```
java Freq if it is to be it is up to me to delegate
```

The program yields the following output:

```
8 distinct words:
{to=3, me=1, delegate=1, it=2, is=2, if=1, be=1, up=1}
```

Suppose that you'd prefer to see the frequency table in alphabetical order. All you have to do is change the implementation type of the `Map` from `HashMap` to `TreeMap`. Making this four-character change causes the program to generate the following output from the same command line:

```
8 distinct words:
{be=1, delegate=1, if=1, is=2, it=2, me=1, to=3, up=1}
```

Are interfaces cool, or what?

Like the Set and the List interfaces, Map strengthens the requirements on the equals and hashCode methods so that two Map objects can be compared for logical equality without regard to their implementation types. Two Map objects are equal if they represent the same key-value mappings.

By convention, all Map implementations provide constructors that take a Map object and initialize the new Map to contain all the key-value mappings in the specified Map. This standard Map constructor is entirely analogous to the standard collection constructor for Collection implementations. The caller can create a Map of a desired implementation type that initially contains all the mappings in another Map, regardless of the other Map's implementation type. For example, suppose that you have a Map named m. The following one-liner creates a new HashMap initially containing all the same key-value mappings as m:

```
Map copy = new HashMap(m);
```

Bulk Operations

The clear operation does exactly what you think it does: It removes all the mappings from the Map. The putAll operation is the Map analog of the Collection interface's addAll operation. In addition to its obvious use of dumping one Map into another, it has a second, more subtle use. Suppose that a Map is used to represent a collection of attribute-value pairs; the putAll operation, in combination with the standard Map constructor, provides a neat way to implement attribute map creation with default values. Here's a static factory method demonstrating this technique:

```
Map newAttributeMap(Map defaults, Map overrides) {
    Map result = new HashMap(defaults);
    result.putAll(overrides);
    return result;
}
```

Collection Views

The Collection view methods allow a Map to be viewed as a Collection in three ways:

- keySet: The Set of keys contained in the Map.
- values: The Collection of values contained in the Map. This Collection is not a Set, as multiple keys can map to the same value.
- entrySet: The Set of key-value pairs contained in the Map. The Map interface provides a small nested interface called Map.Entry, the type of the elements in this Set.

The Collection views provide the *only* means to iterate over a Map. Here's an example illustrating the standard idiom for iterating over the keys in a Map:

```
for (Iterator i=m.keySet().iterator(); i.hasNext(); ) {
    System.out.println(i.next());
}
```

The idiom for iterating over values is analogous. Here's the idiom for iterating over key-value pairs:

```
for (Iterator i=m.entrySet().iterator(); i.hasNext(); ) {
    Map.Entry e = (Map.Entry) i.next();
    System.out.println(e.getKey() + ": " + e.getValue());
}
```

At first, many people worry that these idioms might be slow because the Map has to create a new Collection object each time a Collection view operation is called. Rest easy: There's no reason that a Map can't always return the same object each time it is asked for a given Collection view. This is precisely what all the Java 2 SDK's Map implementations do.

With all three Collection views, calling an Iterator's remove operation removes the associated entry from the backing Map, assuming that the backing map supports element removal to begin with. With the entrySet view, it is also possible to change the value associated with a key, by calling a Map.Entry's setValue method during iteration, again assuming that the Map supports value modification to begin with. Note that these are the *only* safe ways to modify a Map during iteration; the behavior is unspecified if the underlying Map is modified in any other way while the iteration is in progress.

The Collection views support element removal in all its many forms: the remove, removeAll, retainAll, and clear operations, as well as the Iterator.remove operation. (Yet again, this assumes that the backing Map supports element removal.)

The Collection views do *not* support element addition under any circumstances. It would make no sense for the keySet and the values views, and it's unnecessary for the entrySet view, as the backing Map's put and putAll provide the same functionality.

Fancy Uses of Collection Views: Map Algebra

When applied to the Collection views, the bulk operations (containsAll, removeAll, and retainAll) are a surprisingly potent tool. Suppose that you want to know whether one Map is a submap of another, that is, whether the first Map contains all the key-value mappings in the second. The following idiom does the trick:

```
if (m1.entrySet().containsAll(m2.entrySet())) {
    ...
}
```

Along similar lines, suppose that you want to know whether two Map objects contain mappings for all the same keys:

```
if (m1.keySet().equals(m2.keySet())) {
    ...
}
```

Suppose that you have a map representing a collection of attribute-value pairs and two sets representing required attributes and permissible attributes. (The permissible attributes include the required attributes.) The following snippet determines whether the attribute map conforms to these constraints and prints a detailed error message if it doesn't:

```
boolean valid = true;
Set attributes = attributeMap.keySet();
if(!attributes.containsAll(requiredAttributes)) {
    Set missing = new HashSet(requiredAttributes);
    missing.removeAll(attributes);
    System.out.println("Missing attributes: " + missing);
    valid = false;
}

if (!permissibleAttributes.containsAll(attributes)) {
    illegal = new HashSet(attributes);
    illegal.removeAll(permissibleAttributes));
    System.out.println(Illegal attributes: " + illegal);
    valid = false;
}

if (valid) {
    System.out.println("OK");
}
```

Suppose that you want to know all the keys common to two Map objects:

```
Set commonKeys = new HashSet(a.keySet());
commonKeys.retainAll(b.keySet);
```

A similar idiom gets you the common values and the common key-value pairs. Extra care is needed if you get the common key-value pairs, as the elements of the resulting Set, which are Map.Entry objects, may become invalid if the Map is modified.

All the idioms presented thus far have been nondestructive; that is, they don't modify the backing Map. Here are a few that do. Suppose that you want to remove all the key-value pairs that one Map has in common with another:

```
m1.entrySet().removeAll(m2.entrySet());
```

Suppose that you want to remove from one Map all the keys that have mappings in another:

```
m1.keySet().removeAll(m2.keySet());
```

What happens when you start mixing keys and values in the same bulk operation? Suppose that you have a Map, managers, that maps each employee in a company to the employee's manager. We'll be deliberately vague about the types of the key and the value objects. It doesn't matter, so long as they're the same. Now suppose that you want to know who all the individual contributors, or nonmanagers, are. The following one-liner tells you exactly what you want to know:

```
Set individualContributors = new HashSet(managers.keySet());
individualContributors.removeAll(managers.values());
```

Suppose that you want to fire all the employees who report directly to a particular manager, Herbert:

```
Employee herbert = ... ;
managers.values().removeAll(Collections.singleton(herbert));
```

Note that this idiom makes use of Collections.singleton, a static factory method that returns an immutable Set with the single, specified element.

Once you've done this, you may have a bunch of employees whose managers no longer work for the company (if any of Herbert's direct reports were themselves managers). The following code tells you all the employees whose manager no longer works for the company:

```
Map m = new HashMap(managers);
m.values().removeAll(managers.keySet());
Set slackers = m.keySet();
```

This example is a bit tricky. First, it makes a temporary copy of the Map, and it removes from the temporary copy all entries whose (manager) value is a key in the original Map. Remember that the original Map has an entry for each employee. Thus, the remaining entries in the temporary Map comprise all the entries from the original Map whose (manager) values are no longer employees. The keys in the temporary copy, then, represent precisely the employees we're looking for.

There are many, many more idioms like the ones contained in this section, but it would be impractical and tedious to list them all. Once you get the hang of it, it's not that difficult to come up with the right one when you need it.

Multimaps

A *multimap* is like a map but can map each key to multiple values. The Collections Framework doesn't include an interface for multimaps, because they aren't used all that commonly. It's a fairly simple matter to use a Map whose values are List objects as a multimap. This technique is demonstrated in the next code example, which reads a dictionary containing one word (all lowercase) per line and prints out all the *permutation groups* that meet a size criterion. A *permutation group* is a bunch of words, all of which contain exactly the same letters but in a different order. The program takes two arguments on the command line: the name of the dictionary file and the minimum size of permutation group to print out. Permutation groups containing fewer words than the specified minimum are not printed.

There is a standard trick for finding permutation groups: For each word in the dictionary, alphabetize the letters in the word (that is, reorder the word's letters into alphabetical order) and put an entry into a multimap, mapping the alphabetized word to the original word. For example, the word "bad" causes an entry mapping "abd" into "bad" to be put into the multimap. A moment's reflection will show that all the words to which any given key maps form a permutation group. It's a simple matter to iterate over the keys in the multimap, printing out each permutation group that meets the size constraint.

The following program is a straightforward implementation of this technique. The only tricky part is the alphabetize method, which returns a string containing the same characters as its argument, in alphabetical order. This routine (which has nothing to do with the Collections Framework) implements a slick *bucket sort*. It assumes that the word being alphabetized consists entirely of lowercase alphabetic characters:

```
import java.util.*;
import java.io.*;

public class Perm {
    public static void main(String[] args) {
        int minGroupSize = Integer.parseInt(args[1]);

        // Read words from file and put into simulated multimap
        Map m = new HashMap();
        try {
            BufferedReader in =
                new BufferedReader(new FileReader(args[0]));
            String word;
            while((word = in.readLine()) != null) {
                String alpha = alphabetize(word);
```

```
                List l = (List) m.get(alpha);
                if (l==null)
                    m.put(alpha, l=new ArrayList());
                l.add(word);
            }
        } catch(IOException e) {
            System.err.println(e);
            System.exit(1);
        }

        // Print all permutation groups above size threshold
        for (Iterator i = m.values().iterator(); i.hasNext(); ) {
            List l = (List) i.next();
            if (l.size() >= minGroupSize)
                System.out.println(l.size() + ": " + l);
        }
    }

    private static String alphabetize(String s) {
        int count[] = new int[256];
        int len = s.length();
        StringBuffer result = new StringBuffer(len);
        for (int i=0; i<len; i++)
            count[s.charAt(i)]++;
        for (char c='a'; c<='z'; c++)
            for (int i=0; i<count[c]; i++)
                result.append(c);
        return result.toString();
    }
}
```

Running the program on an 80,000-word dictionary takes about 16 seconds on an aging UltraSparc 1. With a minimum permutation group size of eight, it produces the following output:

```
9: [estrin, inerts, insert, inters, niters, nitres, sinter,
    triens, trines]

8: [carets, cartes, caster, caters, crates, reacts, recast,
    traces]

9: [capers, crapes, escarp, pacers, parsec, recaps, scrape,
    secpar, spacer]

8: [ates, east, eats, etas, sate, seat, seta, teas]
```

```
12: [apers, apres, asper, pares, parse, pears, prase, presa,
    rapes, reaps, spare, spear]

 9: [anestri, antsier, nastier, ratines, retains, retinas,
    retsina, stainer, stearin]

10: [least, setal, slate, stale, steal, stela, taels, tales,
    teals, tesla]

 8: [arles, earls, lares, laser, lears, rales, reals, seral]

 8: [lapse, leaps, pales, peals, pleas, salep, sepal, spale]

 8: [aspers, parses, passer, prases, repass, spares, sparse,
    spears]

 8: [earings, erasing, gainers, reagins, regains, reginas,
    searing, seringa]

11: [alerts, alters, artels, estral, laster, ratels, salter,
    slater, staler, stelar, talers]

 9: [palest, palets, pastel, petals, plates, pleats, septal,
    staple, tepals]

 8: [enters, nester, renest, rentes, resent, tenser, ternes,
    treens]

 8: [peris, piers, pries, prise, ripes, speir, spier, spire]
```

Many of these words seem a bit bogus, but that's not the program's fault; they're in the dictionary file.

Object Ordering

A List l may be sorted as follows:

```
Collections.sort(l);
```

If the list consists of String elements, it will be sorted into alphabetical order. If it consists of Date elements, it will be sorted into chronological order. How does the Java programming language know how to do this? It's magic. Well, no. String and Date both implement the Comparable interface, which provides a *natural ordering* for a class, allowing objects of that class to be sorted automatically. The following table summarizes the Java 2 SDK classes that implement Comparable.

Table 62   Java 2 SDK Implementing `Comparable`

Class	Natural Ordering
`Byte`	Signed numerical
`Character`	Unsigned numerical
`Long`	Signed numerical
`Integer`	Signed numerical
`Short`	Signed numerical
`Double`	Signed numerical
`Float`	Signed numerical
`BigInteger`	Signed numerical
`BigDecimal`	Signed numerical
`File`	System-dependent lexicographic on path name
`String`	Lexicographic
`Date`	Chronological
`CollationKey`	Locale-specific lexicographic

If you try to sort a list whose elements do not implement `Comparable`, `Collections.sort(list)` will throw a `ClassCastException`. Similarly, if you try to sort a list whose elements cannot be compared *to one another*, `Collections.sort` will throw a `ClassCastException`. Elements that can be compared to one another are called *mutually comparable*. Although elements of different types can be mutually comparable, none of the SDK types listed here permit interclass comparison.

This is all you need to know about the `Comparable` interface if you just want to sort lists of comparable elements or to create sorted collections of them. The next section will be of interest to you if you want to implement your own `Comparable` type.

Writing Your Own Comparable Types

The `Comparable` interface consists of a single method:

```
public interface Comparable {
    public int compareTo(Object o);
}
```

The `compareTo` method compares the receiving object with the specified object and returns a negative integer, zero, or a positive integer as the receiving object is less than, equal to, or greater than the specified object. If the specified object cannot be compared to the receiving object, the method throws a ClassCastException.

The following class representing a person's name implements Comparable:

```java
import java.util.*;

public class Name implements Comparable {
    private String firstName, lastName;

    public Name(String firstName, String lastName) {
        if (firstName==null || lastName==null) {
            throw new NullPointerException();
        }
        this.firstName = firstName;
        this.lastName = lastName;
    }

    public String firstName()    {return firstName;}

    public String lastName()     {return lastName;}

    public boolean equals(Object o) {
        if (!(o instanceof Name))
            return false;
        Name n = (Name)o;
        return n.firstName.equals(firstName) &&
                n.lastName.equals(lastName);
    }

    public int hashCode() {
        return 31*firstName.hashCode() + lastName.hashCode();
    }

    public String toString() {
        return firstName + " " + lastName;
    }

    public int compareTo(Object o) {
        Name n = (Name)o;
        int lastCmp = lastName.compareTo(n.lastName);
        return (lastCmp!=0 ? lastCmp :
                firstName.compareTo(n.firstName));
    }
}
```

To keep the example short, the class is somewhat limited: It doesn't support middle names, it demands both a first and a last name, and it is not internationalized in any way. Nonetheless, it illustrates several important points.

- Name objects are *immutable*. All other things being equal, immutable types are the way to go, especially for objects that will be used as elements in Sets or as keys in Maps. These collections will break if you modify their elements or keys while they're in the collection.

- The constructor checks its arguments for null. This ensures that all Name objects are well formed, so that none of the other methods will ever throw a NullPointerException.

- The hashCode method is redefined. This is *essential* for any class that redefines the equals method. (Equal objects must have equal hash codes.)

- The equals method returns false if the specified object is null or of an inappropriate type. The compareTo method throws a runtime exception under these circumstances. Both of these behaviors are *required* by the general contracts of the respective methods.

- The toString method has been redefined to print the name in human-readable form. This is always a good idea, especially for objects that will be put into collections. The various collection types' toString methods depend on the toString methods of their elements, keys, and values.

Since this section is about element ordering, let's talk more about Name's compareTo method. It implements the standard name-ordering algorithm, where last names take precedence over first names. This is exactly what you want in a *natural ordering*. It would be confusing if the natural ordering were unnatural!

Take a look at how compareTo is implemented, because it's quite typical. First, you cast the Object argument to the appropriate type. This throws the appropriate exception (ClassCastException) if the argument's type is inappropriate. Then you compare the most significant part of the object (in this case, the last name). Often, you can just use the natural ordering of the part's type. In this case, the part is a String, and the natural (lexicographic) ordering is exactly what's called for. If the comparison results in anything other than zero, which represents equality, you're done: You just return the result. If the most significant parts are equal, you go on to compare the next-most-significant parts. In this case, there are only two parts: first name and last name. If there were more parts, you'd proceed in the obvious fashion, comparing parts until you found two that weren't equal or you were comparing the least-significant parts, at which point you'd return the result of the comparison.

Just to show that it all works, here's a little program that builds a list of names and sorts them:

```
import java.util.*;

class NameSort {
    public static void main(String args[]) {
        Name n[] = {
            new Name("John", "Lennon"),
            new Name("Karl", "Marx"),
            new Name("Groucho", "Marx"),
            new Name("Oscar", "Grouch")
        };
        List l = Arrays.asList(n);
        Collections.sort(l);
        System.out.println(l);
    }
}
```

If you run this program, here's what it prints:

```
[Oscar Grouch, John Lennon, Groucho Marx, Karl Marx]
```

There are four restrictions on the behavior of the compareTo method, which we won't go over now because they're fairly technical and boring and are better left in the API documentation. It's really important that all classes that implement Comparable obey these restrictions, so read the documentation for Comparable if you're writing a class that implements it. Attempting to sort a list of objects that violate these restrictions has undefined behavior. Technically speaking, these restrictions ensure that the natural ordering is a *total order* on the objects of a class that implements it; this is necessary to ensure that sorting is well defined.

Comparators

What if you want to sort some objects in an order other than their natural order? Or what if you want to sort some objects that don't implement Comparable? To do either of these things, you'll need to provide a Comparator, an object that encapsulates an ordering. Like the Comparable interface, the Comparator interface consists of a single method:

```
public interface Comparator {
    int compare(Object o1, Object o2);
}
```

The compare method compares its two arguments and returns a negative integer, zero, or a positive integer according to whether the first argument is less than, equal to, or greater than the second. If either of the arguments has an inappropriate type for the Comparator, the compare method throws a ClassCastException.

Much of what was said about Comparable applies to Comparator as well. Writing a compare method is nearly identical to writing a compareTo method, except that the former gets both objects passed in as arguments. The compare method has to obey the same four technical restrictions as Comparable's compareTo method, for the same reason: A Comparator must induce a *total order* on the objects it compares.

Suppose that you have a class called EmployeeRecord:

```
public class EmployeeRecord implements Comparable {
    public Name name();
    public int empNumber();
    public Date hireDate();
            ...
}
```

Let's assume that the natural ordering of EmployeeRecord objects is Name ordering (as defined in the previous example) on employee name. Unfortunately, the boss has asked us for a list of employees in order of seniority. This means that we have to do some work but not much. Here's a program that will produce the required list:

```
import java.util.*;

class EmpSort {
    static final Comparator SENIORITY_ORDER = new Comparator() {
        public int compare(Object o1, Object o2) {
            EmployeeRecord r1 = (EmployeeRecord) o1;
            EmployeeRecord r2 = (EmployeeRecord) o2;
            return r2.hireDate().compareTo(r1.hireDate());
        }
    };

    // Employee Database
    static final Collection employees = ... ;

    public static void main(String args[]) {
        List emp = new ArrayList(employees);
        Collections.sort(emp, SENIORITY_ORDER);
        System.out.println(emp);
    }
}
```

The Comparator in the program is reasonably straightforward. It casts its arguments to EmployeeRecord and relies on the natural ordering of Date applied to the hireDate accessor method. Note that the Comparator passes the hire date of its second argument to its first, rather than vice versa. The reason is that the employee who was hired most recently is least senior: Sorting in order of hire date would put the list in *reverse* seniority order. Another way to achieve the same effect would be to maintain the argument order but to negate the result of the comparison:

```
return -r1.hireDate().compareTo(r2.hireDate());
```

The two techniques are equally preferable. Use whichever looks better to you.

The Comparator in the preceding program works fine for sorting a List, but it does have one deficiency: It cannot be used to order a sorted collection, such as TreeSet, because it generates an ordering that is *not compatible with equals*. This means that this comparator equates objects that the equals method does not. In particular, any two employees who were hired on the same date will compare as equal. When you're sorting a List, this doesn't matter, but when you're using the Comparator to order a sorted collection, it's fatal. If you use this Comparator to insert multiple employees hired on the same date into a TreeSet, only the first one will be added to the set. The second will be seen as a duplicate element and will be ignored.

To fix this problem, simply tweak the Comparator so that it produces an ordering that *is compatible with equals*. In other words, tweak it so that the only elements that are seen as equal when using compare are those that are also seen as equal when compared using equals. The way to do this is to do a two-part comparison (as we did for Name), where the first part is the one that we're interested in (in this case, the hire date), and the second part is an attribute that uniquely identifies the object. In this case, the employee number is the obvious attribute. Here's the Comparator that results:

```
static final Comparator SENIORITY_ORDER = new Comparator() {
    public int compare(Object o1, Object o2) {
        EmployeeRecord r1 = (EmployeeRecord) o1;
        EmployeeRecord r2 = (EmployeeRecord) o2;
        int dateCmp = r2.hireDate().compareTo(r1.hireDate());
        if (dateCmp != 0) {
            return dateCmp;
        }

        return (r1.empNumber() < r2.empNumber() ? -1 :
                (r1.empNumber() == r2.empNumber() ? 0 : 1));
    }
};
```

One last note: You might be tempted to replace the final return statement in the Comparator with the simpler

```
return r1.empNumber() - r2.empNumber();
```

Don't do it unless you're *absolutely sure* that no one will ever have a negative employee number! This trick does not work in general, as the signed integer type is not big enough to represent the difference of two arbitrary signed integers. If i is a large positive integer and j is a large negative integer, i - j will overflow and will return a negative integer. The resulting Comparator violates one of the four technical restrictions that we keep talking about (transitivity) and produces horrible, subtle bugs. This is not a purely theoretical concern; people get burned by it.

SortedSet Interface

A SortedSet is a Set that maintains its elements in ascending order, sorted according to the elements' *natural order* or according to a Comparator provided at SortedSet creation time.[1] In addition to the normal Set operations, the Set interface provides operations for

- Range view: Performs arbitrary *range operations* on the sorted set.
- Endpoints: Returns the first or the last element in the sorted set.
- Comparator access: Returns the Comparator, if any, used to sort the set.

The SortedSet interface follows:

```
public interface SortedSet extends Set {
    // Range-view
    SortedSet subSet(Object fromElement, Object toElement);
    SortedSet headSet(Object toElement);
    SortedSet tailSet(Object fromElement);

    // Endpoints
    Object first();
    Object last();

    // Comparator access
    Comparator comparator();
}
```

Set Operations

The operations that SortedSet inherits from Set behave identically on sorted sets and normal sets, with two exceptions.

- The Iterator returned by the iterator operation traverses the sorted set in order.
- The array returned by toArray contains the sorted set's elements in order.

---

[1] Natural order and comparators are discussed in a previous section, Object Ordering (page 496).

Although the interface doesn't guarantee it, the `toString` method of the Java 2 SDK's Sorted-Set implementations returns a string containing all the elements of the sorted set, in order.

Standard Constructors

By convention, all `Collection` implementations provide a standard constructor that takes a `Collection`, and `SortedSet` implementations are no exception. This constructor creates a `SortedSet` object that orders its elements according to their natural order. In addition, `SortedSet` implementations provide, by convention, two other standard constructors.

- One takes a `Comparator` and returns a new (empty) `SortedSet` sorted according to the specified `Comparator`.
- One takes a `SortedSet` and returns a new `SortedSet` containing the same elements as the given `SortedSet`, *sorted according to the same* `Comparator` or using the elements' natural ordering, if the specified `SortedSet` did too. Note that the compile-time type of the argument determines whether this constructor is invoked in preference to the ordinary `Set` constructor and not the runtime type!

The first of these standard constructors is the normal way to create an empty `SortedSet` with an explicit `Comparator`. The second is similar in spirit to the standard `Collection` constructor: It creates a copy of a `SortedSet` with the same ordering but with a programmer-specified implementation type.

Range-View Operations

The range-view operations are somewhat analogous to those provided by the `List` interface, but there is one big difference. Range views of a sorted set remain valid even if the backing sorted set is modified directly. This is feasible because the endpoints of a range view of a sorted set are absolute points in the element space rather than specific elements in the backing collection, as is the case for lists. A range view of a sorted set is really just a window onto whatever portion of the set lies in the designated part of the element space. Changes to the range view write back to the backing sorted set, *and vice versa*. Thus, it's okay to use range views on sorted sets for long periods of time, unlike range views on lists.

Sorted sets provide three range-view operations. The first, `subSet`, takes two endpoints, like `subList`. Rather than indices, the endpoints are objects and must be comparable to the elements in the sorted set, using the set's `Comparator` or the natural ordering of its elements, whichever the set uses to order itself. Like `subList`, the range is *half open*, including its low endpoint but excluding the high one.

Thus, the following one line of code tells you how many words between "doorbell" and "pickle," including "doorbell" but excluding "pickle," are contained in a `SortedSet` of strings called `dictionary`:

```
int count = ss.subSet("doorbell", "pickle").size();
```

Similarly, the following one-liner removes all the elements beginning with the letter "f":

```
dictionary.subSet("f", "g").clear();
```

A similar trick can be used to print a table telling you how many words begin with each letter:

```
for (char ch='a'; ch<='z'; ch++) {
    String from = new String(new char[] {ch});
    String to = new String(new char[] {(char)(ch+1)});
    System.out.println(from + ": " +
                    dictionary.subSet(from, to).size());
}
```

Suppose that you want to view a *closed interval*, which contains both its endpoints instead of an open interval. If the element type allows for the calculation of the successor of a given value in the element space, merely request the subSet from lowEndpoint to successor(highEndpoint). Although it isn't entirely obvious, the successor of a string s in String's natural ordering is s+"\0" (that is, s with a null character appended).

Thus, the following one-liner tells you how many words between "doorbell" and "pickle," including "doorbell" *and* "pickle," are contained in the dictionary:

```
int count = ss.subSet("doorbell", "pickle\0").size();
```

A similar technique can be used to view an *open interval*, which contains neither endpoint. The open-interval view from lowEndpoint to highEndpoint is the half-open interval from successor(lowEndpoint) to highEndpoint. To calculate the number of words between "doorbell" and "pickle," excluding both:

```
int count = ss.subSet("doorbell\0", "pickle").size();
```

The SortedSet interface contains two more range-view operations, headSet and tailSet, both of which take a single Object argument. The former returns a view of the initial portion of the backing SortedSet, up to but not including the specified object. The latter returns a view of the final portion of the backing SortedSet, beginning with the specified object and continuing to the end of the backing SortedSet. Thus, the following code allows you to view the dictionary as two disjoint "volumes" (a–m and n–z):

```
SortedSet volume1 = dictionary.headSet("n");
SortedSet volume2 = dictionary.tailSet("n");
```

Endpoint Operations

The SortedSet interface contains operations to return the first and the last elements in the sorted set, called (not surprisingly) first and last. In addition to their obvious uses, last allows a workaround for a deficiency in the SortedSet interface. One thing you'd like to do with a SortedSet is to go into the interior of the set and to iterate forward or backward. It's easy enough to go forward from the interior: Just get a tailSet and iterate over it. Unfortunately, there's no easy way to go backward.

The following idiom obtains in a sorted set the first element that is less than a specified object o in the element space:

```
Object predecessor = ss.headSet(o).last();
```

This is a fine way to go one element backward from a point in the interior of a sorted set. It could be applied repeatedly to iterate backward, but this is very inefficient, requiring a lookup for each element returned.

Comparator Accessor

The SortedSet interface contains an accessor method, called comparator, that returns the Comparator used to sort the set or null if the set is sorted according to the *natural order* of its elements. This method is provided so that sorted sets can be copied into new sorted sets with the same ordering. This method is used by the standard SortedSet constructor, described previously.

SortedMap Interface

A SortedMap is a Map that maintains its entries in ascending order, sorted according to the keys' *natural order*, or according to a Comparator provided at SortedMap creation time. Natural order and Comparators are discussed in the section Object Ordering (page 496). The Map interface provides operations for the normal Map operations and for

- **Range view:** Performs arbitrary *range operations* on the sorted map
- **Endpoints:** Returns the first or the last key in the sorted map
- **Comparator access:** Returns the Comparator, if any, used to sort the map

```
public interface SortedMap extends Map {
    Comparator comparator();
    SortedMap subMap(Object fromKey, Object toKey);
    SortedMap headMap(Object toKey);
```

```
        SortedMap tailMap(Object fromKey);
        Object first();
        Object last();
    }
```

This interface is the Map analog of SortedSet.

Map Operations

The operations that SortedMap inherits from Map behave identically on sorted maps and normal maps, with two exceptions.

- The Iterator returned by the iterator operation on any of the sorted map's Collection views traverse the collections in order.
- The arrays returned by the Collection views' toArray operations contain the keys, values, or entries in order.

Although it isn't guaranteed by the interface, the toString method of the Collection views in all the Java 2 Platform's SortedMap implementations returns a string containing all the elements of the view, in order.

Standard Constructors

By convention, all Map implementations provide a standard constructor that takes a Map, and SortedMap implementations are no exception. This constructor creates a SortedMap object that orders its entries according to their keys' natural order. Additionally, SortedMap implementations, by convention, provide two other standard constructors.

- One takes a Comparator and returns a new (empty) SortedMap sorted according to the specified Comparator.
- One takes a SortedMap and returns a new SortedMap containing the same mappings as the given SortedMap, *sorted according to the same* Comparator or using the elements' natural ordering, if the specified SortedMap did too. Note that it is the compile-time type of the argument, not its runtime type, that determines whether this constructor is invoked in preference to the ordinary Map constructor!

The first of these standard constructors is the normal way to create an empty SortedMap with an explicit Comparator. The second is similar in spirit to the standard Map constructor, creating a copy of a SortedMap with the same ordering but with a programmer-specified implementation type.

Comparison to SortedSet

Because this interface is a precise Map analog of SortedSet, all the idioms and code examples in the section Object Ordering (page 496) apply to SortedSet, with only trivial modifications.

Implementations

Implementations are the data objects used to store collections, which implement the *core collection interfaces* described in the section <u>Interfaces</u> (page 470). This section describes three kinds of implementations: general-purpose implementations, the public classes that provide the primary implementations of the core collection interfaces; wrapper implementations, used in combination with other types of implementations (often the general-purpose implementations) to provide added functionality; and convenience implementations, mini-implementations typically made available via *static factory methods*, which provide convenient, efficient alternatives to the general-purpose implementations for special collections (such as *singleton* sets).

Additionally, you can build your own implementations, based on the Java 2 SDK's *abstract implementations*. This topic is described in the section <u>Custom Implementations</u> (page 520). An advanced topic, it's not particularly difficult, but relatively few people will need to do it.

General-Purpose Implementations

The general-purpose implementations are summarized in the following table. The table highlights their regular naming pattern: Names are all of the form `Implementation Interface`, where `Interface` is the *core collection interface* implemented by the class, and `Implementation` signifies the data structure underlying the implementation.

Table 63　　Naming Patterns of the General-Purpose Implementations

Implementations					
		Hash Table	**Resizable Array**	**Balanced Tree**	**Linked List**
Interfaces	`Set`	HashSet		TreeSet	
	`List`		ArrayList		LinkedList
	`Map`	HashMap		TreeMap	

Java 2 Platform v 1.2 and v 1.3 provide two implementations of each interface, with the exception of `Collection`, which has no direct implementations but serves as a least-common denominator for the other collection interfaces. In each case, one implementation is clearly the primary implementation: the one to use, all other things being equal. The primary implementations are `HashSet`, `ArrayList`, and `HashMap`. Note that the `SortedSet` and the

`SortedMap` interfaces do not have rows in the table. Each of those interfaces has one implementation (`TreeSet` and `TreeMap`) and is listed in the `Set` and the `Map` rows.

The implementations have not only consistent names but also consistent behavior, implementing all the *optional operations* contained in their interfaces. All permit `null` elements, keys, and values. Each one is not synchronized. All have *fail-fast iterators*, which detect illegal concurrent modification during iteration and fail quickly and cleanly rather than risking arbitrary, nondeterministic behavior at an undetermined time in the future. All are `Serializable`, and all support a public `clone` method.

The fact that the new implementations are unsynchronized represents a break with the past: `Vector` and `Hashtable` were synchronized in the Java 2 SDK prior to version 1.2. The new approach was taken because collections are frequently used when the synchronization is of no benefit. Such uses include single-threaded use, read-only use, and use as part of a larger data object that does its own synchronization. In general, it is good API design practice not to make users pay for a feature they don't use. Further, unnecessary synchronization can result in deadlock under certain circumstances.

If you need a synchronized collection, the *synchronization wrappers*, described in the section <u>Wrapper Implementations</u> (page 511), allow *any* collection to be transformed into a synchronized collection. Thus, synchronization is optional for the new collection implementations, whereas it was mandatory for the old.

As a rule of thumb, you should be thinking about the interfaces, not the implementations. That is why there are no programming examples in this section. For the most part, the choice of implementation affects only performance. The preferred style, as mentioned in the section <u>Interfaces</u> (page 470), is to choose an implementation when a collection is created and to immediately assign the new collection to a variable of the corresponding interface type or to pass the collection to a method expecting an argument of the interface type. In this way, the program does not become dependent on any added methods in a given implementation, leaving the programmer free to change implementations at the drop of a hat, if performance concerns so warrant.

The general-purpose implementations are briefly discussed here. The performance of the implementations is described with such words as *constant, log, linear, n log(n)*, and *quadratic*. These words refer to the *asymptotic upper bound* on the *time complexity* of performing the operation. All this is quite a mouthful, and it doesn't matter much if you don't know what it means. If you're interested, refer to any good algorithms textbook. One thing to keep in mind is that this sort of performance metric has its limitations. Sometimes, the nominally slower implementation may be faster for the collection size that you're using. When in doubt, measure the performance.

Set

The two general-purpose Set implementations are HashSet and TreeSet. It's very straight-forward to decide which of these two to use. HashSet is much faster (constant time versus log time for most operations) but offers no ordering guarantees. If you need to use the operations in the SortedSet or if in-order iteration is important to you, use TreeSet. Otherwise, use HashSet. It's a fair bet that you'll end up using HashSet most of the time.

One thing worth keeping in mind about HashSet is that iteration is linear in the sum of the number of entries and the number of buckets (the *capacity*). Thus, it's important to choose an appropriate initial capacity if iteration performance is important. Choosing a capacity that's too high can waste both space and time. The default initial capacity is 101, and that's often more than you need. The initial capacity may be specified by using the int constructor. The following line of code allocates a HashSet whose initial capacity is 17:

```
Set s= new HashSet(17);
```

HashSets have one other tuning parameter, called the *load factor*. If you care deeply about the space consumption of your HashSet, read the HashSet documentation[1] for more information. Otherwise, just live with the default. If you accept the default load factor but want to specify an initial capacity, pick a number that's about twice the size that you expect the Set to grow to. If your guess is way off, it may have to grow, or you may waste a bit of space, but either way, it's no big problem. If you know a prime number of about the right size, use it. If not, use an odd number. Or use an even number. It doesn't really matter much; these things might make the HashSet perform a wee bit better, but nothing to write home about.

TreeSet has no tuning parameters. With the exception of clone, neither HashSet nor TreeSet has any operations other than those required by their respective interfaces (Set and TreeSet).

List

The two general-purpose List implementations are ArrayList and LinkedList. Most of the time, you'll probably use ArrayList. It offers constant time positional access and is just plain fast, because it does not have to allocate a node object for each element in the List, and it can take advantage of the native method System.arraycopy when it has to move multiple elements at once. Think of ArrayList as Vector without the synchronization overhead.

If you frequently add elements to the beginning of the List or iterate over the List to delete elements from its interior, you should consider using LinkedList. These operations are constant time in a LinkedList but linear time in an ArrayList. But you pay a big price! Posi-

---

[1]   The API documentation for HashSet is available on the CD that accompanies this book and online here:
      http://java.sun.com/j2se/1.3/docs/api/java/util/HashSet.html.

tional access is linear time in a `LinkedList` and constant time in an `ArrayList`. Furthermore, the constant factor for `LinkedList` is much worse. If you think that you want to use a `LinkedList`, measure the performance with both `LinkedList` and `ArrayList`. You may be surprised.

`ArrayList` has one tuning parameter, the *initial capacity*. It refers to the number of elements the `ArrayList` can hold before it has to grow. There's not much to say about it. The only `ArrayList` operations that are not required by `List` are `ensureCapacity` and `trimToSize`, which alter the excess capacity, and `clone`.

`LinkedList` has no tuning parameters and seven optional operations, one of which is `clone`. The other six are `addFirst`, `getFirst`, `removeFirst`, `addLast`, `getLast`, and `removeLast`. They make it a bit more convenient to use a `LinkedList` as a queue or as a double-ended queue (*dequeue*), but they also prevent you from easily switching representations when you discover that `ArrayList` is faster.

If you need synchronization, a `Vector` will be slightly faster than an `ArrayList` synchronized with `Collections.synchronizedList`. But `Vector` has loads of legacy operations, so be extra careful to always manipulate the `Vector` with the `List` interface, or you'll be stuck with it for life.

If your `List` is fixed in size—that is, you'll never use `remove`, `add`, or any of the bulk operations other than `containsAll`—you have a third option that's definitely worth considering. See `Arrays.asList` in the section <u>Convenience Implementations</u> (page 514) for more information.

Map

The two general-purpose `Map` implementations are `HashMap` and `TreeMap`. The situation for `Map` is *exactly* analogous to `Set`. If you need `SortedMap` operations or in-order `Collection` view iteration, go for `TreeMap`; otherwise, go for `HashMap`. Everything else in the section <u>Set</u> (page 510) also applies to `Map`.

Completeness requires that we mention `Hashtable`. As with `Vector` and `ArrayList`, if you need synchronization, a `Hashtable` will be slightly faster than a `HashMap` synchronized with `Collections.synchronizedMap`. Again, `Hashtable` has loads of legacy operations, so be extra careful always to manipulate it with the `Map` interface, or you'll be stuck with it for life.

Wrapper Implementations

Wrapper implementations delegate all their real work to a specified collection but add extra functionality on top of what this collection offers. For *design patterns* fans, this is an example of the *decorator* pattern. Although it may seem a bit exotic, it's really pretty straightforward.

These implementations are *anonymous*: Rather than providing a public class, the Java 2 SDK provides a *static factory method*. All these implementations are found in the `Collec-tions` API, which consists solely of static methods.

Synchronization Wrappers

The synchronization wrappers add automatic synchronization (thread safety) to an arbitrary collection. Each of the six core collection interfaces has one static factory method:

```
public static Collection synchronizedCollection(Collection c);
public static Set synchronizedSet(Set s);
public static List synchronizedList(List list);
public static Map synchronizedMap(Map m);
public static SortedSet synchronizedSortedSet(SortedSet s);
public static SortedMap synchronizedSortedMap(SortedMap m);
```

Each of these methods returns a synchronized (thread-safe) `Collection` backed by the specified collection. In order to guarantee serial access, *all* access to the backing collection must be accomplished through the returned collection. The easy way to guarantee this is not to keep a reference to the backing collection. Creating the synchronized collection like this does the trick:

```
List list = Collections.synchronizedList(new ArrayList());
```

A collection created in this fashion is every bit as thread-safe as a normally synchronized collection, such as a `Vector`.

In the face of concurrent access, it is imperative that the user manually synchronize on the returned collection when iterating over it. The reason is that iteration is accomplished via multiple calls into the collection, which must be composed into a single atomic operation. The idiom to iterate over a wrapper-synchronized collection is:

```
Collection c =
        Collections.synchronizedCollection(myCollection);
synchronized(c) {
    Iterator i = c.iterator(); // Must be in synchronized
                               //  block!
    while (i.hasNext()) {
        foo(i.next());
    }
}
```

Note that failure to follow this advice may result in nondeterministic behavior.

The idiom for iterating over a `Collection` view of a synchronized `Map` is similar; however, it is imperative that the user manually synchronize on the synchronized `Map` when iterating over any of its `Collection` views rather than synchronizing on the `Collection` view itself.

```
Map m = Collections.synchronizedMap(new HashMap());
    ...
Set s = m.keySet();  // Needn't be in synchronized block
    ...
synchronized(m) {  // Synchronizing on m, not s!
    Iterator i = s.iterator(); // Must be in synchronized block
    while (i.hasNext()) {
            foo(i.next());
    }
}
```

One minor downside of using wrapper implementations is that you do not have the ability to execute any noninterface operations of a wrapped implementation. So, for instance, in the preceding `List` example, one cannot call `ArrayList`'s `ensureCapacity` operation on the wrapped `ArrayList`.

Unmodifiable Wrappers

The unmodifiable wrappers are conceptually similar to the synchronization wrappers but simpler. Rather than adding functionality to the wrapped collection, they take it away. In particular, they take away the ability to modify the collection, by intercepting all the operations that would modify the collection and throwing an `UnsupportedOperationException`. The unmodifiable wrappers have two main uses:

- To make a collection immutable once it has been built. In this case, it's good practice not to maintain a reference to the backing collection. This absolutely guarantees immutability.
- To allow "second-class citizens" read-only access to your data structures. You keep a reference to the backing collection but hand out a reference to the wrapper. In this way, the second-class citizens can look but not touch, while you maintain full access.

Like the synchronization wrappers, each of the six core collection interfaces has one static factory method.

```
public static Collection unmodifiableCollection(Collection c);
public static Set unmodifiableSet(Set s);
public static List unmodifiableList(List list);
public static Map unmodifiableMap(Map m);
public static SortedSet unmodifiableSortedSet(SortedSet s);
public static SortedMap unmodifiableSortedMap(SortedMap m);
```

Convenience Implementations

This section describes several mini-implementations that can be more convenient and more efficient than the general-purpose implementations when you don't need their full power. All the implementations in this section are made available via static factory methods or exported constants rather than public classes.

List View of an Array

The Arrays.asList method returns a List view of its array argument. Changes to the List write through to the array and vice versa. The size of the collection is that of the array and cannot be changed. If the add or the remove method is called on the List, an Unsupported-OperationException will result.

The normal use of this implementation is as a bridge between array-based and collection-based APIs. It allows you to pass an array to a method expecting a Collection or a List. However, this implementation also has another use. If you need a fixed-size List, it's more efficient than any general-purpose List implementation. Here's the idiom:

```
List l = Arrays.asList(new Object[size]);
```

Note that a reference to the backing array is not retained.

Immutable Multiple-Copy List

Occasionally, you'll need an immutable List consisting of multiple copies of the same element. The Collections.nCopies method returns such a List. This implementation has two main uses. The first is to initialize a newly created List. For example, suppose that you want an ArrayList initially consisting of 1,000 null elements. The following incantation does the trick:

```
List l = new ArrayList(Collections.nCopies(1000, null));
```

Of course, the initial value of each element needn't be null. The second main use is to grow an existing List. For example, suppose that you want to add 69 copies of the string fruit bat to the end of a List. It's not clear why you'd want to do such a thing, but let's just suppose you did. Here's how you'd do it:

```
lovablePets.addAll(Collections.nCopies(69, "fruit bat"));
```

By using the form of addAll that takes both an index and a Collection, you can add the new elements to the middle of a List instead of at the end.

Immutable Singleton Set

Sometimes, you'll need an immutable *singleton* Set, which consists of a single specified element. The Collections.singleton method returns such a Set. One use of this implementation is to remove all occurrences of a specified element from a Collection:

```
c.removeAll(Collections.singleton(e));
```

A related idiom removes from a Map all elements that map to a specified value. For example, suppose that you have a Map, profession, that maps people to their line of work. Suppose that you want to eliminate all the lawyers. This one-liner will do the deed:

```
profession.values().removeAll(Collections.singleton(LAWYER));
```

One more use of this implementation is to provide a single input value to a method that is written to accept a Collection of values.

Empty Set and Empty List Constants

The Collections class provides two constants, representing the empty Set and the empty List, Collections.EMPTY_SET and Collections.EMPTY_LIST. The main use of these constants is as input to methods that take a Collection of values, when you don't want to provide any values at all.

Algorithms

The *polymorphic algorithms* described in this section are pieces of reusable functionality provided by the Java 2 SDK. All of them come from the Collections class, and all take the form of static methods whose first argument is the collection on which the operation is to be performed. The great majority of the algorithms provided by the Java platform operate on List objects, but a couple of them (min and max) operate on arbitrary Collection objects. This section describes the following algorithms:

- Sorting (page 516)
- Shuffling (page 518)
- Routine Data Manipulation (page 519)
- Searching (page 519)
- Finding Extreme Values (page 519)

Sorting

The sort algorithm reorders a List so that its elements are in ascending order according to an ordering relation. Two forms of the operation are provided. The simple form takes a List and sorts it according to its elements' *natural ordering*. If you're unfamiliar with the concept of natural ordering, read the section <u>Object Ordering</u> (page 496).

The sort operation uses a slightly optimized *merge sort* algorithm. This algorithm is

- **Fast:** This algorithm is guaranteed to run in n log(n) time and runs substantially faster on nearly sorted lists. Empirical studies showed it to be as fast as a highly optimized quicksort. Quicksort is generally regarded to be faster than merge sort but isn't *stable* and doesn't *guarantee* n log(n) performance.

- **Stable:** That is to say, it doesn't reorder equal elements. This is important if you sort the same list repeatedly on different attributes. If a user of a mail program sorts the inbox by mailing date and then sorts it by sender, the user naturally expects that the now contiguous list of messages from a given sender will (still) be sorted by mailing date. This is guaranteed only if the second sort was stable.

Here's a trivial program that prints out its arguments in lexicographic (alphabetical) order:

```
import java.util.*;

public class Sort {
    public static void main(String args[]) {
        List l = Arrays.asList(args);
        Collections.sort(l);
        System.out.println(l);
    }
}
```

Let's run the program:

```
java Sort i walk the line
```

The following output is produced:

```
[i, line, the, walk]
```

The program was included only to show you that algorithms really are as easy to use as they appear to be.

The second form of sort takes a Comparator in addition to a List and sorts the elements with the Comparator. Suppose that you wanted to print out the permutation groups from our earlier example in reverse order of size, largest permutation group first. The following example shows you how to achieve this with the help of the second form of the sort method.

Recall that the permutation groups are stored as values in a Map, in the form of List objects. The revised printing code iterates through the Map's values view, putting every List that passes the minimum-size test into a List of Lists. Then the code sorts this List, using a Comparator that expects List objects, and implements reverse-size ordering. Finally, the code iterates through the sorted List, printing its elements (the permutation groups). The following code replaces the printing code at the end of Perm's main method:

```
        // Make a List of permutation groups above size threshold
    List winners = new ArrayList();
    for (Iterator i = m.values().iterator(); i.hasNext(); ) {
        List l = (List) i.next();
        if (l.size() >= minGroupSize)
            winners.add(l);
    }

        // Sort permutation groups according to size
    Collections.sort(winners, new Comparator() {
        public int compare(Object o1, Object o2) {
            return ((List)o2).size() - ((List)o1).size();
        }
    });

        // Print permutation groups
    for (Iterator i=winners.iterator(); i.hasNext(); ) {
        List l = (List) i.next();
        System.out.println(l.size() + ": " + l);
    }
}
```

Running the program on the same dictionary in the section Map Interface (page 487), with the same minimum permutation group size (eight), produces the following output:

```
12: [apers, apres, asper, pares, parse, pears, prase, presa,
     rapes, reaps, spare, spear]

11: [alerts, alters, artels, estral, laster, ratels, salter,
     slater, staler, stelar, talers]

10: [least, setal, slate, stale, steal, stela, taels, tales,
     teals, tesla]

 9: [estrin, inerts, insert, inters, niters, nitres, sinter,
     triens, trines]
```

9: [capers, crapes, escarp, pacers, parsec, recaps, scrape,
   secpar, spacer]

9: [anestri, antsier, nastier, ratines, retains, retinas,
   retsina, stainer, stearin]

9: [palest, palets, pastel, petals, plates, pleats, septal,
   staple, tepals]

8: [carets, cartes, caster, caters, crates, reacts, recast,
   traces]

8: [ates, east, eats, etas, sate, seat, seta, teas]

8: [arles, earls, lares, laser, lears, rales, reals, seral]

8: [lapse, leaps, pales, peals, pleas, salep, sepal, spale]

8: [aspers, parses, passer, prases, repass, spares, sparse,
   spears]

8: [earings, erasing, gainers, reagins, regains, reginas,
   searing, seringa]

8: [enters, nester, renest, rentes, resent, tenser, ternes,
   treens]

8: [peris, piers, pries, prise, ripes, speir, spier, spire]

Shuffling

The shuffle algorithm does the opposite of what sort does, destroying any trace of order that may have been present in a List. That is to say, this algorithm reorders the List, based on input from a source of randomness, such that all possible permutations occur with equal likelihood, assuming a fair source of randomness. This algorithm is useful in implementing games of chance. For example, it could be used to shuffle a List of Card objects representing a deck. Also, it's useful for generating test cases.

This operation has two forms. The first takes a List and uses a default source of randomness. The second requires the caller to provide a Random object to use as a source of randomness. The code for this algorithm is used as an example in the section List Interface (page 479).

Routine Data Manipulation

The Collections class provides three algorithms for doing routine data manipulation on List objects. All these algorithms are pretty straightforward.

- reverse: Reverses the order of the elements in a List.
- fill: Overwrites every element in a List with the specified value. This operation is useful for reinitializing a List.
- copy: Takes two arguments—a destination List and a source List—and copies the elements of the source into the destination, overwriting its contents. The destination List must be at least as long as the source. If it is longer, the remaining elements in the destination List are unaffected.

Searching

The binary search algorithm searches for a specified element in a sorted List. This algorithm has two forms. The first takes a List and an element to search for (the "search key"). This form assumes that the List is sorted into ascending order according to the natural ordering of its elements. The second form of the call takes a Comparator in addition to the List and the search key and assumes that the List is sorted into ascending order according to the specified Comparator. The sort algorithm can be used to sort the List prior to calling binarySearch.

The return value is the same for both forms. If the List contains the search key, its index is returned. If not, the return value is (-(insertion point) - 1), where the *insertion point* is the point at which the value would be inserted into the List: the index of the first element greater than the value or list.size() if all elements in the List are less than the specified value. This admittedly ugly formula guarantees that the return value will be >= 0 if and only if the search key is found. It's basically a hack to combine a Boolean (found) and an integer (index) into a single int return value.

The following idiom, usable with both forms of the binarySearch operation, looks for the specified search key and inserts it at the appropriate position if it's not already present:

```
int pos = Collections.binarySearch(l, key);
if (pos < 0) {
    l.add(-pos-1);
}
```

Finding Extreme Values

The min and the max algorithms return, respectively, the minimum and maximum element contained in a specified Collection. Both of these operations come in two forms. The simple form takes only a `Collection` and returns the minimum (or maximum) element according to the elements' natural ordering. The second form takes a `Comparator` in addition to the `Collection` and returns the minimum (or maximum) element according to the specified `Comparator`.

These are the only algorithm the Java platform provides that work on arbitrary `Collection` objects, as opposed to `List` objects. Like the `fill` algorithm, these algorithms are quite straightforward to implement and are included in the Java platform solely as a convenience to programmers.

Custom Implementations

Many programmers will never need to implement their own collections classes. You can go pretty far using the implementations described in the previous sections of this appendix. Someday, however, you might want to write your own implementation of a core collection interface.

Reasons to Write Your Own Implementation

The following list of kinds of collections you might implement is not intended to be exhaustive.

- **Persistent:** All of the built-in collection implementations reside in main memory and vanish when the VM exits. If you want a collection that will still be present the next time the VM starts, you can implement it by building a veneer over an external database. Such a collection might conceivably be concurrently accessible by multiple VMs, because it resides outside the VM.

- **Application specific:** This is a very broad category. One example is an unmodifiable `Map` containing real-time telemetry data. The keys might represent locations, and the values could be read from sensors at these locations in response to the `get` operation.

- **Highly concurrent:** The built-in collections are not designed to support high concurrency. The synchronization wrappers (and the legacy implementations) lock the *entire* collection every time it's accessed. Suppose that you're building a server and need a `Map` implementation that can be accessed by many threads concurrently. It is reasonably straightforward to build a hash table that locks each bucket separately, allowing multiple threads to access the table concurrently, assuming that they're accessing keys that hash to different buckets.

- **High performance, special purpose:** Many data structures take advantage of restricted usage to offer better performance than is possible with general-purpose implementations. For example, consider a `Set` whose elements are restricted to a small, fixed universe. Such a Set can be represented as a *bit-vector*, which offers blinding fast performance as well as low memory usage. Another example concerns a List containing long runs of identical element values. Such lists, which occur frequently in text processing, can be *run-length encoded;* runs can be represented as a single object containing the repeated element and the number of consecutive repetitions. This example is interesting because it trades off two aspects of performance: It requires far less space but more time than an ArrayList.

- **High performance, general purpose:** The engineers who designed the Collections Framework tried to provide the best general-purpose implementations for each interface, but many, many data structures could have been used, and new ones are invented every day. Maybe you can come up with something faster!

- **Enhanced functionality:** Suppose that you need a Map or a Set implementation that offers constant time access and insertion-order iteration. This combination can be achieved with a hash table, all of whose elements are further joined, in insertion order, into a doubly linked list. Alternatively, suppose that you need an efficient *bag* implementation (also known as a *multiset*): a Collection that offers constant time access while allowing duplicate elements. It's reasonably straightforward to implement such a collection atop a HashMap.

- **Convenience:** You may want additional convenience implementations beyond those offered by the Java platform. For instance, you may have a frequent need for immutable Map objects representing a single key-value mapping or List objects representing a contiguous range of Integers.

- **Adapter:** Suppose that you are using a legacy API that has its own ad hoc collections API. You can write an *adapter* implementation that permits these collections to operate in the Java Collections Framework. An adapter implementation is a thin veneer that wraps objects of one type and makes them behave like objects of another type, by translating operations on the latter type into operations on the former.

How to Write a Custom Implementation

Writing a custom implementation is surprisingly easy with the aid of the *abstract implementations* furnished by the Java platform. Abstract implementations, skeletal implementations of the core collection interfaces, are designed expressly to facilitate custom implementations. We'll start with an example, an implementation of Arrays.asList:

```
public static List asList(Object[] a) {
    return new ArrayList(a);
}

private static class ArrayList extends AbstractList
                    implements java.io.Serializable {
```

```
    private Object[] a;
        ArrayList(Object[] array) {
            a = array;
        }

    public Object get(int index) {
        return a[index];
    }

    public Object set(int index, Object element) {
        Object oldValue = a[index];
        a[index] = element;
        return oldValue;
    }

    public int size() {
        return a.length;
    }
}
```

Believe it or not, this is almost exactly the implementation contained in the Java 2 SDK. It's that simple! You provide a constructor and the `get`, `set`, and `size` methods, and `AbstractList` does all the rest. You get the `ListIterator`, bulk operations, search operations, hash code computation, comparison, and string representation for free.

Suppose that you want to make the implementation a bit faster. The API documentation for the abstract implementations describes precisely how each method is implemented, so you'll know which methods to override in order to get the performance you want. The performance of the preceding implementation is fine, but it can be improved a bit. In particular, the `toArray` method iterates over the `List`, copying one element at a time. Given the internal representation, it's a lot faster and more sensible just to clone the array:

```
public Object[] toArray() {
    return (Object[]) a.clone();
}
```

With the addition of this override and a similar one for `toArray(Object[])`, this implementation is *exactly* the one found in the Java 2 platform. In the interests of full disclosure, it's a bit tougher to use the other abstract implementations, because they require you to write your own iterator, but it's still not that difficult.

The abstract implementations can be summarized as follows:

- `AbstractCollection`: A `Collection`, such as a *bag*, that is neither a `Set` nor a `List`. At a minimum, you must provide the `iterator` and the `size` method.
- `AbstractSet`: A `Set`. Its use is identical to `AbstractCollection`.

- AbstractList: A List backed by a random-access data store, such as an array. At a minimum, you must provide the positional access methods (get(int) and, optionally, set(int), remove(int), and add(int)) and the size method. The abstract class takes care of listIterator (and iterator).

- AbstractSequentialList: A List backed by a sequential-access data store, such as a linked list. At a minimum, you must provide the listIterator and the size methods. The abstract class takes care of the positional access methods. (This is the opposite of AbstractList.)

- AbstractMap: A Map. At a minimum, you must provide the entrySet view. This is typically implemented with the AbstractSet class. If the Map is modifiable, you must also provide the put method.

The process of writing a custom implementation follows.

1. Choose the appropriate abstract implementation class from the preceding list.

2. Provide implementations for all the class's abstract methods. If your custom collection is to be modifiable, you'll have to override one or more concrete methods as well. The API documentation for the abstract implementation class will tell you which methods to override.

3. Test and, if necessary, debug the implementation. You now have a working custom collection implementation!

4. If you're concerned about performance, read the abstract implementation class's API documentation for all the methods whose implementations you're inheriting. If any of them seem too slow, override them. If you override any methods, be sure to measure the performance of the method before and after the override! How much effort you put into tweaking the performance should be a function of how much use the implementation will get and how performance-critical the use. (Often this step is best omitted.)

Interoperability

In this section, you'll learn about two aspects of interoperability: compatibility and API design.

Compatibility

The Collections Framework was designed to ensure complete interoperability between the new collection interfaces and the types that have traditionally been used to represent collections: Vector, Hashtable, array, and Enumeration. In this section, you'll learn how to transform traditional collections to new collections and vice versa.

Upward Compatibility

Suppose that you're using an API that returns traditional collections in tandem with another API that requires objects implementing the collection interfaces introduced in Java 2 Platform version 1.2. To make the two APIs interoperate smoothly, you'll have to transform the traditional collections into new collections. Luckily, the Collections Framework makes this easy.

Suppose that the old API returns an array of objects and that the new API requires a Collection. The Collections Framework has a convenience implementation that allows an array of objects to be *viewed* as a List. You use Arrays.asList to pass an array to any method requiring a Collection or a List:

```
Foo[] result = oldMethod(arg);
newMethod(Arrays.asList(result));
```

If the old API returns a Vector or a Hashtable, you have no work to do at all, because Vector has been retrofitted to implement the List interface, and Hashtable has been retrofitted to implement Map. Therefore, a Vector may be passed directly to any method calling for a Collection or a List:

```
Vector result = oldMethod(arg);
newMethod(result);
```

Similarly, a Hashtable may be passed directly to any method calling for a Map:

```
Hashtable result = oldMethod(arg);
newMethod(result);
```

Less frequently, an API may return an Enumeration that represents a collection of objects. Although there is no direct support for translating an Enumeration into a Collection, it's a simple matter to create a Collection containing all the elements returned by an Enumeration:

```
Enumeration e = oldMethod(arg);
List l = new ArrayList;
while (e.hasMoreElements()) {
    l.add(e.nextElement());
    newMethod(l);
}
```

Backward Compatibility

Suppose that you're using an API that returns new collections in tandem with another API that requires you to pass in traditional collections. To make the two APIs interoperate smoothly, you have to transform the new collections into traditional collections. Again, the Collection Framework makes this easy.

Suppose that the new API returns a `Collection` and that the old API requires an array of `Object`. As you're probably aware, the `Collection` interface contains a `toArray` method, designed expressly for this situation:

```
Collection c = newMethod();
oldMethod(c.toArray());
```

What if the old API requires an array of `String` (or another type) instead of an array of `Object`? You just use the other form of `toArray`, the one that takes an array on input:

```
Collection c = newMethod();
oldMethod((String[]) c.toArray(new String[0]));
```

If the old API requires a `Vector`, the standard collection constructor comes in handy:

```
Collection c = newMethod();
oldMethod(new Vector(c));
```

The case in which the old API requires a `Hashtable` is handled analogously:

```
Map m = newMethod();
oldMethod(new Hashtable(m));
```

Finally, what do you do if the old API requires an `Enumeration`? This case isn't common, but it does happen from time to time, and the `Collections.enumeration` method was provided to handle it. This static factory method takes a `Collection` and returns an `Enumeration` over the elements of the `Collection`:

```
Collection c = newMethod();
oldMethod(Collections.enumeration(c));
```

API Design

In this short but important section, you'll learn a few simple guidelines that will allow your API to interoperate seamlessly with all other fine APIs that follow these guidelines. In essence, these rules define what it takes to be a good citizen in the brave new world of collections.

In-Parameters

If your API contains a method that requires a collection on input, it is of paramount importance that you declare the relevant parameter type to be one of the collection interface types. See the section Interfaces (page 470) for more information on interface types. Never use an implementation type, as this defeats the purpose of an interface-based Collections Framework, which is to allow collections to be manipulated without regard to implementation details.

Further, you should always use the least-specific type that makes sense. For example, don't require a List or a Set if a Collection would do. It's not that you should never require a List or a Set on input; it is correct to do so if a method depends on a property of one of these interfaces. For example, many of the algorithms provided by the Java platform require a List on input because they depend on the fact that lists are ordered. As a general rule, however, the best types to use on input are the most general: Collection and Map.

Caution: Never, ever define your own ad hoc collection class and require objects of this class on input. By doing this, you'd lose all the benefits provided by the Collection Framework.

Return Values

You can afford to be much more flexible with return values than with input parameters. It's fine to return an object of any type that implements or that extends one of the collection interfaces. This can be one of the interfaces or a special-purpose type that extends or implements one of these interfaces.

For example, one could imagine an image-processing package that returned objects of a new class that implements List, called ImageList. In addition to the List operations, ImageList could support any application-specific operations that seemed desirable. For example, it might provide an indexImage operation that returned an image containing thumbnail images of each graphic in the ImageList. It's critical to note that even if the API furnishes ImageList objects on output, it should accept arbitrary Collection (or perhaps List) objects on input.

In one sense, return values should have the opposite behavior of input parameters: It's best to return the most specific applicable collection interface rather than the most general. For example, if you're sure that you'll always return a SortedMap, you should give the relevant method the return type of SortedMap rather than Map. SortedMap objects are both more time consuming to build than ordinary Map objects are and also more powerful. Given that your module has already invested the time to build a SortedMap, it makes good sense to give the user access to its increased power. Furthermore, the user will be able to pass the returned object to methods that demand a SortedMap, as well as those that accept any Map.

Deprecated Thread Methods

$\mathbf{J}$OSH Bloch[1] wrote the following article to explain why the Thread.stop, Thread.suspend, Thread.resume, and Runtime.runFinalizersOnExit methods were deprecated in the 1.1 release of the Java™ platform.

Why Is Thread.stop Deprecated?

Thread.stop is deprecated because it is inherently unsafe. Stopping a thread causes it to unlock all the monitors that it has locked. (The monitors are unlocked as the Thread-Death exception propagates up the stack.) If any of the objects previously protected by these monitors were in an inconsistent state, other threads may now view these objects in an inconsistent state. Such objects are said to be *damaged*. When threads operate on damaged objects, arbitrary behavior can result. This behavior may be subtle and difficult to detect, or it may be pronounced. Unlike other unchecked exceptions, ThreadDeath kills threads silently; thus, the user has no warning that his or her program may be cor-

---

[1] Josh Bloch is a Senior Engineer at Sun Microsystems and the designer of the Collections package.

rupted. The corruption can manifest itself at any time after the actual damage occurs, even hours or days in the future.

Could I Catch the ThreadDeath Exception and Fix the Damaged Object?

In theory, perhaps, but it would *vastly* complicate the task of writing correct multithreaded code. The task would be nearly insurmountable for two reasons:

1. A thread can throw a ThreadDeath exception *almost anywhere*. All synchronized methods and blocks would have to be studied in great detail, with this in mind.

2. A thread can throw a second ThreadDeath exception while cleaning up from the first (in the catch or finally clause). Cleanup would have to repeated until it succeeded. The code to ensure this would be quite complex.

In sum, it just isn't practical.

What about Thread.stop(Throwable)?

In addition to all the problems noted previously, this method may be used to generate exceptions that its target thread is unprepared to handle, including checked exceptions that the thread could not possibly throw, were it not for this method. For example, the following method is behaviorally identical to Java's throw operation but circumvents the compiler's attempts to guarantee that the calling method has declared all the checked exceptions that it may throw:

```
static void sneakyThrow(Throwable t) {
    Thread.currentThread().stop(t);
}
```

What Should I Use Instead of Thread.stop?

Most uses of stop should be replaced by code that simply modifies a variable to indicate that the target thread should stop running. The target thread should check this variable regularly and return from its run method in an orderly fashion if the variable indicates that it is to stop running. This is the approach recommended in the chapter <u>Threads: Doing Two or More Tasks at Once</u> (page 269). To ensure prompt communication of the stop request, the variable must be volatile, or access to the variable must be synchronized.

For example, suppose that your applet contains the following start, stop, and run methods:

```
private Thread blinker;

public void start() {
    blinker = new Thread(this);
```

```
        blinker.start();
    }

    public void stop() {
        blinker.stop();   // UNSAFE!
    }
    public void run() {
        Thread thisThread = Thread.currentThread();
        while (true) {
            try {
                thisThread.sleep(interval);
            } catch (InterruptedException e){
            }
            repaint();
        }
    }
}
```

You can avoid the use of Thread.stop by replacing the applet's stop and run methods with:

```
    private volatile Thread blinker;

    public void stop() {
        blinker = null;
    }

    public void run() {
        Thread thisThread = Thread.currentThread();
        while (blinker == thisThread) {
            try {
                thisThread.sleep(interval);
            } catch (InterruptedException e){
            }
            repaint();
        }
    }
}
```

How Do I Stop a Thread That Waits for Long Periods?

That's what the Thread.interrupt method is for. The same "state-based" signaling mechanism shown previously can be used, but the state change (blinker = null, in the previous example) can be followed by a call to Thread.interrupt to interrupt the wait:

```
    public void stop() {
        Thread moribund = waiter;
        waiter = null;
        moribund.interrupt();
    }
```

For this technique to work, it's critical that any method that catches an interrupt exception and is not prepared to deal with it immediately reasserts the exception. We say *reasserts* rather than *rethrows* because it is not always possible to rethrow the exception. If the method that catches the InterruptedException is not declared to throw this (checked) exception, it should "reinterrupt itself" with the following incantation:

```
Thread.currentThread().interrupt();
```

This ensures that the Thread will raise the InterruptedException again as soon as it is able.

What If a Thread Doesn't Respond to Thread.interrupt?

In some cases, you can use application-specific tricks. For example, if a thread is waiting on a known socket, you can close the socket to cause the thread to return immediately. Unfortunately, there really isn't any technique that works in general. *It should be noted that in all situations in which a waiting thread doesn't respond to Thread.interrupt, it wouldn't respond to Thread.stop, either.* Such cases include deliberate denial-of-service attacks and I/O operations for which thread.stop and thread.interrupt do not work properly.

Why Are Thread.suspend and Thread.resume Deprecated?

Thread.suspend is inherently deadlock prone. If the target thread holds a lock on the monitor protecting a critical system resource when it is suspended, no thread can access this resource until the target thread is resumed. If the thread that would resume the target thread attempts to lock this monitor prior to calling resume, deadlock results. Such deadlocks typically manifest themselves as "frozen" processes.

What Should I Use Instead of Thread.suspend and Thread.resume?

As with Thread.stop, the prudent approach is to have the "target thread" poll a variable indicating the desired state of the thread (active or suspended). When the desired state is suspended, the thread waits, using Object.wait. When the thread is resumed, the target thread is notified, using Object.notify.

For example, suppose that your applet contains the following mousePressed event handler, which toggles the state of a thread called blinker:

```
private boolean threadSuspended;

Public void mousePressed(MouseEvent e) {
    e.consume();

    if (threadSuspended)
        blinker.resume();
    else
        blinker.suspend();   // DEADLOCK-PRONE!
    threadSuspended = !threadSuspended;
}
```

You can avoid the use of Thread.suspend and Thread.resume by replacing the preceding event handler with:

```
public synchronized void mousePressed(MouseEvent e) {
    e.consume();

    threadSuspended = !threadSuspended;

    if (!threadSuspended)
        notify();
}
```

You can also add the following code to the run loop:

```
synchronized(this) {
    while (threadSuspended)
    wait();
}
```

The wait method throws the InterruptedException, so it must be inside a try-catch clause. It's fine to put it in the same clause as the sleep. The check should follow (rather than precede) the sleep so the window is immediately repainted when the thread is "resumed." The resulting run method follows:

```
public void run() {
    while (true) {
        try {
            Thread.currentThread().sleep(interval);

            synchronized(this) {
                while (threadSuspended)
                    wait();
            }
```

```
        } catch (InterruptedException e){
        }
        repaint();
    }
}
```

Note that the notify in the mousePressed method and the wait in the run method are inside synchronized blocks. This is required by the language and ensures that wait and notify are properly serialized. In practical terms, this eliminates race conditions that could cause the "suspended" thread to miss a notify and to remain suspended indefinitely.

Although the cost of synchronization in Java is decreasing as the platform matures, it will never be free. A simple trick can be used to remove the synchronization that we've added to each iteration of the "run loop." The synchronized block that was added is replaced by a slightly more complex piece of code that enters a synchronized block only if the thread has been suspended:

```
if (threadSuspended) {
    synchronized(this) {
        while (threadSuspended)
            wait();
    }
}
```

The resulting run method is:

```
public void run() {
    while (true) {
        try {
            Thread.currentThread().sleep(interval);

            if (threadSuspended) {
                synchronized(this) {
                    while (threadSuspended)
                        wait();
                }
            }
        } catch (InterruptedException e){
        }
        repaint();
    }
}
```

In the absence of explicit synchronization, threadSuspended must be made volatile to ensure prompt communication of the suspend request.

Can I Combine the Two Techniques to Produce a Thread That May Be Safely "Stopped" or "Suspended"?

Yes, it's reasonably straightforward. The one subtlety is that the target thread may already be suspended at the time that another thread tries to stop it. If the stop method merely sets the state variable (blinker) to null, the target thread will remain suspended (waiting on the monitor) rather than exiting gracefully, as it should. If the applet is restarted, multiple threads could end up waiting on the monitor at the same time, resulting in erratic behavior.

To rectify this situation, the stop method must ensure that the target thread resumes immediately if it is suspended. Once the target thread resumes, it must recognize immediately that it has been stopped and exit gracefully. Here's how the resulting run and stop methods look:

```java
public void run() {
    Thread thisThread = Thread.currentThread();
    while (blinker == thisThread) {
        try {
            thisThread.sleep(interval);

            synchronized(this) {
                while (threadSuspended && blinker==thisThread)
                    wait();
            }
        } catch (InterruptedException e){
        }
        repaint();
    }
}

public synchronized void stop() {
    blinker = null;
    notify();
}
```

If the stop method calls Thread.interrupt, as described earlier, it needn't call notify as well, but it still must be synchronized. This ensures that the target thread won't miss an interrupt due to a race condition.

What about Thread.destroy?

Thread.destroy has never been implemented. If it were implemented, it would be deadlock prone in the manner of Thread.suspend. (In fact, it is roughly equivalent to Thread.suspend without the possibility of a subsequent Thread.resume.) We are not implementing it at this time, but neither are we deprecating it (forestalling its implementation in future). Although it would certainly be deadlock prone, it has been argued that there may be circumstances when a program is willing to risk a deadlock rather than to exit outright.

Why Is Runtime.runFinalizersOnExit Deprecated?

Because it is inherently unsafe. It may result in finalizers being called on live objects while other threads are concurrently manipulating those objects, resulting in erratic behavior or deadlock. Although this problem could be prevented if the class whose objects are being finalized were coded to "defend against" this call, most programmers do *not* defend against it. They assume that an object is dead at the time that its finalizer is called.

Further, the call is not "thread safe" in the sense that it sets a VM-global flag. This forces *every* class with a finalizer to defend against the finalization of live objects!

APPENDIX **E**

Reference

THIS appendix contains reference information on several topics.

Java Programming Language Keywords

Table 64 lists all the keywords in alphabetical order. These words are reserved; that is, you cannot use any of them as names in your programs. Note that true, false, and null are not keywords but rather reserved words, so you cannot use them as names in your programs either.

Table 64   Java Programming Language Keywords

abstract	double	int	strictfp **
boolean	else	interface	super
break	extends	long	switch
byte	final	native	synchronized

Table 64   Java Programming Language Keywords

case	finally	new	this
catch	float	package	throw
char	for	private	throws
class	goto *	protected	transient
const *	if	public	try
continue	implements	return	void
default	import	short	volatile
do	instanceof	static	while

* Indicates a keyword that is not currently used.
** Indicates a keyword that was added to the Java 2 Platform.

Operator Precedence

Table 65 lists the operators in the Java programming language. Operators higher in the table have higher precedence than do those lower in the table. Operators on the same line have the same precedence.

Table 65   Operator Precedence

Operator Category	Operators
Postfix operators	[] . (params) expr++ expr--
Unary operators	++expr --expr +expr -expr ~ !
Creation or cast	new (type)expr
Multiplicative	* / %
Additive	+ -
Shift	<< >> >>>
Relational	< > <= >= instanceof
Equality	== !=
Bitwise AND	&
Bitwise exclusive OR	^
Bitwise inclusive OR	|

Table 65   Operator Precedence

Logical AND	&&
Logical OR	||
Conditional	? :
Assignment	= += -= *= /= %= ^= &= |= <<= >>= >>>=

When operators of equal precedence appear in the same expression, a rule must govern which is evaluated first. In the Java programming language, all binary operators except for the assignment operators are evaluated in left-to-right order. Assignment operators are evaluated in right-to-left order.

The <APPLET> Tag

This section gives the complete syntax for the <APPLET> tag.

Note: The information in this section does *not* apply if you are writing applets that use the Java™ Plug-in, such as Swing applets. Simply put, Netscape Navigator browsers require the <EMBED> tag and Microsoft Explorer browsers use the <OBJECT> tag in place of the <APPLET> tag. You can read more about deploying applets using the Java Plug-in online at `http://java.sun.com/products/plugin/`.

When you build <APPLET> tags, keep in mind that such words as APPLET and CODEBASE can be entered either as shown or in any mixture of uppercase and lowercase letters. In the following, entries in boldface indicate something you should type in exactly as shown, except that letters don't need to be uppercase. Entries in italic indicate that you must substitute a value for the word in italics. Brackets ([and]) indicate that the contents within the brackets are optional. Parentheses ((and)) indicate that you must choose exactly one of the separated contents.

```
< APPLET
[CODEBASE = codebaseURL]
(CODE = appletFile | OBJECT = serializedApplet)
[ARCHIVE = archivesList]
[ALT = alternateText]
[NAME = appletInstanceName]
WIDTH = pixels HEIGHT = pixels
[ALIGN = alignment]
```

```
    [VSPACE = pixels] [HSPACE = pixels]
    >
    [< PARAM NAME = appletParameter1 VALUE = value >]
    [< PARAM NAME = appletParameter2 VALUE = value >]
    . . .
    [alternateHTML]
    </APPLET>
```

CODEBASE = codebaseURL

This optional attribute specifies the base URL of the applet—the directory or the folder that contains the applet's code. If this attribute is not specified, the document's URL is used.

CODE = appletFile

This attribute gives the name of the file that contains the applet's compiled Applet subclass. This file is relative to the base URL of the applet and cannot be absolute. Either CODE or OBJECT must be present.

OBJECT = serializedApplet

This attribute gives the name of the file that contains a serialized representation of an applet. The applet will be deserialized. The init method will *not* be invoked, but its start method will be. Attributes that are valid when the original object was serialized are *not* restored. Any attributes passed to this Applet instance will be available to the applet. We advise you to exercise very strong restraint in using this feature. An applet should be stopped before it is serialized. One of CODE or OBJECT must be present.

ARCHIVE = archivesList

This optional attribute describes one or more archives containing classes and other resources that will be preloaded. The classes are loaded by using an instance of an AppletClassLoader with the given CODEBASE.

ALT = alternateText

This optional attribute specifies any text that should be displayed if the browser understands the <APPLET> tag but can't run applets.

NAME = appletInstanceName

This optional attribute specifies a name for the Applet instance. Naming applets makes it possible for applets on the same page to find and to communicate with each other.

WIDTH = pixels HEIGHT = pixels

These required attributes give the initial width and height in pixels of the applet display area, not counting any windows or dialogs that the applet brings up.

ALIGN = alignment

This required attribute specifies the alignment of the applet. Its possible values are the same (and have the same effects) as those for the <IMG> tag and are the following: LEFT, RIGHT, TOP, TEXTTOP, MIDDLE, ABSMIDDLE, BASELINE, BOTTOM, and ABSBOTTOM.

VSPACE = pixels HSPACE = pixels

These optional attributes specify the number of pixels above and below the applet (VSPACE) and on each side of the applet (HSPACE). They're treated in the same way as the <IMG> tag's VSPACE and HSPACE attributes.

< PARAM NAME = appletParameter1 VALUE = value >

Use of a <PARAM> tag is the only way to specify an applet-specific parameter. Applets read user-specified values for parameters by using the getParameter method.

alternateHTML

If the HTML page containing this <APPLET> tag is viewed by a browser that doesn't understand the <APPLET> tag, the browser will ignore the <APPLET> and <PARAM> tags. It instead will interpret any other HTML code between the <APPLET> and </APPLET> tags. Java-compatible browsers ignore this extra HTML code.

In the online version of this tutorial, we use alternate HTML to show a snapshot of the applet running, with text explaining what the applet does. Other possibilities for this area are a link to a page that is more useful for the applet-disabled browser or text that taunts the user for not having a compatible browser.

POSIX Conventions for Command Line Arguments

Command line arguments in a program may cause that program to be unportable (that is, it will not be 100% Pure Java). If a program requires command line arguments, it should follow the POSIX conventions for them. The POSIX conventions are summarized here.

- An *option* is a hyphen followed by a single alphanumeric character, like this: -o.
- An option may require an argument, which must appear immediately after the option: for example, -o argument or -oargument.
- Options that do not require arguments can be grouped after a hyphen, so, for example, -lst is equivalent to -t -l -s.
- Options can appear in any order; thus, -lst is equivalent to -tls.
- Options can appear multiple times.
- Options precede other nonoption arguments: -lst nonoption.
- The -- argument terminates options.
- The - option is typically used to represent one of the standard input streams.

Integrated Development Environments

The Java 2 SDK software comes with a minimal set of tools. Serious developers are advised to use a professional Integrated Development Environment (IDE) with Java 2 SDK software. Table 66 lists several professional integrated development environments.

Table 66   Integrated Development Environments with Java 2 SDK Software

Sun Microsystems Forte™ for Java,™ Community Edition	`http://www.sun.com/forte/ffj/ce/`
Borland JBuilder™	`http://www.borland.com/jbuilder/`
Sybase PowerJ™	`http://www.sybase.com/products/powerj/` `jdk.html`
WebGain Visual Café™	`http://www.webgain.com/Products/` `Expert_Edition/VisualCafe_Expert_Edition.htm`
Oracle JDeveloper™	`http://www.oracle.com/tools/jdeveloper/`
Metrowerks CodeWarrior™ for Java,™ Professional Edition	`http://www.metrowerks.com/desktop/java/`

Check the Java 2 platform Web site for details:

```
http://java.sun.com/j2se/
```

Path Help

This section includes instructions on setting the PATH and CLASSPATH environment variables on Win32 and UNIX platforms. Consult the installation instructions included with your installation of the Java 2 SDK software bundle for current information.

After installing both the Java 2 SDK software and documentation, the SDK directory will have the structure shown below. The docs directory is created when you install the SDK documentation bundle.

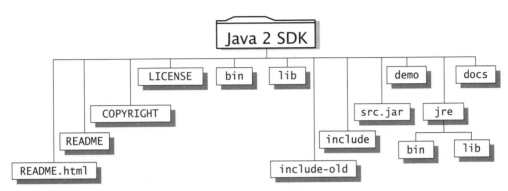

Figure 125 The file structure of the Java 2 SDK software bundle. Note that the bin directory contains both the compiler and the interpreter.

Update the PATH Variable (Win32)

You can run the Java 2 SDK software just fine without setting the PATH variable. Or, you can optionally set it as a convenience.

Set the PATH variable if you want to be able to conveniently run the SDK executables (javac.exe, java.exe, javadoc.exe, and so on) from any directory without having to type the full path of the command. If you don't set the PATH variable, you need to specify the full path to the executable every time you run it, such as:

```
C: \jdk1.3\bin\javac MyClass.java
```

> **Note:** It's useful to set the PATH permanently so it will persist after rebooting. To set it permanently, add the full path of the jdk1.3\bin directory to the PATH variable. Typically, this full path looks something like C:\jdk1.3\bin. Set the PATH as follows, according to whether you are on Windows NT/2000 or Windows 95/98.

Setting the PATH Permanently (Windows NT/2000)

From the Start menu, select the Control Panel > System > Environment, and look for "Path" in the User Variables and System Variables. If you're not sure where to add the path, add it to the right end of the "Path" in the User Variables. A typical value for PATH is:

```
C:\jdk1.3\bin
```

Capitalization doesn't matter. Click Set, OK, or Apply.

The PATH can be a series of directories separated by semicolons (;). Microsoft Windows looks for programs in the PATH directories in order, from left to right. You should have only one bin directory for the Java 2 SDK in the path at a time (those following the first are ignored), so if one is already present, you can update it to 1.3.

The new path takes effect in each new Command Prompt window you open after setting the PATH variable.

Setting the PATH Permanently (Windows 95/98)

To set the PATH permanently, open the AUTOEXEC.BAT file and add or change the PATH statement as follows: Start the system editor. From the Start menu, select Run and enter sysedit in the textbox; then click OK. The system editor starts up with several windows showing. Go to the window that displays AUTOEXEC.BAT.

Look for the PATH statement. (If you don't have one, add one.) If you're not sure where to add the path, add it to the right end of the PATH. For example, in the following PATH statement, we have added the bin directory at the right end:

```
PATH C:\WINDOWS;C:\WINDOWS\COMMAND;C:\JDK1.3\BIN
```

Capitalization doesn't matter. The PATH can be a series of directories separated by semicolons (;). Microsoft Windows searches for programs in the PATH directories in order, from left to right. You should have only one bin directory for the Java 2 SDK in the path at a time (those following the first are ignored), so if one is already present, you can update it to 1.3.

To make the path take effect in the current Command Prompt window, execute the following:

```
C: \>c:\autoexec.bat
```

To find out the current value of your PATH, to see whether it took effect, at the command prompt, type:

```
C: \>C:\path
```

Check the CLASSPATH Variable

The CLASSPATH variable is one way to tell applications written in the Java programming language (including the SDK tools) where to look for user classes. (The -classpath command line switch is the preferred way.) If your machine does not have the CLASSPATH variable set, you can ignore the rest of this step. To check this, run the set command from the DOS prompt:

```
C:> set
```

If CLASSPATH does not appear in the list of settings, it is not set.

If your CLASSPATH variable is set to a value, you may want to clean up your CLASSPATH settings. The Java 2 SDK works fine even if CLASSPATH is set for an earlier version of the SDK software, as long as it contains the current directory ".". However, if your CLASSPATH contains classes.zip (which was only in JDK 1.0.x and JDK 1.1.x) and you don't plan to continue using those earlier versions, you can remove that setting from the CLASSPATH. In any case, if CLASSPATH is set, it should include the current directory—this makes it possible to compile and to run classes in the current directory.

Update the PATH Variable (UNIX)

You can run the Java 2 SDK just fine without setting the PATH variable, or you can optionally set it as a convenience. However, you should set the path variable if you want to be able to run the executables (javac, java, javadoc, and so on) from any directory without having to type the full path of the command. If you don't set the PATH variable, you need to specify the full path to the executable every time you run it, such as:

```
% /usr/local/jdk1.3/bin/javac MyClass.java
```

To find out if the path is currently set, execute:

```
% which java
```

This will print the path to the java tool, if it can find it. If the PATH is not set properly, you will get the error:

```
% java: Command not found
```

To set the path permanently, set the path in your startup file.

For C shell (csh), edit the startup file (~/.cshrc):

```
set path=(/usr/local/jdk1.3/bin $path)
```

For ksh, bash or sh, edit the profile file (~/.profile):

```
PATH=/usr/local/jdk1.3/bin:$PATH
```

Then load the startup file and verify that the path is set by repeating the which command:

For C shell (csh):

```
% source ~/.cshrc
% which java
```

For ksh, bash, or sh:

```
$ . $HOME/.profile
$ which java
```

Checking the CLASSPATH variable

The CLASSPATH variable is one way to tell applications, including the SDK tools, where to look for user classes. (The -classpath command line switch is the preferred way.) If you never set up the CLASSPATH variable for an earlier version of the SDK, you can ignore this step. Otherwise, you may want to clean up your CLASSPATH settings.

The Java 2 SDK will work fine even if CLASSPATH is set for an earlier version of the SDK. However, if your CLASSPATH contains classes.zip for an earlier version, and you don't plan to continue using that version, you can remove that setting from the CLASSPATH now. If CLASSPATH is set but doesn't include the current directory, you should add the current directory to the CLASSPATH value.

To modify the CLASSPATH, use the same procedure you used for the PATH variable in the previous step and do one of the following.

- Remove classes.zip from the CLASSPATH. Leave any application-specific settings and the current directory, "." If CLASSPATH is set but doesn't include the current directory, you should add the current directory to the CLASSPATH value.)
- Remove the CLASSPATH environment variable entirely. (With the Java 2 SDK, the default value is "." [the current directory]. For specific applications, you can use the -classpath command line switch.)

Index

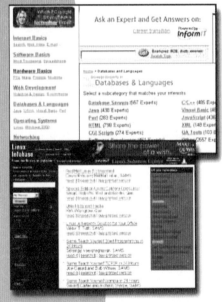

Register
Your Book

at www.aw.com/cseng/register

You may be eligible to receive:

- Advance notice of forthcoming editions of the book
- Related book recommendations
- Chapter excerpts and supplements of forthcoming titles
- Information about special contests and promotions throughout the year
- Notices and reminders about author appearances, tradeshows, and online chats with special guests

Contact us

If you are interested in writing a book or reviewing manuscripts prior to publication, please write to us at:

Editorial Department
Addison-Wesley Professional
75 Arlington Street, Suite 300
Boston, MA 02116 USA
Email: AWPro@aw.com

Addison-Wesley

Visit us on the Web: http://www.aw.com/cseng

The Java™ Series

ISBN 0-201-70433-1

ISBN 0-201-31005-8

ISBN 0-201-70323-8

ISBN 0-201-70393-9

ISBN 0-201-74622-0

ISBN 0-201-48558-3

ISBN 0-201-43299-4

ISBN 0-201-75282-4

ISBN 0-201-75484-3

ISBN 0-201-71623-2

ISBN 0-201-31002-3

ISBN 0-201-31003-1

ISBN 0-201-48552-4

ISBN 0-201-71102-8

ISBN 0-201-70329-7

ISBN 0-201-30955-6

ISBN 0-201-31000-7

ISBN 0-201-31008-2

ISBN 0-201-63456-2

ISBN 0-201-70277-0

ISBN 0-201-31009-0

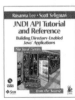

ISBN 0-201-70502-8

ISBN 0-201-32577-2

ISBN 0-201-43294-3

ISBN 0-201-70267-3

ISBN 0-201-74627-1

ISBN 0-201-70456-0

ISBN 0-201-77580-8

ISBN 0-201-71041-2

ISBN 0-201-43321-4

ISBN 0-201-43328-1

ISBN 0-201-70969-4

ISBN 0-201-72617-3

Please see our web site (http://www.awl.com/cseng/javaseries)
for more information on these titles.

The Java Tutorial CD-ROM

The *Java Tutorial* CD-ROM that accompanies this book is loaded with development kits and documentation, including the content and code of all three books: *The Java Tutorial*, *The Java Tutorial Continued*, and *The JFC Swing Tutorial*. Where the release version is not noted, the most recent release at the time of printing is included.

Table 67   Development Kits on *The Java Tutorial* CD-ROM

Development Kits	Version(s)
Java 2 Platform (formerly known as the "JDK") *The latest release is version 1.3.*	Standard Edition, v 1.3 Standard Edition, v 1.2
Java Development Kit (JDK)	1.1.8
Java Runtime Environment (JRE)	1.3, 1.2
Java Foundation Classes (JFC) *includes Swing 1.1*	1.1.1, 1.1
Java Servlet Development Kit (JSDK)	2.0
Java Accessibility Utilities	1.3

Table 68   Documentation on *The Java Tutorial* CD-ROM

Documentation	Version(s)
The Java Tutorial	in PDF and HTML
Java Programming Language API Documentation	1.3
JFC 1.1 API Documentation	1.1
The Swing Connection	
The Java Platform White Paper	

Table 69   Specifications on *The Java Tutorial* CD-ROM

Specifications
Java 2D User Guide
Servlet Specification
JDBC 1.2 and 2.1 Core API Specifications

Table 70   Miscellaneous on *The Java Tutorial* CD-ROM

And more...
Java Code Conventions
Java Programming Language Glossary

The README.html file on the CD-ROM is the central HTML page that links you to all of its contents. To view this page, use the Open Page command or its equivalent in your Internet browser. On some platforms, you can simply double click on the HTML file to launch it in your browser.

You can check out the latest Sun Microsystems Java^{TM} programming language product releases at: http://java.sun.com/products/index.html. If you sign up for the Java Developer Connection,[1] you will receive free, early access to such products, including the latest Java platform.

See this book's Web page at: http://java.sun.com/docs/books/tutorial/uiswing/index.html for pointers to the latest versions of this content.

---

[1] http://developer.java.sun.com/